FRONTPAGE™ 97
WEB DESIGNER'S GUIDE

Supercharging
World Wide Web Sites with the
FrontPage™ Visual Publishing System

WAITE GROUP PRESS™
A Division of
Sams Publishing
Corte Madera, CA

Gary L. Allman
Jason Ledtke
Michael C. Stinson

PUBLISHER: Mitchell Waite
ASSOCIATE PUBLISHER: Charles Drucker

ACQUISITIONS MANAGER: Jill Pisoni
ACQUISITIONS EDITOR: Joanne Miller

EDITORIAL DIRECTOR: John Crudo
PROJECT EDITOR: Andrea Rosenberg
CONTENT EDITOR: Russ Jacobs
COPY EDITOR: Deidre Greene/Creative Solutions
TECHNICAL REVIEWER: Jeff Bankston

PRODUCTION DIRECTOR: Julianne Ososke
PRODUCTION MANAGER: Cecile Kaufman
PRODUCTION EDITOR: Kelsey McGee
SENIOR DESIGNER: Sestina Quarequio
DESIGNERS: Karen Johnston, Jil Weil
PRODUCTION: Chris Barrick, Jenaffer Brandt, Jeanne Clark, Michael Dietsch, Lisa Pletka, Shawn Ring
COVER IMAGE: Clayton J. Price/The Stock Market

Printed in the United States of America
97 98 99 • 10 9 8 7 6 5 4 3 2 1

Library of Congress Cataloging-in-Publication Data
Allman, Gary L., 1970-
    FrontPage 97 web designer's guide / Gary L. Allman, Jason Ledtke, Michael C. Stinson.
      p.   cm.
    Includes index.
    ISBN 1-57169-027-1
    1. FrontPage (Computer file) 2. World Wide Web servers—Computer programs.
    3. Electronic publishing. I. Ledtke, Jason, 1973-   II. Stinson, Michael C., 1948-
    III. Title.
    TK5105.888.A38   1996
    005.75—dc20   96-36320
                                                        CIP

Dedication

This book is dedicated to my parents, Gary and Bernadette Allman. The greatest compliment one could ever give me is that I am just like you! You're the greatest! I love you!

— Gary L. Allman

For my parents, who never push but always support.

— Jason Ledtke

To our daughter Megan, born June 9, 1996. Before her birth she inspired us. Now she fills our days with joy, smiles, and laughter.

— Michael C. Stinson

About the Authors

Gary L. Allman

Gary L. Allman is vice president of technology at preEmptive Solutions Inc., an Internet technologies consulting firm; an SAP Basis Specialist with the Dow Chemical Company; and a lecturer on Microsoft applications. He is currently a Microsoft Certified Product Specialist for Windows 95 and Windows NT and received his B.S. in computer science from Central Michigan University. Gary has worked with Windows for more than six years, has led various development efforts at the Dow Chemical Company, and is author of Altaris FTS Wizard!, a full-text search indexing wizard for the Windows help engine.
In his spare time (yeah, right), Gary enjoys playing basketball and traveling with his wife, Chanthy. He can be reached via e-mail at gallman@preemptive.com.

Jason Ledtke

Jason Ledtke is a graduate student at Central Michigan University. His greatest labor of love is reading books, magazines, and Web pages in a heroic attempt to stay current on the fast-moving topics of Internet technology. He also takes an interest in object-oriented design and development and at any given moment has at least two or three programming projects in the works. Since 1990, he has had at least one email address and has been found lurking in newsgroups or surfing the Web since 1993. He hopes to join or start a small consulting firm specializing in Internet technology and development when he finishes college. When not hunched over a computer, Jason can be found backpacking in the mountains, trying to learn a new guitar tune, or sprinting to class (late as usual). Jason's e-mail address is Jason_Ledtke@msn.com, and he can be found on the Web at http://www.getnoticed.com.

Michael C. Stinson

Michael C. Stinson is a professor of computer science at Central Michigan University. He received his doctorate from Louisiana State University, his master's from Michigan State University, and his bachelor's degree from Central Michigan University. He has been a NASA Fellow at the Jet Propulsion Laboratory, a visiting scientist at Argonne National Laboratory, and a visiting scientist at the Software Engineering Institute at Carnegie-Mellon University. He was a member of the IEEE and ANSI Joint Pascal Committee that standardized Extended Pascal and Object Pascal. Michael currently researches and consults in total
quality management for software, object-oriented software measures, and Web development. He can be contacted at stinson@cps.cmich.edu.

Table of Contents

Contents

Chapter 9: The FrontPage Explorer 193

Chapter 10: Navigation 221

Chapter 13: FrontPage Software Developer's Kit 305

Acknowledgments

I would like to first and foremost thank my parents, for without their love and respect I would not be who I am today. Special thanks go to my dear wife, Chanthy (T) Vongphasouk, for all of her love and support during those late nights (okay, now I'll clean up the office!). I would also like to thank Andrea Rosenberg for her extreme patience and great attitude during those critical deadlines (a joy to work with), and Jill Pisoni for allowing me this opportunity. I can't even express how many thanks I owe you! In addition, I would like to thank Michael and Julie Stinson; Jason Ledtke; Paul Týma (UBG) for teaching me the ropes; Susan Hagen, Pamela Anderson Bowen, and the STIC Team of Dow Chemical; Timothy and Valerie Allman, Stephan Franklin, Chanhom (you're always there), and Rodney Sikkema, Tim and Cathy Hoch (a partridge and a pear tree), the editorial staff, and Waite Group Press for all of their help—eternal gratitude.

—Gary L. Allman

First, I would like to thank everyone who put up with me constantly talking about this book for the last few months. Everyone's input, support, and tolerance were critical in this project. I owe a very special thank you to my folks, who helped me move three times in the last four months. I'd also like to especially thank Anne Marie for her special patience and understanding during this time. You are all very special people in my life.

A big thank you goes to the outstanding team of editors at The Waite Group. Without Andrea, Jill, and a bevy of technical and content editors, there's no way this book would have ever been produced. You guys did a great job helping this novice author through his first work.

I'd also like to give a special thanks to Gambino, Sarah, Jeff, Jane, Chris, and Tim for lending their ears, proofreading copy, bouncing ideas around, or just for their incredible support. Without friends like you, I would go insane. Thank you all.

—Jason Ledtke

First and foremost, I must acknowledge my wife Julie, who made the supreme effort to learn FrontPage with me in order to write this book. Every word attributed to me is at least equally attributable to her.

I would like to thank Gary Allman and Jason Ledtke for their assistance and quality effort. It is students like these who make teaching a noble and worthwhile profession.

Thanks to my parents, Robert and Edith Stinson, for their love and strength of character. Thanks to my uncle, Dr. Donald Stinson, for my profession and many of my values. Thanks to Dr. Subhash Kak for inspiration and faith in me as a student.

I also need to thank Andrea Rosenberg, Jill Pisoni, and The Waite Group staff for their efforts and patience in this endeavor. Their labors are truly a gift to this text.

—Michael C. Stinson

Introduction

Would you jump out of a plane without a parachute? You probably wouldn't make an attempt without first being prepared and ensuring you had every item possible to make your jump enjoyable. To many people, getting on to the Internet, surfing the World Wide Web, and building their own Web sites are much like jumping out of a plane—the experience is unforgettable but can go awry if you're not prepared.

Welcome to *FrontPage™ 97 Web Designer's Guide*. This book is designed to provide you with all of the tools and information necessary to use Microsoft FrontPage and establish yourself on the Internet. Following our skydiving metaphor, consider this book as all the pre-jump training you will need and, most important, your parachute in exploring FrontPage and Web site maintenance.

Who Are You?

If you desire to exploit FrontPage and explore Web site design and management, *FrontPage 97 Web Designer's Guide* is for you. This book provides a complete reference on Microsoft FrontPage and its relationship to the Internet. The book is organized with an increasing level of presentation. From beginning topics, exploring the World Wide Web, TCP/IP, HTML, and FrontPage, to more advanced items including programming in VBScript, JavaScript, and Java, and developing your own Web templates using the FrontPage Web Developer's Kit, this book will appeal to you whether you are a Web novice or an experienced Webmaster.

What Does This Book Contain?

FrontPage 97 Web Designer's Guide has everything you need to start using Microsoft FrontPage right away. More important, the book is designed so that you can immediately jump right to the chapters that address your experience level. If you see a chapter of interest, go there. The following chapters progress from introductory material to increasingly advanced topics.

Chapter 1: The New Generation

Explore why FrontPage represents the new generation of Web authoring tools. You'll learn about the architecture of FrontPage and how its components can be used to effectively create and manage various aspects of the Web management process—from page creation to site automation.

Chapter 2: Making the Connection

Delve into the various avenues for connecting to the Internet and setting up a Web server, including working with Internet Services Providers and getting an access account. In addition, you'll gain background on various hardware and software network components and how they relate to the Internet and World Wide Web.

Chapter 3: Web Development

Familiarize yourself with the history of publishing methods and the natural evolution to Web publishing. You will be provided with a concise approach to effective Web development. This chapter will focus on the development process and illustrate potential pitfalls.

Chapter 4: HTML Made Easy

Explore Hypertext Markup Language and integration into FrontPage from its basic components to some of the more popular tags that have exploded the popularity of browsers such as Netscape Navigator and Microsoft Internet Explorer.

Chapter 5: Installing Microsoft FrontPage

This chapter walks you through an install of FrontPage. Focus is on installation options, the Server Extensions, administration, and understanding the required networking components.

Chapter 6: Designing Your Web Site

Webs are the end result of a FrontPage project: You want your Web site to be the ultimate online experience and draw flocks of readers. Because online publishing is more than combining text and pictures, there are common pitfalls to avoid. This chapter will focus on some basic design considerations and the specifics of creating FrontPage titles.

Chapter 7: FrontPage Editor

This chapter will detail how to develop high-quality, feature-rich pages using the FrontPage Editor. Focus is on the drag-and-drop design environment, usability features, and conversion of existing documents. In addition you will work the Personal Home Page wizard to create your own simple Web page.

Chapter 8: WebBots

You and other Web developers may wish to extend your Webs by offering interactive features including forms and full-text searching. This chapter details how the FrontPage Web Robots (WebBots) can perform many of these functions effortlessly, allowing designers to focus on the look and feel rather than the functionality of a Web page.

Chapter 9: The FrontPage Explorer

Once you decide on a Web, the fun really begins as you need to create, update, and copy your Web. In this chapter you will learn how to maintain a Web site from within the FrontPage Explorer. Focus is on the various interface views (graphical, details, To Do List) and link management. Here you are exposed to the powerful templates included with Explorer and will learn how to build a robust Web with little effort.

Chapter 10: Navigation

In order to read an online Web title, you need navigation tools. This chapter explains the concept of buttons and links, their design, and how they are used to navigate within titles and provide a gateway to other information.

Chapter 11: Multimedia

Sound and music turn the average Web page into a multimedia adventure. Here you will learn about image types, audio file formats, and the process for incorporating sound and music into your titles.

Chapter 12: A FrontPage Project

Here you can close the door and get down and dirty with your Web project. In this chapter you will build a Web site from the ground up by using FrontPage for creation and editing, incorporating a registration form, and linking your pages together.

Chapter 13: FrontPage Software Developer's Kit

To all the techies out there who really want to know what makes FrontPage tick and how to change it, this chapter is for you. Here you will learn to use the FrontPage Software Developer's Kit(SDK) to completely control the Web development process and customize FrontPage to your needs. This chapter details the importance of the SDK and OLE and its application as the underlying architecture of FrontPage and demonstrates how to exploit FrontPage's extensible environment.

Chapter 14: Scripting—Easy as 1...VB

Just when Web pages needed someone else to do the automation tasks, Microsoft created Visual Basic Scripting Edition (VBScript). In this chapter you will learn how to exploit its object architecture to add functionality and automate your pages. Here you'll learn how to use VBScript to unleash the power of ActiveX, Java, and objects on the Web.

Chapter 15: Brewing Java and JavaScript

Care to drink a cup? Coffee metaphors aside, Java is quickly becoming the de facto programming language for the Internet. Read this chapter to learn how to enhance your Web pages by infusing them with Java and JavaScript. This chapter will illustrate how to combine the best of both worlds to create Web masterpieces.

Chapter 16: Forms and Security

Do you want to interact with your readers and protect your Web and them alike? Well, read this chapter to learn how to implement forms and security. Here you'll explore various form functions, how to create them using FrontPage, and how to work with the FrontPage form WebBots. In addition, you will review different Web security issues, different types of cryptography, and security protocols.

Chapter 17: CGI Overview

Did you ever wonder just how Web sites seem to tailor their pages to your needs based on your interaction with the site? From catalogs to registration forms, Common Gateway Interface (CGI) compatible programs are at work. In this chapter you will learn the specifics of CGI programming, various methods of creating CGI scripts, and how to implement CGI using FrontPage. As a bonus, you'll learn the secret to how FrontPage's WebBots really work.

Chapter 18: The Road Ahead

This chapter examines potential new features in store for the World Wide Web in addition to trends and challenges in store as the environment matures.

Appendix A: HTML Tags

This section lists the available HTML tags, including the latest Microsoft and Netscape extensions, that are available for further extension of your Web pages.

Appendix B: Visual Basic Script Reference

This section is a compilation of the VBScript objects and language reference. Use it as a quick reference to the components of the VBScript language.

Appendix C: JavaScript Keys

This section is a compilation of the JavaScript objects and language elements. You'll find this section an invaluable reference during your JavaScript development.

Appendix D: Additional Resources

One of the best ways to gain proficiency in your exposure to FrontPage and Web mastery is to review what others have already done in this field. This section provides you with numerous resources to point you in the right direction.

System and Software Requirements

Since Microsoft FrontPage was designed for the Windows 95 and Windows NT 3.51 and greater, you should have these operating systems on your computer. In addition, it is a good idea to have a World Wide Web browser for viewing your Web pages, so Microsoft Internet Explorer is included on the enclosed compact disc (CD-ROM).

The CD-ROM

The CD-ROM includes sample code, where applicable, from each chapter, in addition to numerous applications that have proven invaluable during the development of this book. Refer to the installation section or review the file **README.TXT** on the CD-ROM for more information regarding the structure of the CD-ROM contents and how to install the various applications.

Jump In

As with most things, to jump right in is the best way to learn about FrontPage and the enclosed CD-ROM content. You're now equipped (parachute and all) to venture into the world of FrontPage and the World Wide Web! So, go right to the chapters that most interest you. See you on the Web!

Installation

FrontPage 97 Web Designer's Guide Release Notes © 1997 The Waite Group, Inc.

These release notes document the contents and installation of the accompanying CD-ROM components.

Requirements

To view the graphics (`.PCX`) and text (`.TXT`) files, you need the following:

◁ A personal computer with a minimum 486 microprocessor running Microsoft Windows 95 or later, or Microsoft Windows NT 4.0 or later

◁ 8-16 MB of RAM

Additional requirements for the included applications can be located in the setup documentation for each application.

Installation Notes

Each application has its own setup requirements and instructions. Please refer to the documents that are included in those subdirectories. Instructions are usually included in a file called **README.TXT** or **SETUP.TXT**.

CD-ROM File Structure and Contents

Each directory prefixed with **FPP*** will include all images (***.PCX**) and code segments (***.TXT**), if applicable, referenced in the book.

```
\FPP
  |ñREADME.HTM              — HTML version of this installation
  |ñREADME.TXT              — Text version of this installation
  \ñSHARWARE.TXT            — Definition of SHAREWARE
     |__ \3RDPARTY
     |      |__ \ACROBAT    — Acrobat Reader and ActiveX Control
     |      |__ \ANBUTTON   — Animated ActiveX button
     |      |__ \CHART      — Charting ActiveX Control
     |      |__ \CYBERGO    — Cybergo ActiveX Control
     |      |__ \FP97EXT    — FrontPage 97 Server Extensions
     |      |__ \FPSDK20    — FrontPage 97 SDK 2.0
```

```
|       |__ \GRADIENT          — Gradient ActiveX Control
|       |__ \IASSIST           — Internet Assistant for Word
|       |    |__ \WRDIE16      — Windows 3.x version
|       |    \__ \WRDIE32      — Windows 95/NT version
|       |__ \JDK               — Java Developer's Kit 1.0.2 for Windows 95/NT
|       |__ \LABEL             — Label ActiveX Control
|       |__ \LOOKATME          — Farallon's Look@Me ActiveX Control
|       |__ \LVIEWPRO          — LView Pro Graphics editor
|       |    |__ \LVIEWPRO.16  — Windows 3.x version
|       |    \__ \LVIEWPRO.32  — Windows 95/NT version
|       |__ \MARQUEE           — Marquee ActiveX Control
|       |__ \PNTSHOP           — Internet Assistant for Word
|       |    |__ \WIN3XNT3.51  — Windows 3.x and NT 3.51 version
|       |    \__ \WIN95NT4.0   — Windows 95 and NT 4.0 version
|       |__ \POPUP             — Menu Popup ActiveX Control
|       |__ \POPUPWIN          — Window Popup ActiveX Control
|       |__ \PRELOAD           — Preloader ActiveX Control
|       |__ \SURROUND          — Surround video ActiveX Control
|       |__ \TEXTPAD           — Text editor
|       |__ \TICKER            — Ticker tape ActiveX Control
|       |__ \TRACK             — Tracking ActiveX Control
|       |__ \VIVO              — Vivo Player ActiveX Control
|       |__ \WHAM!             — Waveform Hold and Modify sound editor
|       |__ \WINFRAME          — Window Frame ActiveX Control
|       |__ \WINZIP            — Nico Mak Computing Windows Zipper
|       |    |__ \WIN3X        — Windows 3.x and NT 3.51 version
|       |    \__ \WIN95-NT     — Windows 95 and NT 4.0 version
|       \__ \XFERPRO           — Internet format decoder
|__ \EXPLORER                  — Microsoft Internet Explorer
|__ \MISC                      — Support files for README.HTM
|__ \SOURCE
    |__ \CHAP01                — Chapter 1 Materials
    |__ \CHAP02                — Chapter 2 Materials
    |__ \CHAP03                — Chapter 3 Materials
    |__ \CHAP04                — Chapter 4 Materials
    |__ \CHAP05                — Chapter 5 Materials
    |__ \CHAP06                — Chapter 6 Materials
    |__ \CHAP07                — Chapter 7 Materials
    |__ \CHAP08                — Chapter 8 Materials
    |__ \CHAP09                — Chapter 9 Materials
    |__ \CHAP10                — Chapter 10 Materials
    |__ \CHAP11                — Chapter 11 Materials
    |__ \CHAP12                — Chapter 12 Materials
    |__ \CHAP13                — Chapter 13 Materials
```

```
|__ \CHAP14          — Chapter 14 Materials
|__ \CHAP15          — Chapter 15 Materials
|__ \CHAP16          — Chapter 16 Materials
|__ \CHAP17          — Chapter 17 Materials
|__ \CHAP18          — Chapter 18 Materials
|__ \APPENDA         — Appendix A Materials
|__ \APPENDB         — Appendix B Materials
|__ \APPENDC         — Appendix C Materials
\__ \APPENDD         — Appendix D Materials
```

Note: Some of the software included on the bundled CD-ROM, including Microsoft ActiveX Controls Gallery, are shareware, provided for your evaluation. If you find any of the shareware products useful, you are requested to register it as discussed in its documentation and/or in the About screen of the application. Waite Group Press has not paid the registration fee for this shareware.

The New Generation

In this chapter you will learn:

What Microsoft FrontPage Is and How It Can
Help You Design and Manage Your Web Site

The Architecture of FrontPage

The Components of the FrontPage User Interface

The Details of the FrontPage WebBots

The Tools Available to Customize FrontPage
for Your Environment

Unless you have been at a pajama party hosted by Rip Van Winkle, you have, no doubt, heard of the World Wide Web or (now clichéd) the Information Superhighway, which has become one of the hottest topics in the history of computers. The Web, so vast and offering so much potential for information access, has become a veritable sea of opportunity. Fortunately, you don't have to float in this sea alone, for Microsoft has thrown you an anchor. In fact, if you look closely, you'll discover a yacht in Microsoft FrontPage, the lead runner of the New Generation of Web-authoring tools.

Why FrontPage?

The World Wide Web (also known as the Web), since its 1989 inception by Tim Berners-Lee, has exploded exponentially. On the Internet, the Web contains a global network of computers that can access interactive information which is served on machines called *Web servers*. Individuals can also access this information using *Web browsers* via command-driven or point-and-click interface access.

Doubling in size annually, the Internet already has more than 50 million users worldwide. With the Web's meteoric success, people and businesses scramble to generate their own Web pages. Most, however, have found that the creation and maintenance of their pages is more work than they anticipated. For instance, Hypertext Markup Language (HTML), the language used to create Web pages, requires potential authors to learn tags and perform some programming in order to make interactive pages.

Learning and maintenance curves created a new software development environment—Web authoring tools. Numerous tools, from the basic to the advanced, are on the market to assist in the development of Web pages. However, the strengths and weaknesses of each of these myriad tools vary, depending on the task at hand. Vermeer Technologies, Inc., saw an opportunity in this market and conceived FrontPage to allow users flexibility and ease in generating pages for the World Wide Web. Coincidentally, Microsoft saw that FrontPage represented a new generation of Web development tools and promptly purchased Vermeer. Microsoft tailored its new acquisition, FrontPage, to share the MS Office look and feel. In one fell swoop, Web novices and professionals alike were caught in the buzz of Microsoft FrontPage.

FrontPage makes creating an interactive Web page much easier because it brings Web authoring to the masses. A visual publishing system, it was created with the designer and developer in mind. Designers will laud FrontPage because it requires neither programming nor HTML coding. Web pages are developed within a drag-and-drop design environment which will invite a whole new audience of Web enthusiasts into the World Wide Web arena. FrontPage generates HTML code which can be viewed on any platform via a standard HTML browser, including Netscape Navigator and Microsoft Internet Explorer. FrontPage extends this support to Web servers as well; FrontPage's server extensions can support Webs on various server platforms, including Microsoft Internet Information Server and Netscape Server.

The Client/Server Authoring System

The FrontPage architecture is much like two brothers. The FrontPage Client components (Explorer, Editor, and To Do List) represent the younger brother, who can handle most of the requests and tasks required to build and maintain your Web site. Occasionally, the server extensions must perform some tasks: Much like the elder brother helping the younger reach the cookies on the top shelf, the server extensions enable the FrontPage Client components to provide you with the same automation functionality on the server that you have when using FrontPage as standalone on your desktop. Figure 1-1 illustrates the FrontPage client/server architecture.

The FrontPage client portion consists of FrontPage Editor, Explorer, and the To Do List. For the most part, Web authors will use these ever-visible components of FrontPage to accomplish their work. FrontPage, however, does rely on its big brother, the server extensions, to handle some of the special tasks which the FrontPage Client cannot handle alone. The special tasks are small executables which reside on the Web server and are engineered to work with various Windows and UNIX Web servers.

When used in tandem, the FrontPage client/server components provide a powerful set of tools to unleash the power of the Web and the ability to create exciting Web sites.

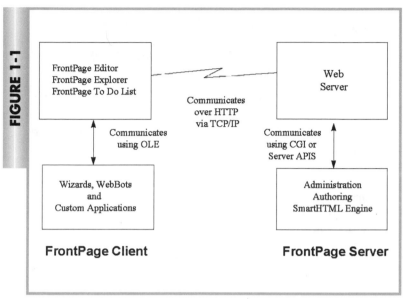

FIGURE 1-1

FrontPage client/server architecture

Security Model

FrontPage contains a flexible security model which provides support in specific areas:

◁ Control of Web access at the end-user, author, and administrative levels.

◁ Proxy support to permit and restrict authoring through a firewall.

◁ Encryption of all client/server communications.

Security Permissions

FrontPage provides security checking through server extensions which control access at end-user, author, and administrative levels.

At the end-user level, FrontPage can restrict individuals from browsing the Web. At the author level, it may restrict unauthorized individuals from accessing, updating, and maintaining the Web. The administrative security level can restrict users from maintaining security permissions.

How does FrontPage accomplish this security scheme? At the lowest level, FrontPage will use the existing security mechanism provided by the Web server. This allows FrontPage to support various Web servers without requiring rewrite of its security scheme. At a higher level, administrators may define access using combinations of user names, passwords, and a list of Internet Protocol (IP) addresses.

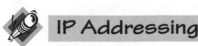

IP Addressing

IP is a component of the network protocol TCP/IP. Some specifics of TCP/IP will be discussed in Chapter 2, "Making the Connection."

Proxy Configuration

The lack of inherent security is one of the greatest threats imposed by the Internet. All serious Internet users, business and individuals alike, use firewalls as one step in restricting unauthorized Internet and Intranet traffic.

A firewall permits or restricts specific traffic between networks. Individuals who use a firewall can provide Intranet access and protect their information from the outside world, while allowing traffic outside the firewall. To handle the permit/restrict process, a proxy server, designated by a machine and optional port number, may be employed. For authoring through or within a firewall, FrontPage supports the specification of a proxy server and lists of servers which may be accessed without going through the proxy server.

Encryption

FrontPage's extensive use of the server extensions results in network traffic which can be perused by prying, hacker eyes. FrontPage encrypts all communication between its client and server components to address this security risk.

Note

FrontPage's security encryption is good, but is susceptible to tampering by professional hackers. For this reason, FrontPage will be enhanced to support the stronger Secure Sockets Layer (SSL) and/or Private Communications Technology (PCT) encryption and authentication standards.

The FrontPage User Interface

The FrontPage user interface is one of the first items that grabs your attention. The interface will be familiar territory for previous users of Microsoft products such as Windows and MS Office 95. Like a sleek limousine, the FrontPage user interface is well-polished and ready to take you wherever your Web authoring journey leads. The components of the user interface include the following:

◁ **FrontPage Explorer**—Provides an overview of your Web with graphical links and utilities for Web management.

◁ **FrontPage Editor**—The editing and design environment for individual pages. Serves as a Web browser for viewing and copying existing Web pages.

◁ **To Do List**—Provides a central task list for singular or multiple Web authors to provide project updates and action items.

◁ **Wizards and templates**—Facilitate your work aesthetically and efficiently: Wizards walk you through many tasks, and templates allow you to use existing styles or page definitions to design pages quickly.

FrontPage Explorer

Figure 1-2 illustrates the Explorer in action. The Explorer provides you with the complete picture of your Web. This Web-at-a-glance view can be toggled to provide a range of additional views, including graphical links and an element list. Another bonus of the Explorer is its relationship to the rest of the FrontPage client components. From the Explorer, you can launch any of the client components, including the Editor, To Do List, templates, wizards, and WebBots.

The FrontPage Explorer provides, but is not limited to, the following features:

◁ Graphical, hierarchical, and file views of the elements that make up your Web page

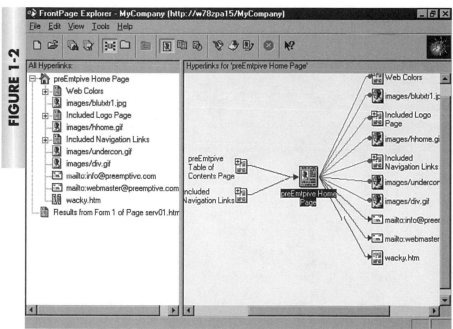

FIGURE 1-2

FrontPage Explorer

◁ Web site wizards and Web site templates for automating Web maintenance tasks

◁ Drag-and-drop hyperlinks including pages, images, and other file types

◁ Backlink autofix for documents that have been moved or renamed

◁ Security permissions and Secure Sockets Layer (SSL) support

◁ Web site copying between Web servers and hardware/software platforms

◁ Link validation to identify and repair broken links

◁ A Getting Started Wizard to assist in management of your Webs

◁ Support for external source management tools (for example, Visual SourceSafe)

FrontPage Editor

Like a captain at the helm, the FrontPage Editor, as shown in Figure 1-3, provides you with the power and assurance to edit your Web pages and ride the sea of Web design. The Editor provides a WYSIWYG editing environment, which enables you to see page elements much as they will appear within the end-user's browser. The Editor provides a powerful and inviting editing environment, much as do the other Microsoft Office components.

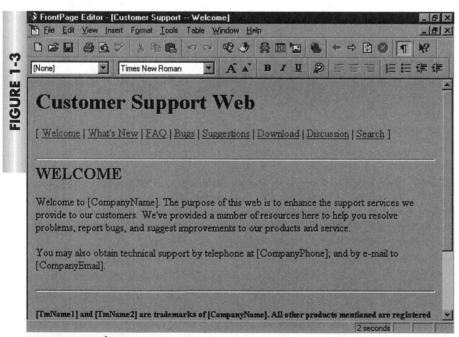

FIGURE 1-3

FrontPage Editor

Some FrontPage Editor features follow:

◁ WYSIWYG page and form editing

◁ Creating customized Web pages quickly with page wizards and templates

◁ Web components that automate many tasks without programming

◁ Point-and-click hyperlink editing

◁ Creating clickable image maps

◁ Conversion of RTF and HTML documents

◁ Graphic conversion to GIF and JPEG

◁ Creating transparent and interlaced GIF images for enhanced image display on your pages

◁ Reversing changes to your pages with multiple level Undo

◁ Viewing and capturing Web pages with a navigable Web browser

◁ Autodetecting a previous edit of your page, so that you can save it under a new name

FrontPage To Do List

Anyone who has ever maintained a Web site (you will soon be one of these folks) knows that it becomes quite difficult to manage a Web and all of the outstanding tasks necessary to complete and maintain the site. Fortunately, FrontPage includes a To Do List to help you manage the tasks for your Web completion. Figure 1-4 illustrates the To Do List interface. Many FrontPage wizards assist as well by automatically adding necessary tasks to your To Do List.

Some of the features included with the To Do List follow:

◁ Lists critical items such as task name, priority name, and so forth in a detailed column

◁ Sorts by category

◁ Allows task reassignment

◁ Moves you to the point on your page that requires work when you click the task

◁ Automatically prompts for completed tasks

◁ Detects authors trying to perform the same task

◁ Views completed tasks historically

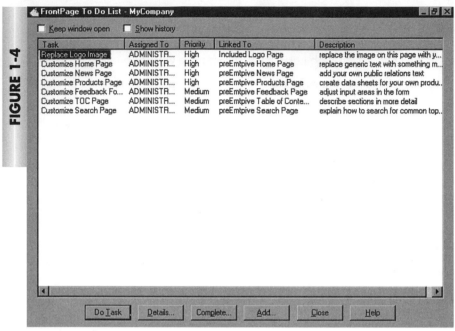

FIGURE 1-4

FrontPage To Do List

FrontPage Wizards and Templates

Imagine that you have your own little Web genie which will perform "Web wishes" for you. Wizards are miniprograms which prompt you for information and choices in order to design your pages and/or Web as you wish. A FrontPage wizard acts very much as a genie: Your wish in Figure 1-5 can't be granted without a little participation on your part. The wizard

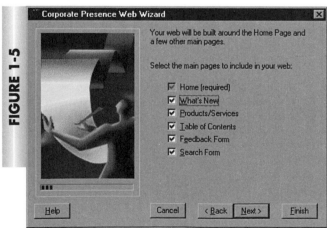

FIGURE 1-5

FrontPage wizard in action

prompts you by offering one or more dialog boxes for you to enter information. The beauty of a wizard lies in its ability to generate one or more pages to start customization. Potentially, this can save you many hours of development time.

Some of the wizards included with FrontPage follow:

◁ **Corporate Presence Wizard** generates a Web site for your company or organization

◁ **Discussion Web Wizard** builds a threaded discussion group into a new or existing Web

◁ **Personal Home Page Wizard** creates a single page just for you

◁ **Frames Wizard** allows you to create a form that implements HTML framesets

◁ **Form Page Wizard** allows you to build and customize a form to gather user input

Perhaps the most frequently asked wizard questions revolve around the creation of custom wizards. Using the FrontPage *Software Developer's Kit* (SDK) and a programming language, such as Microsoft Visual Basic or Visual C++, you can create your own wizards that you can invoke from within FrontPage.

Although wizards can be used to programmatically build Web pages, FrontPage also provides more than 20-page templates to infuse pages with your particular style. Templates can considerably shorten page editing time while giving your Web an individual look and feel. You can easily create your own templates without programming by using the documentation included in the FrontPage SDK.

FrontPage WebBots

Do you ever get that lazy feeling and want someone else to do all your work for you? Although this usually won't happen, FrontPage attempts to grant this wish during Web page authoring: The FrontPage WebBot components are provided for your automation needs.

What Are WebBots?

Contrary to what you might imagine, a WebBot is not a mechanical spider. A WebBot is an active object that is placed into a page to perform interactive functions that traditionally required custom programming. With WebBots, you can design your Web just like the big shots do, without any programming!

No programming sounds like a myth and demands close examination. Imagine a Web page that prompts you for a search string and then, after the click of a button, finds all of the relevant Web pages that contain the search string. Sound familiar? If you have used a Web search engine, such as Yahoo!, Lycos, or Excite, you probably have performed this task many times. How does the process work? After you clicked that page button, the string was sent to the Web server, a program was invoked to search across a catalog of Web pages, the results were compiled, and a new page with search results was put together and sent back to you. This is a lot of work, and the custom program did much of it. However, you could simply place a Search WebBot into your page, where it would handle the rest.

You don't have to worry about the details of the process, because this slight of hand is performed in the background. Using a WebBot is as simple as selecting the Insert/Bot menu item in the FrontPage Editor. Once you select a WebBot, you will be presented with configuration dialogs to customize the activity or view of the WebBot. After customization, a WYSIWYG representation of the WebBot is placed into your Editor page. At run-time, the WebBot communicates with the FrontPage server extensions to perform any necessary activities.

Included WebBots

To aid in your Web site authoring, FrontPage includes a number of standard WebBots:

◁ **Annotation WebBot** inserts text on a page which can be viewed from the FrontPage Editor, but not from a Web browser. Use an Annotation bot to insert place-holder text or notes to yourself as you create Web pages. Annotation text is displayed in purple and retains the character size and other attributes of the current paragraph style.

◁ **Confirmation Field WebBot** is replaced with the contents of a form field. It is useful on a form confirmation page, where it can echo the user's name or any other data entered into a field.

◁ **Discussion WebBot** allows users to participate in an online discussion. The Discussion bot collects information from a form, formats it into an HTML page, and adds the page to a table of contents and to a text index. In addition, the Discussion bot gathers information from the form and stores it in one of a selection of formats.

◁ **HTML Markup WebBot** substitutes any arbitrary text you supply when you create the bot when the page is saved to the server as HTML. Use this bot to add nonstandard HTML commands to a page.

◁ **Include WebBot** is replaced with the contents of another page in the Web.

◁ **Registration WebBot**, a form bot, allows users to automatically register themselves for access to a service. The Registration bot adds the user to the service's authentication database, and then optionally gathers information from the form and stores it in one of a selection of formats.

◁ **Save Results WebBot**, a form bot, gathers information from a form and stores it in one of a selection of formats. When a user submits the form, the Save Results bot appends the form information to a specified file in a specified format.

◁ **Scheduled Image WebBot** is replaced by an image during a specific time period. The image is no longer displayed when the time period expires.

◁ **Scheduled Include WebBot** is replaced with the contents of a file during a specified time period. The contents of the file are no longer displayed when the time period expires.

◁ **Search WebBot** provides full text-searching capability in your Web at run-time. When the user submits a form containing words to locate, the Search bot returns a list of all pages in your Web that contain matches.

◁ **Substitution WebBot** is replaced by the value of a selected page configuration or Web configuration variable.

◁ **Table of Contents WebBot** creates an outline of your Web, with links to each page. The Table of Contents bot updates this outline each time the Web's contents change.

◁ **Timestamp WebBot** is replaced by the date and time the page was last edited or automatically updated.

FrontPage Customization

After using many of the various WebBots and included Web templates and pages, you may wonder to yourself, "How do I create my own?" Have no fear: FrontPage answers the call by allowing you to create your own Web templates and interact with its interface from within other applications. In this section, you'll take a closer look at customizing FrontPage to do your bidding.

Templates

During your Web maintenance journey, you'll find that plenty of Web pages are quite similar to each other. Some may differ only by a few lines. Wouldn't it be nice if you could create new pages based upon existing pages or predefined formats? FrontPage rushes to the rescue by offering page templates. Templates consist of one or more Web pages and the associated settings that can be used to generate new pages. A number of standard FrontPage templates follows:

◁ Normal Page

◁ Bibliography

◁ Confirmation Form

◁ Directory of Press Releases

◁ Employee Directory

◁ Employment Opportunities

◁ Feedback Form

◁ Frequently Asked Questions

◁ Glossary of Terms

◁ Guest Book

◁ Hot List

◁ Hyperdocument Page

◁ Lecture Abstract

◁ Meeting Agenda

◁ Office Directory

◁ Press Release

◁ Product Description

◁ Product or Event Registration

◁ Search Page

◁ Seminar Schedule

◁ Software Data Sheet

◁ Survey Form

◁ User Registration

◁ What's New

Software Developer's Kit

Although FrontPage provides a bundle of powerful features right out of the box, you will ultimately want to create your own page templates or design your own wizards. Think of the possibilities! You could design a wizard and have people use it within your Intranet to create a uniform Web site! Better yet, wouldn't you like to interact with FrontPage via another executable program? You're in luck: Microsoft has made the FrontPage SDK available for public access at its Web site (`http://www.microsoft.com/frontpage`). You'll find the FrontPage SDK on the companion CD-ROM.

The FrontPage SDK allows you to extend Microsoft FrontPage in the following ways:

◁ End-users or developers can create templates for Webs or individual Web pages. Additionally, developers can use the kit to create an entire Web.

◁ Developers can create customized wizards that can be used to generate Webs or Web pages. The wizards and other programs can use Object Linking and Embedding (OLE) Automation to communicate with the Windows version of the FrontPage client.

In addition, the FrontPage SDK includes documentation and sample programs to aid you in FrontPage customization. The FrontPage SDK documentation includes tips and tricks relating to:

◁ **Templates**—Learn where FrontPage stores its templates, how its template files are stored, the details of the information file, home page management and how to create page, Web, and frameset templates.

◁ **Wizards**—Delve into Camelot and you'll learn more about the FrontPage information file, details on the page and Web wizards, how to pass parameters back and forth, how to construct the user interface, initialization settings, the wizard naming conventions, and how FrontPage interacts with its wizards.

◁ **OLE Automation Overview**—This section introduces you to FrontPage terminology and how it applies to the Editor, Explorer, and To Do List interfaces. In addition, it will expose you to a variety of programming considerations and examples.

◁ **FrontPage Explorer Automation**—If you are a developer or a FrontPage developer wannabe, this section speaks your language. Here you encounter all of the exposed OLE Automation methods for the FrontPage Explorer.

◁ **FrontPage Editor Automation**—Much like the Explorer, the exposed OLE Automation methods are illustrated with C++ and Visual Basic calling conventions.

◁ **FrontPage To Do List Automation**—Following in the Explorer and Editor traditions, the exposed To Do List OLE Automation methods are conveniently detailed.

◁ **Examples**—This section presents additional documentation, sample wizards and templates, instructions for building your own utility programs, and CGI compatibility issues. Additionally, the FrontPage SDK includes numerous Visual Basic and Visual C++ examples so that you can build your own utility programs from working models.

What's New?

FrontPage is considerably different from earlier versions and brings many of the HTML supports that users have requested. The latest enhancements to this version fall into the following categories:

◁ Editor enhancements

◁ Explorer enhancements

◁ Office integration

Editor Enhancements

Perhaps the most revamped and most appealing component of FrontPage is the Editor. Responding to customer feedback, Microsoft provides support for many of the Netscape and Microsoft HTML extensions. The following item categories represent the major Editor modifications for this release:

◁ **General Editor** enhancements include moving between Web pages using navigation buttons, custom page templates, frames support, HTML source viewer and preservation, meta page variables, style pages, and the ability to update Office documents within a Web.

◁ **Layout** enhancements include alternative image displays, break-below images, clickable images, a frames wizard, interlaced image support, table support, and an image alignment preview.

◁ **Toolbar and formatting** enhancements include active link color support, new alignment options, font color properties, support for multiple levels of Undo, and support of text superscripts and subscripts.

General

Take a closer look at some of the general Editor enhancements that are included with FrontPage:

◁ **Back and Reload in Editor** allows you to load multiple Web pages for editing and then move among them with the navigation buttons provided in the Editor, see Figure 1-6. This navigation technique extends the Web browser metaphor, allowing you to work just as you would browse the pages.

◁ **Custom Page Templates**, shown in Figure 1-7, provide a basic functionality, or style, for your page. The Editor allows you to create your own templates easily or to choose from more than 20 included templates.

FIGURE 1-6 Page navigation buttons in the Editor

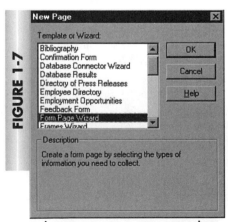

FIGURE 1-7

Selecting a new page template

◁ **Frame Support** is supported by the new Frames Wizard, shown in Figure 1-8, which allows you to arrange multiple pages on an individual page. Frames are very useful for enabling navigation among multiple pages without leaving the original page.

◁ **HTML Viewer and Preservation** enables you to view the HTML code that will be generated by FrontPage and import existing HTML into the Editor. FrontPage can import unsupported HTML code and will preserve this code so that you may incorporate HTML extensions which FrontPage may not natively support.

◁ **Meta Page Variables** features allow you to insert the META and HTTP-EQUIV variables for your page.

◁ **Style Pages** enables you to set the color scheme of a page by using a page property that uses a style page for this information. If you decide to change the color scheme of the style page, all Web pages referencing this style page will automatically be updated.

◁ **Office Document** support allows you to import existing Rich Text Format (RTF) files. If the source RTF file is updated, your pages will also be updated.

Layout

Some of the layout enhancements included with FrontPage are:

◁ **Alternative image representation** allows you to specify an alternative image to be displayed while images are being downloaded. This feature corresponds to the HTML LOWSRC image attribute.

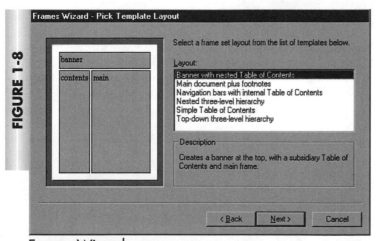

FIGURE 1-8

Frames Wizard

◁ **Break-below images** allow you to specify break tags which work with left- and right-aligned images.

◁ **Clickable images** are supported in two ways for compatibility with browsers which support or do not support client-side images. For compatible browsers, such as Netscape Navigator or Internet Explorer, the Web browser immediately follows a clickable-image hyperlink without requiring additional Web server intervention. However, for incompatible browsers, FrontPage can follow the traditional approach and generate the appropriate HTML to automatically transfer clickable-image processing to the Web server.

◁ **Interlaced image support** has been added for GIF files to enable progressive rendering of an image during its download by right-clicking on an image and selecting the Properties menu item.

◁ **Table support**, shown in Figure 1-9, was perhaps the most requested feature for this version of FrontPage. FrontPage now has a WYSIWYG view of HTML tables and may customize tables by inserting rows or columns, adding images into cells, using fixed or dynamic sizes, splitting or merging cells, aligning a table or individual cells, and providing header cells, spacing, or captions.

◁ **Image alignment preview** allows you to see the effects of alignment changes without closing the alignment dialog box.

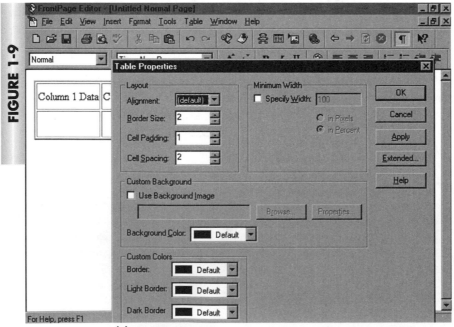

FIGURE 1-9

Customizing tables in FrontPage

Toolbars and Formatting

For Office integration and ease of use, FrontPage now contains the following toolbar and formatting enhancements:

◁ **Active link color** represents the color of a link when you hold down the mouse while you click on a link. FrontPage enables you to modify this color.

◁ **Alignment buttons** have been added to the Formatting toolbar to enable left, right, or center alignment at the click of a button.

◁ **Font color** may be modified for any selection of text by clicking the font color button.

◁ **Multiple level Undo** allows you to undo the last 30 editing actions that you have performed. This feature gives you the freedom to experiment with a page, as well as quick recovery from editing errors.

◁ **Font size** may be changed for any combination of text by clicking this option on the toolbar.

◁ **Superscripts and subscripts** are now supported text elements within the FrontPage Editor.

Explorer Enhancements

The 1.0 FrontPage Explorer provided a strong foundation for Web management. FrontPage now builds on this foundation by adding features that are necessary for management of larger Web sites. The following items represent the major Explorer enhancements for FrontPage:

◁ **Authoring logging** enables administrators to maintain an audit trail of all operations performed on the Web. FrontPage provides the author's name, a date-time stamp, and the operation performed for review by the administrator. This log is also useful for observing the change history of the site.

◁ **Automatic link repair** allows you to move or rename documents and to update all instances of a link within your Web. When you move or rename a file within your Web, FrontPage automatically updates all associated links to this file throughout the Web. FrontPage also maintains a list of all broken links: If you update the broken link, all associated pages may be updated.

◁ **Automatic TCP/IP checking** enables FrontPage to ensure that you have a valid TCP/IP setup and connection during your use. Depending on your connection, FrontPage automatically determines whether or not you are connected to a network or standalone and determines the host name for your session. When necessary, FrontPage launches the Personal Web Server (PWS) to provide server services without displaying error messages, provided your Web server extensions are loaded and configured.

◁ **Discussion group improvements** include the options of viewing all messages in a discussion group to be displayed from FrontPage Explorer and using frames for discussion pages. By enabling message viewing, an administrator may monitor or delete messages. Framed discussion pages, an option within the Discussion Wizard, allows you to develop advanced and aesthetically pleasing discussion pages.

◁ **Getting Started Wizard** provides a helpful dialog that allows you to open existing Webs or create new ones immediately.

◁ **Multiple homing** consists of serving multiple Web domains (such as `cool.guy.com` and `cool.lady.com`) on the same Web server. FrontPage supports the two common methods of implementing multiple homing. In the first implementation, the Web server supports multiple homing intrinsically. In the second implementation, multiple instances of the Web server execute and serve different domains.

Office Integration

Now that FrontPage is officially a member of the Microsoft Office product suite, it sports many of the interfaces and plumbing that the rest of the products include. The following items represent the Office integration enhancements for FrontPage:

◁ **User interface** features include Office-standard formatting toolbars and menu options, as in Figure 1-10. If you have used Microsoft Word or any of the other Office products, you will feel instantly familiar with the FrontPage user interface and its extensive use of wizards and property page dialogs. In addition, the Web navigation tools have been modified to reflect Microsoft Internet Explorer to extend the Web browsing metaphor across the Office suite.

◁ **Spelling checker** utilities abound in many editors. However, FrontPage uses the Microsoft Office spelling checker for seamless integration.

◁ **Windows 95 style help** is available throughout FrontPage. Tabbed dialogs and context-sensitive help features usually place you no more than a click away from answers to your questions.

◁ **Uninstall** capability is expected in most of today's applications. FrontPage is no exception; it includes a robust uninstall utility to ensure proper removal in case you want to delete FrontPage.

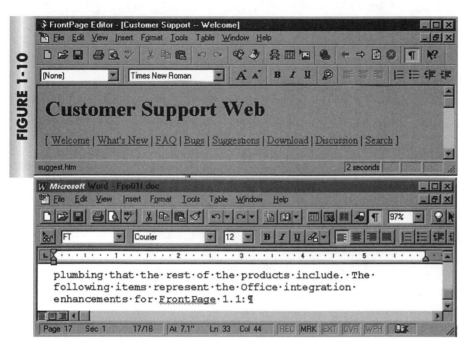

FIGURE 1-10

FrontPage and Word authoring interface

Where to Go from Here

You now have seen many of the features that constitute FrontPage as it leads the way in the new generation of Web authoring tools. This chapter has only touched on these components and features; read on and ride your FrontPage yacht into deeper waters so that you can develop and maintain your Web page *extraordinaire*!

Making the Connection

2

In this chapter you will learn:

Types of Internet Connections
Helpful Hardware and Software in Connecting to the Net
Internet Services
Internet Service Providers (ISPs)
Questions to Ask Prospective ISPs
SLIP, CSLIP, and PPP Accounts
Online Services

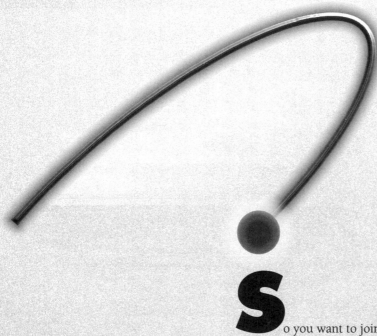

So you want to join the ranks of the cyber-nauts that have steadily increased since the blast-off of the Internet. You, too, yearn to experience all the techno-services the Net offers: to surf the World Wide Web (WWW or Web), have your own Web page, join discussion groups, and communicate via e-mail. How do you make this wonderful dream come true? How will you find your way through the cyber-jargon and the endless variety of services and connections? Although seemingly a daunting task, it is indeed possible to weave through the mysterious maze of Internet choices: Just click your heels together three times, then read the rest of this chapter.

First, A Little Cyber-Jargon

Before your voyage through cyberspace, you need to understand some general terms that pop up over and over in computer books and magazines.

◁ Internet—The Net is composed of many and various computers world-wide that are linked to share data. The Internet offers services such as FTP, Telnet, Usenet, e-mail, and WWW access (discussed later in this chapter). Information Superhighway and Global Information Organization are other synonyms for the Internet.

◁ Internet Service Provider—ISPs resell Internet services. They provide Internet connectivity, access, content development services, and other networking services. ISPs purchase Internet feeds from major Internet sources. They are equipped with many telephone lines, banks of modems, computers, and other hardware. In this chapter, all types of providers, except online service providers, are referred to as ISPs.

◁ Internet Access Provider—It allows customers to indirectly connect to, or access, the Internet through its "middleman" computer. Customers need a telephone line and a modem to connect to an IAP's direct Internet connection.

◁ Internet Presence Provider—It obtains Internet access for customers. IPPs also offer consulting and content development.

◁ Information Provider— It supplies information or services, such as news, stock quotes, and WWW pages, to the Internet.

◁ User— He or she uses or "surfs" the Internet and may also provide information.

◁ Browser—It acts as a translator; this software allows you to read information from a server on the Internet. Browsers (or clients) also translate commands so they will be understood and fulfilled. Each type of Internet service or server demands a particular browser. Two popular WWW browsers are Netscape's *Navigator* and Microsoft's *Explorer*. Free browsers, such as *Mosaic,* can be downloaded from the Internet. Download Mosaic at the following address: `http://www.ncsa.uiuc.edu/SDG/Software/Mosaic/`

◁ Server—It contains information that is accessed by an Internet service such as the WWW, Gopher, or FTP. Each service has a particular kind of server that responds to requests from users. WWW servers are called HTTP (HyperText Transfer Protocol) servers. Figure 2-1 shows the relationship between servers and browsers.

◁ World Wide Web (WWW)—It is an Internet service or application that enables users to share visual information. The WWW contains a large network of data including hypertext documents which may contain images, animation, text, and sound. Links in the documents transport users to associated information and other documents.

Buyer Beware

Now that you are familiar with basic Internet terminology, take a look at the options available to prospective Internet users. The continuous onslaught of service provider and connection choices make informed decisions vital. You must select the hardware, services, and connection that best suit your needs. How fast do you want your modem to be? An individual user will answer this question quite differently than will a large corporation. What services do you need, and will you have the time to use them? Buying cool services like the WWW makes no sense if you only have time to send e-mail messages.

FIGURE 2-1

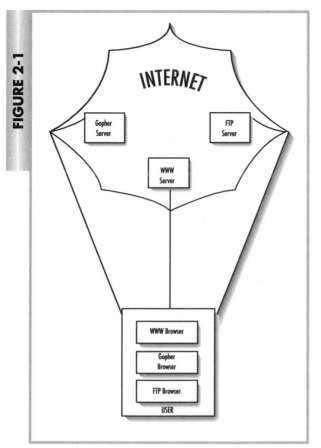

Relationship between servers and browsers

Does your prospective ISP offer the services you want at a competitive price? With so many ISPs available, shopping around can lead to good deals. Do you want merely to access the Net without direct connection, or do you want to connect to it? Do you want to be a user, an information provider, or both? Your answers to these questions can help you find the ISP that is right for you.

If all these choices seem overwhelming, don't panic. Start with the basics and work up. Usually one decision will lead to another. Although this method may work fine for individuals, large organizations may need an Internet consultant to help them make all the choices needed to get connected.

Helpful Hardware and Software

This section outlines several physical components you will need to connect to the Internet: a computer, a modem, a telephone line, and software.

A Computer

Of course, you need to start off with a good computer. Almost any kind of computer can interface with the Internet, but this book focuses on PCs with the Windows operating system. If possible, get at least a 386 PC with 4MB or more of memory, and Windows 3.1, Windows for Workgroups, or Windows 95. Your monitor should be Super VGA, and a sound card and speakers will allow you to hear all of the neat sound effects of the WWW.

A Telephone Line and Modem

The dominant method of connecting to the Internet is through a PC that has a modem and a telephone line. Computers speak in a digital language which, when converted to analog, readily flows through telephone lines. A modem links your computer to your phone line and changes the digital language of the computer to the analog language of the phone line.

Your modem choice depends on how fast you want your connection to be and how much you want to pay. The following modems are recommended:

V.34 28.8 Kbps (kilobytes per second)—fastest in common use

V.32bis 14.4 Kbps—half as fast as the 28.8 Kbps

Remember that the actual speed of your modem depends on the speed of the modem at the other end of your connection. In other words, to achieve a speed of 28.8 Kbps, you must connect to another modem with at least the same speed. Modem speed is also affected by the quality of telephone lines and other types of line interference. V.34 and V.32bis are standard protocols that are used by most Internet providers so make sure your modem uses one of them.

 Tip

Do not buy a no-name modem. Spend the extra few bucks and get a brand name that will have fewer bugs to slow you down, often better drivers, and better technical support.

If you plan to use the Internet frequently or for business purposes, you may want to give your modem a dedicated phone line. Large organizations that are both users and information providers often opt to connect to the Internet directly through high-speed phone lines. They may obtain dedicated lines, or lease dial-in lines.

The Software

You need a certain type of software to make your Net connection. The software, provided by the ISP, depends on the services you want and the type of connection you choose. For instance, if you want to access the WWW using a SLIP account, you will need SLIP connection software, a TCP/IP translator (Winsock), and a Web browser. Certain operating systems, such as Windows 95 and NT, come with their own connection software.

Services Galore

The Internet package from your ISP will probably include

◁ An account on your ISP's system where you can store files and communicate with the Net

◁ An e-mail address which allows you to send and receive messages from users all over the world

◁ A Usenet feed which allows you to participate in e-mail discussion groups

◁ Other services you have chosen

You can have a variety of services on your Internet account. Some services, such as e-mail and Usenet, may come with your account. Others, such as the WWW, you may have to request at extra cost.

Commercial online services operate outside the Internet. These companies act as ISPs and also offer their own libraries of data and services targeted at particular consumer groups.

Figure 2-2 is a diagram showing the relationship of the various Internet related services. Note that there are seven services within the Web-like structure of the Internet. While BBSs and online services are not Internet services, they are satellite services that can access or connect to the Net. The following paragraphs explain the services related to the Internet.

FIGURE 2-2

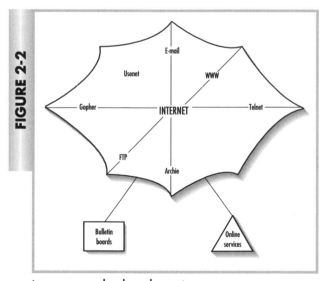

Internet and related services

E-mail

E-mail is the basic Internet service and usually comes with your Internet account. E-mail, or electronic mail, is the elemental tool used for communication on the Net. E-mail allows you to correspond with any of millions of users worldwide. To use e-mail, you need an e-mail address which is supplied by your service. The address consists of your *account name* and the ISP's *domain name*.

If your name were Mary Smith, your account name, or login, might be msmith. Your ISP assigns you an account name or may permit you to select your own. Your ISP has its own domain name. For example, in the domain name cosmic.com, *cosmic* is the provider's name, and *.com* means that it is a commercial provider. Putting it all together, your e-mail address would be

`msmith@cosmic.com`

An e-mail address allows you to be located easily by other users on the Net. Your incoming e-mail messages go first to your ISP's computer, which in turn routes them to your e-mail inbox. You receive e-mail through your connection with your ISP.

Tip

Make checking and answering your e-mail messages the first order of business after you login. Unanswered e-mail is bad Internet etiquette!

Usenet News

The Usenet News service may come with your Internet account. Usenet is a discussion group network. You can choose to talk with any of the thousands of special interest groups that exist on the network. When you select one or more groups to join, you are *subscribing* to these groups. Topics of newsgroups cover social issues, the sciences, business, recreation, and vacation ideas, as well as hobby areas like crafts, gardening, and cats. You can ask experts for advice on parenting, or discuss the plot and characters of your favorite television show.

When you subscribe to a special interest group, the title of that group appears at the top of the screen, followed by questions and comments from other users. You can send answers privately to a specific user, or publicly to the group so everyone can read them. Usenet provides an open forum where people can share their thoughts and opinions on a variety of subjects. Experts can answer questions such as, "What kind of truck should I buy?" or "How should I discipline my child?"

Note

After you spend some time on the Usenet network, you will probably encounter the terms *flaming, flamer, flame war,* and *firefighter.* These words

refer to the angry clashing of opinions that often occurs in discussion groups. Flamers give rude and insulting responses and firefighters attempt to stop flame wars. Try to avoid these controversial situations.

FTP

File Transfer Protocol is an Internet information service that facilitates the transmission and downloading of files from computer to computer. With FTP, you are able to receive files from other computers hooked up to your ISP's computer, or from computers outside of this system. The external computers are called *remote* machines.

When you access remote computers through FTP, log in as anonymous or FTP and use your e-mail address as the password. You can then either download files from a directory, or transmit your files into a directory.

Tip

WWW pages can be stored at FTP anonymous sites: Most Web browsers know how to retrieve Web pages from the inexpensive anonymous sites.

Telnet

Telnet's Internet information service, like that of FTP, allows you to access remote computers. Telnet is more restricted; you cannot simply login as *anonymous* on Telnet: You need an account at a remote site. With that remote account, you can interface with all areas of the remote machine. The anonymous FTP login, however, restricts you to certain directories. Most users don't have accounts at remote sites and don't Telnet very often. However, you can Telnet your own computer when you are away.

Tip

Some remote sites bypass the account restriction and let anyone Telnet to them. These sites will either tell you how to login, or you can simply enter *demo* or *guest* for a login.

World Wide Web

The World Wide Web is a service offered within the Internet. Its graphical interface and point and click capabilities allow users to incorporate pictures, graphics, sound, and animation into their Web sites. You can access libraries of information on the Web, as well as business, commercial, and personal Web sites which offer information on virtually any subject. Many search engines are offered on the Web. Table 2-1 lists a few of them.

Table 2-1 WWW search mechanisms

Search Mechanism	Notes
http://www.yahoo.com	Searches by subject
http://www.yahooligas.com	Searches by subject; geared to children
http://www.altavista.digital.com	Searches by keyword
http://www.lycos.com	Searches by subject and keyword

Archie

Archie, an Internet search application, has sites that contain large databases that represent what is available in particular sections of the Internet. Enter the site name and a single search word to access an Archie site. You receive a list of file names containing that word and the files' sources. Use FTP to download the files you want. Because each Archie site represents a specific portion of the Internet, file lists from two Archie sites will be quite different from each other.

Note

You do not need the Archie application on the WWW, which has its own search mechanisms. However, different search engines may give different results.

Gopher

The Gopher Internet information service facilitates the downloading of documents and searches databases. An FTPdirectory or list often contains columns of coded file names. Gopher directories display complete descriptions along with the file names so you find what you need quickly and easily. Gopher can also access and search other databases.

Tip

WWW browsers have the ability to access Gopher sites. Because of the visual graphics capability of the WWW, many users prefer to access Gopher sites from Web browsers rather than Gopher browsers. To access a Gopher site from a Web browser, type in Gopher:// then the Gopher address.

Bulletin Board Systems (BBSs)

Many BBSs have Internet gateways that only allow you to send and receive e-mail and download files from other bulletin board users. Some offer WWW access with text-based Web browsers or graphical browsers. As more and more BBSs acquire Web browsers, BBSs will become an alternative entryway to the Web.

Online Services

National companies that provide online communication and information services, online services usually enable customers to use Internet services, such as e-mail, Usenet, and Gopher. Most online services offer Internet access, including the WWW. Online services promote their own libraries of data and services that target particular consumer groups, unlike traditional ISPs. Among the available services are America Online's extensive selection of children's games and Prodigy's access to current issues of *Newsweek* magazine. Other services include stock quotes, airline reservations, and shopping. Although these services cost extra, they may be higher in quality than similar services on the Internet. Online services tend to restrict content and control discussion group themes to present a certain atmosphere to customers. Popular Online services include America Online, CompuServe, Prodigy, Microsoft Network, Delphi Internet, and Genie Online Services. Online service rates are generally higher than those of ISPs. Online services and ISPs are compared later in this chapter. Table 2-2 is a quick reference list of Internet related services.

Table 2-2 Quick list of Internet related services

Service	Explanation
e-mail	Allows you to send and receive electronic messages from world wide users
Usenet	Is a discussion group network made up of thousands of special interest groups
FTP	Facilitates transmission and downloading of files between local and remote computers
Telnet	Allows access of a remote computer if you have an account at that site
WWW	Is an information network with a graphical user interface
Archie	Searches; Archie sites contain databases of files available in specific sections of the Internet
Gopher	Facilitates downloading of documents and searches databases
BBSs	Allow you to send and receive e-mail, and download files from other users; many now offer WWW access
Online services	Have their own libraries of data and services; most offer e-mail and Usenet, as well as some kind of Internet access

The Right Connection

At first glance, you may think that selecting an Internet connection is an easy decision. You don't care how you're connected, just so you're connected, right? Sorry, it's not that simple.

Do you want Internet access or do you want a connection to the Net? You access the Internet by terminal emulation through your ISP's computer. When you download files from the Net, they first go to your provider's computer and then are transferred to your computer. Compared with a direct connection to the Net, this process can be slow. Another limitation to terminal emulation is that you cannot use quick, graphic point-and-click applications the way Web surfers do. All of your interfaces are text and keystroke based. On the upside, terminal emulation puts fewer computing demands on your PC, and costs less than a direct connection.

Your ISP connects you directly to the Net with an Internet connection. Internet connections are generally faster than Internet access and allow graphical Web surfing to your heart's content through a direct TCP/IP connection. TCP/IP stands for *Transmission Control Protocol/Internet Protocol*, the language of the Internet: It allows different types of computers to talk to each other. Direct Internet connection requires client software that supports TCP/IP. Figure 2-3 illustrates the difference between Internet access and an Internet connection. Types of accounts based on these two methods are discussed in the next section.

FIGURE 2-3

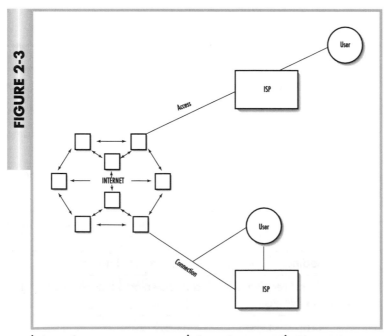

Internet access versus an Internet connection

Note

If you are a member of a Local Area Network (LAN), such as a university or an employer, you may be granted access to the Net. No monthly charges or major decisions are required on your part, but you must comply with time and content restrictions imposed by the LAN manager.

Shell Accounts

Also called UNIX shell accounts or Internet shell accounts, shell accounts use dial-up access through modems, which allows users to communicate with the Internet via their ISP's computer. As text-only interfaces to the Net, shell accounts have no graphics, sound, or point-and-click capabilities. Shell accounts require software such as Procomm or Kermit. A shell account interface is built into the Windows 95 software package. An advantage of a shell account is that, unhindered by graphics, users can move around the Net faster and can sometimes download files faster.

SLIP, CSLIP, and PPP Accounts

SLIP, CSLIP, and PPP accounts do the same thing: The protocols allow direct dial-up connection to the Internet by supporting TCP/IP. SLIP stands for Serial Line Internet Protocol, CSLIP is compressed SLIP, and PPP is Point to Point Protocol. If both you and your ISP run SLIP or PPP software, your computer will become a corner of the Internet. SLIP/PPP accounts have the ability to use any PC Internet client, such as Netscape, to view all the high-tech graphics of the Web, and are the accounts of choice among most users.

Tip

If you want a SLIP/PPP account, a CSLIP or a PPP account that has similar speed. PPP is a newer protocol, and has better error correction and data handling than CSLIP.

A SLIP or PPP account requires SLIP or PPP connection software, the TCP/IP translator, a Web browser, and other Internet clients. All of these are lumped together in a TCP/IP *stack*. A stack is a compilation of connection components. TCP/IP software that can coordinate this stack include Trumpet Winsock (shareware available from `http://www.trumpet.com.au`), and Microsoft's Dial-Up Networking (included in Windows 95). Figure 2-4 shows a simplified illustration of a TCP/IP stack for a SLIP/PPP account.

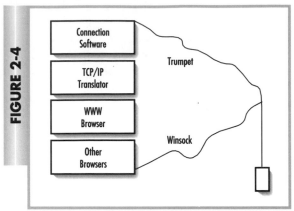

FIGURE 2-4

TCP/IP stack for a SLIP/PPP account

Tip

You may want an Internet account that provides shell and SLIP/PPP access so you can switch back and forth. Use the shell account to gather information quickly. Use the SLIP/PPP account for Net surfing.

Connection Options for Information Providers

An information provider may be an individual, a small business, or a large corporation, but it must supply information and/or services to the Internet. Since this requires a direct connection to the Net for this purpose, many smaller information providers opt for a dial-up SLIP/PPP connection through an ISP. Large companies may bypass the ISPs and obtain dedicated lines, which are permanent, direct, Internet connections. Several high-speed options are available for dedicated connections.

◁ Leased line—Telecommunications companies charge to install a dedicated line: The information provider installs the hardware that links its network to the Internet. Leased lines offer several bandwidth choices; the higher the bandwidth, the faster and more expensive the line.

◁ ISDN (Integrated Services Digital Network)—An ISDN modem connects a computer to a wall outlet. ISDN digital connections are several times faster than traditional modems, and are becoming more and more popular with information providers.

◁ Frame Relay and SMDS (Switched Multimegabit Data Service)—An information provider can lease a line for a specified amount of time, a good choice for companies whose customers are active only during business hours.

◁ Cable—Cable companies in the future will provide Internet connections through cable television. Despite limits on fast delivery of data, cable service can be several times faster than modems or ISDN.

Other Considerations for Information Providers

If you are an information provider, establishing a domain name and leasing Web space are important points to consider.

Domain Name

Information providers who have direct connections to the Internet have domain names that help users find their sites. A domain name is a simple, descriptive Web site name that you register as yours and yours only. Users often try to guess domain names when looking for specific companies on the Web. A good example of a simple, descriptive domain name is

`sun.com`

The *sun* stands for Sun Microsystems, and the *.com* suffix is the domain type. Table 2-3 lists several common domain name suffixes.

Table 2-3 Common domain name suffixes

Suffix	Description
.com	Commercial user
.edu	Educational institution
.net	Network provider
.gov	U.S. Government
.org	Non-profit organization
.mil	U.S. Military

If you do not establish a domain name, your Internet address must be your IP number. An IP number is composed of four groups of one- to three-digit numbers. Needless to say, users will find it harder to memorize an IP number than a domain name, and your site will get less traffic.

Tip

Register your domain name so it will be yours and yours alone. To register, contact the people at the Internet address: RS.internic.net.

Leasing Web Space

Some information providers lease Web space from an ISP instead of establishing their own servers. There are benefits to leasing.

◁ The ISP is responsible for solving problems that arise. Also, the ISP does all the work of connecting you to the Internet and maintaining your account.

◁ The ISP can alias e-mail and Web access to your domain name. E-mail will come directly to your account through the domain name that you registered to your ISP.

Leasing Web space from an ISP is the choice of many information providers, but some organizations choose to be their own ISP and establish in-house servers for security reasons and to maintain complete control of their Internet presence. Table 2-4 lists some Web server sources.

Table 2-4 Internet sources for Web servers

Source	Notes
http://www.w3.org/hypertext/WWW/Daemon/Overview.html	W3 Server Software
http://www.yahoo.com/Computers/World_Wide_Web/HTTP/	Computers: WWW: HTTP
http://sunsite.unc.edu/boutell/faq/www_faq.html	World Wide Web FAQ

FrontPage Web Server

Your computer can act as your individual server through the FrontPage program. The obvious advantage is that you use your machine, instead of an ISP, as a server. Another advantage is that you can test the links in your Web pages before sending them to another server.

The Quest for an Internet Service Provider

The last stop on the road to the Internet is the ISP. (Skip this section if you are planning for a large organization that that will directly connect to the Internet through its own server.) Don't select an ISP casually. Because ISPs vary greatly in quality, as well as in services and types of connections they offer, it pays to shop around. In this section, local and national ISPs will be discussed. To help you in your ISP choice, lists of questions to ask yourself and your provider are included. At the end of the chapter, ISPs and commercial online services are compared.

ISPs in a Nutshell

The most common way to connect to the Internet is through an ISP. Users connect to their ISPs' computers that are already on the Internet. A massive array of chain links is formed that truly resembles a net.

ISPs get on the Net by purchasing expensive Internet feeds. They must purchase telephone lines, computers, and other hardware in order to sell commercial access. In addition, ISPs need full knowledge of UNIX systems, servers, networks, routing, user accounts, and WWW structure, as well as to have good business sense. Increasing competition between ISPs has caused many to fall by the wayside because of poorly maintained systems, frequent machine crashes, inadequate technical support, and bad business decisions.

Local and National ISPs

Both local and national ISPs generally offer the same services, such as SLIP/PPP accounts with speeds of 14.4 Kbps and 28.8 Kbps. One benefit of local ISPs is that your dial-up number will be a local call, so you might not run up large phone bills. Another advantage is that you may be able to have a face-to-face relationship with your ISP. If you can check out its headquarters and meet the managers and support staff, you will have an idea of the quality of the ISP.

National ISPs have the built-in cost of long distance charges, so they will generally be more expensive than local ISPs. However, some national ISPs have local dial-in numbers in some cities.

 Tip

Some national ISPs have 800 dial-up numbers, but usually add a surcharge to offset the cost of this expense.

National ISPs have support lines you can call, but you may have problems getting through, depending on time of day and how many support people are on duty. An advantage of national ISPs is that they are usually less expensive than commercial online services. Therefore, they are well-suited for people in small towns with no local ISPs. If you are interested in a national ISP, check out whether they have a local dial-up number in your area. You may be able to access a national ISP simply by making a local call. See the end of this chapter for Table 2-6, which lists some national ISPs.

Tip

If your local ISP does not provide the services or quality you are looking for, a national ISP with a local dial-up number is a good alternative.

Quiz Yourself

Figure 2-5 illustrates a number of important points you should think about before launching into your ISP search. The following questions will help you narrow the field by clarifying the services you will require.

◁ *Are you able to install and configure your own Internet software?* Let's face it, not all of us are cybertechs. Often, the installation and configuration of networking software gets pretty messy. There is nothing wrong with passing this task to an experienced support person from a local ISP. If you don't mind taking instructions over the phone, a national ISP is acceptable.

◁ *What services do you need?* Many ISPs offer most of the services listed in the previous section. However, some ISPs may not be full service. It helps if you first choose the services you can't live without, then list the rest in order of priority.

◁ *What type of connection do you need?* Probably a moot question, because you are reading a book on creating your own Web pages and will, obviously, want WWW access. You will need a SLIP/PPP connection to the Internet, which is now offered by most national and local ISPs. If you are a large information provider, you may want your own server and a dedicated line (see the section in this chapter titled "Connection Options for Information Providers").

◁ *What type of interface would you like?* Most users want a user-friendly, point-and-click interface to the Internet like those provided by graphical user interfaces. However, some ISPs may only offer a text-based menu system.

◁ *If you want a Web site, how much work can you do yourself?* Will you create your own home page, and are you willing to provide your own site registration, promotion, and maintenance? If you are not able to do some or all of these tasks, you must pay someone else to do them.

◁ *Will your Web site be simple or complex?* A simple home page will have one or two screens of text, a logo, and a couple of local links. Many ISPs are well-equipped to do this for you, in addition to promoting and maintaining your site, at a reasonable price. If you want a complex home page with multiple external links, lots of images, audio, and video, you may have to pay someone else an arm and leg for it. The more of this you can do yourself, the more affordable it will be.

Quiz Your Provider

Don't be afraid to barrage your prospective ISP with questions. The ISP is there to serve you, and if it seems hesitant to answer your queries, look elsewhere. The following questions will give you a good start.

◁ *What are the support hours?* It is important to know the likelihood of getting help when you need it. It's also helpful to know if the support people are knowledgeable. As a test, call the ISP's support line and ask the hardest question you can imagine. If you get a detailed answer, you can relax. If you get silence or stuttering, look elsewhere.

◁ *What is the ratio of customers to phone lines?* The answer to this question will indicate the probability of your getting a busy signal when you want to dial up the Internet. If the ratio is between 5 to 1 and 10 to 1, it is acceptable. A ratio of more than 10 to 1 is your cue to run fast and run far.

FIGURE 2-5

Quiz yourself before your ISP search

Tip

To further test an ISP, call its access number several times a day for a week. If you get more than two busy signals, look elsewhere.

◁ *What are the rates?* When it comes to Internet service, you get what you pay for. ISP rates vary depending on types of service and connection, speed of access, user interface, and other factors. ISP pricing choices will include one or more of the following:

Flat rate—One price for unlimited access
Time block—Charges for blocks of time
Time rate—By the minute or by the hour pricing
Use rate—Price per use of service

Information providers that lease Web space may have to pay fees for users that visit their Web sites. An ISP will usually offer a certain number of free access or *hits* per month. After this number, there is a per hit charge.

Tip

If you want your ISP to help you design your WWW home page, check out your ISP's home page first to see if it looks professional. Bad grammar, misspelled words, and poor design indicate unskilled, untalented designers.

Finally, an acid test for any prospective ISP is to find out if other people like it. If you have a friend who is already hooked up to the Internet, post a memo on a local bulletin board or local discussion group about the provider in question. Customers of this provider will be only too eager to tell you their opinions.

ISPs Versus Online Services: The Race is On!

In the old days, ISPs and commercial online services were like apples and oranges. Each offered their customers their own distinct services, and each had their own pricing based on services offered. ISPs offered users an economical raw view of the Net with traditional Internet connections. Online services promoted their own data libraries along with various consumer services aimed at specific target markets. Now all that has changed. The increase in the number of ISPs and online services available, coupled with the increase in computer users, has caused a firestorm of competition. Both types of providers have made changes in their services as well as changes in how they present themselves to the public. The results of all these changes is a steady closing of the gap between ISPs and online services. The following sections and Figure 2-6 detail pros and cons of both types of providers.

Instant ISPs

ISPs offer a direct connection to the Internet at a reasonable price. In the past, ISPs have not been known for their technical support, nor ease of installation and use.

◁ Now ISPs claim to offer better technical support than online services, and most provide entry-level packages, such as Netcom's NetCruiser, for easier use.

◁ ISPs suggest that they offer more and better services and better Internet access through a more direct connection. Online services may need to pass your Internet feed through their own computer system before it reaches the Internet, which can slow things down.

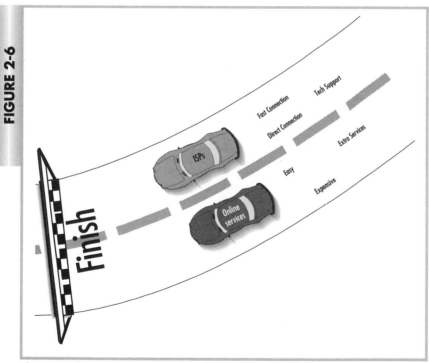

FIGURE 2-6

The race between ISPs and online services

◁ ISPs have faster access to the Net. Most now offer 28.8 Kbps connections as well as ISDN access at 128 Kbps.

◁ ISPs do not restrict Internet content or monitor discussion groups as online services do.

◁ ISP rates are generally cheaper than online services. Their flat rate plans let you surf the Net for hours on end for one monthly fee.

◁ Many ISPs have made their interfaces more user friendly.

 Tip

If you spend lots of time on line, you will want a flat rate. If not, stay with the service you like if your bill is under $20.00 per month.

Onward Online Services

As competition heats up, online services offer much more than their own brand of content and services. Table 2-7 lists some of the larger online services. In an attempt to surpass the ISPs, online services are providing more services at a lower cost.

◁ Some online services let users directly connect to the Internet with full access to the WWW, FTP, Telnet, and Gopher. However, the number of newsgroups is restricted and there are limits on e-mail transfers.

◁ Some online services offer proprietary formats that allow users to create their own simple home pages.

◁ Online service software minimizes installation and configuration hassles. All you need is a computer, a modem, and a credit card. (You may need to download certain files so you can connect to the Internet directly and browse the Web.)

◁ Although online services may have lower monthly minimum charges than ISPs, they usually allow fewer hours for that cost at a higher price per hour.

◁ An online service can concentrate computer power for a specific event such as a nationwide online conversation with a movie star, or an online concert. Large-scale events such as these would overload the lines of ISPs.

◁ Online services exclusively offer access to copyrighted material such as *The New York Times, Business Week,* and *Money Magazine.*

◁ Specialized services provided may include a portfolio-tracking service, airline reservations, access to popular magazines, encyclopedias, and family-oriented resources.

◁ Some online services, such as America Online and Prodigy, allow parents to restrict their children's access to certain areas.

◁ Online services restrict their content and monitor discussion groups in order to create a certain atmosphere for their customers.

◁ Some offer 28.8 Kbps connections; most offer 14.4 Kbps connections.

◁ Many have established more user-friendly interfaces.

The Bottom Line

Online services offer the easiest, most expensive way to the Internet. They have services and libraries of data that cannot be obtained elsewhere. If you have the money, and can live with possibly a slower access speed and content limitations, consider an online service.

ISPs offer cheaper, higher-speed access to the Internet. User friendliness in installation and interface will continue to be implemented as ISPs compete with online services. If you need high speed access at a reasonable price, without all the bells and whistles, consider an ISP.

Where is the Internet?

Even though the Internet seems to be the talk of the town, your town may not have a local ISP. This is usually the case in smaller cities as opposed to large metropolitan areas which may have multiple providers. Since ISPs don't do much advertising, you may have to do some digging to find a provider at a reasonable cost.

Most universities now have Internet access that you can use free. You can't use their connection for commercial purposes, but you can do research, and obtain their help in finding a provider.

Look for local usergroups and BBSs in the back of computer magazines, such as *Computer Shopper*. Other good sources for usergroups and BBSs are computer stores, junior colleges, and universities. If you find a usergroup in your area, attend a meeting and ask for advice. Check out BBSs: Some offer limited access to the Net.

If you can get access to the Net through a friend, local library, or university, there are many sites on the Internet that can help you find an ISP. Some of these sites are listed in Table 2-5. Tables 2-6 and 2-7 list some national ISPs and online services.

 Tip

Before you opt for an online service, compare their charges with a long distance call to a nearby provider in your region. Also remember that some national ISPs have local dial-up numbers in many cities.

Table 2-5 Internet sources for ISPs

Source	Notes
nis.nsf.net	On the Internet via FTP
directory: /internet/providers/	
http://www.yahoo.com	On the WWW
category: Internet Presence Providers	
http://www.thelist.com	On the WWW
mail-server@bts.com	On the Internet; send e-mail and include phrase, get PUB nixpub.long
http://wings.buffalo.edu/world/	The Virtual Tourist

Table 2-6 Some larger national ISPs

ISP	Phone
internetMCI	800-955-5210
Netcom	800-353-6600
Portal	800-433-6444
PSINet	800-744-0852
Pipeline USA	800-453-7473
UUNet	800-488-6383

Table 2-7 Some larger commercial online services

Online Service	Phone
America Online	800-827-6364
AT&T Interchange Online Network	800-299-9699
CompuServe Information Service	800-848-8199
Delphi Internet	508-323-1000

Online Service	Phone
GEnie Online Services	800-638-9636
The Microsoft Network	206-882-8080
Prodigy	914-448-8000

Web Development

3

In this chapter you will learn:

A Comparison of the Web with More Traditional Publication Media

Unique Characteristics of Web Publications Important to Successful Publications

Seven Discrete Steps in Web Development and Publishing and How They Are Related

What Attracts People to Web Sites and Keeps Them Coming Back

Some Common Pitfalls to Avoid When Considering Publishing on the Web

Some Considerations for Determining Your Cyberspace Needs

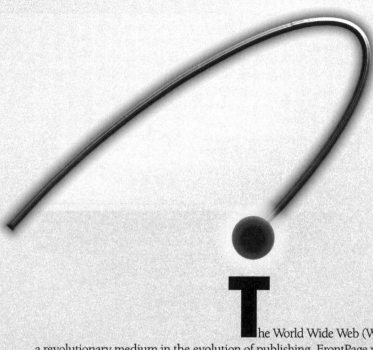

The World Wide Web (WWW or Web) represents a revolutionary medium in the evolution of publishing. FrontPage provides you with almost everything you need to use this new medium effectively, but there is a lot more to developing on the Web than merely creating your own site. The Web is unique and requires special treatment. Web development is an involved process that requires planning and organization.

Figure 3-1 shows a progression of publishing throughout history. There is a number of major epochs; electronic publishing, particularly on the Web, is one. The earliest publications were cave paintings and wood or stone carvings. Early media did not travel well, if at all, which limited their availability. Handwritten material was more portable, but not very durable. It was less time-consuming to produce, but remained labor intensive. The printing press dramatically cut the labor required to produce a document. The reduction in labor allowed mass productions of a publication to be made quickly and at a lower cost. Hence, it was possible to create a great number of copies of a work, so that a publication could be made widely available. Physical proximity with a hard copy was still required. A summary of the qualities of various publication methods is shown in Table 3-1. It is important that you be aware of these so that you can more easily contrast them with the capabilities of the Web. This exposure helps you see the potential and the pitfalls of new media. By examining the history of publication, you can more easily identify the direction in which it is headed today.

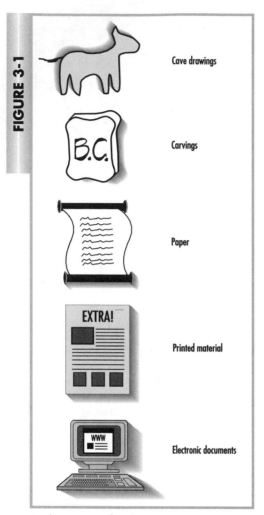

FIGURE 3-1

Cave drawings

Carvings

Paper

Printed material

Electronic documents

A diagram of advancements in publishing

Table 3-1 The qualities of various publishing methods

Method	Labor	Availability	Durability
Cave paintings and carvings	Most labor-intensive form of publishing	Extremely poor; requires physical proximity	Very durable, lasting thousands of years
Handwritten documents	Intensive labor required	Not widely available due to labor involved	Moderate to poor; often need special care

Method	Labor	Availability	Durability
Printed documents	Mass production removes most need for labor	Very common; physical proximity with a copy still required	Poor to durable; bound material better protected
Web documents	Distribution is automated and almost effortless	Immediately available to any location with the proper facilities	Requires maintenance, most of which is automated

The Web and electronic document publishing enable documents to be created dynamically, updated easily, and distributed nearly instantaneously to any location with the proper facilities. Of course, the facilities needed for this type of information exchange (computers and communication capabilities) are relatively expensive today, but paper was also very expensive when it was first invented. Web computers, inexpensive computers ($500 U.S. or less) designed for Internet connectivity, should be available by the time you read this book. They may be the catalyst needed to cement the Web and Web publications into our lifestyles. In the same way the printing press revolutionized the availability of information, the Internet and the Web make it cheap and easy to reach a broad audience in a timely fashion. For these reasons, the Web is growing at a momentous pace and may become a new standard for publishing.

Overview of the Development Process

Because the Web is a unique medium, important differences between Web publications and traditional publications must be considered. Traditional publications are fixed. No changes can be made to them once they are complete. Because a Web publication resides in only one place and is then dynamically distributed from that place, it can be updated easily. Changes to Web publications are immediately available and replace the previous resources. Additionally, the Web is much more competitive for users' attention. It's very easy to switch from one Web document to another; it's more difficult to set down one book and then pick up another. It's also very difficult to map a clear path through the Web. Book readers can be anticipated to open a volume and then read each page until the end of the book is reached. Because of the hypertext nature of the Web, you can never predict with certainty the route a user will follow through the Web. People can—and will—jump into the middle of your document, especially because of the addition of full text search to much of the Web.

Web publishing and traditional publishing methods share many similarities, however. Writing a Web page is not the same as writing a magazine article, designing a CD-ROM cover, or creating a computer program's interface, but it does share qualities with all these media. Some techniques from each of these fields can be borrowed when considering Web development. The layout for a good Web page would not make a good layout for a magazine article, but the ideas at work are similar, and the information expressed may be the same. An outstanding graphic for the Web requires different thought and design than a CD-ROM cover, but the principles for a visually pleasing CD-ROM package apply to Web graphics. The interface to the Web is different from the interface to most Graphical User Interface (GUI) programs, but the techniques used to make GUI programs more user-friendly may work to make your Web site more understandable.

Because of the differences between publication media, Web development requires a unique process. Unlike most previous publishing processes, the process of Web development is cyclical. It has a starting point, but not necessarily an ending point. When a book is published, a very definite process is (or at least should be) followed. The same is true of Web publishing, except that the process is continuous. A book's publication culminates with a finished product that cannot be changed. Revised editions of a book may be printed, but the original product remains. One of the greatest strengths of the media is that when a Web site is published, it can—and should—change over time. If a Web site does not change, there is little reason for it to be visited more than once, unless it is intended as a reference (and even references often need changing). This dynamic quality is unique to the Web and requires cyclic Web development process. An outline for the Web development process is shown in Figure 3-2.

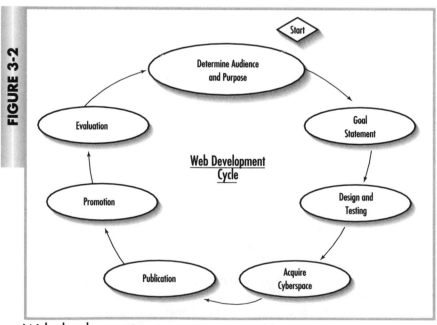

FIGURE 3-2

Web development process

The first step in developing a Web site is to determine your audience and your purpose for Web site development. After that is decided, you must write a clear, concise goal for your Web site. It is appropriate to outline your design and test it with sample Web sites. If these test sites do not reflect your goals, then you need to reconsider the design or reevaluate your goals. Once testing is complete, you will need to acquire some cyberspace based on your anticipated needs (Chapter 2, "Making the Connection," discusses this in greater detail). If the Web resources available to you cannot adequately support your design, you will need to redesign your site, possibly with a new mission, or get new resources. Once you have acquired space on the Web, you can begin publishing your site, testing it as you go. Keep your goals and design in mind, and stick with them as the site comes together. If your publication does not match the design or purpose of your site, you should reconsider these variables. After the creation is complete, not before, publicize your site. Then evaluate the response you receive. If your site is not being used as was originally intended, determine if you need to change your target audience, purpose, goals, design, publication, or some combination of these factors. Periodically reevaluate your Web site's usage to see if it still meets your goals, then react accordingly.

The Web development process builds upon itself (see Figure 3-3). You need to make sure that you do the groundwork before diving in to create your Web site. If you fail to identify your audience and purpose, your goals will be askew, and the resulting Web site may not satisfy your needs. Your Web site is most likely to be successful if you build it with a solid foundation and continue to build upon that foundation.

FIGURE 3-3

Publication

Design

Goal Statement

Purpose and Audience

The foundation relationship between design stages

Determination of Audience and Purpose

Before considering anything else, you must ask yourself two questions in the same breath: "Who is my audience?" and "What do I want to share with them?" If you cannot answer these questions, your Web site is bound to meander and lack content. Your answer to one question is also dependent on the other. The content may be valuable, but if it's directed at the wrong audience, it will not be well received. On the other hand, if the audience at whom you are directing your site does not care about your subject matter, you are also stuck.

The Web has grown large enough to contain a wide variety of individuals, so aim your site at a specific segment. As of April 1996, most estimates show there to be about 20 million people who use the Web, a number growing at a phenomenal pace, doubling almost annually. It would be very difficult to create a Web site interesting to all these users, so you need to target a portion of them. Web users are a diversified community, so you should not expect to find only computer power users. Many other audiences need catering to as well, as the success of such sites as CNN Interactive (`http://www.cnn.com`), ESPNET (`http://espnet.sportszone.com`), Suck (`http://www.suck.com`), and MSNBC (`www.msnbc.com`) indicate.

You might not even desire an Internet Web site. One of the hottest areas in networking is intranets. Intranets are networks, supported internally to an organization, and do not allow users from the Internet to connect into them. Intranets are becoming very popular ways for a corporation to keep its employees informed of current events and to allow them to exchange information with one another.

When you know something about your audience, you must consider your purpose for Web site development. The biggest problem with the Web today seems to be user letdown. Many people coming to the Web can be heard using the old Wendy's slogan, "Where's the beef?" That's because people are flocking to the Web and not bringing anything with them. Cyberspace is cheap, and the Web community is starting to suffer for it. No one wants another useless home page that provides nothing valuable and leads to other similarly useless sites. The best way to add value is to have a purpose for your site.

The number one cause of this waste of resources is that people approach the Web with the purpose of being on the Internet. This is a classic example of media hype ruining a great new potential, and it falls under the same umbrella as the emperor's new clothes. The Web is hot and new, but it cannot remain that way if there is no value in it. For example, imagine that during the great land rush of the 1800s all the American settlers staked out a plot of land, said, "Here I am, World!", and then just waited for things to happen. They would be disappointed, and the potential benefit from those resources would never be reached. The same goes for the Web. If you want to stake out your cyberspace plot, you need to work that plot to make it valuable. Cyberspace is cheap and is worth only the value that you add to it: If you do not put anything into it, no one will get anything out of it.

The best way to add value to the Web is to create a site with a purpose. Decide what information you intend to provide and what value it will be to your audience. If you do not have a good reason to put a site on the Web, why waste the effort by doing so? With this in mind, here are some things to avoid when determining the purpose of your Web:

◁ To be on the Internet is not a purpose. It is the worst reason of all, and leads to the devaluation of the Web as a medium of information exchange. People don't care who is on the Web, only about what they can get from the Web. If you don't provide valuable content, your Web site will fail.

◁ To advertise XYZ is not a very good reason either. Internet users will not flock to your site simply because it exists; it must provide something. If you wouldn't sit and watch television commercials all day, why expect Web surfers to do the same? If advertising is your only goal, rent advertising space from content providers; it will get you a better return for your dollar and do more to enrich the Web. Otherwise, provide something of value, such as coupons, product feature listings, customer support information, contact information, or amusing stories.

◁ Entertainment is one of the hardest goals for a successful Web builder. Often, attaining this goal requires something very innovative, spectacular, or unusual. Fortunately, these are three categories the Web excels in, but that also means competition is fierce.

Once you have avoided those pitfalls, consider the following advice:

◁ Promotion of special events or schedules are excellent uses of the Web because of the Web's dynamic character. For example, a cinema's movie schedule changes frequently, and it is difficult to keep this schedule available to the public. Advertising in newspapers can get expensive, and serves more to convey information than to promote the theater. Special phone lines announcing schedules can require customers to wait long periods to find out information about only one or two shows. Because the Web overcomes all these limitations, theater schedules are excellent items for the Web. Web sites are easy to keep current, and may include special promotional items such as online coupons, multimedia previews, movie reviews, or even an online bulletin board where customers can post their own opinions of particular shows.

◁ Product information is often a good use of the Web, especially for companies that compete in fast-moving markets, because they can leverage the dynamic capabilities of the Web. Online catalogs will probably be huge on the Web. It would be very easy for a large mail order company to digitize its whole catalog and make it freely available on the Web for a fraction of the cost of a physical printing. Even more important, it would be easy for a small merchandising company to place an equally impressive catalog on the Web for the same low cost. Cyberspace is cheap, and small companies can easily compete with large ones in this market. As secure Internet transaction technologies improve, this trend may gain momentum.

Goal Statement

The goal statement is really nothing more than a concrete commitment to your purpose and audience. It should be a concise and to-the-point summary of your audience and purpose for Web site construction. The goal statement follows naturally from the work you did determining these factors.

Goal statements help eliminate the "let's do everything" syndrome when designing a Web site. Often, during the design stage, inspiration strikes and you think, "Wouldn't it be great if I added...." Inspiration can strike when you are not quite finished with your last great idea. To help curb the tendency toward the never-finished Web site, use the goal statement as your guide. Write down your ideas; perhaps they can be implemented later, if they fit into your Web goals. In the meantime, your goal statement will help keep you on track.

The goal statement should include a reference to both the audience and the purpose of the Web site. A good goal statement would read something like the following:

◁ "To present information to potential customers about our product's quality, warranty, and capabilities."

◁ "To provide an up-to-date schedule of events and list of sponsors for the annual festival."

◁ "To promote war gaming and attack [sic] fellow war gamers to our hobby shop by providing a list of resources, bulletin boards for member exchange, and an online MUD." (A multi-user dimension—MUD—is an online game.)

Designing and Testing

After a clear goal has been established for the Web, designing and testing can begin. This is a crucial intermediate step. First, the general format of the Web's pages should be outlined. Then the common attributes, the look and feel, should be specified. For example, decide what elements are going to be common on every page, such as menu bars, sounds, standard graphics (such as the company logo), and links to a directory. It helps to sketch a sample page on a sheet of paper to illustrate your style ideas. After this, create a blueprint for your Web site. FrontPage has an excellent tool for this—Web Explorer. Use the Explorer to create an outline of your Web before you use the Editor to make a page. This blueprint will give you a complete directory of information that will be available on your Web site and how the site will be organized. After the design is mapped out, samples of select pages should be created for testing. Create a few pages following the design you have outlined and see how people react to them. The Web has the luxury of testing, which other media often lack. It's difficult and expensive to print sample magazine articles or CD covers, but it's cheap and easy with electronic publications, like a Web site, to create such samples to gauge their reception.

The design of a Web site can be very involved. In fact, Chapter 6, "Designing Your Web," is devoted to the subject, so focus now on the process, not the design techniques. When designing a Web site, be sure to keep the following things in mind:

◁ The viewers may not always follow the path you prefer. They may jump into the middle of your Web site. For this reason, you need to make sure that navigation is simple, clear, and consistent.

◁ Follow a constant pattern. Design your pages so they all have a similar look and feel. Change of styles can be disorientating, so be kind and stick with a theme.

◁ Design the layout for the entire site at once. Before you even build a page, you should know how your entire Web site will be laid out and how any single page fits into the grand scheme for your site.

◁ Consider what graphics you would like to use. Many large, colorful graphics can look impressive, but the drawback is download time and usability problems with text-only browsers. Be sure to make appropriate trade-offs.

◁ Decide if you plan on using clickable image maps, and if you plan on supplementing them with text links for nongraphical browsers.

◁ Determine if you want to use custom colors for your site's background and links and what those colors should be. If you want to use background images or special colors, be sure they work well together.

◁ Determine what special gimmicks you plan to include, if any, and how they will fit into your design. Make sure they fit into the goals of your Web site.

◁ Keep in mind how the intended audience will view your site. If your site is to be part of an intranet and will not be exposed to the Internet in general, you may be able to add more features and gizmos, because the connection speed would be quite fast.

◁ Watch security issues. Don't put valuable company secrets or private personal data on the Internet.

◁ Remember, you don't have to do everything at once. If you want to establish a presence on the Web quickly, keep your site small and filled with content. You can add bells and whistles later.

After creating your design, you should test it. Use the FrontPage Editor to flesh out a portion of your site, following the design specifications you have outlined, then move around among them. Have someone else look at the test site and navigate through it. Do not tell the user what to do; see if he or she can figure it out independently. If one user has trouble, so will others. A design often looks good on paper, but the implementation may be awkward. What seems clear to you may not be so clear to others. It's best to find out early, while there is still little investment of time or money and it's easy to make corrections to the design.

Don't forget to keep your goal statement in mind during this phase. Ask yourself if the design presents the information needed to reach your goals. Ensure that your design considers the audience. These are all concerns that can be addressed while testing. If your goal is not being met or your audience is not being addressed, go back and rethink your design or reconsider your goals.

Acquire Cyberspace

The target audience, goals, andsite design are the bases for identifying the kind of resources you need to build your Web site. A feel for the size of your site, the kinds of traffic to expect (or hope for), where the visitors will come from, and how they will log on, will help you decide what capacities your site will require and what kinds of accommodations to make.

If your requirements for an Internet Web site are small, you may want to rent space from an Internet Service Provider (ISP). The prices for this service vary based on your location and needs. The advantages of using an ISP include the following:

◁ There is no need to hire additional staff to maintain the server or Internet connection, because the ISP should have dedicated staff performing these duties.

◁ Some ISPs offer excellent technical support.

◁ There is no need for dedicated hardware (such as a server) or leased lines (although you may want a leased line connecting you to your ISP).

◁ Many ISPs will register a custom domain name (such as `mycompany.com`) for you for a fee (usually $100 to $200).

◁ ISPs are often less expensive than maintaining your own server and connection.

There are also disadvantages of using an ISP to support your site. These include the following:

◁ Some ISPs will allow only preapproved CGI scripts or won't allow them at all (this is discussed later).

◁ The ISP may not be using the FrontPage Server Extensions, so you may not be able to edit your sites or use most WebBots directly.

◁ Some ISPs limit the amount of changes you can make to your sites in a given period of time.

◁ The pricing scheme used may make it difficult to estimate the cost of the service, or the cost may vary wildly based on the number of hits your site receives.

◁ Sometimes the ISP imposes constraints on the size of your site.

◁ There may not be very good technical support.

◁ It is difficult to upgrade the capacity of your sites (for example, server capabilities, connection speeds).

Be sure to weigh your needs with these complex issues when choosing how best to connect to the Internet. Once you have made a decision, get the ball rolling early; it often takes a long time to get connected, whether you are connecting to the Internet directly or using an ISP. It could take months just to get an official domain name.

Publication

Publication is the building of your site in a final form. Up until now, you should have built only enough to test your design. Now you will complete it. FrontPage provides excellent tools for publishing and maintaining your Web sites. Indeed, that is its biggest selling point. Discussions on using the FrontPage Editor and other tools for Web construction and publication are provided in Chapters 5 through 10, so they are not covered here. Look through those chapters as you build your Web site. For now, suffice it to say that you construct your Web site during this phase, and FrontPage is an outstanding tool for doing so.

The most important thing to keep in mind when building your Web site is your design. Stick to it! Your final work should follow from your design in the same manner your design follows your goals, which depend upon your audience and purpose. Remember, your Web site is built on the foundations laid in the previous stages of development, so stick with them. Straying from your previous work will hamper the success of your site in the long run, so refer back often!

Promotion

Once your site is completed, not before, you should begin promoting it. There are two common mistakes made concerning promotion. The first is that people publicize a site before it is finished. If many individuals rush to see your site before it is completed, they will leave in disappointment, never to return. No one likes to see a site that may have great potential but is littered with "under construction" graphics or constantly apologizing for a lack of content. The other great mistake is failure to publicize. Many individuals do not think to advertise their site. The fact is, if no one knows your Web site is there, it might as well not exist.

With this in mind, what should be done when the time is ripe to announce your Web site to the world? Two mechanisms can be employed for this purpose: traditional advertising and announcements on the Web. Most traditional advertising is directed at your target audience and the Internet has already attracted those most likely to use your Web site. By targeting both segments, approximately equivalent in effectiveness, your promotion—and therefore your Web site—is more likely to be successful.

The first mechanism for Web site promotion is traditional media. For example, if you are a hobby shop owner developing a Web site for your business, put up flyers in the store.

You might also want to include your site's Universal Resource Locator (URL) in any advertisements you normally make. Movie theaters could include their URLs in their daily advertisements in the paper. Just about any business would benefit by putting its URL on business cards and stationery, just like a postal address. Other traditional media include billboards, posters, yellow page ads, and television and radio commercials. You could maintain a Web site that contains information that might interest potential employers and list the URL on your resume. The important theme found here is that your Web site is promoted by leveraging existing traditional advertising strategies, not replacing them.

Another great location to promote your site is the Internet itself, especially when you consider that most users will come from the Internet. There are numerous places to advertise your Web site, including news groups, indexing sites (such as Yahoo!), and mail servers.

Announcements advertising your site should be made to pertinent news groups. It's a good idea to seek out only those newsgroups that would most likely contain parties interested in your Web site. Be careful; if you post your announcement to many news groups that do not want to hear what you have to say, you will be guilty of *spamming*, and will get flamed from the readership of these newsgroups. The term spamming comes from a Monty Python skit in which the characters continuously chant "spam," to the annoyance of all. *Flaming* is a form of punishment unique to the Internet. If you upset someone, he or she may send you a nasty e-mail. If you upset enough people, you will receive a lot of nasty e-mail messages. And if you do something very offensive (like spamming newsgroups), you will receive so much nasty mail that you will not be able to tell which mail is valuable and which is flame material, you'll spend all day sifting through your mailbox, and your system administrator will not be pleased. With all this in mind, be sure to announce your site only to those news groups that would be most interested in it. News groups such as `comp.infosystems.www.announce` are specially dedicated to announcements, and they should be included in your postings.

Additionally, make sure that your Web site is indexed by all the big-name search sites, such as Yahoo!, Excite, Lycos, and Alta Vista. They all have special forms to fill out to submit your URL to their index. In addition, quite a few Web pages are dedicated to promoting Web sites, and a great number of them are free.

Filling in all those submission forms can be quite a chore. Fortunately, a number of free sites on the Web allow you to submit your URL advertisements automatically to many different sources simultaneously. These sites contain a single form that you fill in with all the information pertinent to your site (URL, description, author, etc.), which they then submit to many appropriate resources automatically. For example, the Submit-it site (`http://www.submit-it.com`) contains a form that can automatically submit your URL and related data to 16 (at last count) different locations, many of which are big-name search sites. If that's not enough, wURLd (`http://www.ogi.com/wurld/`) is another great free advertising site that can submit information to another 16 sites (some of which are duplicates). You are on your own for news groups, though.

If you want even more exposure, you will need to do some submissions manually. It's nearly impossible to give a decent listing of sites that you should (let alone could) notify of your new Web site, because that list is constantly changing. By the time you read this book, any list printed would be out of date, or well on its way. Check out Law World (`http://www.lawworld.com/pracprof/announce/`) for a current list of hot advertising locations. You may also wish to consider renting a billboard on someone else's site. Selling advertising space has become a method of making a Web site profitable, and many of the high-traffic sites sell such space.

If you think all that advertising sounds like a lot of work, you are right. You might want to hire someone to promote your site for you. Many consultants specialize in promotion and would love the business. Investment of a modest fee allows you to advertise your URL at about 300 locations in the Internet (including news groups, mailing lists, and Web indexes). You can easily find a listing of Web promotion agents by searching for Web Promoters at your favorite search site, such as Yahoo!.

If you perform major revisions of your site, you may want to reannounce it. Many search facilities have special change forms to fill out to update your listing in their directories. You may also want to reannounce your site to the news groups periodically to attract users who may have just come to the Internet. Once a year is often enough for such reannouncements; more often than that can be a nuisance.

Evaluation

The next (and not necessarily the final) step is to evaluate your Web site to make sure it's meeting your goals and expectations. This step is often the longest portion in the developmental process, because it represents a relatively stable state in the life cycle of your Web site. Check the usage of your Web site often to make sure it's meeting your goals. If it fails to do so, you may need to go back and rethink your goals, change your design, change your publication, change your promotion strategies, or some combination of these.

Many servers support a number of tools allowing you to track site usage variables, such as number of hits, what documents are viewed most, bandwidth used, and peak usage periods. Unfortunately, at the time of this writing, the personal Web server shipping with FrontPage does not include these tools. Because FrontPage can work with many different servers, you should check and see if any tracking utilities are available (or built-in) for the server you are using. The information provided by these tools can be invaluable in determining the usage of your Web site and can quickly point out potential weak spots in your design.

There are other resources you can use to evaluate Web site usage. Many sites support guest lists, where the viewer has the opportunity to supply his or her name, e-mail address, and the like, on a form that adds the information to a log. You can use this log to get a feel for your users and communicate directly with them. Be careful though; many Web surfers are tired of filling these forms out and are leery of them. This fear has been fanned by sites that sell their lists of names to promoters. Use this technique with moderation, for fear of scaring away viewers. Nevertheless, logs can be a valuable tool.

Evaluate the feedback you receive from your Web site. Listen to suggestions sent to you by viewers and act upon them. If someone takes the time to write, his or her ideas are probably worth hearing. Most people would refer to these corrections as a separate step in the development process called maintenance. In reality, maintenance should be a repeat of the development process just outlined. Maintenance is not just a single step, it is the repeat of all the steps already listed. Whenever your evaluations point out differences between your Web site's intended design, goals, audience, or purpose, you should walk through the entire development process again, making changes where appropriate. This keeps your Web site current and helps you meet your goals.

You are probably ready to dive in to your first project! The potential the Web provides is very exciting: Throughout this chapter, you've probably had a chance to think of some great ideas for your Web site. Now comes the time to start learning the tools you'll be using for your publication.

HTML Made Easy

4

In this chapter you will learn:

Basic HEAD Elements of HTML

Basic BODY Elements of HTML

How a Browser Renders Various HTML Documents

Types of Links

Accessing HTML Code in FrontPage

Limitations of HTML

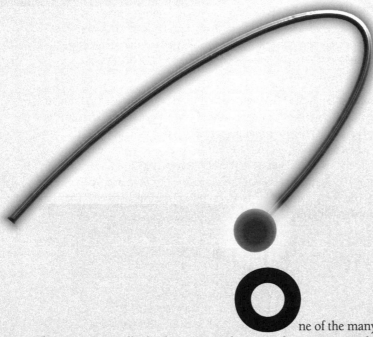

ne of the many benefits of FrontPage is that it automatically displays your Web page in the manner you desire. FrontPage will translate your page design and text in a format called Hypertext Markup Language (HTML), which will then be translated by the Web browser into the Web page of your dreams. Knowing that FrontPage does all the work, why should you bother to learn about the elements and format of HTML?

As a race car driver needs to learn about the mechanics of his or her car's engine, the FrontPage designer should learn about the workings of HTML. The following pages present a powder puff course in the basic levels of HTML (Levels 0 and 1) so you will know the driving forces of your Web page and how you can achieve the ultimate performance for your efforts.

There are several important benefits of being familiar with what's under the hood of the HTML format:

1. You will know the limitations HTML places on the applications of FrontPage. When parts of your page do not appear exactly as you want them to, this is probably due to HTML limitations. For example, you may want to choose the font size of your text. If HTML cannot control this parameter, it is up to the Web browser to choose the font. This chapter discusses which parameters HTML has power to control.

2. General knowledge of HTML allows you to update it with new features that will improve the look and style of your Web page. Being able to install new features yourself will make your Web page stand out in a crowd because of its new and unique design details.

3. Sometimes, to make subtle changes to your page that make it just right, you may need to access HTML directly using an editor. Being familiar with the process behind HTML and having a general knowledge of its components will allow you to add desired structure or design components that do not fall under the FrontPage umbrella. This direct access to HTML becomes more and more valuable as the complexity of your Web page increases.

It is worthwhile to know a little about HTML and how it works. HTML is a markup language, which means it structures a document in a standardized way so that it can be interpreted by a variety of Web browsers. An HTML document is simply a text document with extra marks on it that indicate structure, style, graphics, sounds, and links to other resources. A Web browser translates the marks and text of an HTML document into a specific page layout (Figure 4-1). Different Web browsers lay out the same document in a variety of ways, depending on the specifics of their programs. This is when being familiar with HTML will give you more power to control all aspects of your Web page.

A Brief History of HTML

HTML was created in the image of its mother, Standard Generalized Markup Language (SGML). SGML came into existence to remedy problems that arose from varying types of computers and increased traffic on the Internet. For example, if Jack and Jill had different types of word processors, and Jack sent Jill a document over the Internet, Jill would have to find a way to convert it so her computer could read it. This often turned out to be a painful task. SGML's mission was to banish file incompatibility from the Net. It used a universal format and created easy-to-change documents. For example, Jill's document might have 100 headings. Using SGML, she marks each heading. Oops! She forgot to bold all the headings! Does she have to go back and bold each one? No! With the SGML tags already in place, all she has to type is a simple command and her task is complete.

HTML is based on the ideals of SGML. Using HTML, the designer marks up text to divide it into parts and show its structure. Then the Web browser takes over and translates the text into a well-organized, stylish document.

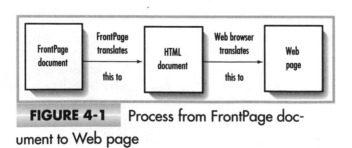

FIGURE 4-1   Process from FrontPage document to Web page

Lesson 1: HTML Highlights

HTML is a markup language that marks the structural elements of a document, such as headers, titles, and paragraphs. These markers are called *tags*; they direct the Web browser in the construction of the layout. The content or text of your Web page is placed between the various tags.

As you will see in the upcoming examples, brackets (< and >) are used to make tags that mark the boundaries of *elements*. An element is composed of a start tag, an end tag, and whatever comes between, for example:

```
<P>
```

This is the paragraph element. It allows you to create blocks of text in your Web page. When your paragraph ends, an end tag is used.

```
</P>
```

Some elements are delineated by just one tag, for example:

```
<LI>
```

This is the list element. It marks the beginning of each item in a list.

Other examples of elements are the head, title, and body, but elements can also be comments, images, and document structure. *Attributes* are placed inside element tags and specify information from other files that will be included in the element, for example:

```
<IMG Src= "source of image">
```

In the above example, Src (source) is an attribute of IMG (image). Src tells you the source of the image.

It may be useful to think of the HTML format as an onion and HTML elements as successive layers of onion skin. For instance, the outer layer of onion skin consists of the all-encompassing HTML element, which starts with the <HTML> tag and ends with the </HTML> tag. All other elements and components of the file are enclosed within this major HTML element. A deeper layer of onion skin is the HEAD element, which in turn encompasses the TITLE element of a still deeper layer. Likewise, the BODY element encloses the P (paragraph) element, and so on. Thus, a simplified yet practical way to think about the HTML structure is that of elements within elements. To understand the basics of HTML, look at a bare bones example in Listing 4-1, then see how it is displayed by a typical Web browser in Figure 4-2.

Listing 4-1 Simple example of an HTML document

```
<HTML>
<HEAD>
        <TITLE> My Home Page </TITLE>
</HEAD>
<BODY>
      <P> Live Long and Prosper </P>
</BODY>
</HTML>
```

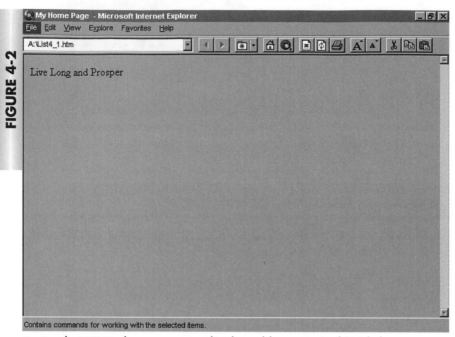

FIGURE 4-2

A simple HTML document, as displayed by a typical Web browser; the TITLE element is located in the browser's title bar

In Listing 4-1, the brackets (**<** and **>**) mark the boundaries of a tag. The letters inside a tag are not required to be all caps or all lowercase; the Web browser will interpret **<TITLE>** or **<title>** or **<TiTLE>** the same way. However, characters *between* the tags are case sensitive—not as easy going. Typing between the tags should look like your finished Web page. For example, this is correct:

```
<TITLE> My Home Page </TITLE>
```

This is incorrect:

```
<TITLE> my home Page </TITLE>
```

Note

There is an exception to every rule! File names and other addresses *inside* tag brackets are case sensitive.

Other points to ponder in this simple HTML document example:

◁ Several tags have matching tags with a slash (/) in front of the word. This type of tag marks the end of an element.

◁ HTML documents are bounded by <HTML>, which is the start tag, and </HTML>, which is the end tag. This is a fairly new convention and may not be present in older HTML documents.

◁ Two other major tag pairs in the example are <HEAD> with </HEAD> and <BODY> with </BODY>. These tags mark the beginning and end of the HEAD and BODY elements.

◁ Now to the deeper layers of onion skin. The TITLE element is enclosed in the HEAD element and is bounded by the tags <TITLE> and </TITLE>. In Listing 4-1, the title is My Home Page and will appear on the title bar of the browser.

◁ The <P> tag is the paragraph tag. It is used simply to separate blocks of text and may or may not require an end tag, such as </P>, depending on which Web browser you are using. We use end tags in our examples. (End tags are ignored by browsers that don't require them.)

◁ Because extra spacing is automatically taken out of HTML files, you can type two tags right next to each other, such as:

```
<HEAD> <TITLE>
```

or you can place one on top of the other:

```
<HEAD>
<TITLE>
```

You can use the format that is easier for you to understand. Indenting is not mandatory, but is used for clarity.

Figure 4-2 shows the simple HTML example using a typical Web browser. To view any file in your system using your browser, type `File://` followed by the file path name in the location window.

It's Elementary!

Let's review what you have mastered so far. The combination of a `<tag>` and a `</tag>`, plus whatever comes between these two, is called an element. Thus, `<HTML>` . . . `</HTML>` forms the major HTML element of the document, which encompasses all other elements. This element is used to signal the Web browser that it is working with an HTML document. You saw from Listing 4-1 that the HTML element has within it the HEAD element `<HEAD>` . . . `</HEAD>` and the BODY element `<BODY>` . . . `</BODY>`. Furthermore, the TITLE element `<TITLE>` is contained within the HEAD element, and the P element is contained within the BODY element.

Now let's discuss other HTML elements and work through more examples. The two main divisions of every HTML document are the HEAD element, which contains important background information, and the BODY element, which contains the text that will be displayed by the Web browser. First, examine the HEAD element.

Lesson 2: Head First

Important background information such as the title and additional indexing information can be found in the HEAD element. The HEAD element starts with the tag **<HEAD>** and ends with the tag **</HEAD>**. Components of the HEAD element are not displayed by the Web browser; therefore, you will not see them on your Web page. These behind-the-scene notes are used by the browser in a number of ways. Links may signal connections with another document and a Uniform Resource Locator (URL), which is the address of that other document. The TITLE is the most important HEAD element because it allows other users to track and access your Web page easily.

Don't confuse the TITLE with a header (H1, H2,...). The TITLE element will appear in the title bar but not in your Web page. A header will appear as a heading in a larger font in your Web page.

Tip

Comments add valuable background information to an HTML document, but are not displayed in your Web page. They are usually placed directly after the major <HTML> tag at the beginning of the document and before the <HTML> tag. < ! – –marks the beginning of a comment, and – – >marks the end of a comment. For example:

```
< ! – – Author: Cindy Bankston – – >
< ! – – Company: Home Pages Are Us – – >
< ! – – Date: May 10, 1996 – – >
< ! – – Comment: Get approval – – >
```

Comments should be used to document complex pages for easy maintenance.

Table 4-1 lists basic HEAD elements.

Table 4-1 HEAD elements

Element	Description
TITLE	For tracking/accessing of Web page
BASE	Identifies URL of documents in Web page
ISINDEX	Signals Web browser that document can be searched
LINK	Describes connection between your document and other documents
*Href	Identifies other document
*Name	Names the link
*Rel	Describes relationship to other document

Element	Description
*Rev	Describes relationship to other document
*Urn	Uniform resource name
*Methods	HTTP methods the other document supports
META	Meta-information
*Http-equiv	Connects META element to a protocol
*Name	Classifies the information in the document
*Content	Names the content
NEXTID	Identification code
*N	Defines the next identification code

TITLE

The TITLE element helps users identify and track your Web page (especially when using hot lists, bookmarks, and spiders). Usually, the Web browser will print the title in the title bar (but not on the Web page itself). It must be descriptive, less than 50 characters, and cannot contain other HTML formatting elements or attributes. Figure 4-2 shows the title and title bar in the Web browser output from Listing 4-1. Required parts: `<TITLE> characters . . . </TITLE>`.

BASE

The BASE element identifies the URL location of other documents used in your Web page. If a document has been moved from its original location, it is important to indicate its original source. This will make the loading of hypertext links more accurate. The BASE element has one attribute, Href, that identifies the URL of other resources. Example: `<BASE Href= "http://www.cmich.edu" >`.

 Tip

A URL is the location or address of a document or Internet resource. Every type of data on the Web is accessible through URLs. HTML uses URLs in the HEAD element, <HEAD>, to indicate links with other documents. URL addresses are also used in ANCHOR elements, <A>, to identify the location you will leap to when you click on a particular hot spot. Most URLs are composed of lowercase characters, and the length of file and directory names is virtually unlimited. The following is the URL for Waite Group Press: `http://www.waite.com`.

ISINDEX

The ISINDEX element signals the Web browser that a document listed in the BASE element can be searched. For example, using this tag in conjunction with the HEAD tag allows you to search the entire document. The server on which the file is located must be able to support a search. This element can also be found in other parts of the HTML format such as the BODY, BLOCKQUOTE, and LI. Required parts: `<ISINDEX>`.

LINK

The LINK element gives details on the relationship between your current document and other documents or objects. Example: `<LINK Href= "your_info.htm">`. The LINK element has several attributes:

◁ Href: Gives the name of the document the link describes.

◁ Name: Names this link so it can be used as a possible hypertext destination, that is, a location you can jump to.

◁ Rel: Describes the relationship defined by this link. Example: `Rel= "made"` means that the URL given in the Href is the author of the document.

◁ Rev: Similar but opposite to Rel. Example: `Rev= "made"` means that the current document is the author of the URL given in the Href.

◁ Urn: Indicates the document's Uniform Resource Name.

META

The META element provides meta-information, that is, you may add information about information in the current document. Example: `<META Content= "January 4, 1997">`. This element has several attributes:

◁ Http-equiv: Connects the META element to a particular protocol that is created by the HTTP server of the document. Example:
`<META Http-equiv="Due-date">`.

◁ Name: Classifies the information in the document. (This is not the title of the document.)

◁ Content: A name for the content that accompanies the given name. Example:
`<META Content="July 30, 1996">`.

Lesson 3: Body Parts

BODY elements are used to mark the portion of your Web page that will be displayed by the Web browser. Therefore, unlike HEAD elements, BODY elements affect the look and style of your final document. This element begins with `<BODY>` and ends with `</BODY>`. The complexity of your Web page design will dictate how many BODY elements must be used. BODY elements can be divided into six categories as shown in Table 4-2: types of text, types of lists, physical styles, logical styles, images, and other features.

Table 4-2 BODY elements

Element	Description
Types of Text	
H1 , H2, H3, H4 ,H5 ,H6	Headers
PRE	Preformat
BLOCKQUOTE	Separates blocks of text
P	Paragraph
Types of Lists	
LI	Indents each list item
OL	Ordered list; numbers items
UL	Unordered list; bullets items
DIR	Creates several columns of items
MENU	Smaller and tighter than an UL
Physical Styles	
B	Bold
I	Italicize
U	Underline
TT	Typewriter fixed-width font
Logical Styles	
CITE	Citation or author
CODE	Computer code
KBD	Directions to user
SAMP	Renders characters as is
STRONG	Emphasizes; usually bold
VAR	Variable in computer code
Images	
IMG	Image
*Src	Source file of image
*Alt	Characters for nongraphical browsers
*Align	Positions image relative to text

continued on next page

continued from previous page

Element	Description
Other Features	
A	Anchor or link
ADDRESS	Home, office, or e-mail address
BR	Line break
HR	Horizontal line

Types of Text

H1, H2, H3, H4, H5, H6

HEADER elements such as these create headers that decrease in font size from H1 to H6. H5 and H6 are rarely used because of their tiny size. Headers are placed within the BODY and BLOCKQUOTE tags. The use of the headers in an HTML document is shown below. Listing 4-2 shows an example of the use of headers, and Figure 4-3 shows the Web browser output. Required parts: **<H1>characters . . . </H1>**.

Listing 4-2 HTML document using headers

```
<HTML>
<HEAD>
  <TITLE> This is a test page </TITLE>
</HEAD>
<BODY>
 <H1> This is a level H1 header </H1>
 <H2> This is a level H2 header </H2>
 <H3> This is a level H3 header </H3>
 <H4> This is a level H4 header </H4>
 <H5> This is a level H5 header </H5>
 <H6> This is a level H6 header </H6>
</BODY>
</HTML>
```

 Note

The font size of the headers decreases from H1 to H6. Header H1 is often the same as the title of the document. Headers H5 and H6 are rarely used because of their small sizes.

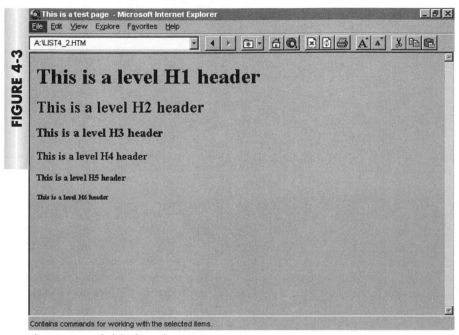

FIGURE 4-3

The six available headers

PRE

The PRE element allows you to preformat a block of text. That is, if you want a poem or a chart to show up on your Web page exactly as you have typed and spaced it, this element signals the Web browser to render it exactly as is (Figure 4-5). PRE has one attribute, width, that allows you to specify the number of characters that can be typed on a line before it will automatically wrap to the next line. The default is 80 characters. See Listing 4-3 for an example of the use of PRE and Figure 4-4 for the browser output. Required parts: `<PRE>characters . . . </PRE>`.

Listing 4-3 HTML document using PRE and BLOCKQUOTE elements

```
<HTML>
<HEAD>
  <TITLE> A Pre and Blockquote example </TITLE>
</HEAD>
<BODY>
 <H2> An example of how pre works </H2>
  <PRE>
     This is how pre works
          it sets the format
                  to the way the text is set.
```

continued on next page

continued from previous page

```
    </PRE>
<H2> An example of how blockquote works </H2>
<BLOCKQUOTE >
        On the other hand you can just type in your thoughts any way you like,
and the blockquote will format them in a style
that would make your mother proud. This tag will set this in a block
no matter how
badly it
 is
entered.
If
you keep typing
it will block all the text.
</BLOCKQUOTE>
</BODY>
</HTML>
```

BLOCKQUOTE

The BLOCKQUOTE element is used to separate a section of text, such as a quote, from the rest of the document. The text is usually indented on both sides and centered. See Listing 4-3 for an example of the use of BLOCKQUOTE and Figure 4-4 for the browser output. Required parts: **<BLOCKQUOTE>characters . . . </BLOCKQUOTE>**.

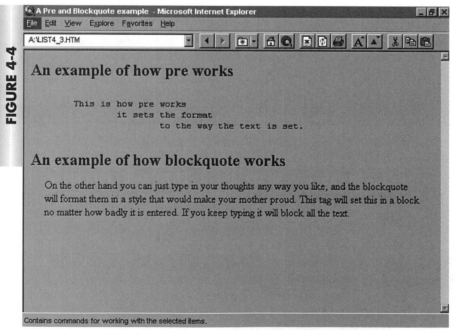

FIGURE 4-4

PRE and BLOCKQUOTE elements as rendered by a Web browser

Note

The PRE element tells the Web browser to render the following text as it is. The BLOCKQUOTE element blocks out a portion of text no matter how you have typed it.

P

The P element separates individual paragraphs by placing a blank line between them. Web browsers require that only one **<P>** be used, either at the beginning or at the end of a paragraph. FrontPage places a **</P>** at the ends of paragraphs for clarity. See Listing 4-4 for an example of the use of the P element and Figure 4-5 for the browser output. An example of how it separates paragraphs is seen in Figure 4-6. Required parts: **<P>characters . . . </P>**.

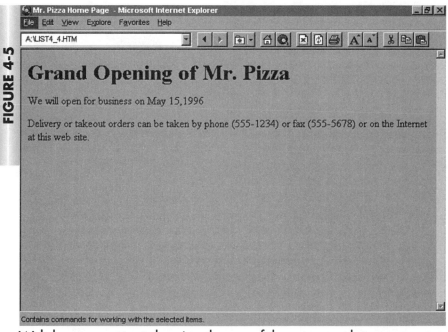

FIGURE 4-5

Web browser output showing the use of the paragraph tags **<P>** and **</P>**

Listing 4-4 HTML document using P

```
<HTML>
<HEAD>
        <TITLE> Mr. Pizza Home Page </TITLE>
</HEAD>
<BODY>
        <H1> Grand Opening of Mr. Pizza</H1>
        <P> We will
 open for business on May 15,1996</P>
        <P> Delivery or takeout orders can be taken
           by phone (555-1234) or fax (555-5678) or
           on the Internet at this Web site. </P>
</BODY>
</HTML>
```

Note

The paragraph tags <P> and </P> come before and after a paragraph and place a blank line between blocks of text. The P element is contained within the BODY element.

Types of Lists

A list is a set of items delineated by numbers or bullets. LIST elements are especially useful when creating outlines. Following are LIST elements that create different types of lists.

LI

The LI element marks each item of a list and causes these items to be indented in the final document. This element is used in conjunction with the UL, OL, MENU, and DIR elements. Listing 4-5 shows an example of the use of the LI element and Figure 4-6 shows the browser output. Required parts: **<LI>** characters.

Listing 4-5 HTML document using LI and OL elements

```
<BODY>
 <H1> A list of the five most popular sports </H1>
 <P>
  <OL>
      <LI> Baseball
      <LI> Football
      <LI> Basketball
      <LI> Hockey
      <LI> Soccer
   </OL>
   </P>
</BODY>
```

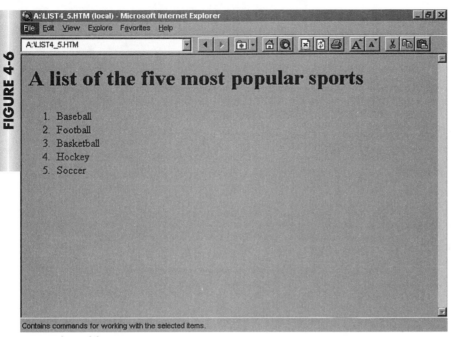

FIGURE 4-6

An ordered list

OL

The OL element is used to render ordered lists. Each item in a series is given a number, as in the main headings of an outline. The LI element is also used to indent items. The Compact attribute can be used with this element to tell the Web browser to group the items closely. Listing 4-5 shows an example of the use of the OL element, and Figure 4-6 shows the browser output. Required parts: **<OL></OL>**.

 Note

The LIST element, LI, comes before each item in a list. An ordered list, OL, places a number in front of each list item.

UL

The UL element allows you to make an unordered list. An unordered list is similar to an ordered list except that the items are bulleted instead of numbered. The UL element comes in handy for items listed under outline headings. The Compact attribute can be used with this element to tell the Web browser to group the items closely. Listing 4-6 shows an example of the use of the UL element, and Figure 4-7 shows the browser output. Required parts: **<UL></UL>**.

Listing 4-6 HTML document using LI, OL, and UL elements

```
<HTML>
<HEAD>
  <TITLE> An Ordered List Example </TITLE>
</HEAD>
<BODY>
 <H1> A list of the five major food groups </H2>
 <H2> and any necessary subheadings </H2>
  <OL>
      <LI> Pizza
        <UL>
          <LI> pepperoni
      <LI> sausage
        <UL>
          <LI> hot Italian
                <LI>
mild Italian
        </UL>
        <LI> mushroom
        </UL>
      <LI> Pop
      <LI> Fries
      <LI> Chips
      <LI> Burgers
  </OL>
  </P>
</BODY>
</HTML>
```

 Note

An unordered list, UL, uses bullets to denote items. Unordered lists can be "nested" inside ordered lists to create an outline.

DIR

The DIR element allows you to create a list of short words or phrases that the Web browser organizes into columns. Each word or phrase should be less than 20 characters. The LI element is used to delineate each item in the list. The Compact attribute can be used with this element to tell the Web browser to group the items closely. A Web browser might group the names below into two columns. Example:

```
<DIR> <LI> Julie
    <LI> Mike
    <LI> John
    <LI> Megan </DIR>
```

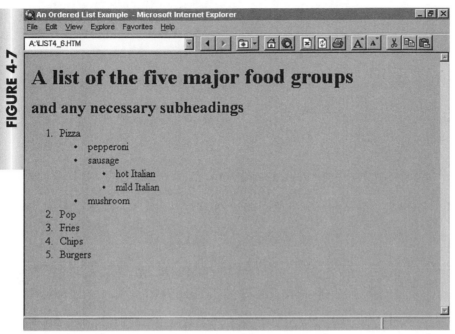

FIGURE 4-7

The ordered list, OL, and unordered list, UL, used to create an outline

MENU

The MENU element creates a list that is similar to an unordered list except that the rendered menu list will appear smaller and tighter. Required elements: **<MENU></MENU>**.

TIP

One of the problem areas in HTML that you should avoid is overlapping tags. For example, if you type in <OL> and then <UL>, then use the end tag </OL> and the end tag </UL>, the ordered list opens and then the unordered list opens. The problem arises when the ordered list is closed while the unordered list is still open. This means that somehow the browser must determine which element contains what. It won't; it will just ignore most of the tags.

It is also important to be sure that you do not leave unnecessary spaces within the element tags. For example, if you entered <BODY> or <BODY>, the tag would not be recognized by the Web browser. The correct way to input the tag is <BODY> without any extra spaces.

Physical Styles

B

The B or BOLD element dictates the appearance of text. Characters placed between `<B>` tags will be bolded. See Listing 4-7 for an example of the use of the B element and Figure 4-8 for the browser output. Required parts: `<B>characters . . . </B>`.

I

The I or ITALICIZE element controls the appearance of text in that characters placed between the `<I>` tags will be italicized. See Listing 4-7 for an example of the use of the I element and Figure 4-8 for the browser output. Required parts: `<I>characters . . . </I>`.

U

The U or UNDERLINE element dictates the appearance of text in that characters placed between the `<U>` tags will be underlined. See Listing 4-7 for an example of the use of the U element and Figure 4-8 for the browser output. Required parts: `<U>characters . . . </U>`.

TT

The TT element creates typewriter fixed-width font text. See Listing 4-7 for an example of the use of the TT element and Figure 4-8 for the browser output. Required parts: `<TT>characters . . . </TT>`.

Logical Styles

CITE

The CITE element marks the citation of a book or another type of document. See Listing 4-7 for an example of the use of the CITE element and Figure 4-8 for the browser output. Required parts: `<CITE>characters . . . </CITE>`.

Listing 4-7 HTML document using B, I, U, TT, and CITE elements

```
<HTML>
<HEAD>
        <TITLE> Some Shakespeare </TITLE>
</HEAD>
<BODY>
        <H1> <B> <U> Sonnet XVIII </U> </B> </H1>
        <P> <I> Shall I compare thee to a summer's day?<BR>
            Thou art more lovely and more temperate...<BR>
        </I> </P>
        <CITE> <TT> William Shakespeare </TT> </CITE>
</BODY>
</HTML>
```

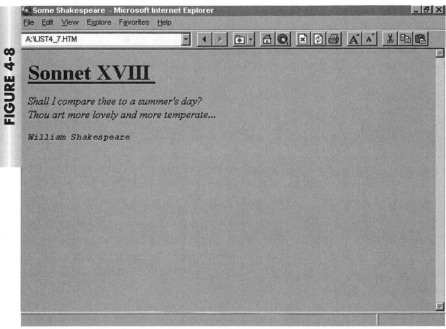

FIGURE 4-8

A browser's rendering of the BOLD, <B>; ITALICIZE, <I>; UNDERLINE, <U>; TYPEWRITER FONT, <TT>; and CITATION, <CITE> elements

Note

Notice that the LINE BREAK element, <BR>, is necessary with a poem format.

CODE

The CODE element indicates computer code usually displayed in a fixed-width font. It could identify a Pascal program that needs to be shown and then converted to Java. Required parts: `<CODE>characters . . . </CODE>`.

KBD

The KBD element tags text or commands that the user is directed to type into the keyboard. These commands might be an instruction set of a form that must be filled out. Required parts: `<KBD>characters . . . </KBD>`.

STRONG

The STRONG element is similar to the BOLD element. It is used to give strong emphasis to a word or phrase that is usually bolded. Required parts:
`<STRONG>characters . . . </STRONG>`.

Images

IMG

The IMG element allows you to place graphical images in your document where this element tag is located. Example: `<IMG Src="images\children\megan.jpg">`. See Listing 4-8 for an example of the use of the IMG element and Figure 4-9 for the browser output. The IMG element has the following attributes:

- ◁ Src: Identifies the source file of the image.

- ◁ Alt: Describes a string of characters that will be displayed in nongraphical browsers.

- ◁ Align: Sets the position of the graphic relative to the text. (This attribute can also be used to position headers—H1, H2, and so forth.)

Align has the following parameters:

- ◁ Top: Text following the graphic is aligned with the top of the graphic.

- ◁ Middle: Text following the graphic is aligned with the middle of the graphic.

- ◁ Bottom: Text following the graphic is aligned with the bottom of the graphic.

Listing 4-8 HTML document using the IMG element

```
<HTML>
<HEAD>
  <TITLE> PIP CAT </TITLE>
</HEAD>
<BODY>
<H1> PIP T. CAT <IMG SRC="PIP2.JPG" ALIGN="middle"> </H1>
<HR>
</BODY >
```

In Listing 4-8, the name of the file with the image is `PIP2.JPG`. This means that this file is a JPEG file, which is explained in detail in Chapter 11, "Multimedia." Suffice it to say here that the browser recognizes a number of image formats and JPEG is one of them. The address of the file is short and simple (`PIP2.JPG`), which tells you it must be located in the same directory as your HTML document (as opposed to another directory at another location such as the WWW).

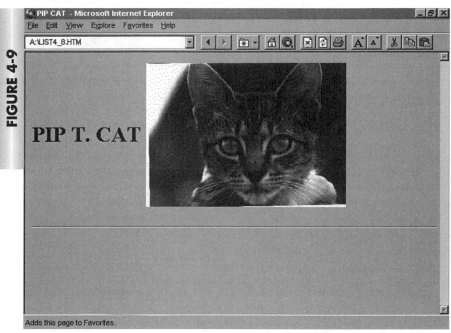

A browser's rendering of the IMAGE, `<IMG>`, element

Other Features

A

A represents the ANCHOR element that links documents. It indicates a hypertext portal that can be entered by clicking on a word or phrase called a *hot spot*. See Listing 4-9 for an example of the use of the A element and Figure 4-10 for the browser output where the hot spots are underlined. Required parts: `<A> characters . . . </A>`. This element has several attributes:

◁ Href: Identifies the location or URL of the hypertext document. It's where you will travel when you click on the hot spot.

◁ Name: Creates a name for the anchor that can be referred to within or outside the document.

◁ Adding a name to the anchored text turns it into a hypertext destination that you or others can "leap" to within your document.

◁ Title: Defines a title for the document indicated in the Href attribute.

◁ Methods: Gives information on the functions that can be performed on the source document.

Listing 4-9 HTML document using the A element

```
<HTML>
<HEAD>
  <TITLE> An Example Using Unordered Lists </TITLE>
</HEAD>
<BODY>
  <H1> The science
Library offers information on: </H1>
<UL>
 <LI> <A Href = "project.htm"> Projects </A> for kids
 <LI> <A Href = "resources"> Online Resources </A> for scientific research
 <LI> <A Href = "visual_aid.htm"> Visual aids </A> for scientific
understanding
 <LI> Specialty areas such as <A Href = "rocks.htm" > Geology </A> and
            <A Href = "stars.htm" > Astronomy </A>
</UL>
</BODY>
</HTML>
```

Note

Within the ANCHOR element, <A>, the Href attribute is used to define the location of the document you will leap to when you click on the hot spot. The hot spot is defined after the Href location, and extra text that accompanies the hot spot word is placed after the anchor end tag, </A>. In Listing 4-9, the hot spots are underlined.

Tip

Hypertext allows you to leap across the vast expanse of cyberspace into another file or document instantly. These magical portals are created in your HTML document using the ANCHOR element, <A>, and Href attribute. The ANCHOR element is where the link is located in your document, and the Href attribute indicates the location *where* you will leap. Next comes your Leap button, or hot spot, which is usually underlined in the final document. Other text that will be displayed is located after the anchor's end tag, </A>. For example:

```
<A> Href= "backyard birds.html" > Backyard Birds </A> and How to
Attract Them
```

will be displayed as: Backyard Birds and How to Attract Them. In this example, Backyard Birds is the link.

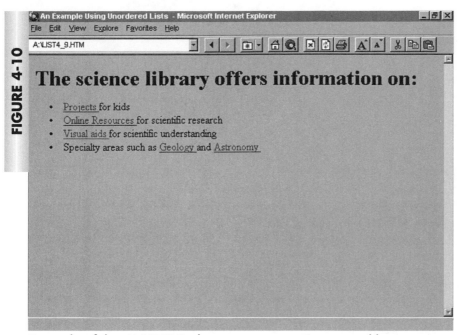

Example of the ANCHOR element, <A>, creating several hot spots, or links, in a document

ADDRESS

The ADDRESS element shows authorship of a document and is usually placed at the end of a Web page. Personal information such as an e-mail address, home address, or office address can be placed between ADDRESS tags. Some Web browsers italicize characters within the ADDRESS tags. Every Web page should have a street or e-mail address at the bottom so other users can contact you. Listing 4-10 shows an example of the use of the ADDRESS element, and Figure 4-11 shows the browser output. Required parts:
<ADDRESS>characters . . . </ADDRESS>.

BR

BR is the LINE BREAK element that allows you to control the amount of text on specific lines. This element comes in handy when writing postal addresses or poems. Listing 4-10 shows an example of the use of the BR element, and Figure 4-11 shows the browser output. Without the BR element, the three lines of text in Listing 4-10 would run together and form one line. Required parts: <BR>.

Listing 4-10 HTML document using ADDRESS and BR elements

```
<ADDRESS>
Clark Kent <BR>
The Daily Planet <BR>
Metropolis, USA 12345
</ADDRESS>
```

Note

A line break, <BR>, is placed where the text should stop for a particular line. There is no <BR> after the last line because the text of the address ends here. Every Web page should have an e-mail address at the bottom so other users can contact you.

HR

The HR element creates horizontal lines in your Web page. Horizontal lines are often used before and after the main body of text or underneath an image. Required parts: **<HR>**.

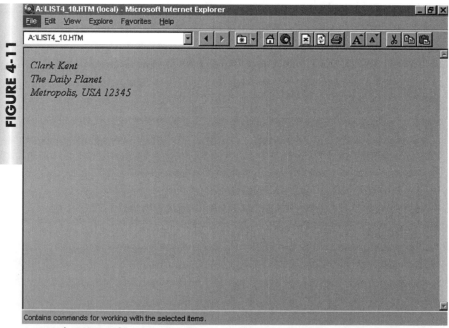

FIGURE 4-11

Example using the ADDRESS, **<ADDRESS>**, and LINE BREAK, **
**, elements to write a postal address

Tip

Because the HTML format uses brackets, < and >, and the ampersand, &, in its code, the problem arises of what to do if you want to use these symbols as part of the text of your Web page. Following are specific sets of characters designed to represent these symbols in HTML:

>   stands for >
<   stands for <
&   stands for &
"   stands for "
     stands for a nonbreaking space, forces a blank space

For example, you would enter the phrase Sugar & Spice as Sugar & Spice.

Lesson 4: A Woven Web Page

Armed with all the basic HTML elements, you are now ready to see them in concert. The following is a simple example of a complete Web page using basic HTML. See whether you can identify the elements. Remember to think of HTML structure as layers of onion skin—elements within elements. The HTML document is shown in Listing 4-11, and the final Web page is displayed as translated by the Web browser in Figure 4-12.

Listing 4-11 A Web page in HTML code

```
<HTML>
<!--Sugar Tree Inc.-->
<!--The Maple Grove Co.-->
<HEAD><TITLE> Springfield's Maple Syrup Festival </TITLE></HEAD>
<BODY>
        <H2 Align="center"> Springfield's Maple Syrup Festival </H2>
        <H3 Align="center"> Saturday and Sunday, April 26 and 27 </H3>
        <P>
        Come celebrate the 35th Annual Maple Syrup Festival! There will be
activities for all: carnival rides, pony rides, crafts and antique shows, a
flea market, parades, jugglers, a teen dance, and our famous pancake, maple
syrup, and sausage meals. Fun for all in Springfield on April 26 and 27!
        </P>
        <STRONG> Don't Miss all the Delicious Food! </STRONG>
    <UL>
            <LI> Pancakes, Maple Syrup, and Sausage
            <LI> Homemade Bean Soup
            <LI> Bratwurst
    </UL>
     For more information contact:
    <ADDRESS>
```

continued on next page

continued from previous page

```
              Maple Syrup Festival <BR>
              3457 Sugar Bush Rd. <BR>
              Springfield, USA 12345
              </ADDRESS>
     </BODY>
     </HTML>
```

In Listing 4-11, the all-encompassing HTML element is first and last. All other elements are contained within this element. Below the HTML element are two comments that list two sponsors of the festival. Within the HEAD element is the TITLE element. The comments and title do not appear in the final Web page, but are for the designer's own information and for easy tracking of the Web page.

The rest of the content and structure elements are placed inside the BODY element. Two header elements, H2 and H3,

are used for the main headings of the page. The Align attribute with the center parameter is placed inside the header elements to center the headings. The P or PARAGRAPH element is used to separate a block of text. The STRONG element is used to emphasize the sentence **Don't Miss all the Delicious Food!** (most browsers emphasize by bolding the characters). Beneath this sentence is an unordered list of the food that will be served at the festival. (Notice that the items are bulleted in the Web browser output, Figure 4-12). The last BODY element is the ADDRESS, which tells users who to contact for further information. (The address is italicized by the Web browser in Figure 4-12.) Notice that the BR

FIGURE 4-12

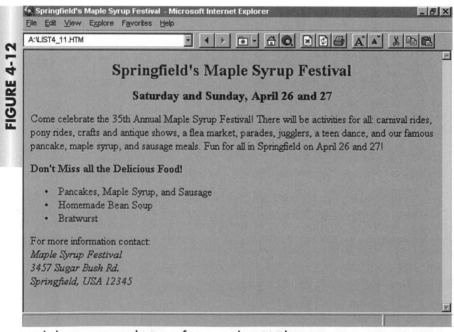

Web browser rendering of a complete Web page

element is used after the first and second lines of the address to signal the ends of those lines. Last, the Web page is wrapped up by using the end tags for BODY and HTML.

If you understand this basic example, you now have the knowledge and power to create your own Web page with HTML! Granted, it lacks a little in the bells and whistles department, but all the basic elements are there that would allow you to go online tomorrow. Although FrontPage will do the work for you on this basic level, having the knowledge and ability to do it yourself will allow you to explore new and advanced HTML features without being overwhelmed.

Lesson 5: Link Up, Link Out

You may want to incorporate hypertext from several different locations into your home page. Hypertext can be images or sound, or it can simply be someone else's Web page. There are two types of locations you can leap to when you click on a hot spot:

◁ A local location on your own computer

◁ An external location on other computers on the Web

The way you link up to these locations is through link addresses. Just as the mail carrier needs your address to deliver your mail, you need specific addresses of other files that will be integrated into your document.

The information in your computer is stored in two types of containers: directories and files:

◁ Directories hold files and other documents

◁ Files hold information such as your home page

Use the names of directories and files to move information around in your computer.

Local Links: Relative and Absolute

When you are on your own computer, you control your destiny. You are the master of all addresses. You create directories and place files in them. Assume that you have set up your directories like those in Figure 4-13. You have a home directory called **dirA** that holds another directory, **dirB**, and a file called **file1.htm**. **DirB** that in turn holds three items: a directory

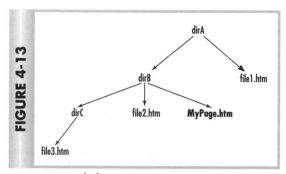

FIGURE 4-13

A typical directory set-up

called `dirC`, a file named `file2.htm`, and a file named `MyPage.htm`. In this situation, you must use two kinds of local links, relative and absolute, to leap from one document to another.

Relative Links

When you put a document address in quotes, the Web browser looks in the directory of your own Web page for that document. Therefore, for `MyPage.htm` in Figure 4-13 to link to `file2.htm`, simply use `HREF="file2.htm"`.

Now the obvious question is, "How do you link to `file3.htm` or `file1.htm`?" These tasks are accomplished by moving around in your computer using forward slashes (`/`) to indicate a change of directory. Moving down to a file below your directory is the easiest. All you do is list the directory and then the file, as in `HREF="dirC/file3.htm"`. This address says "open the directory named `dirC` and link to the file named `file3.htm`."

Moving up in your computer, say to `file1.htm` (Figure 4-13), requires a double dot (`. .`), which means "move up one directory." Therefore, the address `HREF=". ./file1.htm"` would link you to the file in `dirA`.

These addresses are called *relative* because they are all relative to `MyPage.htm`. For a quick reference of how relative addresses work, see Table 4-3.

Table 4-3 Relative addresses

Link	Explanation
`HREF="file2.htm"`	file 2 is in the same directory as your document
`HREF="dirC/file3.htm"`	file3.htm is in dirC, which is contained in the same directory as your document
`HREF="../file1.htm"`	file1.htm is up one directory from your document

Absolute Links

The other way of linking files in your computer is to use absolute addresses. When writing an absolute address, start from the top directory in your system. In Figure 4-13, to link `MyPage.htm` with `file2.htm`, you would use `HREF="/dirA/dirB/file2.htm"`.

Although this method may seem straightforward, it has one major drawback. If you need to change the name of a directory, say `dirA` to `dirMain`, all your absolute links will change (but your relative link will still work).

 Tip

When linking to other documents in your computer, use relative paths to minimize changes in your links.

External Links

Locations of documents outside your computer are often called *remote sites*. Links to these sites make up the many intertwining strands of the WWW. Instead of path names, you use URLs to link with external sites.

Say you are creating a home page for the Maple Syrup Festival. While Net surfing, you find an interesting Web page on how to boil maple sap to make maple syrup. To integrate this information into your home page, you would create a hot spot using its URL. For example:

```
<A HREF="http://www.maple.syrup/" > Boiling Sap </A>
```

As shown in the example, `http://www.maple.syrup/` is the URL of the Web page with the information on boiling maple tree sap. Creating links that allow users to leap to other sources of related information can add depth and variety to your Web page.

Lesson 6: Accessing HTML Directly

The direct use of HTML is often not necessary when using a system such as FrontPage. However, you may wish to use HTML if you intend to add new features to your FrontPage-created HTML page or to make minor adjustments. To access HTML code after it has been created by FrontPage, enter the HTML file by selecting File: Open. The HTML file will have the same name as your Web page file but with the `.htm` suffix. This file can be generated by FrontPage or by an editor. The file should be saved in plain text (ASCII) because the browser will give strange and wonderful responses to files saved in Word, Word Pro, and other word processors.

Tip

A great way to get design ideas for your Web page is to go directly to the source—the Web. Most Web browsers allow you to peek at the HTML code behind Web pages. If you see a particular format or design component that you would like to put in your Web page, you can borrow it by copying the HTML text into your word processor or HTML editor.

Limitations of HTML

However impossible it may seem, limitations do exist on the things you can do with Levels 0 and 1 of HTML. For example, basic HTML cannot make tables, columns of text or graphics, or mathematical equations; include external HTML files; or place a movie into a document. Higher levels of HTML contain these features, and upcoming versions of HTML will be equipped with even more complex structures. HTML can also be limited by your Web browser. For example, Netscape Navigator is currently the only Web browser that allows you to adjust font size, but these limitations change daily. Also, some Web browsers do not recognize new HTML features.

FrontPage News

As stated at the beginning of this chapter, FrontPage 97 will translate your Web page design into HTML, which will then be interpreted by the Web browser into your final Web page. This means that FrontPage will generate all the HTML tags mentioned in this chapter. However, it is worth your while to be familiar with basic HTML techniques so that you may incorporate more advanced features into your Web pages. Although FrontPage 97 does not support all the features of the ever-developing HTML, it does allow you to input all the new HTML features into your FrontPage base document.

This powder puff course in HTML has, perhaps, taken some of the mystery out of this new and developing markup language. Future versions of HTML will remove its current limitations and expand to new worlds of online sound and video, live conferencing, and virtual reality.

Additional Information

For an HTML introduction tutorial, see

`http://www.ncsa.uiuc.edu/demoWeb/html-primer.html`

For general information about HTML, see

`http://www.w3.org/hypertext/WWW/MarkUp/MarkUp.html`

Installing Microsoft FrontPage

5

In this chapter you will learn:

The Components of the FrontPage Publishing Environment

How to Install FrontPage and the Components
Shipped with It

How to Uninstall FrontPage and FrontPage Components

Installing the FrontPage Server Extensions on a Local Host

How to Assign Administrative Accounts Using the
FrontPage Server Administrator

How to Enable/Disable Authoring Capabilities with the
Server Administrator

nstalling Microsoft FrontPage should be as easy as installing a word processor or spreadsheet program, and, if you're like many Web folks, you couldn't wait to get the wrapper off the box and FrontPage installed. This chapter introduces you to the FrontPage components, guides you through a simple installation, shows you how to uninstall FrontPage (should that ever be necessary), teaches you how to install the FrontPage Server Extensions on a Microsoft Windows-based server, and shows you some administrative tasks.

My Setup Program Looks Different—What Gives?

At the time of this writing, the released version of FrontPage was 1.1, and FrontPage 97 was in an early beta stage. Please use the diagrams and walk-throughs as a guide when performing your own installation as the screens of the installation program are subject to change.

FrontPage Components

The Microsoft FrontPage package ships with three components: editing tools (client software), a Web server (Personal Web Server), and a set of programs that enable the editing tools to communicate with the server. This last set of programs is called FrontPage Server Extensions. The FrontPage Web authoring system has three requirements that must be met before it is fully functional. The first requirement is that the client software be installed on your computer. The second requirement is that the computer you are working on have access to a Web server. FrontPage ships with a Web server, so if you don't have access to a Web hosting service, it is possible to use your computer as one. The third requirement is that the Web server you intend to use have the FrontPage extensions installed.

Client Software

The client software is the front end of the FrontPage Web publishing system. The client software comprises the components you see and work with day-to-day. This software includes the FrontPage Explorer, the FrontPage Editor, and the FrontPage To Do utility. The FrontPage Explorer is a program that allows you to navigate your Web sites and view them in a graphical way. It makes it easy to organize the resources your Web sites use and to view them in a way to make them more manageable. The FrontPage Editor is the word processor/layout tool that allows you to easily create the individual documents that make up your Web sites. Odds are, you purchased FrontPage for the features offered by the editor: a WYSIWYG interface and an intuitive environment that closely resembles other products in the Microsoft Office suite. The To Do utility allows you to keep track of your ideas as you develop your Web sites.

Personal Web Server

The Personal Web Server is a basic Web server that completes the FrontPage package by providing everything you need (except the TCP/IP connection) to turn your computer into a Web host. It's a very simple program that's easy to use and configure. It works behind the scenes, delivering your Web documents to the other computers networked to it, be that through a LAN or through the Internet. You may not need the Personal Web Server if you plan on editing only Web sites located on remote hosts. If you want to set up your computer as a host, the Personal Web Server represents a turnkey solution.

Server Extensions

The server extensions are a set of programs that work with the Web server to enable the client software to edit your Web. The server extensions that ship with FrontPage work with the Personal Web Server to allow full functionality of the FrontPage package. If you plan on editing Web sites on a remote host, you must make sure that the server extensions are installed on that host. Server extensions are freely available from Microsoft, and flavors exist to work with many different commercial, shareware, and freeware Web servers operating on many different kinds of systems. If you need server extensions, a good place to start looking for them is **http://www.microsoft.com/frontpage/**. The server extensions that ship with FrontPage also work with servers other than the Personal Web Server. You will learn more about that later.

Lesson 1: Installing FrontPage

Before you begin the installation, you'll need to do several things. First, make sure you have the FrontPage disks or CD-ROM. If you are going to use FrontPage to edit Web sites on a different host computer, you'll need to talk to your Web service provider to make sure that it supports FrontPage extensions. With these steps taken, you'll find that installing FrontPage is as simple as running the setup program. To do this, first exit any programs you may have running, and then click on the Start button and choose Run. When the dialog comes up, make sure your FrontPage CD-ROM is in the drive. Then type the path to the file and click the OK button. The first window the FrontPage Setup program displays is a welcome screen, shown in Figure 5-1. Click the Next button to continue the installation.

Now you must select the location where FrontPage will install the client software. If the default directory chosen is not acceptable, click the Browse... button and select a new destination for these tools. When you are ready to continue, click the Next button.

The FrontPage Setup now offers a couple of installation options, shown in Figure 5-2. The first option is Typical, and the second is Custom. If you want to install all components of the FrontPage package, including the Personal Web Server and its server extensions, choose the typical installation option. If you don't want to set up your personal computer as a Web host or you don't want to install a specific portion of the FrontPage package, choose the custom option.

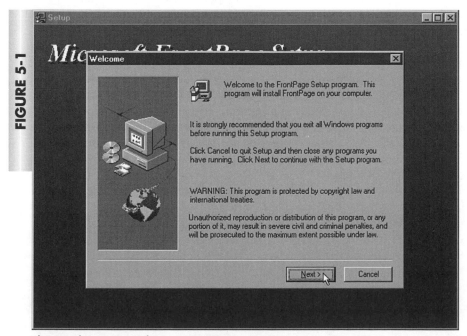

FIGURE 5-1

The Welcome window in FrontPage Setup

FIGURE 5-2

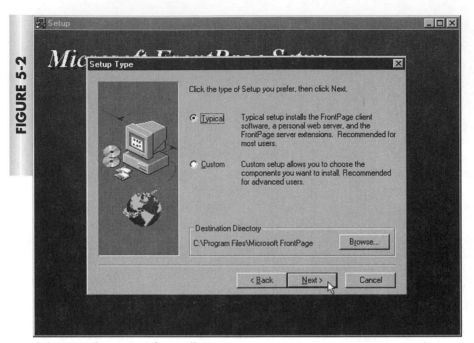

Selecting the type of installation

If you selected the custom installation option, FrontPage Setup will display the window shown in Figure 5-3. Here you can choose the components you would like to install. If you do not plan on setting up your computer as a Web host, there is no need to install the Personal Web Server or the server extensions. If you plan on making your computer a host, but using a server other than the Personal Web Server, you will need to install the server extensions. In all cases, you must make sure that the host you plan to use has a Web server with the FrontPage extensions installed. When you are satisfied with the settings, click the Next button.

If you selected a typical installation or chose to install the Personal Web Server, you'll see the window shown in Figure 5-4. This allows you to customize the location where the server will be installed. The Web sites you create will be stored under this location as well, so if you plan on creating large Web sites, be sure to select a location with enough space to accommodate this growth. If you do not like the default directory the Setup program has chosen, click the Browse... button and choose a new location. When you are happy with the destination directory, click the Next button.

FrontPage Setup will create a program folder on your Start button menu. The default name for this folder is Microsoft FrontPage. To change this folder, select one listed in the Existing Folders list box or enter a new name in the text field above it. When you are satisfied with your selections, click the Next button. The FrontPage Setup will confirm your choices in the Start Copying Files window, shown in Figure 5-5. If you are happy with the selections you've made, click the Next button. If you want to change something, it's not

Choosing FrontPage components to install and the destination of the client software for a custom installation

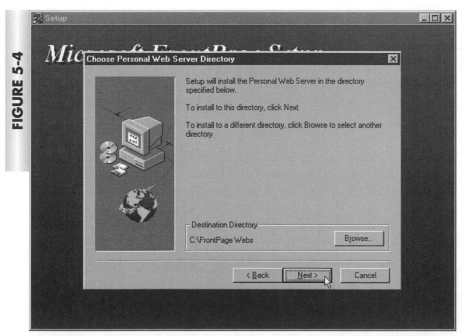

Choosing a location for the server and server extensions

too late. Just click the Back button until you come to the window with the settings you wish to adjust, change them, and continue from there. Once you indicate you are satisfied with your settings, the Setup program will begin installing files from your CD-ROM to the hard drive.

If you chose to install the Personal Web Server and FrontPage Server Extensions, a window will appear after the file is copied, asking you to enter name and password information for the Web administrator, as shown in Figure 5-6. This person will have complete control over the Web sites and will be responsible for assigning names, passwords, and access to the Web sites on that server. It is a good idea to write down this name and password so that you don't forget them in the future. If you happen to forget them, it is possible to uninstall the server extensions and then reinstall them, causing the Setup to request a new name and password for the server administrator. Your old Web sites will not be deleted.

The FrontPage Setup program notifies you when it is finished and displays a dialog with the option to start the FrontPage Explorer right away. Click the Finish button to exit the Setup program.

The first time the FrontPage Explorer is run, it needs to get some information about your machine, including its host name and IP address. A dialog pops up to notify you of this. The Explorer can perform these tasks automatically; all you need to do is click the OK button. If the Explorer successfully identifies these items, a dialog notifying you of success will appear. It should be necessary to perform this task only once.

Your FrontPage Web publishing package should now be installed!

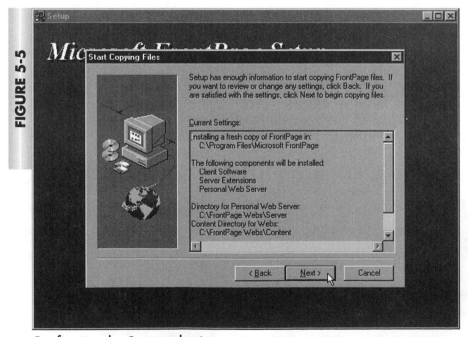

Confirming the Setup selections

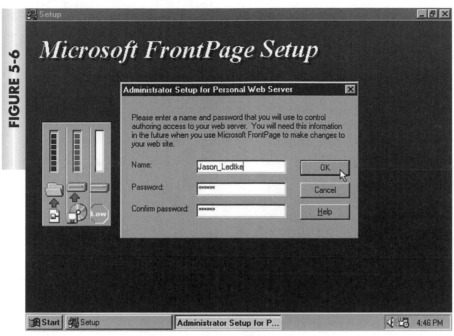

FIGURE 5-6

Entering the name of the Personal Web Server administrator and choosing a password

Lesson 2: Uninstalling FrontPage

If you install options you don't need, it's often easier to uninstall the software and reinstall it rather than try to remove specific components. Additionally, you may want to remove this package one day, so an uninstallation section seems appropriate. Actually, uninstalling is easier than installing!

The first step in removing FrontPage from your system is to open the control panel. This is done by clicking the Start button, choosing Settings, and then choosing Control Panel. Once the control panel is open, double-click on the Add/Remove Programs icon, as shown in Figure 5-7.

This brings up the Add/Remove Programs Properties window. In the list box in the lower part of this window is a list of many applications installed on your system. To remove FrontPage, highlight it by finding it and clicking on it in this box. Then click the Add/Remove button, as shown in Figure 5-8.

This brings up a dialog asking you to confirm the removal of the FrontPage software. Click the Yes button if you want to continue. Your computer will then remove the FrontPage components you have installed locally on your computer. These include the client software, the Personal Web Server, and the FrontPage Server Extensions. When these tasks are finished, you can click the OK button to continue.

Opening the Add/Remove Programs dialog

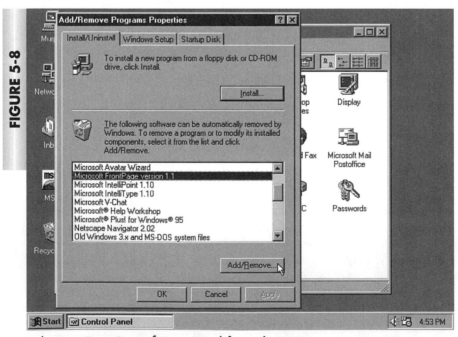

Selecting FrontPage for removal from the system

One nice feature is that, like a Word document or Excel spreadsheet, your creations remain even though you remove the program that created them. Removing FrontPage and the server and server extensions does not affect the Web sites you've already created (other than removing your editing and server capabilities). If the Personal Web Server was installed locally, these Web sites are found in the `C:/FrontPage Webs` directory or the directory you specified during the initial installation. If you want to remove these Web sites, you can delete this directory. If the Web sites were hosted on a machine other than your own, you'll need to delete the Web sites with the FrontPage client software before you uninstall it from your local system.

Lesson 3: Installing the FrontPage Server Extensions on Your Computer

This example assumes that you just installed the FrontPage software, including the server extensions; that you have a different commercial Web server already installed and properly configured on your system; and that you intend to use it to distribute your Web sites. If you installed the Personal Web Server and the server extensions, the Personal Web Server is already properly configured for use with FrontPage. If you plan on using a different computer for hosting your Web site, you should talk to the people responsible for that computer to see if they will install the FrontPage Server Extensions if they have not already done so.

This example adds the FrontPage Server Extensions to a Web server already installed on your system. You will find that this procedure is devastatingly simple. The first step is to run the Microsoft FrontPage Server Administrator. This is done by clicking on the Start button, choosing Programs and then Microsoft FrontPage, and then clicking on Server Administrator. The Server Administrator allows you to perform simple administrative tasks. To install the server extensions, click the Install button.

A dialog box appears asking for the type of Web server to which you wish to add the extensions. Select your Web server from the drop-down list box and then click the OK button as shown in Figure 5-9.

If your server is not listed, you do not have the FrontPage extensions for that server type. Your best bet is to get in touch with your server administrator to identify the correct set of extensions you need. Then download them (free) from Microsoft at `http://www.microsoft.com/frontpage/freestuff/fs_fp_extensions.htm`.

A Server Configuration dialog may appear, asking for more information on your server. If you are using a Netscape server, you will need to enter the port to which the server extensions should be installed. If you are using O'Reilly's WebSite Web server and are using its multihoming features, you will need to enter the domain name for the server host that will contain the server extensions. If you are using the WebSite server but not its multihoming features, you can leave this line blank. If for some reason the extensions were removed from your Personal Web Server and you are reinstalling them now, you will need to supply the location of the server's configuration file. The default location for this file is `c:\FrontPage Webs\Server\conf\httpd.cnf`, but this may be different depending on the location you selected for the server during the Setup.

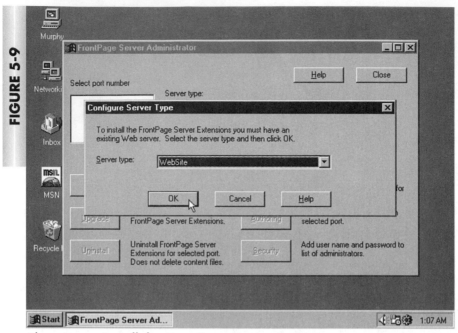

FIGURE 5-9

Choosing to install the FrontPage Server Extensions

After you have entered this information, a dialog will appear (shown in Figure 5-10) requesting confirmation of the information you have entered. If you've entered something incorrectly, click the Cancel button and start over. Otherwise, click the OK button to finish the installation.

You will be prompted for a name and password for the administrator account, as described in Lesson 1. After entering this information, you will have completed the installation of the extensions.

Lesson 4: Assigning Administrator Names and Passwords

To edit a Web site, you must supply a user name and password. If you have access to the FrontPage Server Administrator, you can add user names and passwords to the list of administrators. You can specify which Web sites can be edited by different names and passwords and restrict the locations from which editing is allowed. If you are using FrontPage client software to edit Web sites on a machine other than your own, you will need to set up a user name and password for the Web sites with which you plan to work. Chapter 9, "The FrontPage Explorer," discusses how you can do this remotely through the FrontPage Explorer. To create a new administrator, start the FrontPage Server Administrator. This can be done by clicking

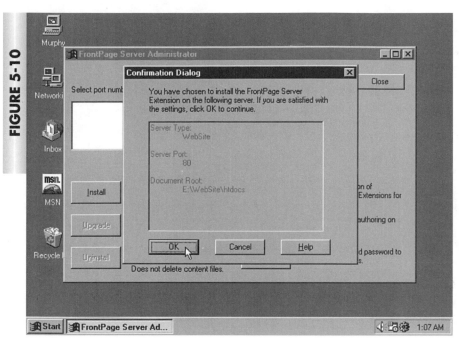

Confirming your selections

the Start button, choosing Programs and then the Microsoft FrontPage start folder, and then clicking on the Server Administrator program. This is the same process described in Lesson 3. Once the Server Administrator is open, click on the Security button, as shown in Figure 5-11.

A dialog appears to enable the creation of new administrators. The top field is the name of the Web site to which the administrator is allowed access. That Web site, and all Web sites under that Web site, then can be edited by supplying the user name and password supplied in the next dialog text fields. If the Web name specified is <Root Web>, then access is given to all the Web sites, because the root is at the top level.

The Advanced button in this dialog allows you to restrict which machines are allowed to edit Web sites. You can restrict which machines can edit your Web sites by their IP address, or you can allow all machines access the default. If you want to enable only a certain machine, or only machines within a certain IP address space, you can determine that here. This could be a good idea if you are concerned about security, but it could be a bad idea if you want people to be able to edit your Web sites from remote locations. No matter what the settings, if a user does not have a valid user name and password for the Web site he or she attempts to edit, the user will be unable to effect changes to that Web site.

If you are satisfied with your selections, click the OK button on the dialog and the Close button on the Server Administrator.

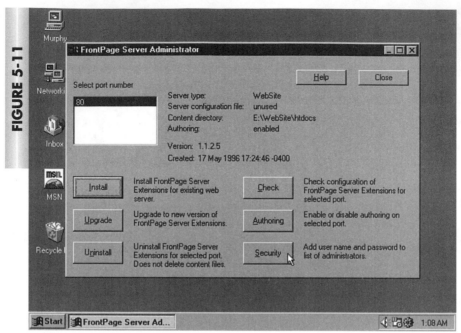

FIGURE 5-11

Adding an administrator

Lesson 5: Controlling Authoring

If you are exposing the Personal Server to the Internet (as opposed to a closed Intranet), you may be concerned about securing the hard work you put into creating your Web sites. FrontPage allows you to disable the authoring features, meaning no person—regardless of his or her password or IP address—will be able to edit the Web sites accessed through a certain port with the FrontPage Client software. The authoring capabilities are a potential security hazard, and this eliminates that hazard. This is great for security, but may prove inconvenient. Anyone with a legitimate desire to edit the Web site will have to get to the server to turn the authoring capabilities back on while he or she edits the site, and turn them off again when he or she is finished.

Toggling the authoring property is as simple as clicking on the Authoring button in the Personal Server Administrator. A dialog appears. Clicking the OK button in this dialog changes the authoring property to the opposite state (enabled if it was disabled, and disabled if it was enabled).

Summary

You should have a fully functional copy of FrontPage installed. You should have access to a server with the FrontPage extensions available for your use. And you should have a good feel for the various FrontPage components. With this in hand, you are ready to do some serious thinking about how to approach the problem of Web site design.

Designing Your Web Site

6

In this chapter you will learn:

The Steps for Designing an Effective Web Site

How to Define Your Design Goals

Three Easy Ways to Make Your Site Stick in the Reader's Mind

How to Provide Navigation in Your Web Site

The Steps to Make Sure That Your Web Site is Accurate and Lively

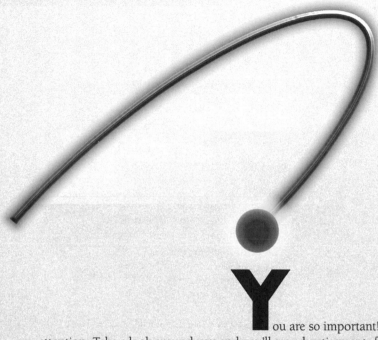

You are so important! Everybody wants your attention. Take a look around you and you'll see advertisements for just about everything from diapers to mouthwash. Turn on the radio and hear the catchy jingle for bologna. Consider the perfume sellers who try to douse you with every perfume and cologne when you walk into a department store. These invasions on your senses are not by chance. They are designed to grab your attention and persuade you to use that product.

How does this extend into the realm of the World Wide Web (WWW or Web)? Well, if you want people to view your Web page, you will have to capture and maintain their interest to "keep 'em coming back for more." This chapter explores the steps involved in creating an effective online publication. First it examines how to target your audience and then tailor your message to fit its needs. You'll learn the fundamentals of graphic design so that you can apply these strategies to your own Web projects.

If you're looking to show your friends, or your boss, just how quickly you can come up with new publication designs, you've come to the right place. The door is open to design secrets that will have you publishing like a guru in no time.

The Design Process

Although it may appear easy enough to get started just by sitting down and plugging away with FrontPage, if you want to design an effective publication, you will have to do a little more work. Before you run away from your PC, screaming at the thought of more work, take a moment to examine things a little more closely.

Designing your pages is a process. Although there are no strict rules, you will fare well to follow these steps:

◁ Define your design goals

◁ Design the flow of information

◁ Follow the three Cs of basic design—simplicity, consistency, and contrast

◁ Design navigation methods

◁ Design your pages

◁ Test and experiment

Define Your Design Goals

The reason you want people to see your pages, besides to show them how cool you are, is that you have something that you want them to experience. In other words, you wish to communicate with your audience. Keep in mind that *how* you communicate this information is just as important as *what* you communicate.

Determine Your Audience

What made you pick up this book? Why do you choose one cola over another? Why did you feel you just had to check out the Dilbert Zone home page, in Figure 6-1, before work today? Give up? Well, there was something basic about the object that attracted you. The reasons why are not as important as the fact that you had a need filled by reacting to the object. For example, you may need a little humor to get your day started (as many often do), so you visit the Dilbert Zone home page. The Dilbert Zone home page is targeted at an audience that appreciates workplace satire and enjoys a good laugh. Just as the Dilbert site has an intended audience, so should your Web site. Understand who will be viewing your site.

Once you have decided to create your online masterpiece, you should determine who the intended audience will be. This is a critical step. If you do not know who your audience is, research and find out. Even if you are your own audience, it is imperative that you tailor the design to fit your audience. Compare the MTV page, in Figure 6-2, to the CNBC Ticker page, in Figure 6-3. The MTV page caters to its younger audience through the use of bright colors, various font styles, and extensive graphics. The CNBC page focuses on the purpose of the page—describing what the CNBC Ticker is all about. Notice the use of uniform colors and traditional typeface, catering to a more mature audience, rather than elaborate graphics.

Once you have determined your audience, consider its background. Are your readers very knowledgeable about the information you intend to present? If so, then you may freely use jargon to which your audience is accustomed. If your audience consists of novices, explain information in more detail or use simpler jargon. Will your readers look to your publication as a source of reference, entertainment, or enlightenment? Designating your audience will make it easier for you to design a publication that meets its needs.

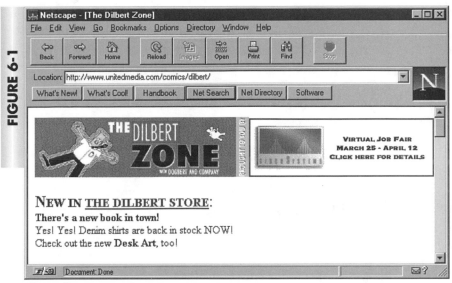

The Dilbert Zone home page
(http://www.unitedmedia.com/comics/dilbert/)

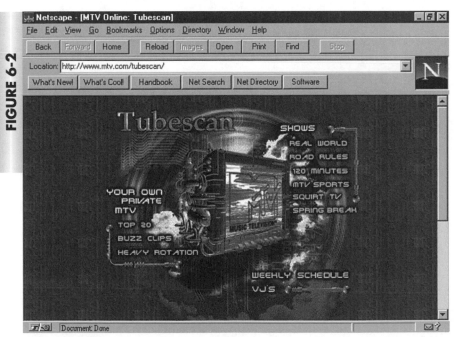

The MTV tubescan page (http://www.mtv.com/tubescan/)

FIGURE 6-3

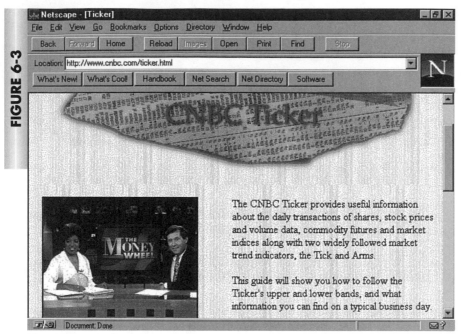

The CNBC Ticker page (`http://www.cnbc.com/ticker.html`)

Establish Your Message

You want your design to present your point in the most attractive and informative manner possible. Your message should contain elements that you want your readers to remember after they have completed viewing your publication.

Think of your Web site as an online publication. What is the purpose of your publication? Is your publication intended to inform (of today's stock prices), to persuade readers to do or react to something (try a new flavor of coffee), or to serve as a reference (encyclopedia entry)? A publication that attempts to persuade may include a feature list and comparisons to lesser brands, whereas an informative publication may present information in an objective manner.

What should your readers learn? Many people surf from one Web site to another and happen to land on various sites by chance. Given this fact, you will want to present your information in the most concise and effective manner as possible. You can do this by using keywords, catch phrases, or graphics to illustrate your message.

Keep in mind that designing an online publication is different than designing for print. Your readers have total controlover what they wish to view and may choose not to scroll through a long document or wait for a large graphic to load. Although the Web is expanding, people are generally restricted by slow phone lines and various display options. Your goal should be to present your message in a manner that caters to the readers' needs rather than exacerbating limitations.

Set the Tone

In acting classes all over the world, actors are asked to express various emotions, but to say only the words "I love you." Although this may seem like a trivial task, actors quickly learn that there are numerous ways to present the exact same information by changing their tone. This same concept applies to online publishing. In the days of the typewriter, how did you express items that you wanted the reader to pay particular attention to? Yes, you used the infamous underline. But isn't there a more imaginative way of conveying tone? Why, yes, there is.

The dawn of word processor programs opened a cornucopia of methods to achieve emphasis, including, but not limited to, bold, italics, fonts, sizes, color, and graphics. The only problem with all these possibilities is that many people attempt to use all of them in the same publication. Many novices even go so far as to make a sentence bold and underlined. So what is a designer to do? You want to reach your audience with a designated message but you don't want to bore, confuse, or offend. What is the best way to do this? Simply put, pick a mood.

Picking a mood will make your life much easier. Consider the New York-style glitzy approach, used by PaperMag in Figure 6-4, compared to the flashy sports motif used by the ESPN SportsZone in Figure 6-5.

FIGURE 6-4

PaperMag exemplifies New York style glitz
(http://www.papermag.com/)

FIGURE 6-5

ESPN SportsZone uses the sports page metaphor
(http://espnet.sportzone.com/)

Notice that the PaperMag page, in Figure 6-4, makes clever use of neon images to provide the user with a flavor of New York's neon Broadway. The reader immediately recognizes this page as "a cool place to be!" Contrast this with ESPN Zone's approach in Figure 6-5. ESPN Zone caters to sports enthusiasts who are used to reading the daily sports pages. How does ESPN do this? ESPN provides many stories and statistics in the sports page format, which makes it very easy for enthusiasts to navigate ESPN Zone.

Disney establishes a playful mood by using cartoon images and references to "fun" and "games" (see Figure 6-6). This approach speaks to children who are looking for a little extracurricular entertainment.

Keep in mind that if your mood is playful, you may wish to incorporate oddly placed shapes around your text to provide a busy effect. If you strive to be more conservative, use uniform fonts and colors. Also notice that effective use of headlines quickly informs the user why he or she should continue to read. White space is also an excellent way to draw attention to a particular object or idea. How do you use white space? If you think about the layout of the text and pictures used in this book, you will quickly see the advantage of white space. If there were a poor use of white space in this book, then all the text and pictures would run together and it would be difficult to determine where one paragraph starts and another begins.

FIGURE 6-6

The Disney page screams "Fun!" (http://www.disney.com)

Design the Flow of Information

What were the first words out of your English teacher's mouth when it came time to write a paper? That's right—start with your outline. Your first thought probably is "Outline? I don't need no stinkin' outline." But this little gem is very useful and time saving. So, what is an outline? It is a skeleton of your publication's structure.

The outline illustrates how your information will flow from topic to topic. This concept not only will save you time and help you organize, but it is one of the foundations of online publishing. If you take a look at this book's table of contents (TOC), you can quickly gauge your points of interest and which pages to view. Consider that with online publications, this TOC may be the chief form of navigation within your publication.

You should initially create an outline to help you organize your thoughts and information flow, but it will be easier to map out your FrontPage project if you already have your structure defined.

The 3 Cs of Basic Design

First, please note that the three Cs actually comprise an S and two Cs. But that wouldn't be as easy to remember, would it? The following rules are valid for design in general but are even more appropriate given the dynamic nature of online publications:

◁ Simplicity

◁ Consistency

◁ Contrast

Simplicity

Think of some of the famous catch phrases of our era: Alka Seltzer's "Plop, plop, fizz, fizz. Oh, what a relief it is" and Nike's "Just Do It." In many cases, a simple picture, such as the Energizer Bunny in Figure 6-7, also elicits a familiar phrase. These phrases are simple and easy to remember. You may remember many famous slogans or catch phrases because of their simplicity.

Remarkably, the human brain remembers best when things are learned in five to seven chunks at a time. This is an important point. If you want people to look at your publication, remember to use a simple phrase of keywords or images to capture their interest.

Why do magazines like the *Globe* or the *Enquirer* garner so many readers? Some may argue that there are a lot of strange people who actually believe Big Foot is Michael Jackson's godfather, but the real reason is that these publications use headlines eloquently. Compare the two Elvis headlines in Figure 6-8.

FIGURE 6-7

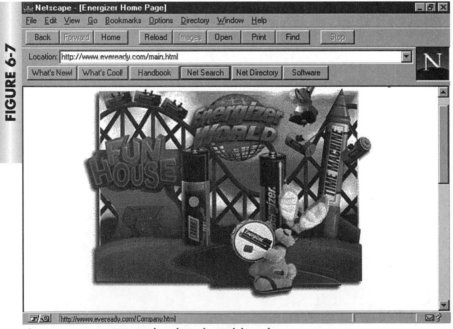

The Energizer Bunny back to his old tricks
(`http://www.everready.com/main.html`)

FIGURE 6-8

Elvis Auditions for Jurassic Park!

Fictional Elvis headlines
(image from `http://www.seas.upenn.edu/~lzeltser/Pics/elvisaurus.jpg`)

"Elvis Auditions for Jurassic Park!" will draw more readers than the second caption, "A False Elvis Siting."

Once you have established headlines as a key component of simplicity, it's time to reexamine the use of elements on a page. The cliché, "a picture is worth a thousand words," follows the simplicity concept. Numerous readers would stop to look at a picture of the Elvisaurus example above.

Another approach to simplicity involves limiting the size of your fonts. Typically, a Web page will be one or two screens of information. Given small screen real estate, you do not want to confuse the reader by using 18 different fonts. A general rule of fonts limits you from one to three per Web page. Why would you want to use more than one font? Well, consider the headline example. Most pages contain one or more headlines and then a story area. If you follow this trend, you will use a headline font and and perhaps one or more story fonts. To provide text variety, spruce up your text with color. Don't go overboard with colors—follow the same one to three rule used with fonts.

More About Graphics and Headlines

Because many online users will be communicating over slow phone lines, it is helpful to offer a headline as well as a picture. This way, your user can follow the gist of your page without waiting for your graphics to load over the phone line.

Consistency

Have you ever looked closely at a McDonalds' advertisement or food wrapper? How about a Gateway computer advertisment? What comes to mind when you look at these items? For McDonalds, you probably think of the golden arches or pictures of a Big Mac; Gateway conjures up cow images and black and white spots on packages. These combined images help relay corporate identity. Such uniform presentation is called *consistency*.

Consistency is one of the key ingredients that will make your online publication stand out from everyone else's. Think of your interests. What do you want people to think when they read your material? If there is a mental image or a theme that you wish to convey, use it throughout your publication. Are you developing a title for your company, family, or class, or for fun? Consider these factors when you wish to make your publication consistent. Simply put, consistency is the repetitive use of design elements. Examine the Microsoft Web pages in Figure 6-9 and Figure 6-10. Although each page conveys a different image, the layout of each page is consistent with the Microsoft Web site.

Repetition is not about going overboard by using your corporate symbol every other word and annoying your readers very quickly. Specifically, repetition involves more than that.

Consider the screen space that you use when you design pages for your publication. Use the same margins throughout your publication, although you don't have to use exact margins. Consider the areas between text and graphics. Typically, you should consistently use the same amount of white space on your page for major graphics, including headlines or symbols. If your readers see your logo at the top of the first page, they generally will expect to see that logo throughout your publication. And if you use images to represent forms of navigation, then use them consistently throughout. You want your readers reveling in the awesome splendor of your page, not wondering why page 2 is different from page 1.

Another consistency issue is the use of fonts and colors. Previously, you learned that a general rule is to use one to three fonts throughout your publication. But consider how you wish to use these fonts. If you use a font for a headline in one place, then use it consistently for that purpose throughout the publication. Let your fonts and colors relay not only the text but also a feeling of what you are trying to convey.

Red is frequently used for emphasis or warning text. Because most readers have come to expect this use of red, you probably should not use this color in your main text. Also, keep your colors consistent with your image. What a mixed image would be conveyed if McDonalds were to display its logo using a competitor's colors rather than its own! If your company's colors are blue and white, try to resist that temptation to use neon green in your logo (no matter how cool you think it may look).

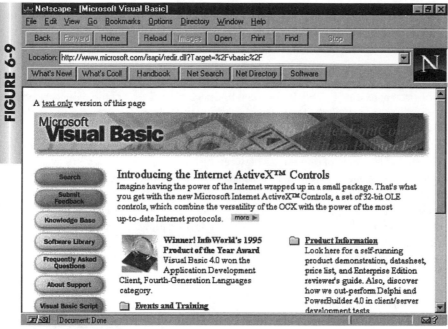

The Microsoft Visual Basic site

The Microsoft Visual Basic scripting site

Contrast

Believe it or not, humans are visually stimulated creatures. You are not convinced? Think about all the people who stand around in each other's offices or in the malls trying to find the hidden pictures in computer art (worse yet, think of all the poor souls who never see the picture—yes, it is a cow in a spaceship). If you're still not convinced, think of one of the reasons you're reading this book. You want to design great-looking online publications so you can show your stuff on the Web. The success of the Web is further testimony to the innate desire to share information visually.

One of the most effective ways to illustrate something is through the use of contrast. Contrast is the illumination of differences between objects to catch the viewer's eye.

The hidden vase image in Figure 6-11 is one of the most famous examples of contrast.

Depending on how you look at the picture, you may see a white vase superimposed on a black background or two black faces on a white background. In either instance, your eye is immediately drawn to the picture and one of the two images jumps out at you. This example illustrates the contrast of color. You don't always have to contrast colors, but it is one of the most effective ways of creating contrast.

Another method of contrast is to use headlines. Yes, your old friend Elvis is visiting again in Figure 6-12 (sort of like in real life, no?). Notice that when the headline is different from the rest of the text, the headline jumps out and grabs the reader's attention.

You can achieve this effect not only through headlines but also through the use of graphics. One tactic that many online magazines use is the headline graphic. The picture tells the user the focus of the article and the headline further explains why the reader should continue. Let that picture do all the talking for you. Figure 6-13 combines the above elements to create an intriguing electronic magazine front page.

If you do not wish to use the graphical approach, there are always the standbys—the fonts. Many publications make effective use of an extremely large or decorated first letter of a paragraph to catch your attention and draw you into their product. You can play with font shapes and sizes to create the appropriate contrast between your bodies of text. However, remember to use contrast sparingly and only where appropriate. For example, if you are developing an online magazine, it may make sense to use a large font for the name of your

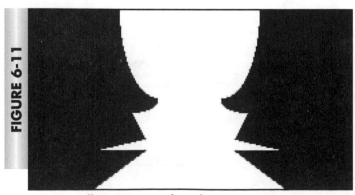

FIGURE 6-11

Contrast illustration (What do you see?)

FIGURE 6-12

I Saw Elvis!

Today I saw Elvis as I was Walking down the street. He said, "Hi. How's it going?"

I saw Elvis!

Today I saw Elvis as I was Walking down the street. He said, "Hi. How's it going?"

Contrast using the headline approach

magazine, but not for minor text elements such as the date or the 10th word of the second paragraph. Figure 6-14 illustrates the clever use of font and text placement to draw attention to the magazine without diverting the reader's attention from the subject at hand. The key to using contrast is to highlight the most important points of your publication to entice the reader into further exploring your paradise.

FIGURE 6-13

CNN Interactive (`http://www.cnn.com/`) effectively uses headlines

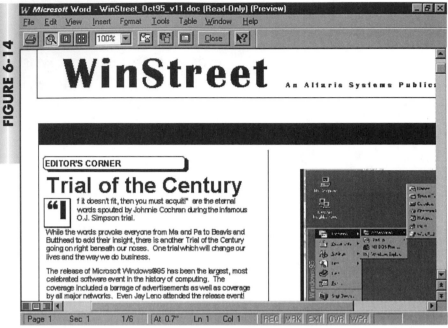

FIGURE 6-14

The WinStreet publication makes use of clever font and text placement

Design Your Navigation Methods

Before you are ready to begin developing your online masterpiece, consider one other major difference between online and printed publications—navigation. Although some people can find the place they want to be through ESP, this section is addressed to the mere mortals of the crowd.

With printed publications, a reader typically uses one or more of the following tools: the table of contents, the index, and page numbers. If the reader desires to go to a specific page, she or he just turns to that page. If unsure to which page to go, the reader consults the TOC or the index to help him or her feel around in the dark. These navigation tools are also at your disposal in the online world. The majority of online publications use these tools. Chapter 10, "Navigation," discusses this topic in detail. For now, give the tried and true elements your attention.

The TOC conveys the structure of your publication and allows users to see the smaller parts that make up the sum of your title. In the online arena, the TOC is available, but tends to be somewhat generalized due to the limitations of screen real estate and length of the page. Because this navigation tool is so frequently used, FrontPage includes an outline control that allows you to emulate a TOC. Some online publications also use indexes within their pages, but this is uncommon because of the power and flexibility of today's text search engines. These engines have become so common that you may decide to do away altogether with an overall index.

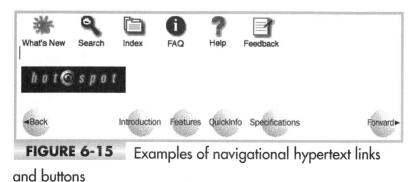

FIGURE 6-15   Examples of navigational hypertext links and buttons

Other navigation tools at your disposal include hypertext links and buttons. Hypertext links are useful little gadgets. A hypertext link consists of a text phrase that, when clicked with the mouse, will take the reader to another part of the document or display a popup window.

This opens up a whole new realm of possibilities for online viewing. You can now use terms or phrases in your title; if viewers want to learn more about that topic or wish to jump to another area, they can just click the phrase. No need for a reader to look up the word or consult the index for related topics, because the functionality is available at the click of a button. This leads to the next tool—buttons.

Buttons are another excellent navigation tool. Like a hypertext link, a button allows the reader to jump to another portion of your publication. A common use of buttons is forward and backward navigation. Online publications do not have physical pages that readers can turn, but if you present readers with a button, they can navigate freely within your document. Figure 6-15 illustrates popular uses of the linking button metaphor.

When developing buttons, most authors use video recorder buttons to represent common actions such as backward, forward, and stop. In some instances, you may wish also to incorporate graphics for your buttons. In the wonderful world of FrontPage, it is now possible for your user to click on your graphic to learn more about a topic.

An effective method of using navigation buttons involves your logo or main page banner. When you use this picture for the first time, you can place a smaller version on subsequent pages, letting the user know that he or she has an instant link back to your main page. Think of the possibilities!

Design Your Pages

With any new adventure, it's great to learn the basics before proceeding: You are almost ready to continue on your journey. The next sections offer a few things for you to keep in mind as you move on to design with FrontPage.

Overall Look and Feel

What will be the overall look and feel of your publication? Of the numerous methods to convey your business or personal touch, which approach will you choose? Whatever you decide, you should be consistent throughout the publication.

Maybe, like many Web explorers, you wonder which looks are available. Or maybe you feel you don't have the creative nature and need a little help to get you rolling. Have no fear: There are sources all around you. Pick up any major magazine or your local newspaper, read billboards, or watch television. Better yet, search the Web and see what other creative individuals, like yourself, have already done. All Web designers had to create a first publication and learned how just like anyone else. Besides, how bad could it be? Okay, there are some wacky ideas out there, but even the wacky ideas are great tutorials. If you think you have an idea but are missing little things, like perhaps graphics, view what others have done and embellish on their approaches. Limitless examples are everywhere. The next time you leave your house, consciously observe just how many great eye-catchers are around you. Examine why they catch your eye and maintain your interest.

Static and Dynamic Stories

As you design your pages, consider the nature of the information on the page. Text that you wish to incorporate into your titles is termed *story*. Why call it story rather than text? Imagine the look on your parents' faces if as a child you had asked them to "present me with some oral text" rather than "tell me a story." Although this may not be the reason text can be called a story, the concept of a story is familiar to most people.

Stories can follow two types of formats: static or dynamic. Static stories are those that you tailor carefully to one or more pages, whereas dynamic stories are simply placeholders for ever-changing content. An example of a static story is an encyclopedia entry for Marilyn Monroe. Although her skirt might not have been static in *Some Like It Hot*, her biography is static. Unless she joins the immortal ranks of Elvis or the Highlander, you can assume that her story remains the same. You can design a page with her biographical information and assume that you will not have to change it. But when you discover some awesome tidbit to add to her biography, you could add it to her page, although it might require some redesigning to fit everything on the page.

A dynamic story offers a separation of design from content. What does this mean? Consider an online daily magazine, where you designate a page to the headline of the day. If you like torture, you might decide to redesign the page every day, but you might prefer to have your news writer update the daily headline and then have your Web administrator update the site. This is not an uncommon occurrence in many sites. How can you simulate the dynamic update of your Web page? The answer lies in FrontPage's ability to import files.

Look at the cool example in Figure 6-16. At first glance, the Web page looks like a typical combination of text. However, the only text that the Web administrator typed was the "Welcome..." and "Today's Features." The rest of the page was imported by FrontPage. How was this accomplished?

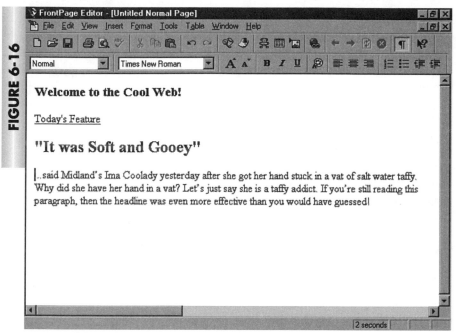

FIGURE 6-16

Imported headline story

◁ Using a word processing program (for example, Microsoft Word), we created a rich text format (.RTF) file called `samp_headline.rtf`.

◁ Using the FrontPage Editor, we created a sample Web page and entered the `"Welcome..."` and `"Today's Features"` lines.

◁ From here, we used the `Insert → File` menu option and selected our previous .RTF file. FrontPage performed the file import, leaving us with the page in the example.

FrontPage's file import functionality will make your life much simpler because it lets you update dynamic pages merely by changing a source document and performing a new import into your Web site.

Number of Pages

As you develop the structure of your title, note the number of pages that you may require. Knowing the number of pages will allow you some flexibility in designing your pages. For example, suppose you are covering a fictional global attack by alien killer electric penguins (a la Monty Python). You are sure this story covers multiple pages, given the plight of the world, so you may want to designate the first page to a large headline and a photograph of the penguins. Subsequent pages could then be designed to have a more text-oriented appeal and to read like a typical article.

Story Flow

Your story flow will be tailored largely on your readers' needs. Historically, the scrolling metaphor has been used in online publishing to allow the user to view information that does not fit in the visible screen area. Although you still find the scrolling metaphor used frequently, many authors use the page-turning metaphor.

The page-turning metaphor follows a traditional approach to reading. When you are finished with a page of information, you turn the page to see the next section of information. This feature is implemented through the use of navigation buttons or hypertext links.

There is no reason that you can't effectively combine the two types of page viewing on a single page. Suppose you have a highlight page, as in Figure 6-17. You could feature the basic highlight but also incorporate the feature story on the same page. If it does not quite fit, the reader can scroll this story for more information. In any case, the main page is at the reader's disposal.

Parts Is Parts

Once you have designated your story flow, consider the structure of the title. Are there any topics that don't fit into the flow of the story? Are there any amusing anecdotes or asides? These may be helpful to the story but do not fit into the main body.

Suppose you are designing a title that will provide detailed instructions to drive from New York City to Los Angeles. One approach is to list the linear steps that can be used for the reader's journey, but that would make for a rather dry title (not *boring,* because there probably is a secret population of individuals who enjoy reading maps in their spare time). You could spice up the journey by adding images of the various states, with links and pop-ups relative to the states and their landmarks. Such a title would serve two purposes. First, it would serve as a direct navigational guide. Second, it would also provide a fantastic journey across America. The Ticketmaster Web page, Figure 6-18, employs a similar navigation map.

Your goal of breaking the title down into individual parts should be to alleviate the reader's task of having to read your story linearly to obtain enjoyment—a lesser feat for printed publications because their readers can put the book down or flip to another page. Online publishing involves a reader's eyes staring at a computer screen, so you want to provide as much exercise as possible for those eyes without popping them out of their sockets.

Graphics, Text, and Audio—Oh My

Determine in advance all the artwork you will need to build your title. The list will include not only works that you plan to emulate (no, not steal—there are little things called copyright laws that you don't wish to violate even if "everyone is doing it") but works that you plan to create from scratch as well. Choose the size and complexity of your artwork carefully because of the limitations of displaying over phone lines, but remember that it is most efficient to gather anything that potentially can be used for your project and toss out nonessential elements later.

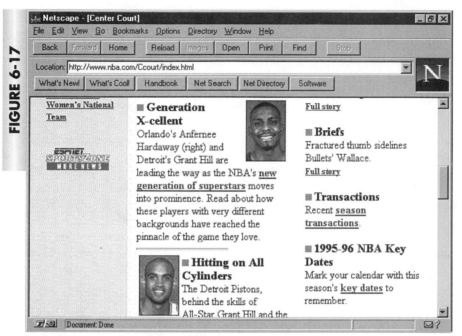

Headline story flow example (http://www.nba.com)

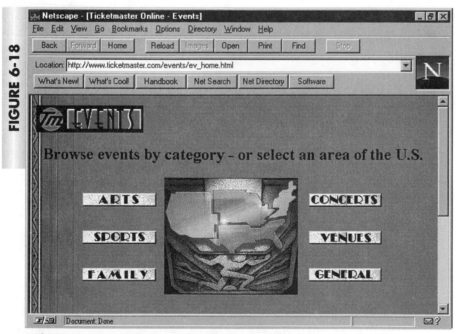

Ticketmaster uses geographical navigation map
(http://www.ticketmaster.com)

The use of text is another component that you should consider. Font sizes and possibilities are endless. Settle on a few that you will be happy with and leave the rest for future projects. Audio is another feature that you can add to make your publication a feast for the senses, but take note that not everyone has a sound card (poor souls) and performance costs are involved with transmitting sound over telephone lines.

Test and Experiment

The final step of the design process is the most fun of all—the testing phase. Feel free to try out ideas and experiment with them. A common approach is to start with a pencil and paper. Take a few moments to jot down some ideas and begin drawing your pages. The pencil and paper allow you the flexibility of discarding designs that you don't like without investing a lot of time on the computer. If you find a particular magazine article or other idea that you would like to emulate, study it carefully. Take notice of the different components of the magazine page and break them apart. This will help you make modifications as you discover the composition of the page. This is very important when working with FrontPage, because you will build your pages by interacting with the components in a toolbox.

Once you have a basic design, it is a good idea to test your ideas on a sample audience and gather feedback, because these people will give you insight that you didn't know was possible. During this phase, let your creative juices flow as you can always revise later. (Although, if your boss has you under a deadline, you may want to remove the Beavis and Butthead cartoons from your page before you complete it.)

Where Next?

In this chapter, you explored the steps required to create an effective publication. By following these design tips, you can design an online publication that is as exciting for you to develop as it is for your readers to explore. The topics illustrate how the groundwork performed in the design process prepares you for using FrontPage. This foundation will propel you into later chapters, where you will tap all the flexibility and power of FrontPage. Strap on your seat belts because the next stops will have you developing your own publications like a veteran in no time!

FrontPage Editor

7

In this chapter you will learn:

How to Plan a Web Site
The Standard Toolbar
The Format Toolbar
The Personal Home Page Wizard
Links
Bookmarks

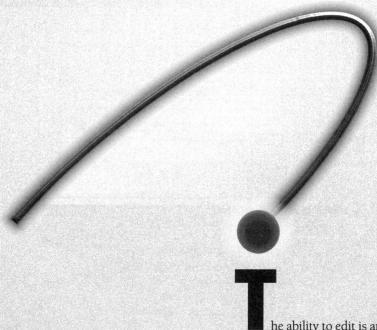

The ability to edit is an indispensable skill that will assist you in developing a professional-looking Web site. Editing involves a seemingly endless number of aspects. A simple analogy to editing a Web site is organizing and handling all the details of producing a motion picture. What will the movie be about? What tools are necessary to make the movie and how are they used? How do you make changes in the movie after work has begun? How do you store the reels of film, then put them together for the final product? This chapter will answer all these questions, only you will be creating a FrontPage Web site instead of a western.

FrontPage Editor (FP Editor) supplies you with all the tools you need to develop an interesting, attractive Web site. The tools are grouped into two main toolbars and several drop-down menus located at the top of the FP Editor screen. Familiarizing yourself with the meanings of the icons in the toolbars and the different features is well worth the time and effort. If you are accustomed to the general style of Microsoft editors such as Word, you will probably move rapidly through this chapter.

Making a Great Movie

Using the similarity between a motion picture and a Web site, we can make a few more comparisons. We have all been to good movies and bad movies, interesting movies and boring movies. If there were a formula for a great movie, Hollywood would pay millions for it. Although a great movie formula might never be found, you can use movie-making techniques to develop home pages.

Many details must be taken care of before a director can start shooting a film. Obtaining the written screenplay, hiring the actors and technicians, and planning the filming locations are only a few of these details. Careful planning is also needed in designing a Web site. The following lesson explains the steps you need to go through before you put your hands to the keyboard.

Lesson 1: Steps to a Well-Planned Web Site

The following techniques are borrowed from the movie makers of Hollywood and will help you build a clear and concise foundation for your home page.

1. Develop a storyline. Just as all movies need some kind of storyline or plot, so does your Web site. In other words, what do you want to say in your home page? Do you want it presented in a conservative or a casual manner? Are you trying to interest others in a personal project or general information? Whatever your mission is, you must be clear about what you are presenting to your viewers.

2. Gather resources and information. The production of a movie requires an endless list of resources, including technicians, tools, makeup, equipment, and actors. Research about all aspects of the movie is also needed. Your Web site may require resources such as pictures, artist sketches, or specific data. You need to make sure you have or can obtain these components before you begin to type.

3. Create a storyboard. A storyboard is a series of pictures created by movie artists to plan exactly how a particular scene will go. To apply this technique to creating a Web site, sketch what you would like your page to look like on a sheet of paper. Add links to additional pages or other URLs. Draw pictures where you would like to place them. Doing this will give you an idea about the continuity or flow of your Web site.

This three-step method will prompt you to ask some specific questions about your Web site. Is it interesting? To whom is it interesting? Are you tailoring your Web site to attract a particular group of viewers? Do you have all the information you need to create an informative, attractive, professional Web site? During Web development, you must always keep your target audience in mind. A great Web site that no one wants to view is a contradiction. Try to think of one great movie that no one went to see.

Lesson 2: Opening FrontPage Editor via FrontPage Explorer

At this point, you are ready to begin the process of developing your Web site by opening a new Web in FrontPage. Follow these steps when initially creating your Web:

1. To open a new Web in FrontPage, click on the Start button at the bottom of the screen, then select Programs | Microsoft FrontPage. This brings you into FrontPage Explorer and the Getting Started with Microsoft FrontPage dialog box, as shown in Figure 7-1.

FIGURE 7-1

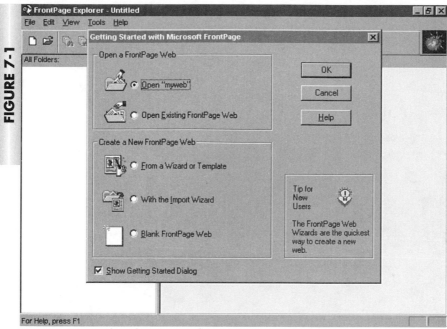

Getting Started with Microsoft FrontPage dialog box

2 In the Create a New FrontPage Web box, select the From a Wizard or Template choice. (You can also import an existing Web at this point, or open a blank Web.) This brings up the New FrontPage Web dialog box.

3. Choose Normal Web, then click on OK. This brings up the Normal Web Template dialog box.

4. Type in the name of your Web in the Name of New FrontPage Web field, then click on OK. This brings up the Name and Password Required dialog box.

5. Type in your name and password, then click on OK. After a short time, you will see the FrontPage Explorer view of your Web Normal Page.

6. Click on the Show FrontPage Editor button in the toolbar to open FP Editor.

Your first view of FP Editor will look like Figure 7-2. Working down from the top of the screen, there is a row of four drop-down menus: File, View, Tools, and Help. Underneath this row is the Standard toolbar, and beneath that is the Format toolbar. The toolbars allow for quick access to the same commands found in the four drop-down menus. At the bottom of the screen is the status bar.

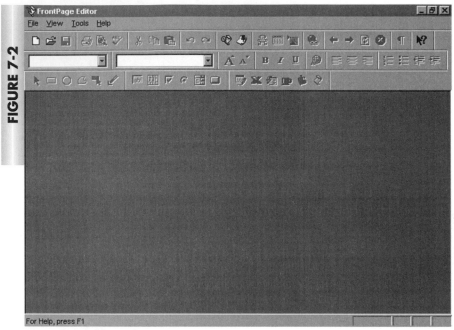

FIGURE 7-2

First view of FP Editor

Once you have opened the editor, there are three ways to open a new page:

1. Click on the File drop-down menu, then select New.

2. Click on the New button in the Standard toolbar.

3. Press CTRL+N.

Tip

Placing your cursor arrow on a button in a toolbar will cause a tool tip to appear near that button that will tell you its purpose.

After you have opened your new page, note that some of the buttons in the toolbars have become darker, indicating that they are now activated. The drop-down menu row has been expanded to include more options: File, Edit, View, Insert, Format, Tools, Table, Window, and Help.

Lesson 3: Fun with Toolbars

There are five toolbars and a status bar in FP Editor. In this chapter, you will learn about the Standard toolbar, the Format toolbar, the Advanced toolbar, and the Status bar. The Image and Form toolbars are specialty toolbars and are discussed in Chapters 11 and 16, respectively.

In FP Editor, you can bring any toolbar into view by selecting View from the row of drop-down menus. From there, you can choose the toolbars that will be visible on your screen. Once the toolbars are visible, you can use the click-and-drag method to move them anywhere on the page. To return them to the top, simply double-click on the solid bar above each toolbar.

Lesson 4: The Standard Toolbar

The Standard toolbar contains basic editing commands you will need, such as Cut and Paste, Save As, and Spell Check. As shown in Figure 7-3, the buttons in this toolbar are grouped into ten sections according to their uses. This lesson explains the Standard toolbar buttons.

1. The first set of buttons deals with creating a new page, opening an existing page, and saving a page. The first button, which looks like a sheet of paper, creates a new normal page when clicked on.

2. The second button is an open folder. This command allows you to open a page that already exists. When you click on this button, the Open File dialog box is brought up. You can either search for a particular file using the Look in feature or type in the file name and type of file in the Other Location tab, then click on OK.

3. The third button, which has a computer disk on it, lets you save the current document. Clicking on this button will bring up the Save As dialog box, where you type in the name of your page, then click on OK.

4. The second set of buttons allows you to print, preview, and spell check the current document. A picture of a printer is on the first of these buttons. When this button is clicked, the Print dialog box will be brought up. Here you enter your printer type and pages you wish to print, then click on OK.

5. The second button in this group contains a magnifying glass on top of a sheet of paper. This is the Print Preview button, which displays a full view of the page(s) you are working on in the browser. From the browser view, you can zoom in to the document to get a closer view, zoom out, or print.

6. The last button in this set contains the letters ABC and a check mark. This button allows you to spell check your current page(s).

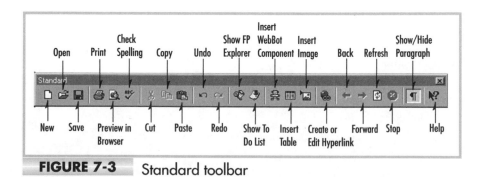

FIGURE 7-3   Standard toolbar

7. The third set of Standard toolbar buttons lets you cut, copy, and paste segments of text. A pair of scissors is on the first button in this group. After you highlight a word or words, this button cuts the word(s) and puts them on a clipboard in case you want to paste the word(s) somewhere else.

 Tip

To highlight a word or words, hold down the left mouse button while dragging the cursor from the beginning to the end of the word or phrase. If you are highlighting only one word, double-click just before the beginning of the word or on the word itself.

8. The second button in this group is the Copy command and has two identical pages on it. This button will copy a highlighted word or words to a clipboard, which will save it or them for you to paste somewhere else. Remember, the clipboard will save only the last item cut.

9. The third button contains a clipboard and a page and will paste whatever you have put on the clipboard at the site of your cursor.

10. The next set of buttons includes the Undo and Redo buttons. The Undo button has an arrow pointing to the left and allows you to undo or reverse your last action or command.

11. The Redo button has an arrow pointing to the right. Use this button if you want to restore what you have just reversed with the Undo button.

12. The next set of Standard toolbar buttons contains the Back to FP Explorer and To Do List buttons. The first button has a scroll on it; it will take you directly to FrontPage Explorer.

13. The other button has a tack on it. This icon will display the To Do List (see Lesson 13 for details about the To Do List).

14. The next group has the Insert WebBot Component, Insert Table, and Insert Image buttons. The first button has a picture of a WebBot on it and brings up the WebBot Components dialog box. For more information on WebBots, see Chapter 8.

15. The second button has a table on it and, when clicked on, displays the table window in which you can select the dimensions of your table.

16. The third button has a tiny mountain scene on it and, when clicked on, brings up the Image dialog box.

17. The next group has only the Create or Edit Hyperlink button. Clicking on this button brings up the Create Hyperlink dialog box which lets you choose what your text will be linked to.

18. The eighth set of Standard toolbar buttons deals with several aspects of hyperlinks. The first button in this group has a left pointer, which sends you back to the previous page in the hyperlink history list.

19. The second button has a right pointer, which sends you forward to the next page in the hyperlink history list.

20. The third button has a page with arrows on it. This button lets you reload the current page or refresh.

21. The last button in this group has a sign with an X on it. This button stops the network operation currently in progress.

22. The next group has a single button with a paragraph symbol on it. This button lets you show or hide paragraph marks, form outlines, and other guides. This button automatically defaults to Hide.

23. The last button contains a question mark and an arrow. This is the Help command. After clicking on this button, you must select the object with which you would like help. The editor will give you information on that object.

Lesson 5: The Format Toolbar and Status Bar

The Format toolbar houses the editing commands that control the appearance and organization of text, such as bold, text size, and alignment. As shown in Figure 7-4, the windows and buttons in this toolbar are grouped into seven sections according to their uses.

1. On the far left of the Format toolbar is the Change Style window. Clicking on this window will display a list of style choices. Unless changed, the current style will default to Normal. To change the style, place the cursor at the beginning of the word you would like to modify, or drag the cursor from the beginning to the end of a phrase or sentence to highlight it. Click on the window to display the style choices, then click on the style you need.

2. The second window is the Change Font window. Clicking on this window will display a list of font choices. To change a font, highlight the text, click on the Change Font window, then select the font you need.

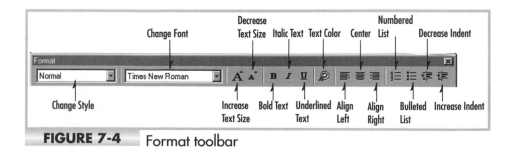

FIGURE 7-4　Format toolbar

3. The first group of buttons controls the size of your text. The first button is a large A with an upward-pointing arrow. Clicking on this icon will increase the size of selected text. The more you click on this button, the larger the text will become.

4. The second button is a smaller A with a downward-pointing arrow. The more you click on this icon, the smaller the selected text will become.

5. The second set of buttons modifies the appearance of one or more words you select. The first button, a bold B, will bold any word that is selected. To select a word or sentence, highlight it by dragging the cursor from the beginning to the end of the text. Then click on the B to bold the highlighted text.

6. The second button in this group, an italic I, will italicize any word or words you select.

7. The third button, an underlined U, will underline any word or words you select.

8. The third group of buttons contains only the Text Color icon. This button sets the color of the word or words selected. Clicking on the Text Color button will bring up the Color dialog box, as shown in Figure 7–5. You can choose from a palette of basic colors, or you can create your own custom color by clicking on the Define Custom Colors button.

FIGURE 7-5

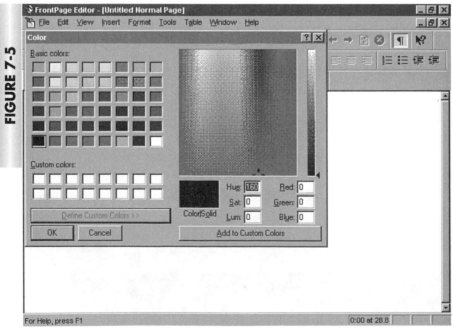

Color dialog box

9. The fourth group of buttons in the Format toolbar deals with alignment of text. The first button in the group aligns a selected word, sentence, or paragraph with the left margin. Select a word or sentence by dragging the cursor from beginning to end of the word or sentence to highlight it. You can select a paragraph by the same method, or by simply placing the cursor at the beginning of the paragraph.

10. The second button centers text.

11. The third button aligns text with the right margin.

12. The last set of buttons in the Format toolbar features lists, types, and indention, and comes in handy when creating outlines. The easiest way to use these buttons is to click on them before typing in text. The first button formats text into a numbered list by automatically placing numbers before list items.

13. The second button formats text into a bulleted list by automatically placing bullets before list items.

14. The third button decreases indention or moves text to the left.

15. The last button increases indention or moves text to the right.

 Tip

Numbered list and bulleted list formatting can be done with toolbar buttons or can be selected in the Change Style window.

16. The status bar is located at the bottom of the FrontPage screen, as shown in Figure 7-2. When the cursor is placed on a button in any of the toolbars, a short explanation appears in the status bar. Usually, these explanations are a bit more detailed than the tool tips that appear near the buttons. The status bar also gives explanations for all the items in the nine drop-down menus at the top of the screen.

 Tip

One or both toolbars can be moved to the bottom of your screen by clicking on them and then dragging them down to the bottom.

Lesson 6: The Advanced Toolbar

Figure 7-6 shows the Advanced toolbar, which has six components that deal with the technical aspects of developing a Web site.

1. The first button has a page and a pencil on it, and allows you to insert HTML code into your Web page. HTML is covered in Chapter 4 and Appendix A.

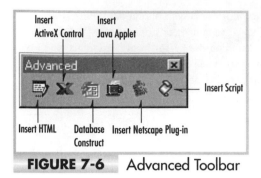

FIGURE 7-6 Advanced Toolbar

2. The second button allows you to insert an ActiveX control object. These are third-party components that can interact with each other, and are based on Microsoft's OLE/COM technology.

3. The third button allows you to insert a database construct so you can link up to databases. This increases the usability of FrontPage forms by allowing easier interfacing with databases.

4. The fourth button allows you to insert a Java applet. See Chapter 15 for more on Java.

5. The fifth button allows you to insert Netscape plug-ins at the cursor. Netscape plug-ins are third-party components based on the Netscape platform.

6. The last button allows you to insert a script at the cursor. See Chapters 14 and 15 for various scripting methods.

Lesson 7: Templates and Wizards

Now that you are familiar with the toolbars in FP Editor, let's move on to a slightly higher level of editing, involving templates and wizards. Throughout your Web site development, you will be confronted with the option of using templates and wizards to speed your work. See Tables 7-1 and 7-2 for lists of general and business templates.

Table 7-1 General templates

General Template	Explanation
Normal page	Creates a blank Web page
Bibliography	Creates a bibliography page that makes references to printed or electronic works
Confirmation form	Creates a page to acknowledge receipt of user input from a Discussion, FormResult, or Registration form

General Template	Explanation
Feedback form	Creates a page on which users can submit comments about your Web site, products, or organization
Frequently asked questions (FAQ)	Creates a FAQ page that answers common questions about some topic
Glossary of terms	Creates a page defining related terms, divided into alphabetized sections
Guest book	Creates a page on which visitors to your Web site can leave their comments in a public guest log
Hot list	Creates a page of links to your favorite sites, divided into categories
Hyperdocument page	Creates a page in a hierarchical document divided into sections
Search page	Creates a page on which users can search for key words across all documents in a Web site
Survey form	Creates a survey form to collect information from readers and store in a file on your Web server
Table of contents	Creates a page with links to every document in your Web site, displayed in an outline format
User registration	Creates a page on which users can self-register for a protected Web site; only useful in a root Web site ('/')
What's new	Creates a page telling users about changes to your Web site over the last couple of months, sorted by date

Table 7-2 Business templates

Business Template	Explanation
Directory of press releases	Creates a directory pointing to all your press releases sorted by date
Employee directory	Creates an alphabetized listing of all employees in your company with a hot-link table of contents
Employment opportunities	Creates a listing of available positions in your company with a form to request more information

continued on next page

continued from previous page

Business Template	Explanation
Lecture abstract	Creates a page describing an upcoming lecture: Use this with the seminar schedule template
Meeting agenda	Creates an agenda for a scheduled meeting
Office directory	Creates a page listing the locations of all your company's offices
Press release	Creates a press release ready for linking into the Press Release template
Product description	Creates a page describing a product according to features, benefits, and specifications
Product or event registration	Creates a page on which users can register for product support or an upcoming event
Seminar schedule	Creates a main page in a hierarchy describing a seminar event: Use with the Lecture Abstract template
Software data sheet	Creates a data sheet describing features and benefits for a software product

A template is a static page that is an example of a standard page type. Templates are like cookie cutters that are designed for a specific use. For example, a page that is often used in developing Web sites is a survey form. FrontPage has created a Survey Form template that requires you only to change or add certain information.

Wizards assist you in creating complex pages by asking you a series of specific questions. With the answers to these questions, a wizard will automatically form a page or set of pages. These pages may be complete or they may form a template you complete on your own. Table 7-3 lists FrontPage wizards.

Table 7-3 FrontPage Wizards

Wizard	Explanation
Database Connector Wizard	Creates an Internet Database Connector file specifying how to connect to, and interpret results from, a database
Form Page Wizard	Creates a form page by selecting the type of information you need to collect
Frames Wizard	Creates a page divided into tiled areas called frames; each frame contains another page or image
Personal Home Page Wizard	Creates a home page customized to meet your needs

Using templates and wizards is a great way to make Web development easier and faster. Following is an example of how to use these little wonders.

1. Select File | New. This brings up the New Page dialog box, as shown in Figure 7-7.

2. Choose the Meeting Agenda template.

3. Read all instructions thoroughly. This may save time and effort later.

4. Fill in any required information. For example, as shown in Figure 7-8, this template requires a date and time for the meeting.

5. Erase instructions at the top of the template.

6. Save your page using the File | Save As command.

Using templates and wizards is an easy way to create interesting and complete Web pages. They allow you to concentrate on the content of your pages because they take care of the basic structure.

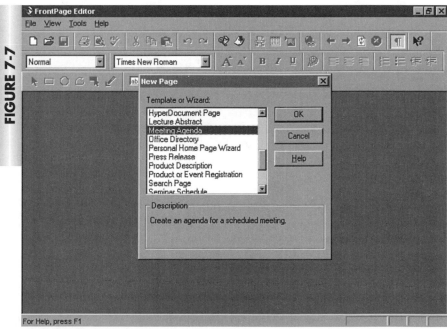

FIGURE 7-7

New Page dialog box

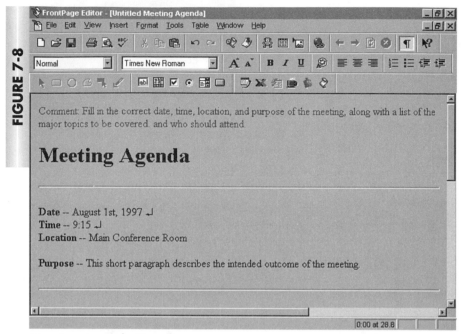

FIGURE 7-8

Meeting Agenda Template

Lesson 7: Opening a Normal Page

There are two ways to get started on your Web site. You can either use the Personal Home Page Wizard or simply open a normal page in the editor. For this lesson, you will open a normal page in FP Editor. The Personal Home Page Wizard is featured in Lesson 9.

When you open a normal page, the editor provides you with a blank page. You are responsible for typing in your home page from scratch. The following steps illustrate this process:

1. In the editor, select File | New. This brings up the New Page dialog box.

2. Choose Normal Page, then click on OK. This will give you a new blank page. Notice in the Format toolbar that the word Normal is displayed in the Change Style window.

3. In your new page, type in My Home Page. Note that this is a very small font.

4. To make your title bigger and bolder, place your cursor at the beginning of the title. Press down the left mouse button and drag the cursor across the words, then lift up on the left mouse button. The words My Home Page should now be highlighted in a complementary color (for example, black will become white).

5. Click on the Change Style drop-down window to display the variety of styles available.

6. Select Heading 1. Now your title is much larger and bolded.

7. Add your name to the text line you just created with a dash to separate the text from your name. Note that the Heading 1 style is continued in your name.

8. To separate the top line from the rest of the page, choose Insert | Horizontal Line. This places a horizontal line at the insertion point, where your cursor is located.

Tip

If there is too much space above the horizontal line, place your cursor at the beginning of the line and press the Backspace key.

9. Make a list on the line below the horizontal line by first clicking on the numbered list button in the Format toolbar.

10. List an interesting feature about yourself. For example, type in Baseball Player.

11. Press the ENTER key, then press the Increase Indent button twice. Now click on the Bulleted List button in the Format toolbar.

12. Type in some details about being a baseball player such as catcher, and batted .283.

13. To add a number 2 to your outline, press the ENTER key after typing in batted .283. You have now added another bullet. To delete the bullet and add a number 2, click on the Decrease Indent button in the Format toolbar twice. This will automatically shift the cursor to the left and insert a number 2.

14. Type in two more features about yourself.

15. Highlight the entire outline, then select Heading 3 from the Change Style window.

16. End the outline by either pressing ENTER twice or pressing CTRL + End (at the same time).

17. Insert another horizontal line below the outline by selecting Insert: Horizontal Line.

18. Below the line, type in your e-mail address so you may be contacted. Figure 7-9 shows your completed home page.

19. Save your work by selecting File | Save As. This brings up the Save As dialog box.

20. In the Page Title field, replace Untitled Normal Page with Homepg1. Note that the page URL consists of up to eight letters of the page title. Click on OK. Now your home page is saved to the current Web site.

Tip

To view this in a browser, hold down the right mouse button and choose Page Properties to get the URL of your page. When you bring up your browser, enter this URL in the location field.

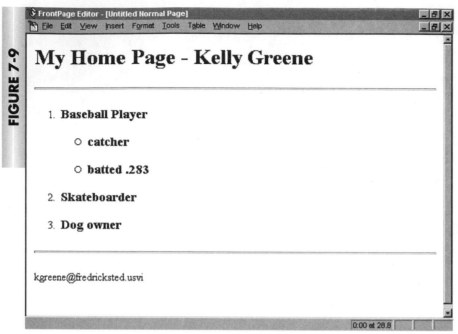

Home page with outline and e-mail address

Lesson 8: Viewing Generated HTML

FrontPage allows you to view the HTML code it generates for your home page. To view the HTML code for the home page in Lesson 7, open `Homepg1.htm`, then select View | HTML. As shown in Figure 7-10, this brings up a dialog box with the HTML code for that page. To exit this screen, click on the Cancel button at the bottom.

Lesson 9: The Personal Home Page Wizard

You learned how to create a home page from scratch in Lesson 7. Here is another way to accomplish the same goal. The Personal Home Page Wizard takes you through a step-by-step process that automatically develops the structure of your page.

1. In FP Editor, select File | New. This brings up the New Page dialog box.

2. Select Personal Home Page Wizard from the list of wizards and templates. This will bring up the first screen of this wizard.

3. As shown in Figure 7-11, the wizard provides you with a list of major sections to choose from: Employee Information, Current Projects, Hot List, Biographical Information, Personal Interests, Contact Information, and Comments and Suggestions. Select the last four choices on this list by clicking on the boxes next to the items. Click on Next.

FIGURE 7-10

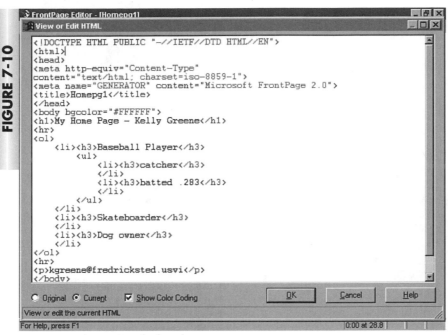

```
FrontPage Editor - [Homepg1]
View or Edit HTML

<!DOCTYPE HTML PUBLIC "-//IETF//DTD HTML//EN">
<html>
<head>
<meta http-equiv="Content-Type"
content="text/html; charset=iso-8859-1">
<meta name="GENERATOR" content="Microsoft FrontPage 2.0">
<title>Homepg1</title>
</head>
<body bgcolor="#FFFFFF">
<h1>My Home Page - Kelly Greene</h1>
<hr>
<ol>
    <li><h3>Baseball Player</h3>
        <ul>
            <li><h3>catcher</h3>
            </li>
            <li><h3>batted .283</h3>
            </li>
        </ul>
    </li>
    <li><h3>Skateboarder</h3>
    </li>
    <li><h3>Dog owner</h3>
    </li>
</ol>
<hr>
<p>kgreene@fredricksted.usvi</p>
</body>
```

○ Original ● Current ☑ Show Color Coding   OK   Cancel   Help

View or edit the current HTML

For Help, press F1   0:00 at 28.8

View or Edit HTML dialog box

4. The next screen allows you to give your home page a title (which will show up at the top of the page) and a URL (which is the name the page will be saved under). Type in Homepage in the Page Title field and enter Homepg2.htm in the Page URL field, then click on Next.

5. This screen lets you choose the format of your home page. There are three format choices: Academic, Professional, and Personal. Select Personal, then click on Next.

6. Figure 7-12 shows the next screen, where you must type some personal interests into the window, then select how you would like the items to be presented: Bulleted list, Numbered list, or Definition list. Select Numbered list, then click on Next.

7. The next screen asks you to type in your contact information, such as your postal, e-mail, and URL addresses and your office, fax, and home phone numbers. Type in the information you choose to give out, then click on Next.

Tip

A word of caution—you do not have to fill in all the contact information requested. Remember, this information will be available to users worldwide.

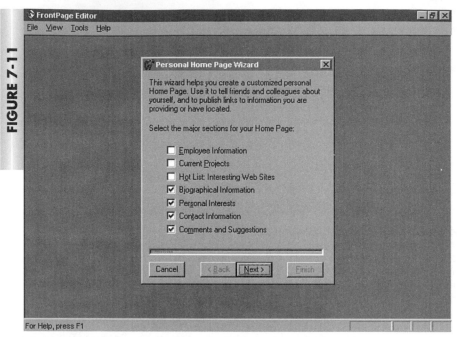

FIGURE 7-11

Major sections list in the Personal Home Page Wizard

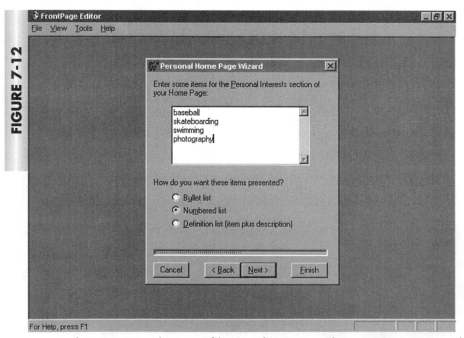

FIGURE 7-12

Personal interests and types of lists in the Personal Home Page Wizard

8. Because you chose a Comments and Suggestions section, this screen asks you to choose how to collect comments and suggestions from readers. Select Use form, store results in Web page, then click on Next.

9. This screen allows you to choose the order of the major sections of your home page. Do this by highlighting the section name, then using the Up and Down buttons to move an item around in the list. When the sections are in the correct order, click on Next, then click on Finish.

10. Now the Personal Home Page Wizard will create a home page according to your specifications. Figures 7-13, 7-14, 7-15, and 7-16 show your home page ready for you to complete.

11. After you have typed in the rest of the information needed, save your page using the File | Save command. You will need this created home page for the next two lessons.

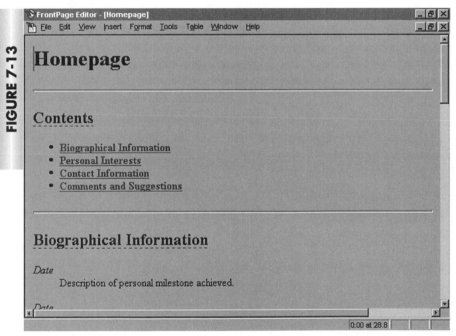

FIGURE 7-13

Homepage, part 1

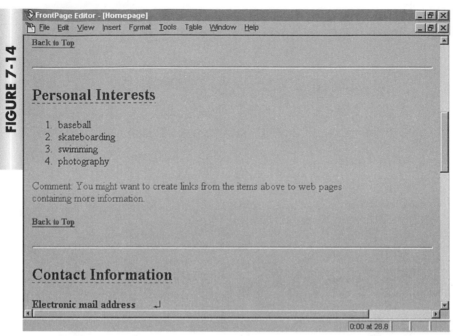

Homepage, part 2

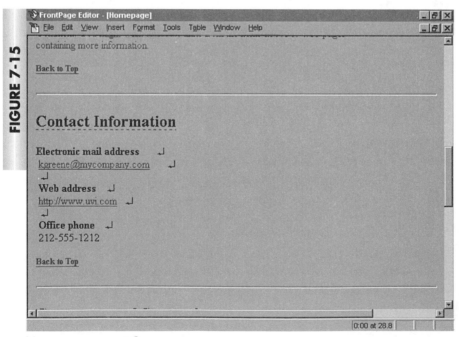

Homepage, part 3

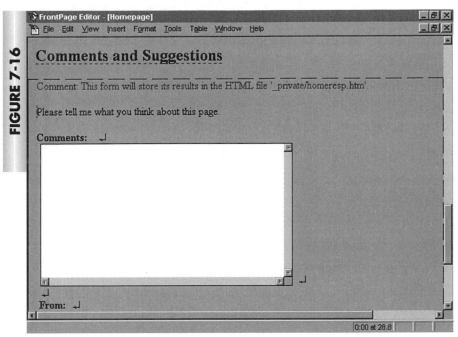

FIGURE 7-16

Homepage, part 4

Lesson 10: Moving from Links to Bookmarks

For this lesson, you will use the home page created by the Personal Home Page Wizard in Lesson 9. Take a minute to glance over this page. Notice that the items listed in the Contents section are underlined. Also, the words **Back to Top** that appear at the bottom of the major sections have been underlined. Underlined text indicates that it is a hot spot. Hot spots are links that transport you to other pages or bookmarks. In this lesson, the hot spots and bookmarks have already been created. You will learn two methods for moving from a hot spot to a bookmark in FP Editor.

Method 1

1. In the home page created in Lesson 9, place your cursor anywhere within the words `Personal Interests` in the Contents section.

2. Click on the right mouse button. As shown in Figure 7-17, this will cause a drop-down menu to appear.

3. From this drop-down menu, choose Follow Hyperlink Forward. This will transport you to the Personal Interest section of the home page. The heading `Personal Interest` is a bookmark.

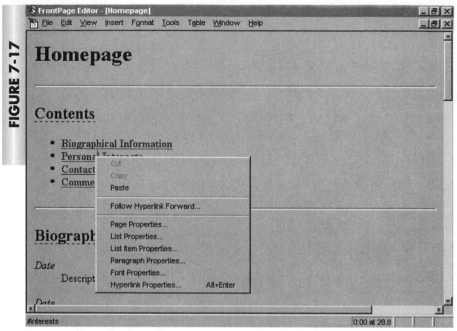

FIGURE 7-17

Format drop-down menu

Method 2

1. Place your cursor on the words Back to Top at the bottom of a major section.

2. While holding down the CTRL key, press the left mouse button. This will transport you to the top of the page to the heading Contents, which is a bookmark.

Lesson 11: Linking Pages

Now you will learn how to create a link from one page to another or a link from a page to a bookmark. You will still be using the home page you created in Lesson 9, but first you will have to go into FrontPage Explorer to open another page in your Web.

1. While Lesson 9's home page is opened in the editor, go to FrontPage Explorer using the FrontPage Explorer button in the Standard toolbar.

2. Choose Normal Page in the All Hyperlinks View, then double-click on Normal Page in the Hyperlinks for Normal Page View. This transports you to this page in the editor.

3. Type in Homepage. Highlight this line with your cursor.

4. Select Edit | Hyperlink. This brings up the Create Hyperlink dialog box, as shown in Figure 7-18.

5. In the Create Hyperlink dialog box, select Homepage in the Open Pages window (this is the title of the page created in Lesson 9). This page is the target of your link. Click on OK. Now Homepage is underlined because it has become a link that will transport you to the Homepage.

Tip

After you create the link and save it, the link will show up in your Web site in FrontPage Explorer.

6. Underneath the line Homepage, use the Indent Right and Bullet List buttons in the Format toolbar to make an indented bulleted list with the items Biographical Information, Personal Interests, Contact Information, and Comments and Suggestions.

7. Highlight Personal Interests. Choose Edit | Hyperlink.

8. In the Create Hyperlink dialog box, select Homepage in the Open Pages window. This is the page containing the bookmark to which you are linking.

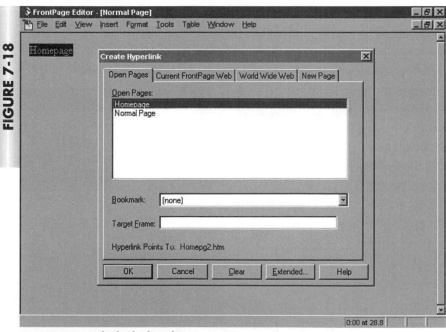

FIGURE 7-18

Create Hyperlink dialog box

9. The Bookmark window lists all the bookmarks that have been created in the current Web site. In the Bookmark window, select Interests. Interests is the name of the bookmark in the Personal Interests section of the Homepage. Click on OK. Now there is a link between the item `Personal Interests` in the normal page and the bookmark `Interests` in Homepage.

 ## Tip

To test a link you have created, place your cursor on the underlined hot spot. Then press the right mouse button and select Follow Link Forward from the format drop-down menu. This will transport you to the other end of the link.

Lesson 12: Creating a Bookmark

A bookmark marks a specific spot in a page as the target of a link. This lesson explains exactly how a bookmark is created. You will use the normal page you opened in Lesson 11, and the page titled Homepage created in Lesson 9.

1. In Normal Page from Lesson 11, type in `Bookmark Example` below the rest of the text.

2. Highlight this line, then choose Edit | Bookmark. This brings up the Bookmark dialog box, as shown in Figure 7-19. Click on OK. Now you have made this line a bookmark. Remember this is just a target of a link—the bookmark is not linked to anything yet.

3. To link the bookmark to something, you need to go to a different page in your Web site. Place the cursor on the link called `Homepage`. Select Tools | Follow Hyperlink. This transports you to the page titled Homepage.

4. At the bottom of this page, above the copyright information, type in `Back to Bookmark`.

5. Highlight this line, then choose Edit | Hyperlink. In the Create Hyperlink dialog box, choose Normal Page in the Open Pages window. Normal Page is the location of the bookmark.

6. Choose Bookmark Example in the Bookmark window. Click on OK. Now you have created a link from the words `Back to Bookmark` in Homepage to the bookmark called `Bookmark Example` in Normal Page.

7. Test your hyperlink by placing the cursor on `Back to Bookmark`, then press the right mouse button and select Follow Link Forward from the Format drop-down menu.

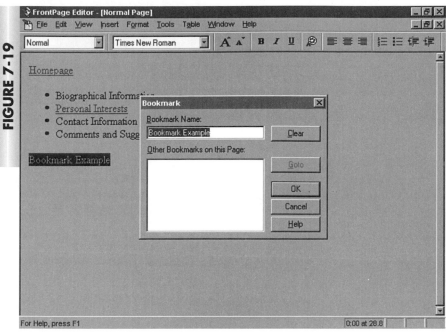

FIGURE 7-19

Bookmark dialog box

Lesson 13: The To Do List

No matter how much you accomplish in a day, there are always things to be done tomorrow. You may keep track of these tasks in your head, or you may jot them down on a piece of paper. FrontPage can create a To Do List for you electronically.

1. Choose Tools | Show To Do List, or click on the To Do List button in the Standard toolbar. This brings up the FrontPage To Do List dialog box.

2. To add an item to the list, click on the Add button. This brings up the Add To Do Task dialog box, as shown in Figure 7-20.

3. In this box, fill in the priority, task name, who it is assigned to, and a brief description of the task. Click on OK.

4. When you have finished your list, click on the Close button in the FrontPage To Do List dialog box. Figure 7-21 shows a To Do List.

FIGURE 7-20

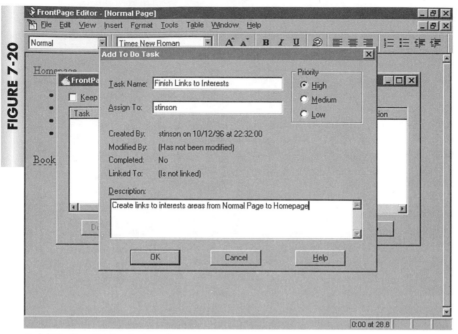

Add To Do Task dialog box

FIGURE 7-21

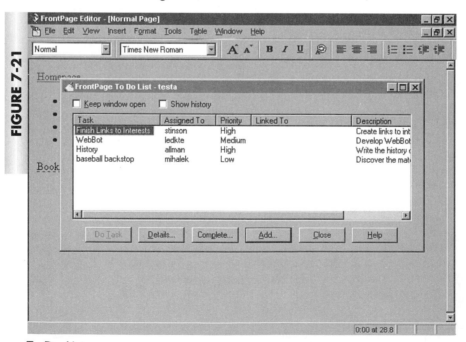

To Do List

Lesson 14: Clip Art

To spice up your pages, FrontPage has provided an array of clip art for you to use. Clip Art categories include buttons, backgrounds, bullets, lines, headers, and miscellaneous. The following steps demonstrate the ease of using clip art in FrontPage:

1. Insert Image. This brings up the Image dialog box.

2. Click on the Clip Art tab, then select Lines in the Category window.

3. After the images are loaded, a selection of line styles will appear. Click on the one you want, then click OK. Now you have added a clip art line to your home page. Figure 7-22 shows the Clip Art tab of the Image dialog box.

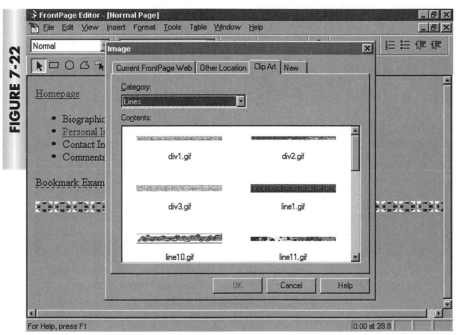

FIGURE 7-22

Clip Art tab of the Image dialog box

Editing Adventures

This chapter should have given you some idea of the flexibility and power of FP Editor. However, there are many more interesting things the editor can do. You can explore these possibilities by using the ever-popular Help button in the Standard toolbar. Just click on the Help button, then select the item you have a question about, such as a toolbar button or a command in one of the main drop-down menus. You can also use the Help command in the row of main drop-down menus. Don't forget about the status bar at the bottom of the screen that gives a brief explanation of any command on which the cursor is placed. Jump into the world of editing and create a dazzling Web site. FrontPage makes editing fun, and it will do much of the work for you.

In the next chapter, you will learn how to save even more editing time and effort by using WebBots.

WebBot Components

8

In this chapter you will learn:

The 13 Different WebBot Components
Shipping with Microsoft FrontPage

The Three Categories into Which They Fall

What Each WebBot Component Does

How to Use Each of the WebBot Components
in Your Web Sites

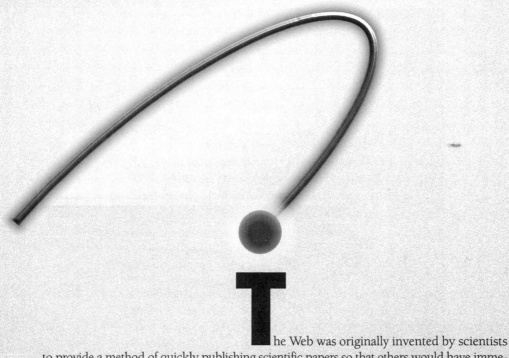

The Web was originally invented by scientists to provide a method of quickly publishing scientific papers so that others would have immediate access to the most recent works. As such, the Web was not originally designed to house the dynamic content we see today. Browsing the Web was originally a one-sided conversation. That changed quickly, however, as methods for creating data on the fly and receiving input were developed, most notably in the form of Common Gateway Interface (CGI) scripting. CGI can be a very powerful tool when developing your Web site because it can be used to automate many tasks, but it is also very complex. That's why FrontPage utilizes WebBot Components (WebBots). WebBots are very powerful because they include the most common CGI functionality, they are easy to use, and they behave the same no matter what server is used (provided that the server has the FrontPage Extensions installed).

What Is a WebBot Component (WebBot)?

FrontPage incorporates some of the most common types of CGI scripts as WebBots. It also adds a few new types of WebBots to make the job of maintaining a Web site a little easier. WebBots are very powerful, flexible, and easy to use. They allow you to add dynamic content to your Web site and gather information from people browsing your site. A WebBot, fundamentally, is a program that runs on the server much like (often exactly like) a CGI script. As such, WebBots place more of a strain on the server than ordinary HTML documents, because they often require special processing.

Note

Previously, you may have heard the term *WebBot* used in the context of the Web. These other WebBots are programs that access the Web, usually searching for information or cataloging the Web. However, when talking about FrontPage, a WebBot component is a unique feature that is not the same nor necessarily related to the more traditional Internet robot. A FrontPage WebBot is more akin to a CGI script than it is to these other devices. For simplicity's sake, we also refer to FrontPage WebBots as *WebBots* in this chapter.

The FrontPage WebBots

FrontPage provides three basic classes of WebBots: editing, organization, and form. All WebBots work to make the job of maintaining Web sites easier by automating many common editing tasks. The Editing WebBot family is the largest group, with seven members. The Organization WebBots provide advanced features for your Web site, such as an automatically updated table of contents or full text search for the entire Web. The Form WebBots are a close-knit bunch that work to gather and store information provided from the user via forms.

The Editing WebBots

The Editing WebBots all operate within the scope of the FrontPage Editor. They work to ease common tasks through automation and resource sharing. These WebBots are the "sliced bread" of the WebBots: They can really simplify your work!

Lesson 1: The Include WebBot

The Include WebBot is the father of this family. If you understand how to use it, the rest of the WebBots in this family seem very familiar. The Include WebBot allows you to add the contents of one document into another.

Although this concept may seem trivial, consider that many of your pages may share common elements. With an Include WebBot, you can create one document to serve as a footer, another to serve as a header, and another for the company logo and address. Rather than repeatedly entering that information for each newly created page for your site, you can use the Include WebBot to add this content in bulk. So if you change a header file which has been included in all of your pages, all you have to do is update the header file and FrontPage will simultaneously update every page in your Web! This allows you to change the entire look and feel of your whole Web site with just a few simple edits! The Include WebBot simplifies the editing process and gives you more time to concentrate on making your pages the best they can be.

Tip

If you change the contents of an included file, you may need to refresh the view of other documents already opened in the FrontPage Editor. This causes the new contents to replace the stale (outdated) Include WebBots.

Creating the Normal Web

For this chapter, you're going to create a new Normal Web site. Once you have done that, open the Home Page (the only one in the site) with the FrontPage Editor. You can easily do this by double-clicking on it in the Hyperlinks view. You will use this Web as a demo throughout this chapter.

Building and Inserting the Header File

In the FrontPage Editor, create a new Normal Page document. From the File menu, choose Page Properties, then change the title of the document to *Header* and press the OK button. Now add some text to represent the header you would like at the top of all your pages in this Web site. If you were making a real Web site, you might want to put a banner, logo, navigation links, or other information in the header as well. There is no limit on what you can put in a page you intend to include elsewhere. Save your work (name the file Header.HTM) when you're finished.

Now go back to the Home Page. From the Insert menu, choose WebBot Component, then select Include from the dialog, as shown in Figure 8-1. When prompted for the URL of the resource to include, enter the URL of the header file created earlier.

The contents of the header file should now appear at the top of this document. Add a couple of lines of text to your document, so it looks something like Figure 8-2. Save your changes to this page, as you'll work with it in the other lessons in this chapter.

Lesson 2: The Timestamp WebBot

The Timestamp WebBot is a special kind of Include WebBot. Its only purpose is to convey the last time the page was edited. This is very convenient for creating those little last modified tags often found near the end of Web pages.

Working from where you left off in Lesson 1, return to editing the Home Page in the FrontPage Editor. At the bottom of the document, enter the text "This page last modified:". Then select WebBotComponent from the Insert menu. Choose a Timestamp WebBot for insertion. You have several choices for the date and time formats, and even have the option of omitting the time. Figure 8-3 shows the options selected.

When you've made your entries, your Normal page should look something like Figure 8-4. Congratulations; you've just learned your second WebBot. Be sure to save your work, because you'll be using this Web in the other examples.

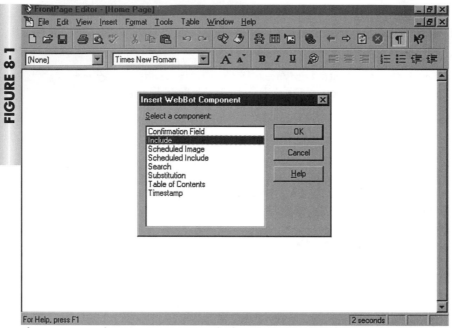

The Insert WebBot Component dialog

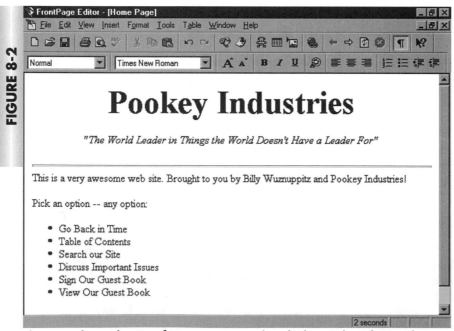

The sample Web site after creating and including a header and text

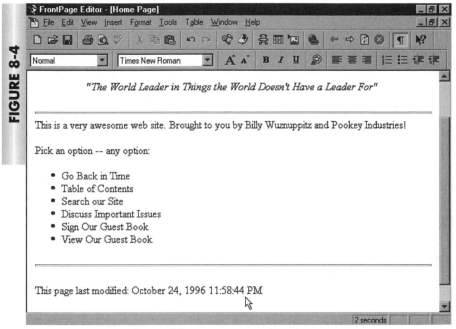

FIGURE 8-3   The Timestamp
WebBot Properties dialog

The Home Page after adding a Last Updated Timestamp

 Tip

You may want to include the last updated part of your Web pages in a footer page, similar to the way you created the header page. The only caveat to this is that the date the Timestamp WebBot shows is the last time that the footer file was edited, not the last time the pages in which the footer is included were edited.

Lesson 3: The Scheduled Include WebBot Component

The Scheduled Include WebBot works just like the basic Include WebBot, except its operation expires after a specified time frame. This can be handy if your company is hosting a contest for a limited period of time and you want to advertise the contest during that period. You can automate the process of displaying and then removing that information.

Working from where you stopped in the last lesson, you will need to edit the Home Page. Create a new file and change its title to Sliced Bread. Add some text to it (if you prefer, try making it look like the text shown in Figure 8-6) and save your work.

Now go back to the Home Page and position the cursor in front of the bottom horizontal rule. Select WebBot from the Insert menu and select a Scheduled Include WebBot from the dialog. Enter the URL of the Sliced Bread document in the topmost text area and then change the starting and ending times for the display. The Scheduled Include WebBot Properties dialog is shown in Figure 8-5.

When you've finished, your Home Page will be similar to Figure 8-6. Be sure to save your work, because you'll use this Web more. The Scheduled Include WebBot will cause this HTML to be displayed within the time frame you specified. After the ending date, the included page will not appear when others browse your site.

Lesson 4: The Scheduled Image WebBot Component

The Scheduled Image WebBot works the same as the Scheduled Include WebBot, except it is meant to add only an image rather than a whole document. This WebBot is especially useful for adding new or updated graphics in front of links to recently modified resources.

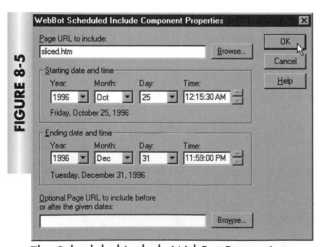

FIGURE 8-5

The Scheduled Include WebBot Properties dialog

FIGURE 8-6

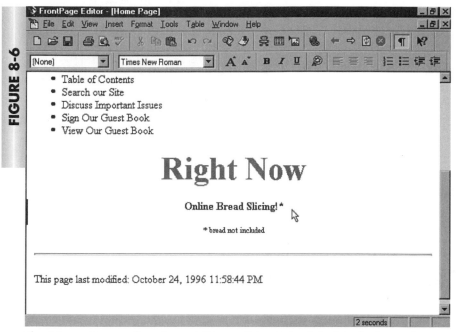

The Home Page after the addition of the Scheduled Include WebBot

In this example, you are going to continue where you stopped with the previous lesson: modifying the sample Web site. First, copy the `undercon.gif` file from your root Web's `\images` directory into your current Web's `\images` directory and refresh your Web. Then open the Home Page in the FrontPage Editor and position the cursor in front of the Go Back in Time bulleted item. Then select WebBot Component from the Insert menu and choose a Scheduled Image WebBot. Notice that the dialog for this WebBot is quite similar to the one for the Scheduled Include WebBot (see Figure 8-5). Select the `undercon.gif` image and then set the time frame for the image's lifespan (we'll stop displaying this on December 31, 2000 07:00:00am).

When you've finished, the Home Page should look similar to Figure 8-7. Now you should save your changes for future lessons.

Lesson 5: The Annotation WebBot Component

The Annotation (purple text) WebBot allows you to add hidden comments to your Web site. The comments are not visible when the page is loaded by normal browsers, but can be seen from the FrontPage Editor. This allows you to make notes and reminders on your pages without cluttering it for your viewers.

Use the Editor to open the Home Page in the Web site from the previous lessons in this chapter. Position the cursor behind the Go Back in Time bulleted entry. Then choose Comment from the Insert menu. You can enter text in the comment area, as shown in Figure 8-8. This text will be visible only to people editing your Web with the FrontPage Editor, where it appears as unformatted purple text. Save your work when you are finished.

FIGURE 8-7

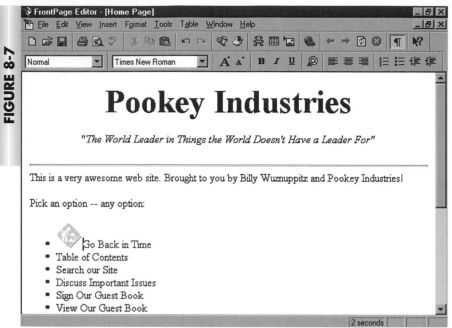

The Home Page after the additions of the first four lessons

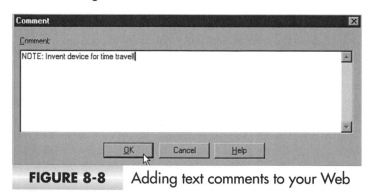

FIGURE 8-8   Adding text comments to your Web pages using the Editor

Lesson 6: The Substitution WebBot

The name, *Substitution WebBot,* can be misleading. The Substitution WebBot allows you to configure variables and place their associated values variables throughout your Web site. It is very much like a light-duty Include WebBot that solely inserts text.

Tip

When given a choice between using the Substitution or Include WebBots, use the Include WebBot when you need the text formatted a certain way or need to include resources other than text and use the Substitution to insert pure text. By using Web parameters and the Substitution WebBot, you can reduce the number of files cluttering up your Web site and the amount of server space your Web site uses.

Open the Home Page in the Web site you have been working with in this chapter. Place the cursor after the date of the last edit and add the word *by*. Then choose WebBot Component from the Insert menu and select a Substitution WebBot. The WebBot Substitution Component Properties dialog contains a list box that holds the variables relevant to this page. Select the **ModifiedBy** variable, as shown in Figure 8-9. This causes the name of the most recent person to edit the Web to be substituted for the **ModifiedBy** variable.

Several default parameters are standard to every Web site. They are listed in Table 8-1. You can configure your own parameters for use in a Web site as well. This is done by selecting Web Settings from the Tools menu of the FrontPage Explorer, then clicking on the Parameters tag of the Web Settings window (shown in Figure 8-10). The custom parameters available to your Web are listed here, along with their corresponding values. You can add a parameter-value combination by clicking the Add button and filling in the associated dialog. Once you create your own variables, they will be listed in the Parameters tab and in the Substitution WebBot Properties dialog, along with the standard variables, which

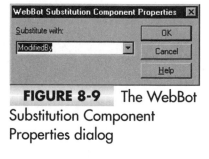

FIGURE 8-9 The WebBot Substitution Component Properties dialog

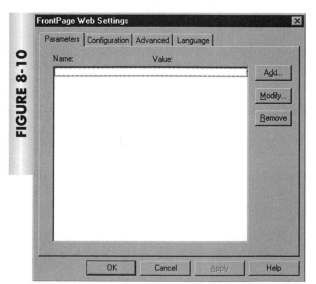

FIGURE 8-10

The custom parameters tab of the Web Settings dialog

are always present. Including them in your Web will cause their values to be inserted into your Web site in the same manner as the default parameters.

Table 8-1 Default Web parameters and their use with the Substitution WebBot

Parameter	Use
Author	Displays the name of the person who originally created the page
ModifiedBy	Displays the login name of the last person to modify the page
Description	Displays the contents of the comments field found in the FrontPage Explorer's Properties dialog box
Page-URL	Displays the URL of the current page in long format

The Substitution WebBot is very much like the Include WebBot, but with some important differences. The Include WebBot inserts an entire HTML document, including formatting. The Substitution WebBot inserts only text. This inserted text can then be formatted differently each time it is used, unlike the Included WebBot insertions. Also, the Substitute WebBot text can be inserted in the middle of a line; the Include WebBot contents cannot. This combination makes both WebBots useful in different situations. Use the Include WebBot when you need to incorporate common preformatted components, such as navigation bars or document footers, into your Web site. Use the Substitution WebBot for bits of information, such as the name of your immediate supervisor or secretary, that are used and formatted distinctly in different parts of the Web site.

Once you have added the name of the last person to modify your Web with the Substitution WebBot, save your work.

Lesson 7: The HTML Markup WebBot

The Web is changing very quickly. New features are appearing all the time. To make FrontPage work with the newest tags as they are introduced, you can use the HTML Markup WebBot. This WebBot allows you to enter HTML directly into your Web. There are some potential hazards here, however: FrontPage cannot verify if the HTML you enter is correct. Also, because it cannot know exactly what the HTML you enter is meant to do, it cannot give you the semi-WYSIWYG display you have come to expect from FrontPage.

You are going to use the same Web as in the previous lessons. Open the Home Page with the FrontPage Editor. Place the cursor at the very bottom of the document and select HTML Markup from the Insert menu. Inside the HTML Markup dialog, enter the text `<!--This is just an HTML comment -->`, as shown in Figure 8-11. This is just an HTML comment and is ignored by browsers, so it will not have any effect on the appearance of your Web outside of FrontPage. Comments like these are used by people hand-coding HTML. They help hand-coders keep organized (or hide bad code). FrontPage doesn't use comments

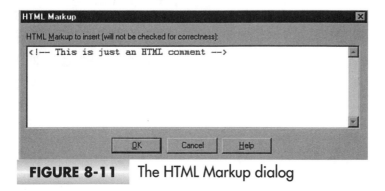

FIGURE 8-11   The HTML Markup dialog

like these because it was designed to shield you from the uglies of HTML. Instead, it provides a similar functionality with the Insert Comment dialog. You could use the HTML Markup WebBot to do something more exciting (like embedding a sound or video clip), but this example illustrates how the HTML Markup WebBot works; it does not teach HTML tags that FrontPage doesn't support. Click OK when you've finished making your changes.

Save your work when you are done, because you will use this Web site again.

The Web Organization WebBots

The Web Organization WebBots add an incredible amount of functionality to your Web site. They can automatically index your entire Web site and make that information available to viewers. Because of their nature, these WebBots tend to use a lot of resources (memory, disk space, and so on). Web sites with a lot of textual information may find their sizes nearly doubled just by adding a Search WebBot, and performing searches may slow server performance in large and busy sites, although your mileage may vary.

The Web Organization WebBots can get stale quickly. When you are editing your site, they aren't always aware of what changes you are making. Changing the structure of your Web site, adding files, removing files, and editing files can cause these WebBots to convey incorrect or misleading information. To update them, select Recalculate HyperLinks from the Tools menu of the FrontPage Explorer. This causes their contents to be regenerated. Do this every time you make changes in a Web site that uses one of these WebBots, or the information they present might be incorrect.

Adding these WebBots to your site can be easily automated using the templates provided with FrontPage. Just open the FrontPage Editor and choose to add a new Table of Contents or Search Page from the list of templates. You can then easily edit these templates to fit the look and feel of your Web site.

Lesson 8: The Table of Contents WebBot

The Table of Contents (TOC) WebBot does exactly what its name suggests: It creates an outline-like TOC of the pages in your Web. Using this WebBot is much easier than trying to create your own TOC, especially in Web sites that change a lot. This WebBot automates the process of creating and updating the table.

Once again, you are going to work with the same Web site you've been editing in the previous lessons in this chapter. Open a new page in the FrontPage Editor and change its title in the Page Properties dialog to Table of Contents. Feel free to add the header file with the Include WebBot, as you did in Lesson 1. Then you can add a TOC WebBot by selecting WebBot from the Insert menu and choosing the Table of Contents WebBot. This brings up the WebBot TOC Component Properties dialog, as shown in Figure 8-12.

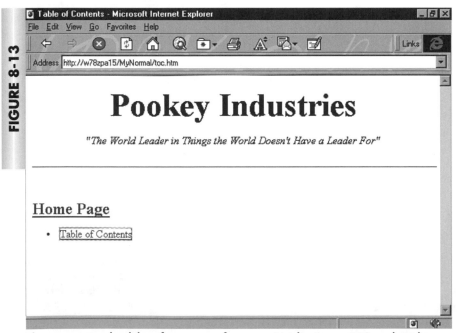

FIGURE 8-12   The WebBot
TOC Component Properties dialog

The generated table of contents for your Web site as viewed with Microsoft Internet Explorer

By default, the TOC WebBot will organize itself by treating the default page (normally `index.htm`) as the highest point in the Web site's hierarchy and then arranging the other page displays based on their relationship to that document. You can select the HTML size of the heading you'd like to use in this dialog as well. There are also three options dealing with how the WebBot should handle displaying the resources in the Web site. Selecting the Show each page only once option prevents the same document from being displayed several times in the TOC. Selecting the Show pages with no incoming links option will cause the TOC to list all files present in your Web site, even if they aren't linked to any other documents. The Recompute TOC option causes FrontPage to regenerate the TOC every time a resource in the Web site is edited. The drawback to this is that the process of recalculating the TOC is involved and can dramatically slow editing performance and responsiveness of your server. If you don't select this option, be sure you recalculate the links after each editing session. This is done by selecting Recalculate links from the Tools menu of the FrontPage Explorer.

After you've added the TOC WebBot, notice that the WebBot does not display the actual TOC; rather, it provides a representation of one. It will display a real TOC when the document is viewed with a browser, as demonstrated in Figure 8-13. You'll notice that the only two files listed are the Normal page and the Table of Contents. The reason for this is that they are the only two documents directly linked in your Web! The header and footer are included in them, but the TOC WebBot is smart enough to realize that they aren't real parts of your Web site and so doesn't include them in the TOC structure.

You may want to add a link back to the Normal page and a footer in this document. Save your work when you have finished making additions. Then open up the Normal page with the editor again and add a link to the TOC page you just created. Save your changes here as well. Because you're finished with this lesson and you opted not to have the TOC WebBot updated after every edit, you should recalculate the links to update the TOC WebBot before exiting.

Lesson 9: The Search WebBot

The Search WebBot has two functions: searching your entire Web site or searching the contents of a discussion group. Because Search WebBots need to index your site, they often create large files that can dramatically increase the size of your Web. You may want to keep that in mind if you don't have a lot of space available on your server.

Working with a Search WebBot from a browser is similar to using Alta Vista™ or another popular index. The difference is that this search covers only your Web site, not the entire World Wide Web. Just enter your search string into the form, and the WebBot will search your site for that information.

Once again, you will be working with the same Web site as before. Open a new document for this site in the FrontPage Editor. Change its title in the Page Properties window to Search Page. Then, if you like, add the header to the top of the document with the Include WebBot just as you did in Lesson 1. To include a Search WebBot, first choose WebBot from the Insert menu. Then select the Search WebBot item. This brings up the WebBot Search Component Properties dialog shown in Figure 8-14.

FIGURE 8-14

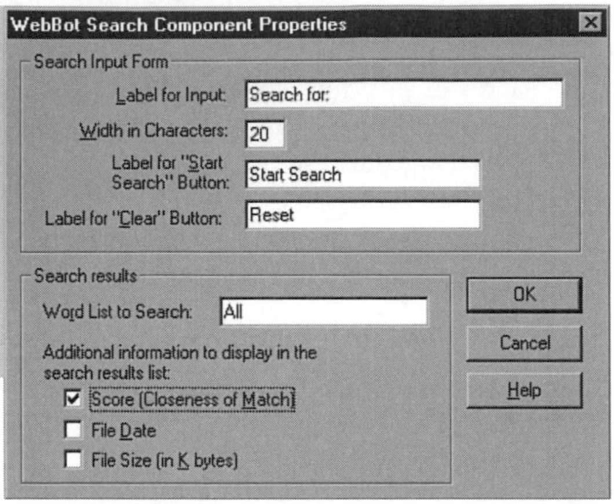

The WebBot Search Component Properties
dialog

You can control the labeling and appearance of the Search WebBot somewhat from the
WebBot Properties dialog. Changing these values modifies the appearance of the Search
Bot's form. You can also specify the word list to search. The default value is all, which causes the WebBot to index your whole Web site. If you'd like it to index the contents of a discussion
WebBot instead, then replace this value with the directory where the articles for the discussion forum are stored. It will start with an underscore (_). The forum was created with
the Discussion WebBot Wizard, as described in Lesson 12. You can display information
about each hit, such as score, date, or file size by selecting these options. The score is a measure of how well the document matches the search string; higher scores indicate the document
is more likely to contain the desired information. The date is the date the file was last modified, and the file size is the size of the hit HTML document.

When you are finished, you may wish to add a footer and a link back to the Normal
page at the bottom of the document, just as you have done with the other pages in this Web
site. Don't forget to save your work. Now that you have created a Search page, go back and
place a link to it in the Normal page, and then recalculate the links from the Explorer to
update the Search and TOC WebBots.

The Form WebBots

Form WebBots are the hidden WebBots. You often don't realize that you are working with
a WebBot when using one of these because they work behind the scenes. Form WebBots
all work with form input, so they don't have much of a visual display in the FrontPage Editor.
The Save Results and Registration WebBots accept data from forms and treat it appropriately. The Confirmation WebBot allows you to repeat the data gathered from form fields

Lesson 10: The Save Results WebBot

The Save Results WebBot takes the input from a form and saves it to a file on the server in one of several formats. To demonstrate this WebBot, you are going to add a guest book to your Web site. You'll often see guest books when browsing the Web. They ask you to submit your name, e-mail address, and comments so that the author has some idea about who is viewing the site and can gather some input. Although you can let FrontPage generate a starter guest book using the File | New Editor menu, for illustration you will be creating your guest book, from scratch, in the same Web site with which you've been working. Open your Web site with the FrontPage Explorer and create a new page in the editor. Change the title of this page to Guest Book in the Page Properties dialog. Add the Header with an Include WebBot and some text inviting the viewer to *Please sign my guest book*.

Now you are ready to add the form. You will want one-line text form fields to collect your guest's name, address, and e-mail address. To create these, just select **one line text box** from the Form Field Items in the Insert menu. Name these fields **GuestName** and **Email**, according to the information they will gather. You'll also want a large scrolling text box for users to enter their comments, which can be added by selecting the menu option **Scrolling text box**. Add Submit and Reset push buttons to the bottom of the form. If you feel you need a refresher on how to do this, review Chapter 7, "FrontPage Editor." Add a link back to the Home Page and a footer. When you've finished, it should look like Figure 8-15.

FIGURE 8-15

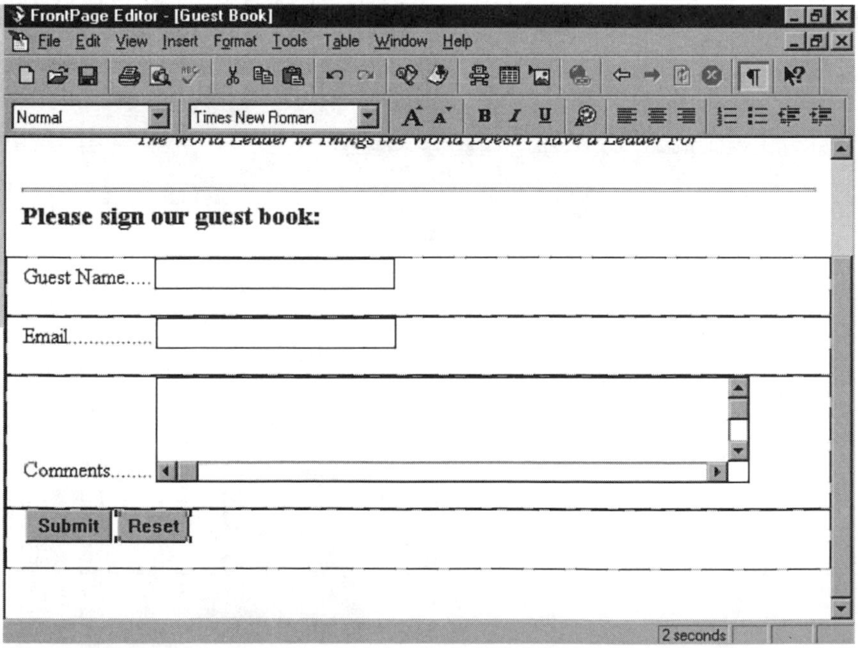

The Guest Book page

Tip

Forms often have a very helter-skelter look. It is difficult to line up the fields in a row with the variable width fonts that most browsers use by default. You have three options to help organize your forms: Place the fields in a table, use fixed-width fonts, or align all form fields on the left. We usually go the route of the fixed-width font because it's easy to work with these fonts. Just select the contents of the form and set the character style to Typewriter—<tt>.

Up to this point, you've created only the form and haven't set up the Save Results WebBot. To do this, right-click the form and select Form Properties from the popup menu. This brings up—what else—the Form Properties dialog. Set the Form Handler to Save Results WebBot. Then click the Settings button. This brings up the Settings dialog shown in Figure 8-16.

You have several options to configure here. First, determine in what format you want to save the results. You can save the results in one of several text database/spreadsheet formats or some type of HTML style so that you can link them right into your Web site. Because you want to display people's comments in a document in your Web site, use the HTML format. Set the WebBot to save the results as HTML by selecting that option in the File Format drop-down list. Then select what other information you'd like saved from the Additional Information box. This data is automatically gathered when a form is submitted, so you don't

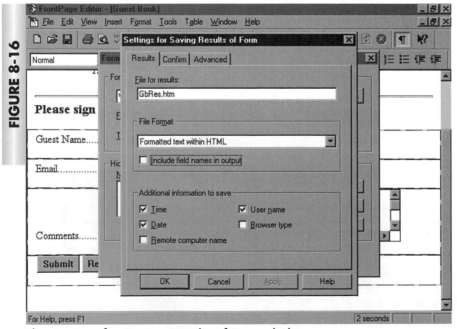

The Settings for Saving Results of Form dialog

need any special fields for it. If you have a special page you would like to use to confirm the results, you can enter its URL here; otherwise, FrontPage will generate its own (you'll add a Confirmation page in Lesson 13, so leave it blank for now). Don't forget to provide a file name for storing the results as well. Because this file is in HTML format, you'll want to use the `.htm` extension.

Under the Advanced tab, you'll find a similar set of dialogs. That's because you can configure the Save Results WebBot to save the data twice, in different formats. This way you aren't faced with the decision of either displaying the data as HTML or saving it in an easily imported format: You can do both. In this case, just one format is fine.

When you are finished, save this page, open the Normal page, and add a link to your new Guest Book form. Also, place a link to the results file your form is generating so the world can see all the great things people are saying about your Web site. Save your changes. Keep in mind that because you have a Search and TOC WebBot in this Web site, you'll want to recalculate links as well.

For a clearer understanding of what you've done, look at Figures 8-17 and 8-18. Figure 8-17 shows the Guest Book form being filled out from a browser. Figure 8-18 shows the HTML file that holds those comments, as well as the comments from previous guests.

Congratulations, you've just learned to use the Save Results WebBot to save data gathered from a form!

Lesson 11: The Registration WebBot

The Registration WebBot is used to automate the process of granting access to Web sites. Recall that you can configure different security settings for each Web site. You can even

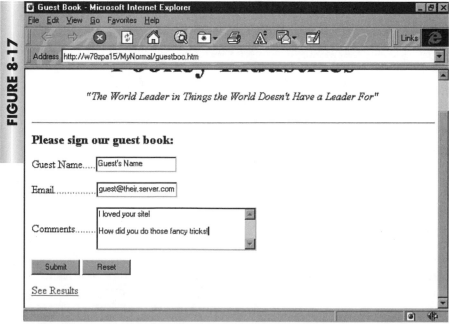

FIGURE 8-17

Filling in the Guest Book form

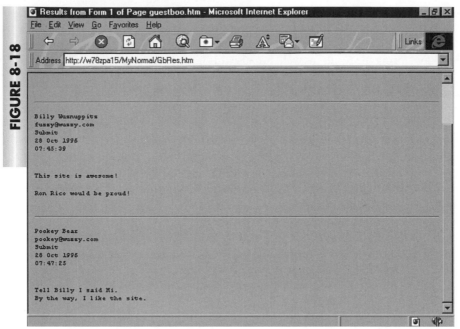

FIGURE 8-18

The HTML results file generated by the Save Results WebBot
used by your guest book

prevent people from viewing the Web site unless they have a valid account name and password. The Registration WebBot can facilitate the process of adding accounts by automatically generating new names and passwords for a Web site based on the input provided in a form.

Once again, you are going to work with the demo Web used in the previous lessons. First make sure the permissions for your Web site would not ordinarily allow others to view it. Open the demo Web site you've been working with in the FrontPage Explorer. From the Tools menu of the Explorer, choose Permissions. In the Settings tab, select the Use unique permissions for this Web option (if it's not already selected), then click the Apply button. Now go to the Users tab and make sure the "Only registered users have browse access" option is selected. Click OK to accept these settings.

Now that your Web site is somewhat secured from the rest of the world, you're going to make an entrance door with the Registration WebBot. Because this WebBot requires form input and is really a one-trick pony (although it is a good trick), you're going to take a little shortcut here and use the User Registration template provided with FrontPage. This way you don't have to go through the whole process of creating the form.

Start by opening the Root Web in the FrontPage Explorer. Then open the editor and select New from the File Menu. Select User Registration from the list of templates. This will generate a new page, the bottom of which is shown in Figure 8-19.

To make this WebBot work, you need to adjust its settings. Start by right-clicking on the form and choosing Form Properties from the popup menu. This brings up the Form

Properties dialog. Click on the Settings button in the Form Handler area. The Settings dialog shown in Figure 8-20 will then appear. Change the Web site name field to the same name as the name of the Web site created for the lessons in this chapter.

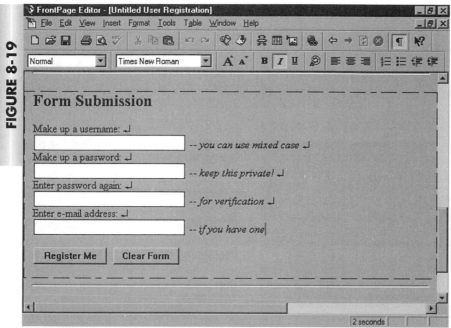

FIGURE 8-19

The bottom of the User Registration template

FIGURE 8-20

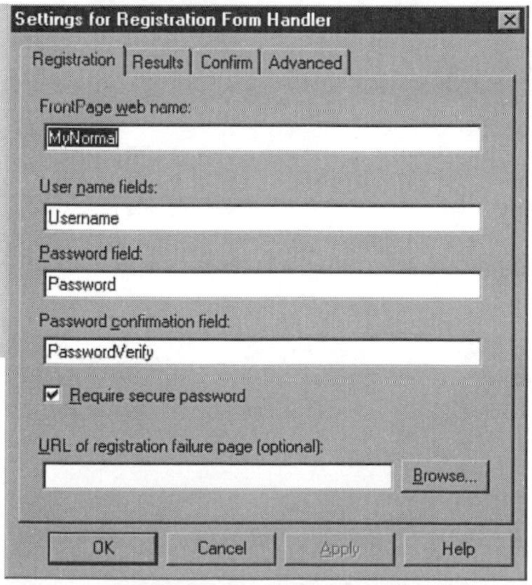

The Settings for Registration Form
Handler dialog

You can configure several other options here as well. If the Require secure password option is selected, then the password the user chooses must be longer than six characters and must not match the user's name. You can also enter a URL to go to in case the registration fails. If you don't enter a URL here and for some reason the registration fails, a default page will be generated describing the error to the user.

The other two tabs in this dialog work just like those for the Save Results WebBot, allowing you to configure what data gets saved, what file it goes to, and the format of that file. Note that the password and user ID information is not saved here, for security reasons. This file is just a log of information about the creation of the accounts, not information that needs to be kept secure.

Once this is complete, the Results WebBot is functional. Save this page, then try viewing it with your favorite browser. You won't be able to view the Web site with the browser until you create an acceptable account and enter the correct name and password. If you try to access a file inside the protected Web site, you'll be prompted for a name and password, as shown in Figure 8-21.

If you don't have a valid account (name and password), you can register for one by filling out the form we just created in the Root Web. This will automatically create an account for the user, with no extra maintenance on your part.

You do not need to save this page, because you won't use it again. If you like, you can also change the permissions on the demo Web site you've been working with, because those changes were made only to demonstrate this WebBot.

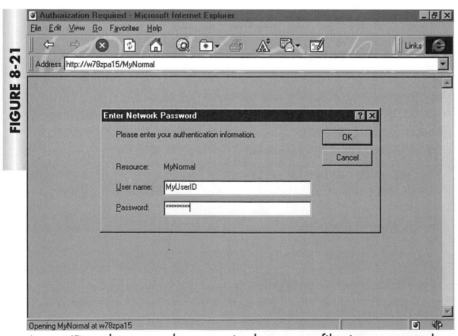

FIGURE 8-21

A user ID and password are required to access files in a protected Web site

Lesson 12: The Discussion WebBot

The Discussion WebBot is a very powerful messaging tool. With it, you can allow people to communicate through your Web site. You can even moderate the discussions (or appoint a moderator). This tool can be very valuable anywhere that feedback needs to be distributed easily. Unfortunately, this nifty functionality comes at the expense of simplicity: The Discussion WebBot is probably the most complex FrontPage WebBot. Fortunately, it comes with some tools to make it more manageable, but it's still tricky.

Because of the complexity of the Discussion WebBot, you're going to create a Discussion WebBot using the Web Wizard provided in the FrontPage Explorer. First, open the Web site with the FrontPage Explorer, if you haven't already done so. Then, choose New Web from the File menu. Select the Discussion Web Wizard, making sure the Add to the current Web option is selected, as shown in Figure 8-22.

The Discussion Web Wizard will guide you through the process of creating a discussion group. First it will display some information about its purpose. Click the Next button and you will be shown your first set of options, as shown in Figure 8-23. The Table of Contents option causes a page with an index of the articles in the Web site to be created and maintained. The Search Form option allows you to include a Search WebBot that looks only at the articles in the discussion forum, not the whole Web site. The Threaded Replies option determines if the postings should be threaded based on the subject matter, similar to the way Internet newsgroups work. The Confirmation Page gives you the option of creating a page that is viewed after the user submits a new article to the discussion forum. For this example, select the options shown in Figure 8-23. When you've finished, click the Next button.

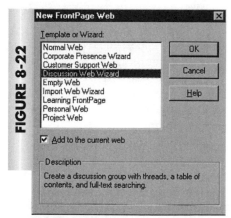

FIGURE 8-22

Add a Discussion WebBot to the current Web site using the Discussion Web Wizard

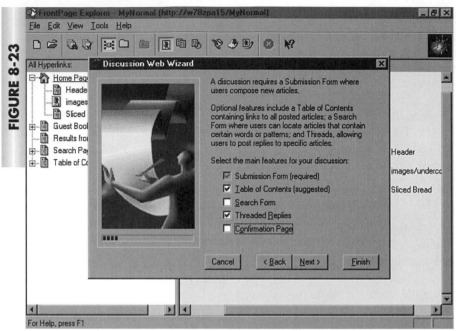

FIGURE 8-23

The first set of options for the Discussion Web Wizard

In the next window, enter the name for your discussion forum. Enter **Bread Maker**, then click the next button. You are then asked to specify what input fields are needed when people post to the discussion forum. Because this is just a general chat forum, you don't want to include category or product fields. Select the Subject and Comments option, then click the next button. Because this is meant to be an open discussion, choose the "No, anyone can post articles" option that comes up next. Clicking the Next button again requires you to enter how you want to sort the postings to your forum. Click the Next button after entering your preference. You are then presented with the option of making the TOC for this Web site become the default for this Web site. Select No here. If you make the TOC for the Web site the default page, your current default will be overwritten.

This brings you to the formatting step of the wizard, as shown in Figure 8-24. Here you can make all sorts of specifications for the pages in the discussion Web site, including selecting one of 13 different backgrounds that come with FrontPage. Enter your preferences, then click the Next button.

Next you are given control over the frames used in your discussion forum. Because this is meant to demonstrate the Discussion WebBot, avoid the added complexity frames bring. Select the No Frames option, then click Next.

That's all for now, so click the Finish button to continue. If you had selected different options, you might have been presented with different screens by the Discussion Web Wizard. All the options are pretty self-explanatory, so you shouldn't have any difficulty using this wizard to configure a discussion Web site with your own preferences.

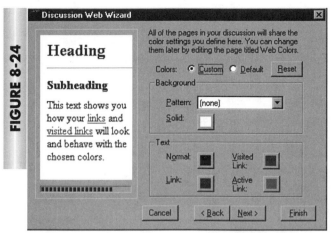

FIGURE 8-24

Configuring the page options for the files in your discussion forum

When you go back to the Explorer, you'll see that several new files have been created. The **Bread Maker TOC** file is the table of contents for the forum. It lists all the articles, arranged by date and subject (because those were the options you selected). The Bread Maker Submissions form document performs exactly as it is named. It contains a form that gathers data and posts the results as an article in the forum. This is where the Discussion WebBot resides. The wizard also generates headers, footers, and color pages for these documents.

Open the Bread Maker Submissions form document with the FrontPage Editor. If you right-click on the form, select Form Properties from the popup menu, and then click the Settings button, you can see the Discussion WebBots settings, as shown in Figure 8-25. Make Bread Maker the title of the discussion. You can also set what values are posted to the articles under the Article tab. If you wish, you can add additional fields to the form and they will be posted to the discussion forum as well.

Open the Home Page with the Editor and add a HyperLink to the Bread Maker TOC file. Save all your changes and recalculate the links. After this is done, you should be able to use your Discussion WebBot. When your visitors go to the Bread Maker TOC document, they'll see something like Figure 8-26, which shows the table of contents for the discussion group. Notice that the discussion is threaded and arranged by date. Clicking one of the links takes the user to the particular article, as demonstrated by Figure 8-27. To post an article of his or her own, the user simply clicks the post link and then fills out the Bread Maker Submission form shown in Figure 8-28. You can modify these documents to fit in with the style of your Web site for a more appealing feel.

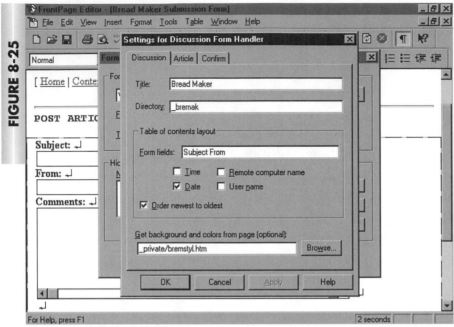

The Discussion WebBots settings

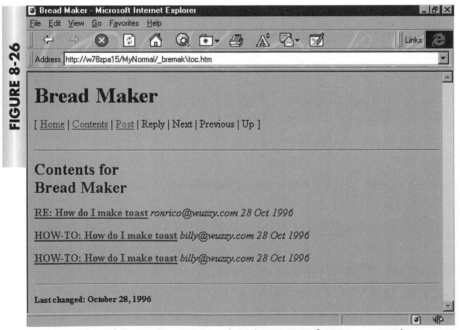

The Bread Maker TOC as viewed with Microsoft Internet Explorer 3.0

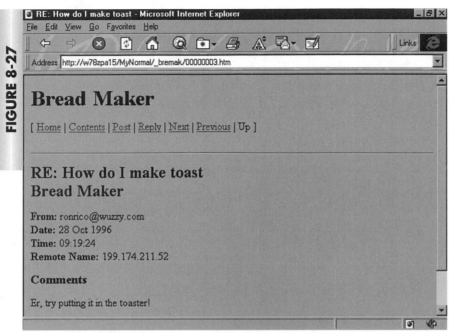

A sample article from the Bread Maker discussion group

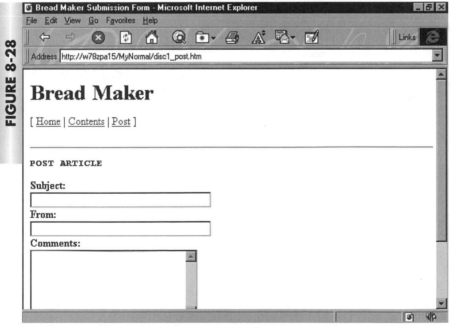

The form to fill out that allows users to add an article to the discussion group

The power the Discussion WebBot brings to your Web site is certainly worth the work! It allows for real user-to-user interaction.

Lesson 13: The Confirmation Field WebBot

When you collect data from your guests using a form, it's customary to echo their input back to them when they've finished. The Registration, Save Results, and Discussion WebBots have some of this functionality built in automatically, but on occasion it's nice to customize confirmation pages so that they fit in with the look and feel of the Web site you've worked hard to create. The Confirmation WebBot is just the tool for this job. It's meant to be used only after form data has been submitted from a Registration, Save Results, or Discussion WebBot; it doesn't have much functionality any other time.

We are going to demonstrate this WebBot by using it to create a confirmation page for your guest book. Open the Web site used throughout this chapter with the FrontPage Explorer. Then create a new Normal page in the editor. Change the title of the page to Confirmation in the Page Properties dialog. If you like, you can include the header file with an Include WebBot and set up some formatting like that used in the rest of the Web site. When you've finished, position the cursor in the body of the document. Type Thanks and then choose WebBot from the Insert Menu. Select Confirmation Field as the type of WebBot. This will bring up the WebBot Confirmation Field Component Properties dialog shown in Figure 8-29.

The Confirmation WebBot echoes data collected from a form, similar to the way the Substitution WebBot works. You can choose which form field gets displayed by entering its name in the text area in the Confirmation WebBot Properties dialog. In this example, you want to echo only the user's name so that you can customize the confirmation page by addressing it specifically to the user. Because the user entered her name in a form element (the one-line text box named GuestName, if you followed Lesson 10), you can use the data in that field to address your message. This is accomplished by entering the field's name (`GuestName`) in the Confirmation WebBot Properties dialog. After adding this to the document, you can add a brief message. You'll probably want to add a link to the Guest Book file as well. Save your work on this page when you've finished.

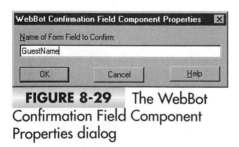

FIGURE 8-29 The WebBot Confirmation Field Component Properties dialog

Now open the Guest Book entry document with the editor. Right-click on the form and select Form Properties from the popup menu. Then click the Settings button to bring up the Settings for Saving Results of Form dialog. In the bottom text area of this dialog, enter the URL of the confirmation page you just created. When the user submits the data, the browser will be taken straight to this page. After you save your work on all these pages and recalculate the links, you should be able to view your Web site with your favorite browser.

Summary

Now you are an experienced user of all the standard FrontPage WebBot Components. You should have a good feel for their use and purpose, and now should be ready to use them in new and creative ways to enhance your Web sites. Congratulations. You've just learned some of the most advanced techniques provided by FrontPage!

The FrontPage Explorer

9

In this chapter you will learn:

How to Perform Basic Functions Such as Creating,
Importing, Copying, Renaming, and Deleting Webs

The Different Symbols and Their Associated Meaning Used
by the FrontPage Explorer

The Different Ways FrontPage Explorer Allows You to
View Webs and Their Uses

How to Use the To Do List with FrontPage Explorer

How to Verify and Recalculate Links

How You Can Configure FrontPage to Use Different
Editors for Different File Types

How to Control Access to a Web Through Administrative,
Authoring, and End User Accounts

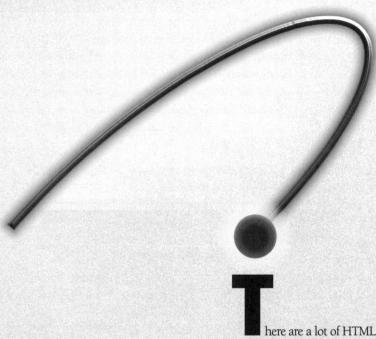

There are a lot of HTML editors. Many companies and shareware programmers have seen the opportunities presented by the Web, and they all want to be the one making the tool you use to create your Web sites. Although these companies create good tools, one vital component is often missing from all but the most advanced Web publishing kits: a tool to help you visually organize your Web site. These other programs are often excellent at helping you write HTML, but they don't include anything that allows you to view your Web site hierarchy, sort out how the individual pages relate, or easily show you what resources are used by your Web site. They don't take into account the big picture, which can be invaluable in helping maintain perspective during development. FrontPage's Explorer is the big-picture tool that is often overlooked in other packages.

With the FrontPage Explorer, you are able to view your entire Web site in shorthand visual format. It allows you to control important aspects of your whole Web from one source, rather than deal with each page separately. The explorer helps you identify broken and missing links, add and remove resources, create and manipulate Web sites, control security settings, and view the contents of the Web site in several different organizational formats. It is a tool for site management, not merely page creation.

Manipulating Webs

The FrontPage Explorer works in terms of Webs. Each Web is stored in its own folder (assuming you're using a Windows 95 or NT HTTP server), and the folders for all Webs are stored in the `FrontPage webs` directory. The `Contents` folder in the `FrontPage webs` directory contains the root web for the server. All other Webs are children of the root web and so are contained in subdirectories of the `Contents` folder. If this seems confusing, consider this: If you created a new Web called `MyNewweb`, its contents would be located in the folder `c:\FrontPage webs\Contents\MyNewweb`. If you were to edit the root web, we would be making changes to files in the `c:\FrontPage webs\Contents` folder. And if you created a new web called `Subweb` to be a child of `MyNewweb`, its resources would be located in the folder `c:\FrontPage webs\Contents\MyNewweb\Subweb`.

Now that you have a clearer understanding of what FrontPage Webs are, you are ready to learn how to manipulate them using the FrontPage Explorer.

Lesson 1: Getting Started

Before you even perform your first piece of page editing, you're probably wondering, "How do I get started?" To aid you inyour quest, FrontPage includes the Getting Started Wizard (see Figure 9-1). Open FrontPage from the Start menu (typically Start | Programs | Microsoft FrontPage). Once FrontPage has started, you are presented with a friendly wizard that will allow you to open/create a Web. This wizard will save you time by allowing you to quickly perform the tasks required in order to get started using FrontPage. However, once you master the tasks to open Webs, you can always suppress this wizard by unchecking the option Show Getting Started Dialog.

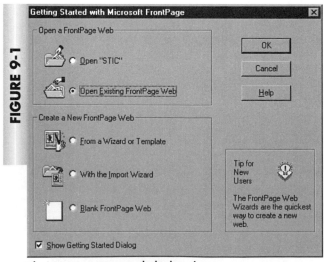

FIGURE 9-1

The Getting Started dialog box

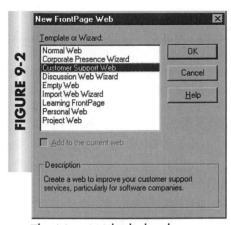

FIGURE 9-2

The New Web dialog box

Lesson 2: Creating Webs

There are four possible methods to create a new FrontPage Web:

◁ Constructing a Web using a wizard or template

◁ Importing an existing Web

◁ Creating a blank Web using the Getting Started dialog

◁ Using the Explorer File | New Web menu option

You must have administrative privileges to create new Webs (Lesson 12 talks more about this). If you create a new Web using a wizard, you have a number of options available to you (see Figure 9-2).

A number of templates and wizards are provided with FrontPage. Table 9-1 lists the templates and their uses. Once you've selected the type of Web you'd like to create, click the OK button. You'll then have to enter the name of the server on which to create the Web (this is usually something like `www.theserver.com`) and a name for the Web. This name may not contain any spaces. The FrontPage Explorer will then create the new Web on your server. This may take a while, especially with a slow connection or a slow and busy server.

Table 9-1 The standard FrontPage templates and wizards

Template or Wizard	Description
Normal Web	This creates a new Web with one empty page. This page is usually named `index.html` or `default.html` and is the default document for the Web.

continued on next page

continued from previous page

Template or Wizard	Description
Corporate Presence Wizard	This wizard presents you with many dialog boxes. Based on your selections, it creates a Web shell for a company site. From there, you can modify and improve the site, making it your own.
Customer Support Web	This creates a Web that mimics a typical customer support site. You can easily edit it to fulfill your customer support needs.
Discussion Web Wizard	This wizard creates a discussion-group Web, based on your preferences. The discussion Webs can include a table of contents and are capable of threading conversations, providing full text searches of all postings, and allowing moderation.
Empty Web	This creates an empty Web. The difference between this and a normal Web is that no default HTML document is created.
Import Web Wizard	This allows you to load documents from an existing directory structure into a new Web.
Learning FrontPage	If you choose to go through the Help tutorial, you'll need to create this Web. (To get to the tutorial, choose Microsoft FrontPage Help Topics from the Help menu, then select the Contents tab in the dialog that follows. The tutorial is in the Learning FrontPage category.)
Personal Web	This sets up a Web with a page that serves as a template for a home page. This single page is geared toward a corporate employee's home page on an intranet.
Project Web	This creates a Web whose purpose would be to track and organize a project. This Web is geared for use on a corporate intranet. It includes such things as a list of team members, project scheduling, and a threaded discussion area.

Once you've created a Web, you canthen edit it to fit your designs. Using the wizards can give you a big head start in configuring a Web. For example, if you know your site is going to contain a discussion, why not use the Discussion Wizard to create it? That way you don't have to spend all your time doing everything from scratch.

Lesson 2: Opening Webs

Opening an existing Web is very simple. Either by using the Getting Started dialog or from the File menu on the FrontPage Explorer, choose the Open FrontPage Web... option or click the Open Web button on the toolbar. This brings up the Open Web dialog. Enter the host name of the server where the Web resides (something like **www.myhost.com**) in the Web Server text area. Then click the List Webs button. In a couple of seconds, a list of Webs hosted by that server will appear in the Webs text area, as shown in Figure 9-3.

Select the Web you wish to open, then click the OK button. You will be prompted for an administrative user ID and a password in order to manage the Web. Once your ID and password are confirmed, the information about that Web will load into the FrontPage Explorer and you'll be able to edit it with the FrontPage Editor or manipulate its contents from within the Explorer.

Lesson 3: Removing Webs

If there is a Web that you no longer want present on your server, first open it as described in Lesson 2. Once the Web is open, select Delete FrontPage Web from the File menu. You must have administrative privileges to delete an entire Web. The Web will then be removed from the server. This may take a little while, so try to be patient (it's hard but it can be done).

Lesson 4: Importing Webs

After you have created your masterpiece Web, you may wish to copy (publish) this Web to another location. In previous versions of FrontPage, this was a tricky process. However, now this process can be performed by opening or creating a Web (see Lesson 2),or choosing Publish FrontPage Web from the File menu (see Figure 9-4).

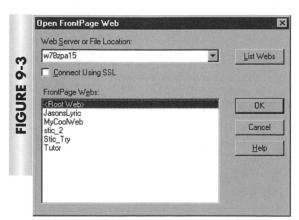

FIGURE 9-3

The Open Web dialog after listing the Webs available on a server

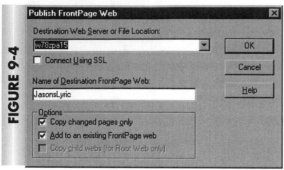

FIGURE 9-4

Publishing your Web using the FrontPage
Publish Web dialog box

Tip

Many servers are configured with a time-out period, usually about 10
minutes. When a process (such as a CGI script) exceeds that time limit, the
server assumes that something went wrong and kills the job. Because the
Copy Web command can take such a long time and uses a hidden script to
achieve its goals, it's possible that the server will stop accepting data
before the whole Web is transferred. You'll need to talk to your Webmaster
or hosting service if you encounter this problem. They can reconfigure the
server so it will work with long tasks such as the Copy Web command.

Once you are presented with the Publish FrontPage Web dialog, enter the name of the
destination server and the name for the Web on that server. Then click the OK button to
publish your Web. In effect, publishing your Web is synonymous to copying. Copying Webs
is a long procedure, and this action may take a long time. If you select the Copy changed
pages only option, you can speed up the process by only updating changed pages on the
target server. Also, if there is already an existing FrontPage Web on the target server, you
can opt to add to that Web by designating this option on the dialog box.

Tip

A good use for the Publish Web command is to set up your machine as a
server using the Personal Web Server shipped with FrontPage. Then, rather
than creating and editing your Web from the destination server, where performance might be slow, create and edit your Webs using your computer as a
temporary server. Because all the functions are being performed by your
computer, you don't have the extra overhead associated with network
communications and traffic, and you'll probably find editing easier because

the server will be more responsive. When you've finished the Web, copy it from
your server (your computer) to its ultimate destination with the Publish Web
command. Make sure the destination server is up and running and has the
FrontPage extensions installed.

If you wish to import a Web from a server that does not have the FrontPage server extensions installed, you may find yourself in a bit of a bind because the FrontPage WebBots
cannot work on a server without these extensions. However, FrontPage will detect this and
attempt to lauch the FrontPage Publishing Wizard (more about this in the next lesson) to
assist you in copying your Web to a server lacking these extensions.

So, it seems that sending your Web out to the world is simple enough, but you may be
wondering how you would ever load in an external Web or files into a new FrontPage Web.
Fortunately, this can be performed by selecting the Import Wizard from the Getting
Started dialog box. First you will be presented with a dialog box prompting you for the
destination of the new Web you are going to create (see Figure 9-5), and this will be followed up with a wizard which will guide you through the process of finding and importing
the appropriate files into your Web (see Figure 9-6).

Lesson 5: Renaming Webs

Renaming a Web is pretty simple, but it is not obvious how to do it. To rename a Web, first
open it as described in Lesson 2. Once it's open, choose Web Settings... from the Tools menu.
In the Web Settings dialog, select the Configuration tab. From here you can easily change
the name of the Web and its title by changing the values in the Name and Title text areas,
as shown in Figure 9-7. When you have finished making changes, click the OK button.
The Web will then be renamed.

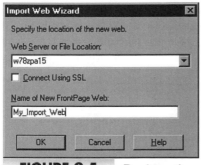

FIGURE 9-5   Designating
the destination server during
the Web/file import process

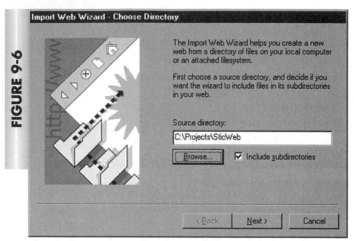

FIGURE 9-6

The Import Wizard will walk you through the steps to import a Web or individual files into your new Web

Lesson 6: Exporting Webs

Few situations require you to export a Web. If the end server you plan to use has the FrontPage Server Extensions installed, then there is no need to save or export a Web to it, because all updates occur automatically. If you're trying to move a Web from one FrontPage-enabled server to another FrontPage-enabled server, simply use the Publish FrontPage Web command, described in Lesson 4.

FIGURE 9-7

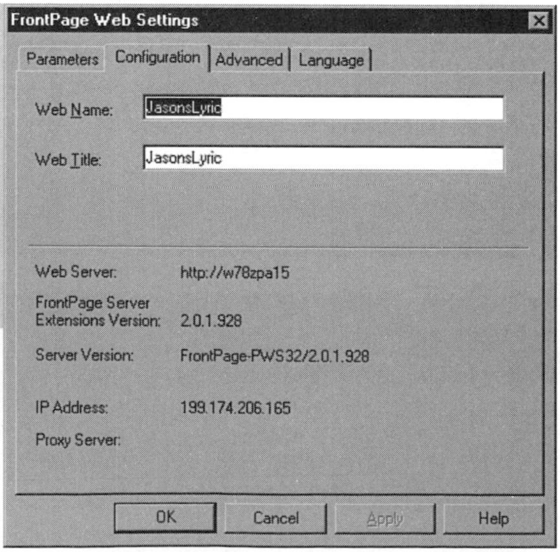

The Configuration tab in the Web Settings dialog

The only time you really need to export a Web is when you need to move a Web from your FrontPage-enabled server to a server that does not have the FrontPage Server Extensions installed. Microsoft provides a free tool for performing just such a task. It's called the Microsoft FrontPage Publishing Wizard. If you File Transfer Protocol (FTP) your files to your host, then this wizard is just what you need. It's available for free download at `http://www.microsoft.com/frontpage/freestuff/fs_fp_pbwiz.htm` and is available on the compact disc (CD-ROM) included in this book.

To install the Publishing Wizard, first close any applications you may be running. Insert the CD-ROM included with the book into your CD-ROM drive, then run the program `D:\PublishingWizard\postweb11a.exe`, where D is the letter of your CD-ROM drive. A dialog will appear asking you to close all running applications. Click the OK button. A Setup dialog will appear, as shown in Figure 9-8. You can change the installation directory and the program group to which the wizard is installed. When you've finished, just click the Installation button, as shown in Figure 9-8. The installation will complete itself. If you wish to uninstall this wizard, open the Add/Remove Programs window from the Control Panel, select the Microsoft FrontPage Publishing Wizard, and click the Uninstall button.

Once the Publishing Wizard is downloaded and installed, you can easily export your Webs to non-FrontPage servers, but keep a number of things in mind. The first problem is that many WebBots will no longer work on the new server. Any WebBot that produces dynamic output will not work in an exported Web. This means pages containing Discussion

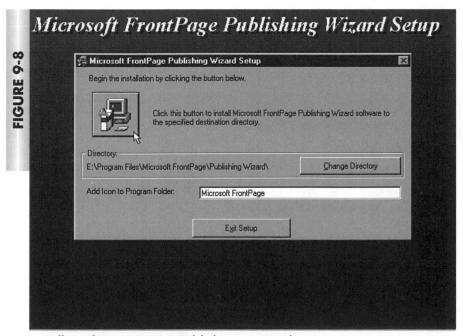

FIGURE 9-8

Installing the FrontPage Publishing Wizard

Bots, Search Bots, Registration Bot, Save Results Bot, and other dynamic bots will not function properly on the new server without special effort. The Publishing Wizard will warn you which files in your Web contain some of these problem bots and present you with options for dealing with them.

To copy a Web to a server that does not have the FrontPage Extensions installed, run the Publishing Wizard. The first screen contains some information about the wizard. Click the Next button when you are ready to continue. The next step, shown in Figure 9-9, requires you to enter the information needed to access the Web server by FTP. Enter the domain name or IP address of the server in the top blank, the directory where the Web should be hosted (usually `public_html`) in the second blank, and your user name and password for that account in the third blank. If you are unsure of any of this information, contact your ISP for help. When you've finished, click the Next button.

The Publishing Wizard will then get a listing of Webs on your local machine. Select the Web you would like to post, then click the Finish button. You can choose to update all the files, update only the files that have changed since your last update, or name the files to update individually, as shown in Figure 9-10. Clicking the Post button will log you on to the server and begin the process of updating these files. If you have Webs containing any of the dynamic bots described earlier, FrontPage will notify you and present you with several options. Depending on your skill and resources, your best bet may be to avoid the Save Results, Registration, Discussion, and Search bots in the first place.

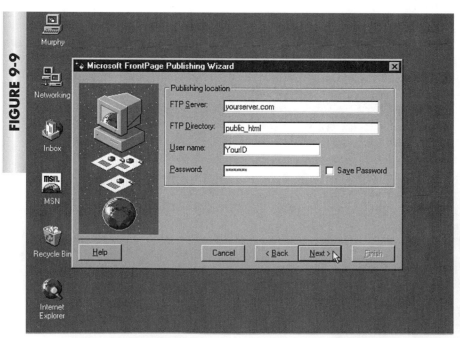

FIGURE 9-9

Entering FTP access information for the FrontPage Publishing Wizard

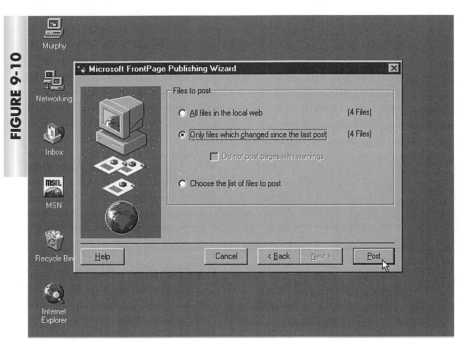

Choosing which files to update

You will not be able to edit files directly from a server that does not have the FrontPage Server Extensions installed. However, you can still edit files locally and export them again at a later time. Another thing to be aware of is that the security functions will no longer work: Anyone with access to that server will be able to view your Webs. You will not be able to control who can view your Webs as you can with a FrontPage-enabled server:

 Tip

You may have noticed that there is no lesson on saving Webs. That's because Webs are dynamically updated. If you rename a file, the change occurs immediately on the server. When you save your changes from the FrontPage Editor, the file is updated on the server. When you add new documents, you can import them immediately (or FrontPage will remind you to import them when you exit). This is why it can sometimes take a little while to perform these simple tasks: There's a lot of communication going on with the server. You never need to save the changes you made to your Web from the FrontPage Explorer because it's already being done for you!

Web Views

In addition to manipulating Webs, the Explorer plays a very important role in organizing them. With the FrontPage Explorer, you have a choice of two different ways to view your Webs: Folder view and Hyperlink view. Both of these views represents a different approach to organizing the resources in your site. In addition to these views, FrontPage Explorer relies heavily on visual symbols to convey information. These symbols give information about the nature of a resource, the status of the links on a page, whether the page has an error, the type of links present, and other useful data. Table 9-2 lists the graphical symbols used by the explorer, as well as what they symbolize.

Table 9-2 FrontPage Explorer symbols and their associated meanings

Symbol	Purpose
	Indicates that there are links present on a page. If the arrow is grayed, the links for that resource are already being listed somewhere else in the window.
	Identifies broken links.
	The Home Page for the Web, often named `index.html`. Only found in Outline view.
	A page that has links.
	Identifies an image.
	Identifies a `mailto:` link.
	A link to something on the World Wide Web. Most commonly, these are links to other sites, but any resource from another Web is represented with this symbol.
	Indicates an error has occurred in the page. Only found in Outline view.
	A page in the current Web. These are normally HTML documents.
	The page centered in link view. Double-clicking brings up the appropriate editor.
	A file other than an HTML document or valid image file.

Now that you have a grasp of the symbolism, let's talk about each of the different views available in the FrontPage Explorer.

The Hyperlink View

The Explorer Hyperlink view represents a hierarchical arrangement of your Web, similar to the Folder view. However, there are some very distinctive differences. In the left pane, the default page is represented at the top of the pane as a small house (as in the home page), with the other resources in the Web listed below it according to their relationships.

You can gather information on how the pages relate to one another by examining their relative positions. Resources used or referenced by a page are indented and listed directly under their referencing page. If a page contains links or resources, it will have a small arrow next to it, unless those resources have already been expanded and displayed. If the arrow next to the Page icon is red, the links it contains are not yet exposed in the Outline view pane. If the arrow is gray, then that particular page (and the material it uses or references) is already displayed somewhere else in the Outline view hierarchy. Remember, your Web pages are often interlinked, which can make it difficult to display the Web in a strictly hierarchical format. This can lead to some confusion initially, but once you get comfortable with the display, you will find it very valuable. If you are a little confused by the Outline view, Lesson 7 should help clear things up.

By right-clicking on a resource listed in the Outline view, you can do such things as delete the resource, open the resource for editing, change the URL (file name) for the resource, or attach comments to a particular resource. If the resource has links, you can expand or reduce the display by clicking the plus and minus symbols in front of each resource. If the outline view is cramped for space or you wish to make more room for the right-side view, you can resize the windows by clicking and dragging the bar dividing the two panes.

Lesson 7: Using the Hyperlink View

For this lesson, you will create a new customer support Web; it should look like the one shown in Figure 9-11.

You are not concerned about anything other than the hyperlink view at this time. Notice that the home page for this Web is the page named Customer Support—Welcome. Immediately underneath it are two pages, respectively called Included Page Header and Included Page Footer. Because these two files are directly below (and indented under) the Customer Support—Welcome page, you know that this page either contains a link to these resources or uses them.

Tip

Notice that the two files underneath the home page are prefaced with the words, Included Page, which indicates that they are probably used by an Include Bot (a way of appending pages), and means that the home page contains these two files. We'll talk more about the Include Bot in the WebBots chapter. You can tell quite a bit about the Customer Support page without even looking at it. The Included Page Header file has a plus symbol in front of it. This indicates that it contains or links to other resources. You can expand

continued on next page

continued from previous page

its contents by clicking the plus symbol. This brings up a listing of eight more pages in the Web, as shown in Figure 9-12. Notice that they, too, contain references to resources. When you click on a plus symbol and it changes to a minus symbol, this indicates that you have expanded the item completely and that there are no more embedded items in the list.

To illustrate further how the hierarchical structure works, expand the What's New resource listing. Notice that the Included Page Header file is not expandable. Once again, that file can be viewed elsewhere at a higher hierarchical level. Notice that the download part of the customer support Web cannot be expanded either, even though its expanded form is not visible anywhere else the Outline view. Because it can be viewed at a higher level (toward the left of the window) somewhere else in the hierarchy, this more distant reference is not allowed to expand. You know that both of these files contain references because they have a plus symbol associated with their icons, unlike the Included Page Footer, which has no associations and therefore has no plus symbol.

FIGURE 9-11

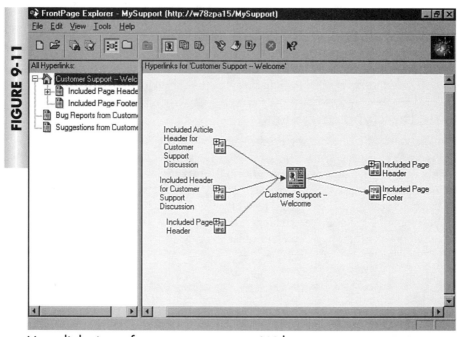

Hyperlink view of a customer support Web

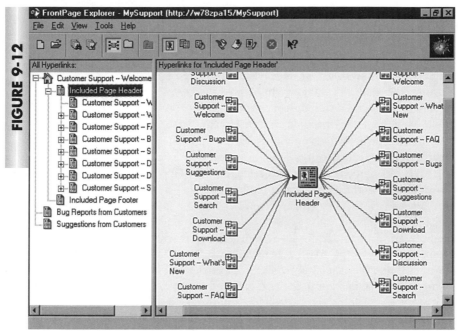

FIGURE 9-12

Viewing the resources of the Included Page Header file

One more thing to note is the two files at the bottom of the Outline view: **Bug Reports from Customers** and **Suggestions from Customers**. These two files are not a normal part of the hierarchy because they are not referenced by any other pages in the Web. These two files serve as repositories for data gathered from forms in the Web. (Chapter 8, "WebBots," talks about how to deposit this data.) You don't want the general public viewing these two files, so links to them are not included anywhere in the Web. Because of this, they fall out of the hierarchy based on the home page and have each started mini-hierarchies. Because they do not reference anything (as illustrated by the lack of plus symbols), they have no sub-items.

Do not delete this Web because you'll use it again in several more lessons in this chapter. You should now have a pretty good understanding of how the left pane of the Hyperlink view organizes your Web. You'll be able to use it to maneuver through your Web quickly and to identify how the resources interrelate easily. Now let's examine the right pane.

The Hyperlink View Revisited

Probably the most eye-catching element of the Hyperlink view is the right pane of the Explorer window.

This panel provides another way of looking at the resources used by the Web. The Hyperlink view emphasizes the relationship between a document, its resources, and the other pages that use it as a resource. The display centers around a single resource. Notice that to the left of this resource documents may be shown with an arrow pointing to the resource of interest. The significance of this arrow is that those documents either contain a link to the main resource or use it in some other fashion. To the right of the main resource lie the resources the item references, illustrated by the arrows pointing from the main resource to the reference resources. The arrows illustrate these relationships. Resources on the left have arrows pointing toward the resources to their right because they use or reference them.

The right pane is associated with the contents of the left pane so that you can pick which resource to treat as the central resource for the right pane of the hyperlink view. By clicking on a resource in the left pane, you make it the center of the right pane. By examining the Hyperlink view, you can identify all the documents that reference various items from the current Web and all the resources they reference. The Hyperlink view is not limited to the same hierarchy as the left pane as it is allowed to display more complete relationship information, and it is also allowed the potentially confusing possibility of viewing repeated sequences of relationships.

Double-clicking on a resource displayed in the right pane will cause it to be opened for editing. You can change the page URL (file name) and add comments from the right pane the same way as in the left pane: Right-click on the resource and then edit its properties. You can expand the relationships of the non-centered item by clicking on the plus symbol in the icon's corner. Hiding expanded relationships is as simple as clicking the minus symbol in the icon's corner. Once again, the items on the left have arrows pointing to the resources on the right that they use.

Lesson 8: Using the Hyperlink View

To demonstrate the Hyperlink view, you will use the same customer support Web as in Lesson 7. If you do not have this Web available, you can easily create a new customer support Web. You will not edit this Web, only view it in different ways. If the Hyperlink view is not showing in the right pane, click the Hyperlink View button so that it is displayed.

Notice that the Customer Support—Welcome (Welcome, for short) page is centered in the display. It is the focal point for your viewing. The three pages on the left contain links to this Web, as illustrated by the arrows leading from them to the Welcome page. These are all the documents in this entire Web that contain links to the Welcome page. To the right of the Welcome page are the only two resources it uses or references, illustrated by the arrows leading from it to them. By focusing the Hyperlink view on a document, you can find all the files in this Web that reference that document, as well as all the files in the Web that it uses. This contrasts with the Outline view because the Outline view shows only the resources a page uses and does not provide an easy method of viewing all the resources that use it. With the Hyperlink view, you can easily get a picture in both directions of what uses a page and what a page uses.

You can view this linking relationship for the other files displayed as well. This can lead to some confusion, but it can also be very useful if you're trying to establish the flow of different resources. For example, from the Hyperlink view, expand the Included Page Header view by clicking on the plus symbol in the upper-left corner of its icon. This lists the eight documents it references. Expand the Customer Support—Welcome page shown at the top of these documents in the same fashion. You can now see the Welcome page shown twice and the Included Page Header document shown twice, as in Figure 9-13. There is no limit to how many times you can expand the resources used by a hyperlink.

FIGURE 9-13

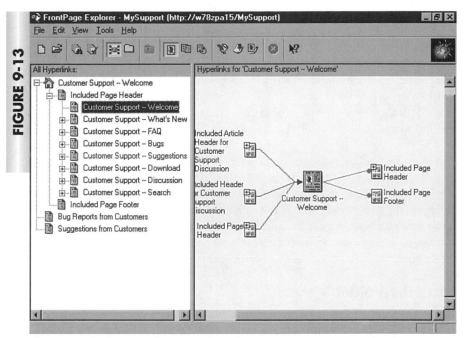

The Hyperlink view does not limit how many times you display a document's related resources

Now let's take a look at a different document. If you click on the Included Page Header document in the Outline view, you'll see that the Hyperlink view rearranges itself to center its display around this document. You can also see that, for this document, the same files that the header links to also link back to the header. Centering the Hyperlink view on the footer (by clicking on it in the Outline view) reveals that nine documents are referencing it, but the footer itself does not reference any resources: It's being used but it is not using anything.

You should now have a clearer understanding of how the Hyperlink view organizes itself. You know how to use this view to examine the relationships shared between documents. You also know that you can open documents for editing by double-clicking on them in Hyperlink view.

The Folder View

The Explorer Folder view is the Swiss army knife view of the Web: It shows everything but isn't very sophisticated. It represents a hierarchical arrangement of your Web similar to the way the Windows 95 Explorer displays a hierarchical view of your computer's file system. It does not concern itself with links or internal organization at all, but rather, focuses only on the contents of the Web. The Folder view display is like the Windows 95 Explorer in that the left pane contains a list of the folders which make up your Web and the right pane displays pertinent information about each file: the title, file name, size, extension, date of the last modification, who modified the file last, the URL, and any comments associated with the file. The Folder view is not the default view for the FrontPage Explorer window, so if you wish to see it, you have to click the Folder View button in the button bar. Figure 9-14 identifies this view.

Because all the views are integrated so only one resource is selected at a time, you can use the Folder view to help you locate files in the Hyperlinks view. To do this, simply right-click on the title of the file you are interested in, then select Show Hyperlinks from the popup menu. The FrontPage Explorer will find and select that file and center it in the Hyperlinks view.

You can also sort the files in the Folder view by clicking on the label bars near the top of the pane. For example, to sort the files in order of size (smallest to largest), simply click on the Size label bar. You can resize the spacing given to each column by clicking and dragging the edges of the label bars as well. In the Summary view, you can also change the file's properties in the same manner as in the other views: Simply right-click the title of the document of interest, select properties from the popup menu, and from there you can edit the URL or add comments.

Lesson 9: Using the Folder View

Because the Folder view is merely a listing of files that does not depend on their relationship, it is the simplest view to understand and the easiest to use. For this lesson, you'll use the customer support Web you created previously. If you have not created a new customer

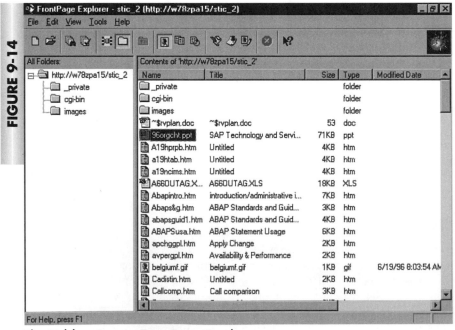

FIGURE 9-14

The Folder view in FrontPage Explorer

support Web, you'll need to do so before following this example (see Lesson 7). Once you've opened the unedited customer support Web, make sure the Folder view is displayed by clicking the Folder View button.

From the Folder view, you can search for a certain file and then select that file as the focus for the Hyperlinks view. To illustrate this, right-click on the file titled **Included Article Header for Customer Support Discussion** (its file name is **cusuahdr.htm**), then select Show Hyperlinks from the popup menu. You'll see the outline hierarchy expanded until the file is exposed. It will be highlighted and the hyperlinks will be displayed in the right pane, centered on that file.

You should now have a pretty good feel for the Folder view. It really is the easiest of all to understand because it's just a listing of files and some of their properties. You'll have no problem using the Folder view to get a quick look at the entire contents of your Web.

Displaying Different Resources

The FrontPage Explorer toolbar includes three buttons whose function may not be obvious. Figure 9-15 shows these three buttons: the Hyperlinks to Images button, the Repeated Hyperlinks button, and the Hyperlinks Inside Page button. These options are also echoed in the View menu. They control what optional resources are displayed in the Outline and Hyperlink views.

The Hyperlinks to Images button determines whether images should be included as special Hyperlinks. If this option is selected, then all images referenced by a page will appear in the Hyperlinks view. The Repeated Hyperlinks button determines whether multiple hyperlinks in a page should be displayed. By default, the Hyperlinks view displays a reference to a source only once, though the source may be referenced many times within a single page. For example, if the Hyperlinks to Images option is turned on, a single resource listing would appear for a graphical bullet used in a bulleted list. If the Repeated Hyperlinks option were selected as well, then there would be one entry for every time the graphic was used: If you used the bullet eight times, the link to that graphic would be repeated eight times for that page. The last option is Hyperlinks Inside Page. If a document references bookmarks within itself, it technically contains links back to itself. Selecting the Hyperlinks Inside Page option causes those internal links to be represented in the Hyperlinks view.

FIGURE 9-15 The resource view option buttons

Cool Features

FrontPage has some very powerful capabilities. Some of these can be fully appreciated only if you've slugged your way through hand-coding a bunch of HTML pages as part of a team or had to change a file name and update every link to that file throughout the entire Web. Fortunately, FrontPage comes with features to smooth such common sticking points. The To Do List makes it easy to coordinate jobs, especially when several people are working on the same Web. In addition, link maintenance in FrontPage is greatly facilitated, even to external links. Also, FrontPage allows you to configure different editors for different file types, a feature that makes Web weaving a little more pleasant.

The To Do List

The To Do List (see Figure 9-16) is just what it claims to be: a utility for organizing your thoughts on how the Web should progress. With the To Do List, you can assign tasks to different individuals, which helps organize a group of people who are working on the Web simultaneously. Some wizards automatically add tasks to the To Do List to help remind you how to complete your Webs. To access the To Do List, simply click the To Do List button on the FrontPage Explorer toolbar. You'll notice this button looks the same for both the Explorer and the Editor. The use of the To Do List is discussed in Chapter 7.

FIGURE 9-16

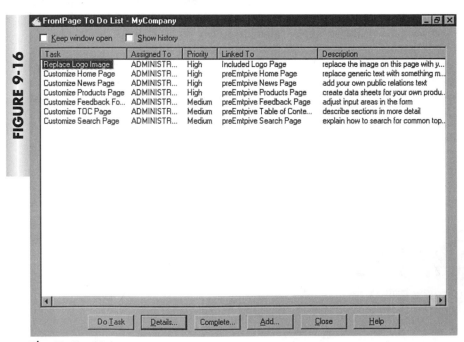

The To Do List

Lesson 10: Verify Links

One of FrontPage's strongest features is its ability to keep track of your links and dynamically update them. If you change the name of a file, FrontPage will give you the option of automatically updating all references to that document throughout your Web so that no links are broken. Equally as impressive, you can have FrontPage go out to the Internet and make sure links to sources outside your Web are valid as well. Of course, it can't dynamically update these, but it can tell you which links are broken so you can fix them.

To demonstrate how to verify links, open a new personal Web with the FrontPage Explorer. Once this is done, select Verify Links from the Tools menu. This brings up the Verify Hyperlinks window, as shown in Figure 9-17.

To check the links, click the Verify button. FrontPage will then attempt to connect with each of the resources the links point to and change the status of those links to represent the success or failure of the attempt. All the links in this example are broken because they are meant only to demonstrate how the template works, not to reference real documents. If the links are OK, then a green dot and the word OK appears in the status column next to the link.

You can easily edit the misformed links from the Verify Links window. To do this, select the link you want to change (most probably a broken link) and click the Edit Link button. From the Edit Link window, you can change the URL the link refers to (preferably to a valid URL). Even better, you can automatically change every instance of that link throughout your Web. When you select this option, FrontPage searches through your entire Web for every instance of that link and replaces it with your new URL. If you prefer, you can edit each page by itself by clicking the Edit Page button, or you can automatically add the task of fixing the link to the To Do List by clicking the Add Task button.

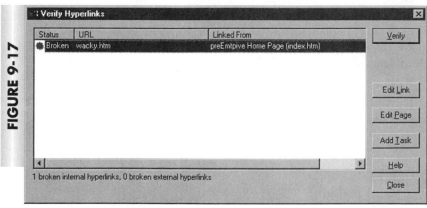

FIGURE 9-17

Explorer can verify links within your Web

Tip

It's a good idea to check on broken links yourself by trying to browse the site with your Web browser. Sometimes a link is listed as broken because it takes too long to retrieve or the request for the document was *throttled*.
Throttling is a method by which some servers improve performance. Rather than trying to fill all requests—dramatically slowing the performance for everyone—the server ignores, or throttles, some requests so it can provide good service to the remainder. Some sites don't like Web robots viewing them, and the FrontPage Explorer is such a robot. In short, just because a link is listed as broken doesn't mean that it is really bad, and you should investigate further before declaring the site dead and removing or changing the link. Because you know which links are good, the job is much simplified.

Lesson 11: Recalculate Links

As you change the names of files, add new links, and change old links, or as other users simultaneously edit the same Web, the FrontPage Explorer's views may become stale. This means that the view you see isn't necessarily the same thing that's on the server. The Recalculate Links command causes the server to go through the Web and regenerate all the files and links: It updates the Web. It also causes the display in the Explorer to be updated. The Recalculate Links tool is especially useful when you have a Search Bot in your Web. Search Bots allow full text searches of the contents of your Web—Chapter 8 discusses them in greater detail. Recalculating links is very important when you've finished editing a Web that contains a Search Bot, because you want it to have an accurate record of your Web.

To recalculate the links in your Web, simply select Recalculate Links from the Tools menu of the FrontPage Explorer. This action may take some time, because the work is done by the server. Large Webs, slow servers, and heavy traffic on the server can all lengthen the amount of time it takes to recalculate links.

Lesson 12: Configuring Editors

One nice feature of FrontPage is its ability to configure different editors to work with different file types. You can use your favorite graphics program to edit graphics, your favorite sound editor to edit sound files, and so on, without changing the default windows' file associations. FrontPage is highly configurable: You could even configure FrontPage to use an HTML editor other than FrontPage Editor. Of course this would be a little dodgey, because you wouldn't be able to use bots or many of the other FrontPage features.

In this lesson, you are going toconfigure FrontPage to use LView Pro for editing GIF and JPEG images. You must install LView Pro to follow this example. LView Pro is provided on the CD-ROM accompanying this book, and can be found in the **LView** directory. To install LView Pro, simply copy the files in the **LView** folder to a folder on your hard drive (something like **c:\program files\LView*.***). To run LView, double-click on the file **lviewpro.exe**.

FIGURE 9-18

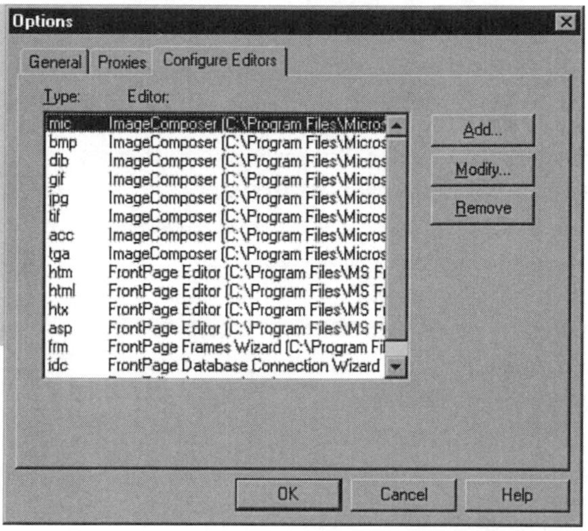

Editors configured for use by FrontPage

To configure different editors for use in FrontPage, select the Configure Editors option from the Tools menu of FrontPage Explorer. This brings up the Configure Editors tab shown in Figure 9-18.

Because you are going to add a new editor, click on the Add button. This brings up the Add Editor Association dialog shown in Figure 9-19. Here, you want to provide the information needed to associate LView Pro with both GIF and JPEG file types. First, associate it with the GIF image format by entering **gif** in the File Type text area. Then add **Image Editor** (or whatever you'd like) to the Editor Name text area. If you know the command line (path) needed to run LView Pro, enter it in the command area; otherwise, click the Browse button and find the **lviewpro.exe** file, then click OK to confirm your settings.

Once you've confirmed your settings, you can see the association listed in the Configure Editors window. Because you also want JPEG images to be opened with LView Pro, associate the file extensions **.jpg** and **.jpeg** with LView Pro in the same manner. When this is completed, whenever you open one of these types of resources with FrontPage Explorer, it will be loaded into LView Pro for editing ease.

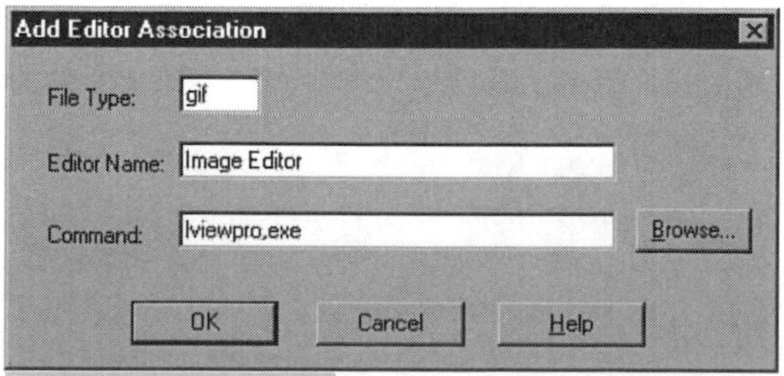

FIGURE 9-19 Associating GIFs with LView Pro

Tip

It is not always necessary to associate file types with certain editors. When FrontPage opens a resource that does not have an editor configured for it, it uses the default Windows associations. The only time you'll want to add associations is when the default Windows association is different from the editor you wish to use or when there is no default Windows association. For example, you may have an image viewing program as the default Windows association for image files, but when you're working with FrontPage, you will want to open images with a graphics editing program (such as LView Pro) so you can edit them instead of merely viewing them.

Security and Access

Aside from the ease of editing and functionality FrontPage provides, it also provides some measure of security. The ability to restrict who can edit and view your Webs allows flexibility in how you can use FrontPage. FrontPage provides three levels of access: Administrator, Author, and End user. These are described more clearly in Table 9-3. You can create separate accounts for each of these levels, allowing some people full administrative control and others editing privileges, and you can even restrict viewing access to those with a valid account. You can also restrict access for each account type by IP address. This could allow only computers using corporate IP addresses access to certain features. Each Web can have a separate set of accounts controlling access and permissions, or you can use the settings for the root Web across the board.

Table 9-3 Access types and their privileges

Access Type	Privileges
End user	Can view and work with Webs through a Web browser. This is standard use and does not allow the ability to edit the Web with FrontPage. By default, the Web is available to everyone.
Author	Authors can view, edit, create, and delete the pages in a Web. They cannot delete entire Webs or create new ones. They have all the privileges of an end user.
Administrator	Administrators have full access to a Web. They can delete the entire Web, add new accounts (administrators, authors, and end users), delete accounts, and add access restrictions, and they have all the privileges of authors and users. The administrator of the root Web has administrative privileges for all Webs.

Lesson 13: Changing Administrators, Authors, and End Users

In this example, you're going to add a new authoring account to a Web. You're going to use the support Web you've looked at in previous lessons in this chapter, but which Web you use really doesn't matter; just don't try to change the access privileges to one that's important! This example assumes you have administrative privileges to the Web you are editing.

First, open the Web with the FrontPage Explorer. Then, from the Tools menu, select Permissions. This brings up the Web Permissions dialog shown in Figure 9-20. Notice that the default setting for the Web is to Use same permissions as root Web. If you want to change access for all Webs, you'll need to open the root Web and make the administrative changes there. In this case, you want only your new author to have access to this Web, so change the option to Use unique permissions for this Web. Before you'll be able to make changes, you'll need to click the Apply button. If you try before that, you will receive an error message.

Now click the Authors tab. Notice that there are no authors listed. That's because (if you just created this Web) you are an administrator and have authoring privileges already. If you click the Administrators tab, you will see your account listed there. There is not always a need to create separate authoring and administrative accounts: Administrators already have authoring privileges. To add an authoring account, click the topmost Add button in the Administrators section and enter in the new account name and password information. When you've finished, you can see the new authoring account is listed in the text box, as shown in Figure 9-21.

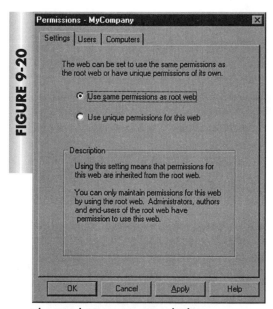

FIGURE 9-20

The Web Permissions dialog

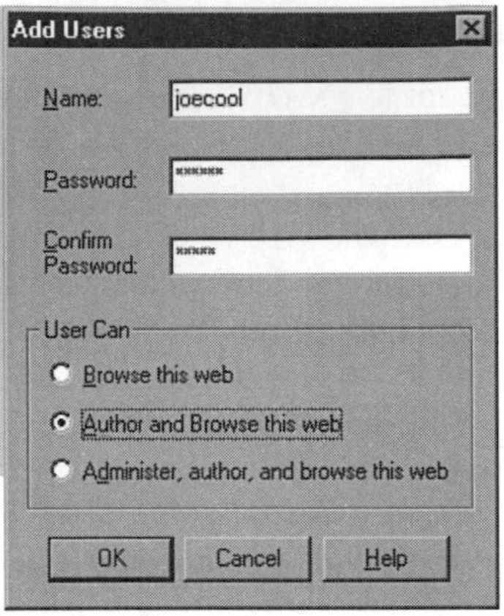

FIGURE 9-21

Adding a new authoring account

You want to protect the Web from crackers, because someone else on the Internet might acquire (or guess) an account name and password. To help secure access privileges, restrict which IP addresses can access this Web for editing. This way, even if someone guesses a correct name and password, he or she would still need to have access to a computer using an acceptable IP address. Restrict access to certain IP addresses by clicking the Add button on the bottom half of the window and entering an IP mask. You can use wild cards (*) to represent any number. Now the authors can access the editing functions only from computers whose IP address fits the mask. It's also a good idea to restrict access for administrators as well, because they have even more control over the Web than editors. It would be wise to limit administration tasks to only one IP address—preferably the host machine itself, if possible. You can create multiple IP address masks for each type of account.

If you click the End Users tab, you'll notice that the Web is set so everyone has access. Because this is a customer service Web, that makes sense. If you created a Web on an intranet for the purpose of sharing information about budget proposals, you might want to restrict access to a certain few by selecting the Registered users only option and then creating names and passwords for each person you wish to have access. Another reason to restrict access could be if you create an e-zine on the Web and want to charge people for a subscription: You could restrict general access by requiring users to have an end user account and password.

Summary

You've learned much about the FrontPage Explorer. You should feel fairly comfortable with its interface; that confidence will grow as you work with it. You should understand the basics of Web manipulation and maintenance. You've learned some of FrontPage's security methods and other advanced features. With this in hand, you should have no problem administering, authoring, and supporting a Web.

Navigation

10

In this chapter you will learn:

What a URL Is and Its Basic Parts

How an IP Address and a Domain Name Relate

Controls Common to Most Graphical Browsers and
Their Functions

How to Browse a Web Using the FrontPage Editor

How to Copy Pages from the Web to Your Web

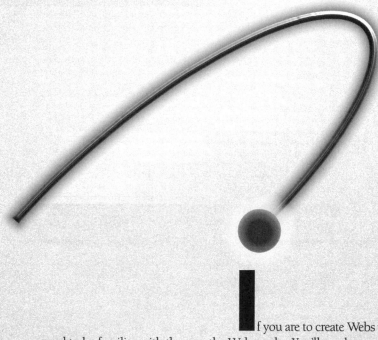

If you are to create Webs with a good design, you'll need to be familiar with the way the Web works. You'll need a good understanding of common functions and how to move from one place to another. Once you've learned the basics of navigation, you'll learn how to apply them to FrontPage. This chapter tries to show you a little about exactly what *there* means. It also discusses the essentials for getting information from there to here. Don't worry, surfing the Web isn't tough, and knowing how to move around on the Web will give you a leg up on learning the best way to handle yourself.

The Foundation of the Web: The URL

The Web was created as a way to move information. The Web's model of information exchange involves linking a phrase, word, image, or part of an image to other resources in the Internet. It's like having a research paper with a built-in bibliography. You can choose to follow the reference to another source, which has more information on a particular concept, or you can continue reading the rest of the document. In the case of the Web, these references are called *links*. In fact, the Web has so many links going in so many different directions that it's safe to say the entire Web is linked to itself: It's really all one large (VERY, VERY

LARGE) interconnected document. By creating your own site, you are adding on to the Web as a whole.

The biggest problem with links is that they need to point to information located on other computers connected via the Internet, meaning they need some way of uniquely identifying each other. Not only that, links need to specify how to retrieve the information they point to. How can they do all this? With a Uniform Resource Locator (URL). A URL represents a way of addressing computers, files, and communications protocols on the Internet. Figure 10-1 shows a sample URL.

The first part of the URL is the *protocol*. The protocol tells the browser how to deal with the rest of the URL. If the protocol is `http://`, that means the document should be retrieved using the HTTP protocol. HTTP is the form of communication the Web uses almost exclusively. Table 10-1 lists some of the common protocols and their uses. This chapter concentrates on the HTTP protocol, but it's nice to know what else is out there.

Table 10-1 Common URL protocols and their functions

Protocol	Use
`http://`	Hypertext documents and others
`https://`	Hypertext documents located on a secure server
`file://`	Used to name a file located on a local disc; the file is opened directly; no Web server is used
`ftp://`	File Transport Protocol—a method of moving files on the Internet that was developed before HTTP and HTML
`gopher://`	A way of organizing information on the Internet into menus; it was in use before the Web became popular
`mailto:`	Starts the mail program associated with your browser; an e-mail address usually follows this protocol
`news:`	Starts a mail reading program associated with your browser; the name of a newsgroup usually follows

Assuming that the protocol is HTTP or a closely related type, the next bit of information contained in a URL is the *host*. The host is a way of addressing computers on the Internet.

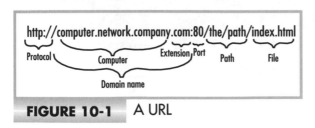

FIGURE 10-1   A URL

Every computer that is connected to the Internet has a special address. This address is called an *IP number*, and it is usually represented by four sets of digits separated by periods, something like this: **204.157.202.86**. Numbers like this are great for computers to work with, but aren't so great for humans. To make things a little easier on us all, organizations have been established to keep track of these numbers and give them out as needed. Another organization keeps track of the host names assigned to each number, making sure that names are not reused. For example, **rs.internic.net** has been assigned to the address **198.41.0.5**. There should be no other site named **198.41.0.5** or **rs.internic.net** anywhere in the world. The IP address **198.41.0.5** may have more than one host name, however, so names other than **rs.internic.net** may refer to that same IP number.

The part of the text that represents the IP number is called the *domain name*. Humans find **rs.internic.net** easier to remember than its associated IP address **198.41.0.5**, and **rs.internic.net** provides easier access to information about the host. Some hosts don't have domain names; you might have to enter the IP address directly if you wish to access these hosts.

Tip

The organizations responsible for IP addressing have realized that unless something is done, all available IP addresses will be used up soon. Because of this, a new standard of IP addressing is being developed. It will be called *IPng*, and it may be in use by the time you read this book. It will be compatible with the current IP addressing system and could create about 8×10^{28} new addresses, enough to give billions and billions of unique IP addresses to every person in the world.

You can often tell something about the organization that owns the domain name by looking at the last little bit. This is called the *extension*. Extensions have specific meanings that allow you to know something about the site. Table 10-2 lists some common extensions and their meanings.

Table 10-2 Common extensions and their meanings

Extension	Meaning
.com	Company
.org	Nonprofit organization
.edu	Educational institution
.uk	In the United Kingdom
.us	In the United States

continued on next page

continued from previous page

Extension	Meaning
.biz	A business (often used instead of .com)
.net	Often an Internet Service Provider or Internet-related service
.au	In Australia
.can	In Canada
.ger	In Germany

Sometimes a number follows the domain name. This number represents the port, or *channel*, the server should be listening to. If the protocol is HTTP (for Web documents), the default port is 80. Sometimes, for security reasons, Webmasters set up servers on a port other than 80. Quite often, this will be port 8080. If no port number is listed in the URL, 80 will be used by default. If the server you want to connect with is listening on a port other than 80, you will not be able to connect unless you specify that port.

After the optional port comes the *path*. The path is the series of directories from the root Web that the server must go through to get to where the file is stored. If the file is stored in the root Web, no path is needed.

After the path comes the *file*. The file is the name of the document you wish to retrieve. The document does not always have to be an HTML document. It could be a GIF, JPEG, AU, or other format file supported by your browser. The file name often is not specified. When this is the case, the default name `index.html` is used.

If all this seems a little confusing, consider this: The URL `http://host.com` is the same as `http://host.com:80/index.html`. Some of the information doesn't need to be expressed because it can be assumed.

The last thing an HTTP URL can contain is a *bookmark*. A bookmark is a place marker inside of a Web page. In some large Web pages, authors place bookmarks to mark certain spots. You can reference these bookmarks by placing a pound sign after the URL, followed by the bookmark name. This will cause that page to load and display the bookmarked part of the document at the top of the browser.

Common Web Elements

The most important elements to be familiar with are links and anchors. No, it's not a game (like *Chutes and Ladders*), but it does have a certain ring to it. The term *link* and the term *anchor* are synonymous. Links are how you use HTML to point to another document. A hypertext link tells the browser, "if the user clicks here, go to this URL." Links are often assigned to text and images and always point to a URL. Bookmarks are related to URLs, and therefore links, in that they mark a certain location in an HTML document. This enables a link to tell the browser not only what document to go to but what part of the document it should look at. Hypertext links (where text is linked to another URL) often appear in the browser underlined and in a special color. If the link has been followed (that is, you've been to that URL before), the link is often a different color.

Because the Web is more than just text, other things can have links too. One of the most common linked objects is graphics. Pictures, or parts of a picture, are often linked to URLs and give the Web a much more human interface. It's easy for us to associate images with their destinations. If you explore the Web a lot, you'll notice that people often use arrows to represent forward and backward in their Webs, and sometimes you'll see little houses representing the home page or other pictures that make the destination clear. You should become comfortable with these common elements.

Common Browser Elements

Even as word processing programs made by different software manufacturers tend to have similar features, Web browsers also share some common functions. You should become familiar with these, because they are important tools. To build effective Webs, you need to know how to move around in them. Most browsers are used from a graphical environment, such as Microsoft Windows, so it makes sense to concentrate on those.

 Tip

Often, you will hear complaints that you should be designing Webs for use with Lynx, a text-based browser. In reality, Lynx is not used very much today, and you shouldn't waste your time trying to please the few people who use a niche browser like Lynx. The real concern is that some browsers (like the very popular Netscape browser) allow you the option of turning off inline graphics—which greatly speeds up how fast a Web page is loaded. This is a common method of *speed surfing*, and you should work to accommodate surfers because they make up a large portion of the Web community.

URL Address Area

Almost every browser in use today lists the URL it is currently addressing. Typing a valid URL in this area will take you to that address. Figure 10-2 points out the URL address area in a popular browser.

FIGURE 10-2

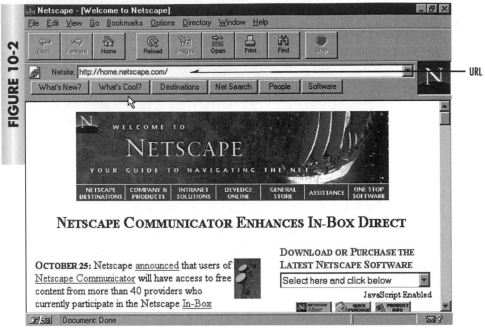
— URL

The URL address area in Netscape Navigator 3.0

Common Buttons

Most graphical browsers sport a button bar that has a lot of common functionality. Some of the most common and important buttons are Back, Forward, Stop, Reload, and Print. Figure 10-3 shows a common browser with these buttons identified. Table 10-3 lists these buttons, along with their functions.

Table 10-3 Common browser buttons and their functions

Button Name	Function
Back	Causes the browser to return to the previous URL.
Forward	If the Back button was pressed, theForward button will move you ahead. The Forward button does not work unless the Back button was pressed first.
Reload	Most browsers store Web pages in a special cache to improve performance. Sometimes a site will change, but the browser will still display the documents stored in the cache. Pressing the Reload button forces the browser to reload the entire document from its original source. This button is often used for sites that change frequently.
Stop	This stops the current page from loading or finishing loading.
Print	This prints the document being viewed.

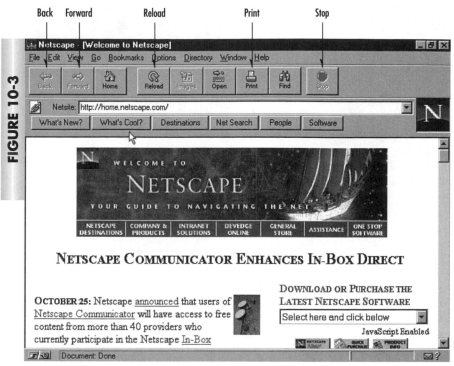

Common browser buttons as shown in Netscape Navigator 3.0

Status Bar

The status bar is a feature found in most Windows programs. It's the small strip at the very bottom of the window, and it is used to convey pertinent information. In most browsers, this area is used to show the URL a link points to. For example, if you move the mouse pointer over a link, the destination URL of that link will be displayed in the status bar. The status bar can also be used to display other messages, such as when the browser is connecting to another host, what it's currently downloading, or the progress made on current transactions.

Navigation with FrontPage

FrontPage, by its nature, must include tools to navigate the Internet. In fact, it is nearly a complete browser in itself. You can use FrontPage to navigate the Web, making it easy to copy information for use in your own Webs, though you need to be cautious of copyright restrictions when doing this sort of thing. You are often better off putting a link in your Web to sites of interest, rather than importing those sites directly.

URL Address Area

There is no true URL address area in FrontPage, at least not in the same way there is in an ordinary browser. You can, however, enter a URL, and FrontPage will take you to that destination. As with any other browser, if you want to get onto the Web, you'll need to be connected.

Lesson 1: Opening a Page with the FrontPage Editor

To browse a Web page with the FrontPage Editor, you'll first need to start the editor. Any site you can browse with a normal browser, you can also browse with the FrontPage Editor, though it may not appear quite the same. When the editor is running, click on the File option in the menu bar; then select Open. Once this is done, the Open File dialog appears. Click on the Other Location tab; then select the From Location option. Type in the URL you wish to go to; then click the OK button. If you are properly connected to the Internet, the FrontPage Editor will open that URL and display the document. Remember, the editor is not like most browsers, so the document may appear a little differently than you've come to expect.

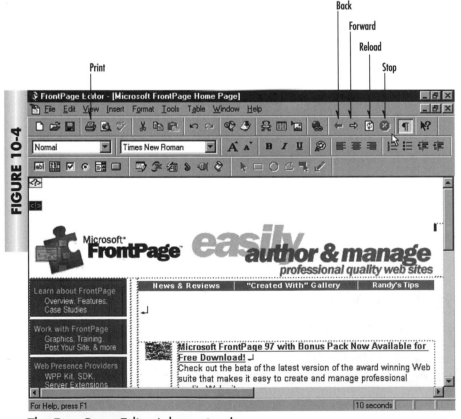

The FrontPage Editor's browsing buttons

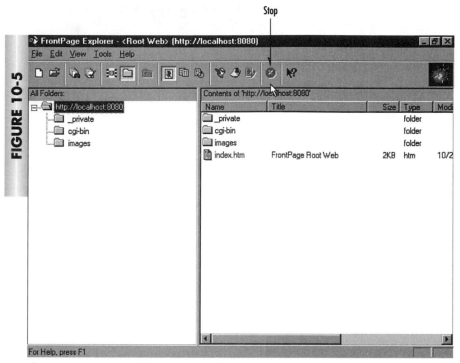

The FrontPage Explorer's Stop button

Common Buttons

The common buttons described earlier are also available in FrontPage and serve the same functions as they would in an ordinary browser. Figure 10-4 shows the FrontPage Editor with the browsing buttons identified. Figure 10-5 shows the FrontPage Explorer with the Stop button identified. If you need a refresher on the function of the these buttons, refer to Table 10-3.

Status Bar

The status bar in the FrontPage Editor serves the same purpose that status bars serve in normal browsers. It displays the destination URL when the mouse cursor is over a link. This is illustrated in Figure 10-6. It might also display other information as you work with the editor. The status bar in the FrontPage Explorer serves a similar function: displaying its current activity as it retrieves documents from the Web.

FIGURE 10-6

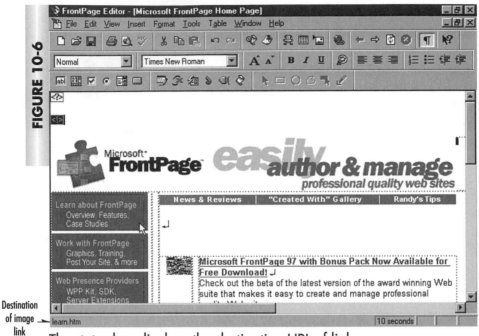

Destination of image link → learn.htm

The status bar displays the destination URL of links

Tips, Tricks, and Nifty FrontPage Web Navigation Features

To use FrontPage effectively, it's important that you understand how to get around in it. There's more to this than just creating pages! Using FrontPage Editor as a browser can save you time. Being able to borrow other sites easily makes it much easier to learn HTML and discover how certain tricks work.

Lesson 2: Navigating the Web with the FrontPage Editor

You can use the FrontPage Editor as a browser. All you need to do to follow links across the World Wide Web is to right-click on the link and then select Follow Link from the popup menu, as shown in Figure 10-7.

Tip

You can also follow links by pressing and holding down the CTRL key while left-clicking on a link. Pressing the CTRL key turns the mouse pointer into a small arrow when it's over a link, making it easier to identify linked objects.

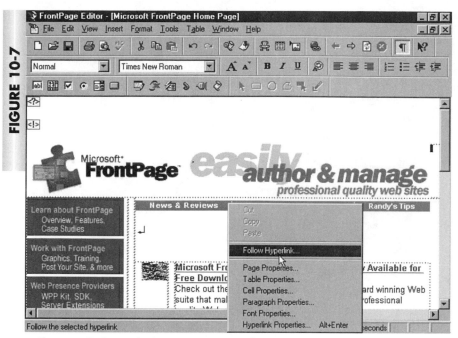

FIGURE 10-7

Following links with the FrontPage Editor

Lesson 3: Copying Web Pages with the FrontPage Editor

If you get to a page you particularly like, FrontPage has the ability to copy the page. First, open the Web you want to store the page in with the FrontPage Explorer. Then open the page you'd like to add to the Web with the FrontPage Editor (as described in Lesson 1). Once it's fully loaded, select Save as from the File menu of the FrontPage Editor. That will save the page from the Net right into your Web.

Tip

It is illegal to steal the work of others from the Web. Most people don't realize that copying entire Webs, individual Web pages, or even single graphic images from other people's sites could constitute copyright infringement. Make sure you have the proper permissions and authority before you start copying any part of other people's work from the Web, especially if you intend to use the works in your own pages.

FIGURE 10-8

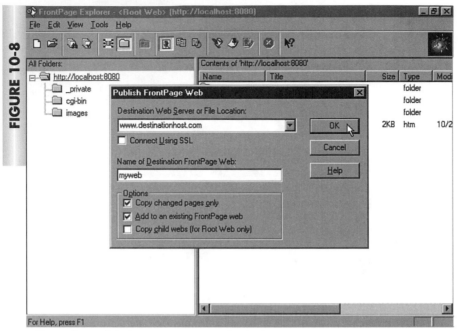

Fill out the Publish FrontPage Web dialog

Lesson 4: Copying Entire Webs

If you have access to a host that has the FrontPage extensions installed, you can copy the entire Web from that host and move it to another host. This is very convenient if your company is adding new servers for its intranets or for moving Webs from one Internet host to another should you change providers. To do this, first open a Web with the FrontPage Explorer as described in Lesson 1. Then select File from the Explorer menu bar and choose Publish FrontPage Web.

This will cause a Publish FrontPage Web dialog to appear, as shown in Figure 10-8. In the Destination Web Server text area, you enter the name of the host to which you wish to copy the Web. The Name of Destination FrontPage Web text area is what you'd like to call the copied Web. This name does not have to be the same as the source Web. If you want to add the contents of this Web to an existing Web, just select the Add to an Existing FrontPage Web option. If the Web you are publishing from is the root Web, you also have the option of copying all of its child Webs as well. When you have entered the appropriate information, click the OK button.

FrontPage will then begin copying materials from the source Web to the destination you specified. Both the source and destination must have the FrontPage Server Extensions installed. When the Web publishing is finished, FrontPage will display a dialog notifying you that the task is completed.

If the source Web you wish to copy from is on a site that does not have the FrontPage extensions installed or you do not have access to that Web, you'll have to copy each page individually, as described in Lesson 3. Once you've copied all the pages, you may need to fix their links so they'll function properly. Additionally, you should keep in mind that FrontPage will not grab things such as CGI scripts or other items it does not readily recognize. You'll have to import those manually, which may not be possible through normal means. Also, many CGI scripts probably won't work. After all, CGI scripts are often made to run on a specific platform, and odds are your platform isn't the same as the one from which the script is coming.

Where to Go from Here?

You know how to move about the Web, understand how to use FrontPage to do it, and even know how to extract information from valuable sites. You should have no problem importing pages from the Web so that you can learn the tricks of the trade right from the source.

Summary

You've learned quite a few tricks for FrontPage in this chapter. You've learned the fundamentals of Web browsing, and you should feel comfortable with the basic browsing abilities of the FrontPage client software. With this in hand, you should be ready to create your Web masterpieces.

Multimedia

In this chapter you will learn:

Displaying Images
Inline Images
Image Formats
Transparent GIF Images
Lossy Compression
Background Images
Sound Files

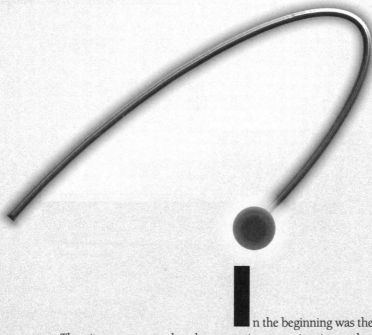

n the beginning was the word, and the word was *text*. Then it came to pass that there were *images*, *animation*, and *sound*, and the people said, "This is good."

Multimedia is a general catchall name that covers the variety of ways information can be presented. Ideally, multimedia is information that is communicated in ways that appeal to your five senses:

◁ Sight

◁ Hearing

◁ Touch

◁ Smell

◁ Taste

In olden days, when handwritten or typed text was king, multimedia was only a twinkle in a handful of inventors' eyes. Then came radio, silent movies, talkies, and television. In the 1960s a Hollywood producer introduced Smell-O-Vision, where smells that corresponded to particular movies were piped into theaters. Though this concept was foul smelling to theater goers, the spirit of multimedia lived on until it found a niche in which it was limited only by the imagination—personal computers.

Computerized multimedia using color, images, audio, and video has vastly improved the interface between machine and user. Multimedia entertains, but it also helps users understand and communicate information more efficiently. Common multimedia tools found in today's PCs include compact discs (CD-ROMs), sound cards, speakers, and motion video cards.

The Internet, the World Wide Web (WWW or Web) in particular, provides a multitude of tools that appeal to the senses, including still and moving graphics, audio, and hyperlinks. This multimedia capability allows companies and individuals to have full-color, dynamic Web pages with worldwide exposure. You, too, can be a part of this cyberspace rainbow if you use FrontPage to create your Web page.

Multimedia on the Web

The main multimedia tools used on the WWW are images and sound. You can use multimedia to add features such as

- Logos
- Buttons
- Photos and drawings
- Graphs and charts
- Signatures
- Sound bytes
- Movies (and animation)

If you can see it or say it, you can add it to your Web site. However, graphics and sound are memory hogs, so use them wisely. The large amounts of memory these features need make fast transmission a must, but some users may have slow computers or slow modems. The more features you add, the more users on the other side of the Web may have to wait to download your Web page.

Graphics

Graphics are saved in files in your computer. These files can have many different types of formats. Each graphic format was created for a specific purpose, such as good color retention or compression capability. Users choose particular formats depending on their needs and wants. The Web generally uses two formats: GIF and JPEG. FrontPage handles both of these formats with ease.

GIF

GIF stands for Graphical Interchange Format and is pronounced like "Jiff" or "Giff" (the pronunciation is the subject of much debate at parties). GIF was originally developed by CompuServe to allow users to exchange pictures online, but it is now the standard format for most images on the Web. The GIF format has a special compression feature that allows it to be reduced for fast transfer. Compression is the "squeezing" of data into a size that can be conveniently stored in your computer. GIF's compression is *lossless*, that is, you don't lose any of the original image when compression takes place. GIF has an 8-bit color format that allows for 256 colors. Because of the limited number of colors, GIF is not the best format to use for photos, but can be used for

- ◁ Drawings
- ◁ Icons
- ◁ Lines, bars, and edges
- ◁ Cartoons
- ◁ Buttons and bullets

Note

GIF is one of the most widely used image formats on the Web. It can store both inline and external images. If you're unsure of which format to use, choose GIF.

JPEG

JPEG, pronounced "jay-peg," stands for Joint Photographic Experts Group. This is a very flexible format that is excellent for multicolor images that need to be compressed. JPEG images use a *lossy* compression algorithm that loses a portion of the data to make it more compressible. Usually, you don't notice the loss unless the image is compressed and decompressed several times. JPEG has a 24-bit color format that can handle a wide variety of colors and hues (up to 16,777,216), thus it is good for detailed, realistic images. JPEG is often used to store the following graphics:

- ◁ Photographs of nature
- ◁ Multicolored images of people and animals
- ◁ Large images

Working with Images

Images are a key element in presenting information on the Web, thus FrontPage makes it easy to include them in your Web page. Table 11-1 shows the types of image files that FrontPage can translate into either GIF or JPEG files. When adding graphics to your home page, you will probably need an editing tool to make adjustments such as changing the size, color, or format; cropping; or rotating your images. These adjustments will give your home page an appealing, professional look.

Table 11-1 Types of image files FrontPage can translate into GIF or JPEG

Format	File Extension
GIF	`.gif`
JPEG	`.jpg, .jff`
Windows & OS/2 BMP	`.bmp`
TIFF	`.tif`
Microsoft Paint	`.msp`
Window Metafile	`.wmf`
SUN Raster	`.ras`
WordPerfect	`.wpg`
Encapsulated PostScript	`.eps`
PCX	`.pcx`
Targa	`.tga`

Lesson 1: Getting Started in Multimedia

This lesson lets you know what you need to get started in multimedia. It is important to be familiar with what kinds of hardware and software are necessary to participate in the cyberworld of images and sound.

Images and audio are two very distinct areas in multimedia. Much time and energy in the development of the computer has been devoted to visual interfaces. This is due to the fact that the traditional form of input is typing, which creates a visual picture. Therefore, your system is probably able to handle images in a wide range of colors and to have software to manipulate images and display them quickly.

Sound is a relatively new direction for computers. Personal computers today can emit a variety of sounds, use voice commands, and some can even take dictation. These new developments are blazing new and exciting trails into multimedia.

Hardware

To use many of the latest features of image processing, you need a good video card with its own memory. More memory usually means a faster display and the capability to display more colors. Most systems have some type of video card, the only variable being its memory size.

To develop and use sound, you need a sound card, which not many people have at this time. This should be a hint to you about how much sound you should use in your Web page. If you have a sound card or plan on getting one, most cards will allow you to hook up head phones and speakers, as well as input sound from a microphone (you can create your own message this way).

To input your own photographs, you will usually need a scanner. Scanners come in several styles, including hand held and flat bed. Invariably, scanners come with software that stores the images. If you don't have a scanner, don't worry about getting one. Usually you can have pictures scanned in at your local copy center for about $10.00 per photo. If you want your image sized, the copy center will often do this at no extra cost. Be sure to ask the copy center to put your image in a format you can use. The JPEG format is recommended for photos.

Storing Files

New users may fall victim to the "I know it's here somewhere" phenomenon, when you create and store a file somewhere, then forget where you put it. It is recommended that you create specific folders for various types of files. For example, develop a folder called `images` and place all your images in this folder. (If you use sound, create an `audio` folder.) If you collect lots of images, create folders within your main folder. This way, whenever you need to search for an image, you'll know exactly where to start, for example, `c:\images\`.

Searching for Files

If you've searched through all the appropriate folders and still can't find a certain file, you need to know how to do a search of your system. You need to have a utility such as a *whereis* program, where you type in the name of the file you are looking for. If you have Windows 95, familiarize yourself with the Find utility that comes up in a menu after you click Start.

If you really want to test your searching prowess, tell a friend to hide a file anywhere on the computer and you, then, try to find it. With the Find utility, you need only a part of the name. Use an asterisk (*) to represent anything at all. For example, if you are looking for `surfing.jpg`, you need only type in `surf*.*`.

Lesson 2: The Image Toolbar

The Image toolbar, as shown in Figure 11-1, allows you to create hotspots with a click of a button. This lesson explains the icons in the Image tool bar.

1. The first button in the Image tool bar has an arrow on it, and is highlighted when an image is selected.

2. The second button is a rectangle, and allows you to draw a rectangular hotspot. Click on this button, then draw a retangular hotspot in your Web page (see Lesson 9 in this chapter).

3. The third button is a circle, and allows you to draw a circular hotspot.

4. The fourth button is a rectangle with an arrow, and indicates the location of a hotspot in an image. Select the image, then click on this button. If there is a hotspot in the image, it will be shown as a circle.

5. The fifth button has a pencil in it, and allows you to make images transparent (see Lesson 5 in this chapter).

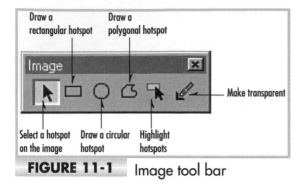

FIGURE 11-1 Image tool bar

Lesson 3: Inline Images in Your Home Page

Web browsers can translate two kinds of images: *inline images* and *external images*. Inline images are embedded directly into your Web page and are displayed when your page is displayed. Most browsers can now display inline images in both GIF and JPEG formats.

External images are not directly displayed in your Web page. They are usually on the other end of a link and can be downloaded by users. When incorporating external images into your Web page, you have a greater variety of image formats to choose from, such as JPEG and PCX.

The obvious question is: Where do images come from? Images can be your own drawings or artwork you scan in. You can also get images from a clip art package, or you can scan in personal photos.

 Tip

Beware of scanning pictures or photos that may be copyrighted. You might need permission from the owners of certain images to use them. The safest way is to use your own images or to use royalty-free clip art.

The FrontPage Editor makes inserting inline images into your Web page a simple process. If your image is ready to be displayed (if not, see Lesson 1) and is in your computer, take the following steps:

1. Click on Insert | Image. This brings up the Image dialog box. See Figure 11-2.

2. In the Other Location tab, click on the From File button, then click on Browse. This brings up another Image dialog box.

3. From the File of type window, use the down arrow to obtain the list of file types. Select your image format type (for example, if your image is in JPEG, select GIF and JPEG). See Figure 11-3.

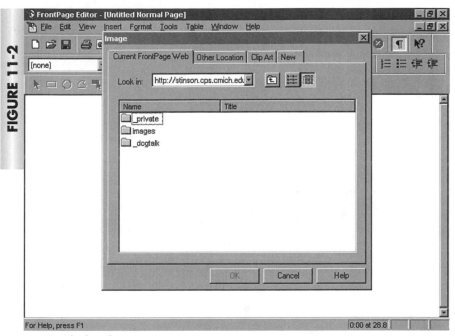

Image dialog box

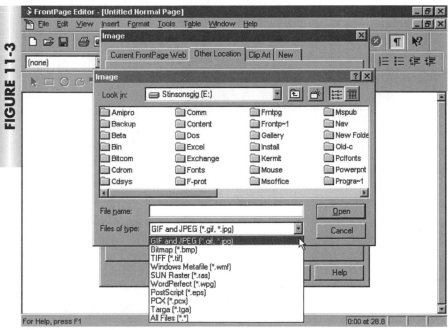

File of type menu

4. Double-click on your system (in Windows 95, this will be My Computer). This brings up a list of your drives.

5. Double-click on the drive where the image is located, then click on any folder where it might be located.

6. Click on the file. Its name will appear in the File name box. See Figure 11-4.

7. Click on Open. Your image will now be displayed in your home page next to the cursor (this is called the *insertion point*). See Figure 11-5 for an example of an image in a Web page.

FIGURE 11-4

Selecting a file

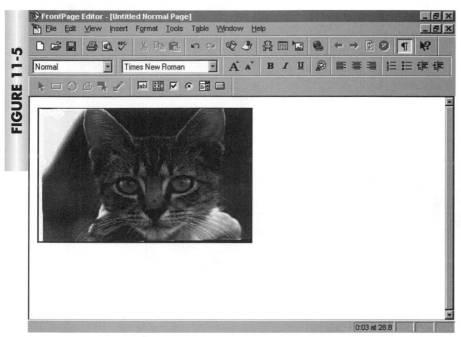

FIGURE 11-5

An image in a Web page

Lesson 4: Text Alternatives

Some users have browsers that do not display images. For these people, you need to provide an alternative to an image, such as a line of text. For example, if you are displaying an image of your cat, you might use the simple message, **Our Cat** or **A Picture of Our Cat Pip**. FrontPage allows you to insert this alternative feature in the following steps:

1. Click on your image.

2. Click on Edit | Image Properties. This will bring up the Image Properties dialog box.

3. Select the General tab. In the area called Alternative Representations, in the box labeled Text, type A great picture of our cat Pip. Figure 11-6 shows the filled-out Image Properties dialog box.

4. Click OK to exit the Image Properties dialog box.

This text will now be displayed for users with nongraphical browsers. You will not see this in your home page, but it will be in the code of the HTML document (to check your HTML document code, select View|HTML from your page in FP Editor).

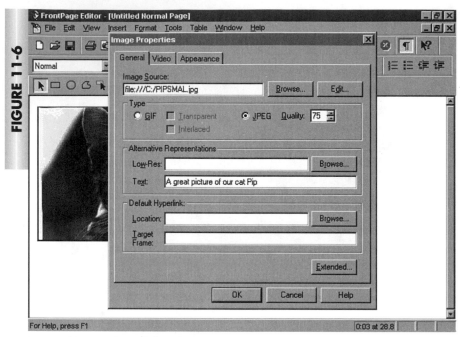

FIGURE 11-6

Image Properties dialog box

Lesson 5: Image Formats

There are two broad categories of image formats: *bit map* and *vector*. Bit-mapped images are the most common and include the GIF and JPEG formats. The bit-map format builds an image point by point. These points of light are called *pixels*. An image is built one pixel at a time, with parallel lines of pixels.

Vector graphics are built by constructing lines. This type of format is mostly used in computer-aided design and manufacturing of boats, cars, and planes. The bit-map format is emphasized here because it can be used for images such as photographs and sketches.

The bit-map format builds images one pixel at a time. Pixels have three basic characteristics: color type, bits per pixel, and compression type.

Color

The primary colors are red, blue, and green. Other colors are formed by mixing together these colors. Generally, you can mix red, green, and blue (RGB) to form most any color you desire, the question being how much of each color you need. Your television works on the same principle. If you put a few drops of water on your TV screen, you will see the three separate colors.

Bits per Pixel

How many colors can you form? This question is answered by the bits per pixel. Bits are individual values that can be either 0 or 1. One bit per pixel gives you two choices (usually black or white). Two bits per pixel gives you four choices (00, 01, 10, and 11). The more bits, the more color choices you have. If you have a choice of eight colors, you have three bits per pixel and these choices: 000, 001, 010, 011, 100, 101, 110, and 111. In the GIF format, you have 256 choices and eight bits per pixel. Other formats such as JPEG require many more bits.

Note

Usually, the more bits per pixel you have, the more of a memory hog your image will be.

Compression

Your computer uses different types of compression to help save space and time when transferring files across cyberspace. There are two basic types of compression: lossless and lossy. Lossless means no data is lost in the compression. GIF files have this type of compression. Lossy is a compression used by JPEG files that decreases size and speeds up the display, but some information is lost (usually this is not noticeable; see Lesson 7).

Two other methods of compression are *run-length* and *LZW*. Run-length simply compresses information such as RRRRR to 5R. LZW stands for Lempel-Ziv & Welch, and is a well-known method that GIF and other files use.

Table 11-2 names some common file formats and the image format, kind of color, maximum size, and compression method for each.

Table 11-2 Common graphic formats and their characteristics

Format	Type	Color	Bits per Pixel	Compression
PCX	Bit map	RGB	Up to 24	Run-length
DXF	Vector	Color table, unrelated to standard models	Up to 24 N/A	N/A
GIF	Bit map	RGB	Up to 24	LZW
PostScript	Metafile	RGB & CMYK	Up to 32	N/A

continued on next page

continued from previous page

Format	Type	Color	Bits per Pixel	Compression
TIFF	Bit map	CMYK & YCbCr (an RGB reconstruction with intensity values)	16	LZW
Windows	Bit map	RGB	1, 4, 8, or 24	Run-length

Tip

If you can't remember where your image file is, most systems have software to help you find it. For example, Windows 95 has a Find feature that is activated from the Start button. If you then choose Files and Folders, you can type in the name of your image (or something close to it) and its location will be displayed.

Lesson 6: Transparent GIF Files with Icons

One advantage of GIF-formatted files is the option of making them *transparent*. Transparent GIF files are files with a specifically chosen background color that is the same as the background of the HTML file. This makes the GIF image appear transparent and it becomes known as a *transparent image*. The image isn't literally transparent; the image now has one color that allows the background to be displayed. You can use this technique in interesting ways, especially if you have a patterned background.

FrontPage allows you to use transparent GIF files with a click of a button (or two). This makes icons, buttons, and other simple graphics much more attractive. To demonstrate this feature, use the **underconstruction** GIF file that comes with FrontPage (this assumes that you have installed FrontPage in the C drive):

1. Obtain the **Undercon.gif** image with the search technique described in Lesson 1, or try this:

   a. Click on Insert | Image. This brings up the Image dialog box.

   b. Click on the Clip Art tab.

   c. In the Category box, use the down arrow and choose Misc.

   d. Click on the underconstruction image. This will place the image at the insertion point on your page. Figure 11-7 shows the image.

2. Use the above method to place another **Undercon.gif** image next to the first one.

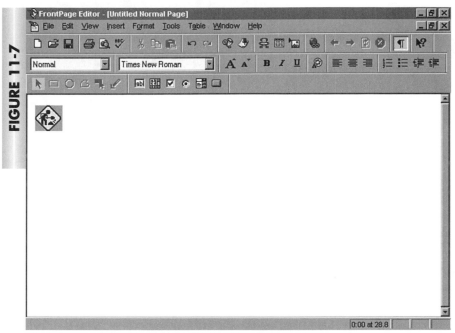

FIGURE 11-7

The `Undercon.gif` image

3. Click on the second image. This highlights and activates the Image tool bar. Figure 11-1 shows the Image tool bar.

4. Click on the pencil image in the Image tool bar. This will now turn your pointer into a pencil as you move over the second image.

5. Use the small arrow next to the eraser to select the color that will be transparent, then click to activate. Figure 11-8 shows the original image and the transparent image.

As you can see, the white background of the second image has been changed to the grey background of your home page. Figure 11-9 shows how this technique works with a sketch.

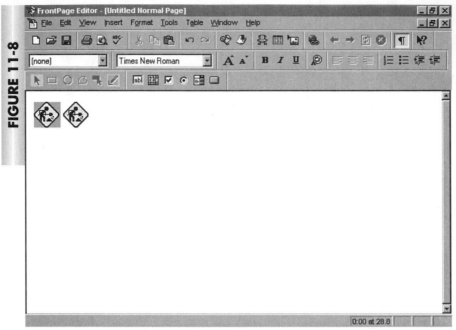

Original image and transparent image of `Undercon.gif`

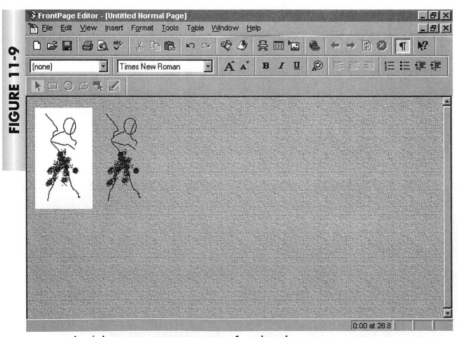

Original and transparent image of a sketch

Lesson 7: Lossy Compression

Sooner or later, all your disk space will be used up by whatever data you have on your computer. This is known as the Law of Expanding Data. The data on your computer disk will require a much larger disk, even if you don't add more data. A temporary solution to the overflow of data on your disk is to compress the data files.

Compression is good for a number of reasons, including reduced storage and faster transmission. But compression is not without a cost. Files that must be compressed must then be decompressed to use them. This process requires time and a special compression program. You may find that there is not enough space left on your drive for a compression program.

You read earlier about lossless and lossy, the two types of compression. Lossless compression simply squeezes some data in the file. For example, KKKKKKK is written as 7K. No information is lost, and the original seven Ks can be obtained by decompressing the 7K. Lossless is designed so that the entire file can be completely restored. On the other hand, lossy compression eliminates the stuff it thinks you can do without. In most cases, if the file isn't compressed too much, lossy provides excellent results. If lossy is used incorrectly, or if it compresses an image file too much, it might ruin your image.

Figure 11-10 has three images contained in it. The first is a JPG file of the Wawa Canada Goose in Ontario, reduced from a larger file to about 220×221 pixels. The middle picture is a compressed version of this image (50×50 pixels). Somehow, 53,460 pixels have been reduced to 2,650 pixels. Information obviously has been lost. This smaller image was then decompressed back to the 220×243-pixel image, as shown in the third image. In the

FIGURE 11-10

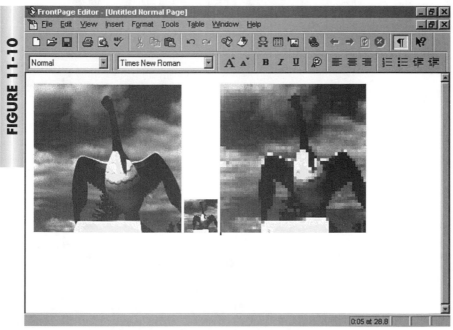

The Wawa Ontario Goose—an example of lossy compression

third image, notice the data that has been lost in this process. The third image is the same size as the original, but it is not as clear and crisp. This is lossy compression. If the original image had not been compressed as much as it was, you probably wouldn't be able to detect a difference between the original and restored images.

Lesson 8: Thumbnails and Alternate Images

Thumbnail images received their name due to their relatively small thumbnail size. These smaller images have two purposes. One is to give an indication of a larger image or other document stored elsewhere, and the other is to preview a larger image as it is being downloaded. Figure 11-11 shows examples of three thumbnail images.

Creating Smaller Images: The Height and Width Attribute

There are two ways to create smaller images. One way is to create and store a smaller image when you create and store the original larger image. If you have an image of 600×800 pixels, you can make an image that is 100×133 pixels as a thumbnail. Notice that the ratio of height to width is maintained. Resizing the original image is accomplished quite easily with most image-handling programs.

FIGURE 11-11

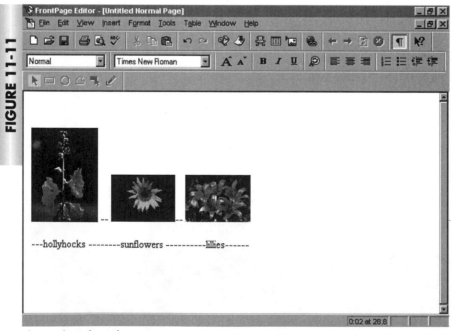

Three thumbnail images

The other method of creating smaller images is to insert HTML into your home page. This information tells the browser to shrink the image into a smaller area. To resize an image using HTML, do the following:

1. In your home page, move the cursor to the insertion point.

2. Click on Insert | HTML Markup. This brings up the HTML Markup dialog box. You can type any legal HTML code here.

3. Type `<img src="images/apicture.gif" width=100 height=133>`. This is an HTML command that allows you to display your image (`apicture.gif`) with the additional width and height attributes.

4. Click on OK to exit the Insert Bot Properties dialog box.

Alternate Images

When visitors to a Web site have to wait for long periods of time while images are downloaded, they tend to get impatient and move on to another Web site. To entice them to wait, you can tease them with a thumbnail image until the original image can be downloaded.

1. In your home page, place the cursor on your original image, then click the right mouse button. This brings up a drop-down menu.

2. Click on Image Properties. This brings up the Image Properties dialog box.

3. In the Alternate Representations box, type the path (address) to your thumbnail image into the Low-Res field.

4. Click on OK to exit the Image Properties dialog box.

 Tip

Some thumbnail images may be too small to be recognized by viewers. Keep this in mind when you create them.

Lesson 9: Speed Up Your Graphics

You may be tempted to add too many large graphics or images to your Web page. Too many graphics and images will make downloading your page very slow, and may cause your Web site visitors to hit the Stop button and move on to faster pastures. The following tips will help you make your Web page visitor-friendly:

◁ Make your images as small as possible.

◁ Use alternate images (Lesson 7).

◁ Use interlaced GIF files.

An interlaced GIF file originally appears with very poor resolution that improves as the entire image is received. This allows the visitor to get the basic image and decide to move on or wait for the rest of the image to be loaded. FrontPage allows you to store any GIF or JPEG file as an interlaced GIF file by choosing this as an option using `Edit:Properties` on an image and choosing `Interlaced`.

What does it mean to make your image as small as possible? Although you might like seeing a half-page image, a passport-size image may be enough to convey meaning to visitors. On the other hand, a piece of art may require an entire screen or more because of its detail. In the end, you have to use your own judgment.

Lesson 10: Clickable Images as Links

One of the most interesting ways to link your Web pages together is to use images as links from one page to another. *Clickable images* are easily created in FrontPage. Your job is to think of creative ways to use them.

Assume you have decided to sell your prize pitbull as a guard dog. Because he is well trained and from a long line of champion vicious guard dogs, you have written a résumé page for him. The bait to get visitors to read about the beast is simply a photo you have scanned in and placed in one of your Web pages. You have your pitbull résumé in a file called `pitres.htm`. To link the résumé to the picture, take the following steps:

1. Click on the image. This will activate the Image tool bar. Notice that the corners of the image have changed color. The corners are now called *handles*.

2. Click on the rectangle button in the Image tool bar. You will use the rectangle to make the entire image a hot spot.

3. Move your cursor inside the image. Notice that the cursor becomes a pencil.

4. Move the pencil to the upper-left corner of the image.

5. Click and hold down the left mouse button. Drag the newly created rectangle across the image to the bottom-right handle. See Figure 11-12.

6. Release the mouse button. The Create Hyperlink dialog box will appear.

7. Click on the Current FrontPage Web tab.

8. In the Page box, select `pitres.htm` and click OK. Figure 11-13 shows the Current FrontPage Web tab of the Create Hyperlink dialog box.

9. Click OK to exit the Create Hyperlink dialog box.

Now anyone wanting information about this killing machine can click on the image and go to the résumé page.

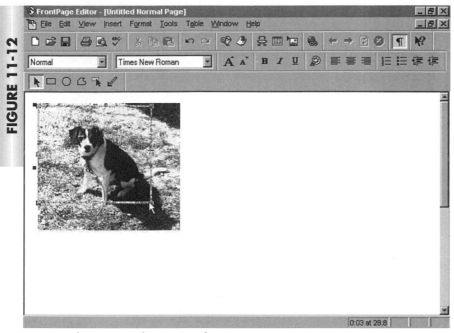

Moving the rectangle across the image

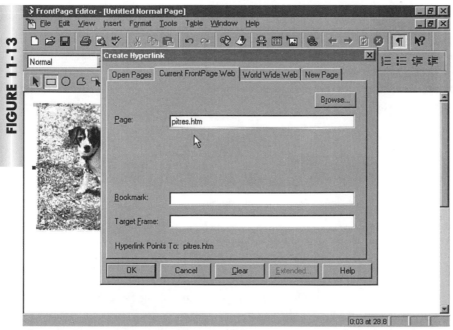

The Current FrontPage Web tab of the Create Hyperlink dialog box

Lesson 11: Background Image for Effect

You might have seen Web sites with background colors and styles that add just the right touch. If you would like your page to have such a design element, you need to look to the Web for an array of patterns and colors, ranging from metallic blue to satin orange. Search the Web for background images. A large number of background images can be found on the Internet by searching with the words **background** and **image** (this is done on many search engines by **background&&image**). You are not restricted by FrontPage; you can download any image from the Web to your computer and use it as a background.

FrontPage 97 has a number of background images available in Clip Art. To add one of these as your background, take the following steps:

1. Click on File | Page Properties.

2. Choose the Background tab.

3. Select the Background Image check box, then click on Browse. This will bring up the Select Background Image dialog box.

4. Click on the Clip Art tab. The background category will be the default.

5. Choose your background from the variety of backgrounds displayed.

6. Click OK to exit the dialog boxes.

Lesson 12: Aligning Text with Images

FrontPage provides many different ways to align your images with your text. Much of this is subjective. Sometimes you will need to try several different ways of aligning your image before you hit on the right one. To align your images, first click on the image, then select Edit | Image Properties. This brings up the Image Properties dialog box. Choose the Appearance tab. Types of inline image alignments are described below and shown in Figure 11-14.

◁ Top: Aligns the top of the image with the top edge of the tallest element (text, image, and so on) in the line.

◁ Texttop: Very similar to top except that the image is aligned with the tallest text element in the line. When the line contains only text, texttop and top are the same.

◁ Middle: Aligns the middle of the image with the baseline of the text. The baseline of the text is the line that the letters rest on.

◁ Absmiddle: Aligns the middle of the image with the absolute middle of the text. This is unlike middle, which aligns the image with the baseline of text, which is lower than the absolute middle of the text.

◁ Bottom: Aligns the bottom of the image with the baseline of the text. In Figure 11-14, notice that the letter p hangs down below the bottom of the image, and so will y and q.

◁ Absbottom: Aligns the absolute bottom of the image with the absolute bottom of the text. The bottom of the image will line up with the bottom of g, j, p, q, or y, again as demonstrated by the letter p. However, if you do not use any of these letters, bottom and absbottom will be exactly the same.

◁ Left: Shifts image to the left margin.

◁ Right: Shifts image to the right margin.

 Tip

For aligning icons or special symbols, use top or middle. For general alignment of images, most people prefer bottom.

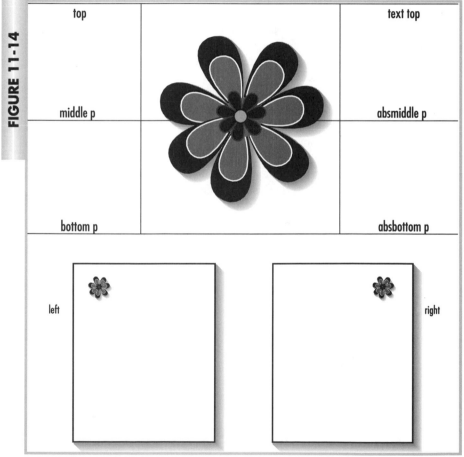

FIGURE 11-14

top   text top

middle p   absmiddle p

bottom p   absbottom p

left   right

Types of alignment

Lesson 13: Audio on Demand

Audio on demand is the solution to the problem of having to wait to download an entire audio file before you can hear it. A new technique of continuous delivery called *streaming* (also called *near-real time*) allows you to listen to sound almost instantly.

Streaming starts the playback of sound after a short buffering period, then plays the entire audio clip to the end. *Buffering* is a technique that stores a few seconds of sound from the file and uses that few seconds to overcome any delay in the transmission of the rest of the file. This allows the sound to be heard soon after it is accessed. This means visitors to your site will be less bored and therefore less inclined to click to the next site.

Why is transmitting sound so slow and difficult? Remember that your 28.8 kbps modem has a throughput (actual data transfer rate) of 3.6 kilobytes (3.6 K) per second on the fastest modems today. This is approximately one-fiftieth the speed of a single-spin compact disc (CD-ROM) drive. Therefore, to achieve CD-ROM quality sound in real time, you must speed up your transfer rate by 50. This is not possible in the foreseeable future, so another approach is needed.

One method used to speed up the transmission of sound is also used for images—compression. You may remember the commercial on television where the man talks very fast. This is a form of audio compression. All the current technologies for streaming audio use a system known as *codecs* (coder/decoders). This system includes a compression part known as an *encoder* and a decompression part known as a *decoder*. The decoder also plays the audio portion at the receiving end (see Figure 11-15).

Codecs uses the lossy compression technique. This is similar to the lossy compression JPEG uses for images. Lossy does not compress by simply throwing away information, but it throws away things that are fairly similar to other things. This might not work well for an orchestra playing classical music, but for your favorite heavy metal group, "The Blaring Head Wounds," it might work just fine. In this lossy technique, the more you need to compress something, the more similar its components appear.

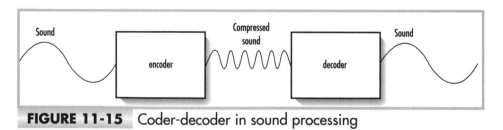

FIGURE 11-15 Coder-decoder in sound processing

Lesson 14: Audio

Although sound adds an exciting dimension to your home page, it slows it down. Audio is a memory-hog. It is large in file size and slow to download.

Most browsers deal with audio as a separate document that uses special applications to run. Therefore, it would not be practical to go through every new type of applet that supports audio.

Internet Explorer supports a special HTML tag that can be used in your FrontPage document. The tag is `<BGSOUND>`. Other browsers such as Netscape simply ignore this tag. To use this tag, you must first develop a `.wav` file that contains your audio message. Suppose you have chosen a message such as `Hello World`. You place it in the file `hworld.wav` in the folder C: audio using a microphone and a sound card.

1. Place your cursor in your Web page.

2. Select Insert | Background Sound. This brings up the Background Sound dialog box.

3. Select the Other Location tab, then click on Browse. This brings up another Background Sound dialog box.

4. Select `My Computer` in the Look in window.

5. Select drive C, then choose the audio folder.

6. Select the `hworld.wav` file, then click Open.

7. In your page, click on the right mouse button, then choose Page Properties from the drop-down menu. This brings up the Page Properties dialog box.

8. In the General tab, in the Background Sound section, increase the Loop size to 2. This will set your sound file `hworld.wav` to play 2 times. Figure 11-16 shows the Page Properties dialog box.

9. Click on OK to exit the Page Properties dialog box. You have now added sound to your Web page.

This approach should be tested by running your browser on a local file and listening to the sounds using your headphones or speakers. You can run a local Web by starting your browser and typing `file:/yourWebname`. This will ensure success when your Web is visited by others.

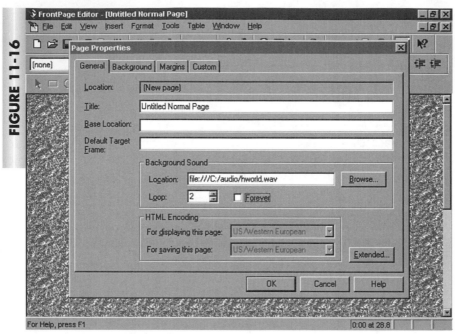

FIGURE 11-16

Page Properties dialog box

Lesson 15: Adding Horizontal Lines Near Images

A great way to set images apart from text is to insert horizontal lines between them. This is another visitor-friendly technique that helps viewers delineate one area from another. Plus, it looks good.

FrontPage allows the inclusion of horizontal lines of various widths, alignments, and thicknesses. To insert a horizontal line, follow these steps:

1. Move the cursor to the insertion point (where you want the line to be).

2. Click on Insert | Horizontal line.

If you wish to change the properties of your line, follow these steps:

1. Place your cursor on the line and click, then select Edit | Horizontal Line Properties. Click on the right mouse botton. This brings up the Horizontal Line Properties dialog box. The parameters you can set are

◁ Width

Percent of Window (0-100%); 100% is the default.

Pixels (specific width based on number of pixels)

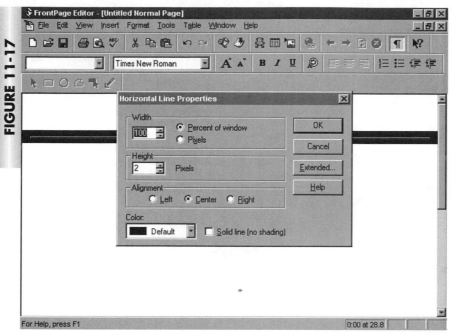

FIGURE 11-17

Horizontal Line Properties dialog box

◁ Height (by pixels); 2 pixels is the default.

◁ Alignment

Left (left-justified)

Center (center-justified); this is the default.

Right (right-justified)

◁ Color (select from a color palette or accept black, the default)

◁ Solid line or shading (shading makes it appear three dimensional; shading is the default)

Figure 11-17 shows the Horizontal Line Properties dialog box.

2. After choosing how you would like your line to appear, click on OK. If you don't like the way it looks, go back to the Horizontal Line Properties dialog box.

Summary

Multimedia was created, and multimedia is good. Multimedia adds tremendous potential to the world of the Web. A few notes of caution: You might have recently purchased a new and fast computer that outperforms 99 percent of all machines that currently reside on the

Web. Although this is a great tool, remember that you develop Web pages not only to please yourself but also to attract an audience. If 99 percent of Web users do not have your speed or display capabilities, then you should develop your pages to accommodate the slower pace of those users. Some Web developers have special pages with features that many browsers are unable to display. Therefore, you should concentrate on making your pages as interesting as possible for the masses, and store your slick ideas until you can use them effectively.

A FrontPage Project

In this chapter you will learn:

To Organize a Web Project
To Create and Develop a Web in FrontPage
To Edit Web Pages
About User Registration Forms
To Link Webs and Web Pages
About Bookmarks

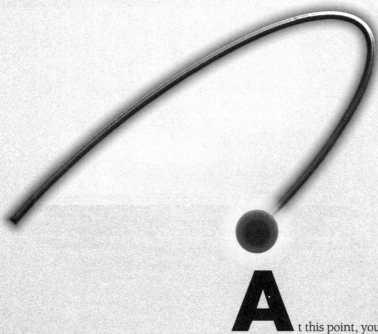

At this point, you have learned quite a bit about all the things FrontPage can do and how it can be an indispensable tool in helping you create a stunning Web site. If you still have doubts about the ease of use and quality of FrontPage, this chapter is sure to change your mind. If you're already sold on FrontPage, get ready to learn more about it. This chapter contains new and exciting lessons.

This chapter gives you a view of the big picture. It is your step-by-step guide for planning and creating a Web project. Along with a detailed explanation of each step, you will be looking over the shoulders of three friends who have decided to create a magazine for display on the World Wide Web (WWW or the Web). Their work will be shown to give you a real-world example of how a Web site is developed.

Steve and Jane are avid gardeners who would like to have a gardening magazine on the Web. They know a lot about plants, but little about the creation of a Web site. Luckily, their friend Ned is an ardent Web surfer and owns a copy of FrontPage. Steve and Jane decide to make Ned a partner in their project if he will help with the technical end of it. Ned enthusiastically accepts, and the project is a go. But before Ned can start his work on the Web site, the three partners have a meeting to discuss aspects of the project, such as the mission statement, roles and responsibilities, magazine layout, and Web structure. Steve puts together the following agenda for this organizational meeting.

Project Organization Agenda

1. Mission statement

2. Roles and responsibilities of members

3. General aspects of the project

4. Structure and look of the project

5. Specific aspects of the project (links, discussion groups, and so forth)

6. Web structure

1. Mission Statement

A mission statement lists the goal or goals of a particular project. It is a must for undertakings that involve more than one person because although each partner has his or her own project duties, each should keep in mind the common thread that holds all partners together. A mission statement should be as specific and to the point as possible. A sentence or a short paragraph is usually all that is needed to define the particular objectives of the activity.

During the organizational meeting, the three partners discuss alternative mission statements. Steve wants this one:

"The purpose of this project is to create an interesting gardening magazine that will be offered on the WWW."

This statement is true, but a bit too general and vague. Ned's mission statement is as follows:

"The purpose of this project is to attract Web surfer-gardeners to a Web site that offers a gardening magazine."

This statement is true also, but still not specific enough. Jane combines the first two ideas, then adds some details:

"The purpose of this project is to create an interactive gardening magazine that will be offered on the WWW. The magazine will have regular and feature articles on particular plants, as well as a page where subscribers can ask an expert their gardening questions."

Everyone agrees to adopt the last statement but to leave it open to modifications as the project evolves.

2. Roles and Responsibilities

Members of a group project need to know exactly what is expected of them. If they have no direction, they tend to feel lost and frustrated, and this leads to low productivity. Even a general directive such as "Let's get this project done" is of little value because members need to understand *how* the project will be done and *who* will do *what*. To help keep morale and productivity high, each member needs his or her own list of responsibilities, coupled with a schedule of when each task should be done.

Jane, Steve, and Ned list their roles and responsibilities as follows:

Jane's role: Gardening writer; responsible for writing regular articles of the magazine—"Perennial of the Month" and "Amazing Annuals"—as well as answering subscribers' questions to Miss Greenthumb. All articles for a particular month will be due on the 20th day of the previous month. Initially, Jane will work with Steve and Ned during the Web-building process.

Steve's role: Gardening writer; responsible for writing two feature articles per month and managing letters to the editors. All articles for a particular month will be due on the 20th day of the previous month. Initially, Steve will work with Jane and Ned during the Web-building process.

Ned's role: Technical coordinator; responsible for creating and maintaining all technical aspects of the Web and Web site. This will include interfacing with the ISP. He will also insert finished articles into the Web each month and will manage the "Letters to the Editor" section. Ned will have one month to build the Web and will work closely with Jane and Steve during this time.

3. General Aspects of the Project

Discussing the general aspects of a project helps bring the overall project into focus. The general aspects include broad details about what the project is all about and a timetable for the initial start-up, as well as any ongoing work. When creating any project, it is best to go from the general to the specific. In other words, first look at the forest, then look at the trees.

Steve takes the following notes during the general discussion of their project:

◁ A monthly gardening magazine offered on the Web

◁ Approximately 10 pages

◁ A page with a form for "Ask Miss Greenthumb"

◁ Regular articles: "Comments to the Editor," "Perennial of the Month," "Amazing Annuals," and "Miss Greenthumb Answers"

◁ Two feature articles per month, such as "Edible Plants" and "What Plants Attract Butterflies to Your Garden"

◁ Ned will have one month to build the Web and set up the Web site. Steve and Jane will work with him during this month, then will have two additional weeks to perfect their articles for the first issue.

◁ Articles for a particular month will be given to Ned no later than the 20th of the month prior to publication.

4. Structure and Look of the Project

The structure and look of a project define certain structural and design elements that will be uniform throughout the project. These elements include page numbers, page color, page background texture, link colors, heading sizes, font, headers, footers, and horizontal lines. A uniform, regular structure must be maintained to present a professional-looking project.

After discussing the various alternatives for the structure and look of their Web magazine, Steve, Jane, and Ned decide on the following elements:

◁ Link colors: blue for unused links; purple for used links

◁ Heading size: heading 2 in drop-down Format menu

◁ Font: 10

◁ Type style: Times

◁ Page color: Gray

◁ No page numbers

◁ No headers or footers

5. Specific Aspects of the Project

Whereas general aspects broadly define a project, specific aspects go one step further and focus on particular details. This process forces project members to think about the elements of a project and exactly how the project will be accomplished. The more specific these details get, the better. For a Web magazine, the content of the magazine as well as aspects of the Web should be discussed at this time.

At the organizational meeting, Jane and Steve come up with a list of things they want to include in the gardening magazine:

◁ Letters to the editors

◁ Regular article: "Amazing Annuals"

◁ Regular article: "Perennial of the Month"

◁ Page with form: "Ask Miss Greenthumb"

◁ Regular article: "Miss Greenthumb Answers"

◁ Two feature articles per month

Ned makes some suggestions based on his knowledge of how Web sites work:

◁ A registration/subscription page

◁ A form on its own page for letters to the editor

◁ A Table of Contents page with links to all articles

◁ A Search form at the bottom of the Table of Contents page

◁ A discussion group

6. Web Structure

When planning a Web project, the structure of the Web needs to be carefully thought out. Drawings and sketches will help you visualize where all the Web components (or pages) are located and how links will connect these components. Your main sketch should have your home page in the center, with radiating arrows symbolizing links. Various pages containing forms or text from your Web are placed at the ends of the arrows. Additional Webs may also be attached to your Web pages via links. Links can also connect your Web to specific pages on the WWW. These aspects need to be considered when planning your Web structure.

Figure 12-1 shows the sketch that Ned draws after a lengthy discussion with his partners. Allowing for modifications during development, Jane, Steve, and Ned agree on this Web structure.

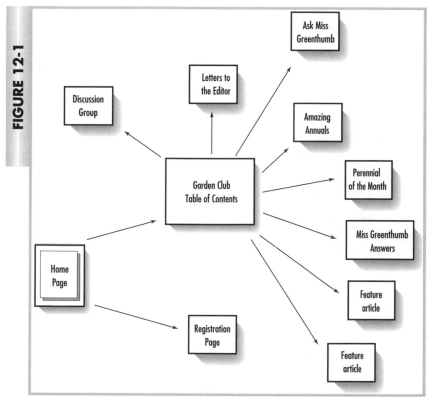

FIGURE 12-1

Web structure for a gardening Web magazine

Developing the Web

Developing your Web means creating it, step by step, with the help of FrontPage. During this process, you will implement all the decisions you made in the discussion-organization phase of the project.

The three partners have had their organizational meeting and have made the decisions about the style and structure of their Web site. Now Ned, with the help of Jane and Steve, will get to work on the Web's structure. FrontPage is indispensable at this point because it allows Ned to bypass the long and tedious process of programming with HTML code.

The following pages illustrate how the Web structure for the Garden Club Web site is developed. For convenience, the steps in the process have been broken down into lessons.

Lesson 1: Opening the Root Web and Your Home Page

The root Web is the master Web. All visitors to your Web site are automatically channeled through the root Web, which contains your home page. From your home page in the root Web, visitors can click on links that will send them to one or more child Webs. A child Web is any Web other than the root Web, and it is an offshoot of the root Web.

Your first step in developing a Web is to create the home page in the root Web. Open the root Web by the following procedure:

1. In FrontPage (FP) Explorer, select File | Open FrontPage Web. This brings up the Open FrontPage Web dialog box.

2. Click on the List Webs button, then select Root Web, then click on OK. This brings up your root Web in FrontPage (FP) Explorer, shown in Figure 12-2.

3. Double-click on FrontPage Root Web in the Hyperlinks for 'FrontPage Root Web' view to bring up your home page in FP Editor. This is the same view you would see in a browser such as Netscape Navigator. Figure 12-3 shows your home page in Netscape Navigator.

Lesson 2: Creating and Editing Your Home Page

When you bring up your home page in the root Web, you will discover that it is already filled with headings and directions. Read them first, then save this original file under the name **orig.htm**. You will save the changes and additions you make to this page to the file **index.htm**. After you have saved the original file, you may edit it as follows:

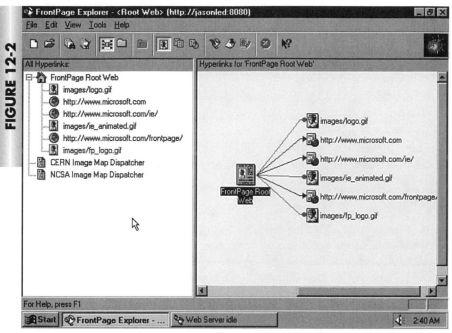

Root Web in FrontPage Explorer

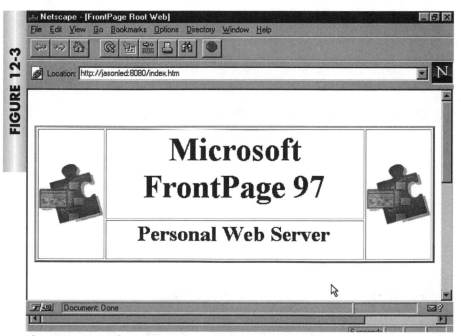

The FrontPage home page in Netscape Navigator

1. Delete the FrontPage Personal Web Server and `microsoft.com` address as you would normally delete things in a word processing program.

2. Delete `Your Home Page Goes Here`.

3. Now to create your home page. Select Heading 1 from the drop-down Format menu (see Figure 12-4).

4. Type in the title of the home page, `The Garden Club`. To make it a little larger, click on the big A in the toolbar. To color the title, click on the Text Color icon in the tool bar. This will bring up the Color dialog box. You can pick a basic color or customize your own color. After you have chosen your color, click on OK to exit.

5. To insert a horizontal line, place the cursor under the title, then select Insert | Horizontal Line.

6. To insert an image logo, place the cursor to the right of the title, then select Insert | Image. This brings up the Image dialog box. Select the Other Location tab. Click on From File, then click on Browse, then select the image file (you will have to create this file). Click on OK. (See Chapter 11, "Multimedia," for more information on inserting images.)

7. To align the title with the top of the image, select the image by clicking on it, then go to Edit | Image Properties. This brings up the Image Properties dialog box. Select the Appearance tab. In the Layout box, choose Top from the Alignment drop-down menu. To place a border around the image, type 2 in the Border thickness field. Click on OK.

8. To put in a date line, place your cursor below the horizontal line. Select the Center and the Italicize buttons in the toolbar. Type in the date, volume number, and issue number, (for example, September 1997, Volume 1, Issue 1).

9. Place the cursor below the date line. Type in a paragraph explaining what the magazine is about and who the editors are.

10. Under this paragraph, you will now create a bulleted list that contains two bullets: Registration and The Garden Club Magazine. (Later, you will make these hot spots and link them to other pages.) Select the Bulleted List icon from the tool bar. Select Heading 4 from the drop-down Format menu (see Figure 12-4). Type in `Registration` and `The Garden Club Magazine`.

11. To save your work, select File | Save As. This brings up the Save As dialog box. Notice that the name of this page, index.htm, already appears in the File Path window. Click on OK.

12. Close the root Web by selecting File | Close FrontPage Web.

   Figure 12-5 shows the top half of the home page.

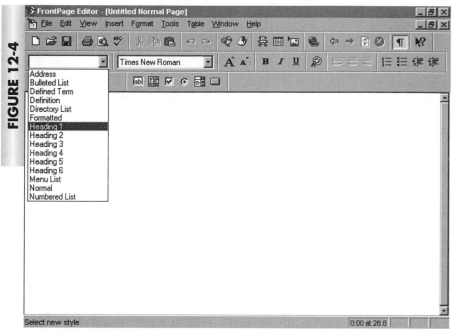

FIGURE 12-4

The drop-down Format menu

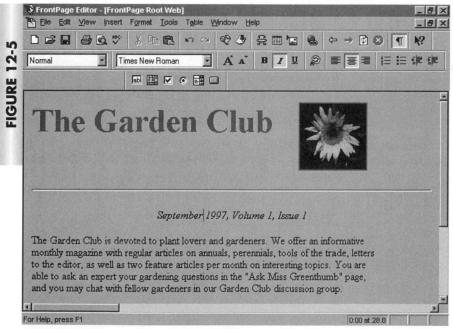

FIGURE 12-5

Home page located in the root Web

Lesson 3: Creating a Registration Page

Now you will create a registration page that visitors have to fill out in order to subscribe to the Web magazine. In the next lesson, you will link it to the home page.

1. In FP Explorer, open up a new Web by selecting File | New FrontPage Web. This brings up the New FrontPage Web dialog box. Select Normal Web then click on OK. This brings up the Normal Web Template dialog box. Type in `Garden Club` in the Name of New FrontPage Web window. Click on OK. (FrontPage may require your name and password at this point.) This is the Web for which users will be registering, the *target Web*.

2. Select Tools | Permissions. This will bring up the Web Permissions dialog box.

3. In the Settings tab, choose Use Unique Permissions For This Web, then click on Apply.

4. Click on the Users tab. Choose Only Registered users have browse access, then click on OK.

5. Close the GardenClub Web by selecting File | Close FrontPage Web.

6. Open your root Web in FP Explorer.

7. Go to FP Editor (while the root Web is still open in FP Explorer) and select File | New. This brings up the New Page dialog box.

8. Choose User Registration, then click on OK. This brings up a registration form with instructions.

9. In the new form, click on any form field in the lower part of the page, then click the right mouse button, then select Form Properties. This brings up the Form Properties dialog box.

10. Click on Settings. This brings up the Settings For Registration Form Handler dialog box.

11. In the Registration tab, type in `GardenClub` in the Web name field. Figure 12-6 shows the Settings for Registration Form Handler dialog box.

12. Click on OK to exit the Settings For Registration Form Handler dialog box.

13. Click on OK to exit the Form Properties dialog box.

14. Now you are able to edit the Registration form. Read then delete the top two paragraphs of instructions.

FIGURE 12-6

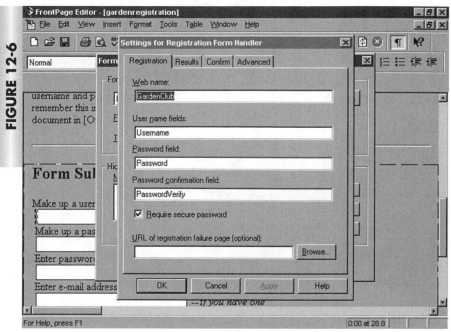

Settings for Registration Form Handler dialog box

15. To find and replace [Other Web] with GardenClub, select Edit | Replace. Type [Other Web] into the Find what field. Type GardenClub into the Replace with field. Click on Replace All. Click on Cancel to exit.

16. A couple of things in the text can be edited to conform to a Web magazine site. In the first line, to be a user of can be changed to for a free subscription to. The sentence about sending articles and postings can be deleted. Figure 12-7 shows the top half of the User Registration form.

17. The author information at the bottom can be edited also. Author information goes here can be deleted, and The Garden Club can be substituted for [OrganizationName]. Figure 12-8 shows the bottom half of the User Registration form.

18. Select File | Save As. Type Gardenreg into the Page Title field, then click on OK.

19. Close the Registration form by selecting File | Close.

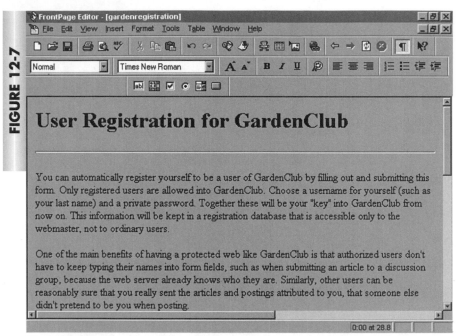

User Registration form (top half)

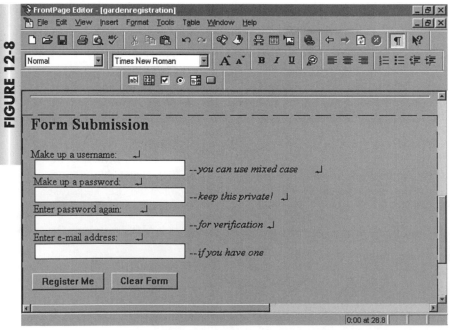

User Registration form (bottom half)

Lesson 4: Creating a Link Between the Registration Form and the Home Page

Now you will create the all-important links between the Registration form you just created and your home page.

1. In FP Explorer, open the root Web.

2. Double-click on FrontPage Root Web in the Hyperlinks for "FrontPage Root Web" view. This will bring up the home page in FP Editor.

3. Select the word Registration in the bulleted list in the home page.

4. Choose Edit | Hyperlink. This brings up the Create Hyperlink dialog box.

5. Select the Current FrontPage Web tab.

6. Click on Browse. Select the Registration form gardenre.htm. (Notice that FrontPage keeps only eight letters of the title.) Figure 12-9 shows the Current FrontPage Web tab of the Create Hyperlink dialog box.

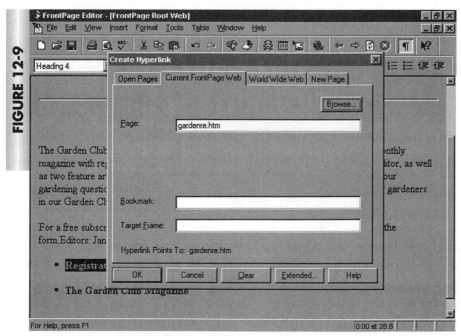

FIGURE 12-9

Current FrontPage Web tab of the Create Hyperlink dialog box

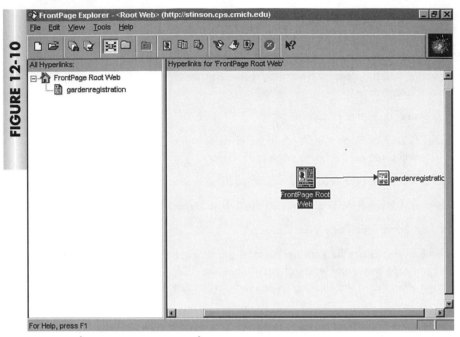

Root Web in FrontPage Explorer

7. Click on OK to exit the Create Hyperlink dialog box. Notice in your home page that the word Registration is now underlined and has changed color, signifying the link.

8. Save the hyperlink by saving the root Web (select File | Save).

9. To view the Web, select Tools | Show FP Explorer. Figure 12-10 shows the root Web in FP Explorer.

Lesson 5: Creating a Child Web

Now you will create the GardenClub page which will be a part of the GardenClub Web. The GardenClub page will be the hub to which all pages of the magazine will link.

1. In FP Explorer, select File | Open FrontPage Web. This brings up the Open FrontPage Web dialog box. Figure 12-11 shows the Open FrontPage Web dialog box.

2. Click on the List Webs button. Select WebGardenClub, then click on OK. This brings up FP Explorer showing the Normal Page you created in the GardenClub Web. (Note: the name of the Web appears in the bar across the top of the page.)

FIGURE 12-11

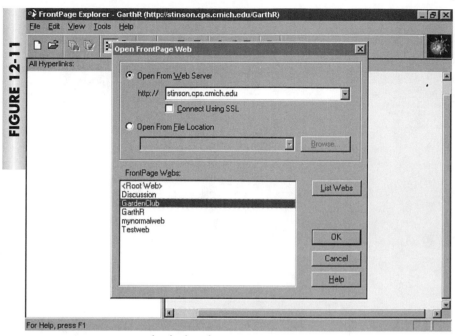

Open FrontPage Web dialog box

3. Edit the page name by double-clicking on Normal Page in the Hyperlinks for Normal Page view. Select File I Save As, then type in GardenClub. Click on OK.

4. Go back to FP Explorer and select File I Close FrontPage Web to save the GardenClub Web.

Lesson 6: Linking a Child Web to the Root Web

Because all visitors to your Web site will come in via the root Web, the GardenClub Web must be linked to it.

1. In FP Explorer, select File I Open FrontPage Web, then select Root Web in the Open FrontPage Web dialog box, then click on OK. This will open your home page in FP Explorer.

2. Double-click on FrontPage Root Web in the Hyperlinks for "FrontPage Root Web" view to open it in FP Editor.

3. Select (or click on) the phrase The Garden Club Magazine.

4. Choose Edit I Hyperlink. This brings up the Create Hyperlink dialog box.

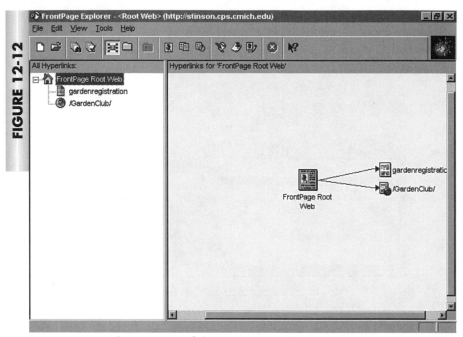

FIGURE 12-12

FrontPage Explorer view of the current Web structure

5. In the Open Pages tab, select GardenClub, then click on OK. This creates a link between the GardenClub Web and the home page, where the hot spot is now underlined and colored. To check the hyperlink, click the right mouse button on the hotspot, then select Follow Hyperlink Forward from the drop-down menu.

6. Save the root Web by selecting File | Save.

7. Select Tools | FrontPage Explorer for a view of the current Web structure, as shown in Figure 12-12.

Lesson 7: Editing the Child Web Page

Now a table of contents needs to be inserted into the new Web Webpage called GardenClub.

1. From FP Explorer, where you were viewing the Web structure in Lesson 6, select File | Open FrontPage Web. This opens the FrontPage Web dialog box.

2. Click on the List Webs button, select GardenClub, then click on OK. This brings up the GardenClub Web in FP Explorer.

3. Click the right mouse button, then select Open from the drop-down menu. This will open the GardenClub page in FP Editor.

4. Copy the Garden Club heading, logo, horizontal line, and date from the root Web and paste them into the GardenClub page.

5. To insert a table of contents, select Heading 2 from the drop-down Format menu (see Figure 12-4). Type in the heading, `Table of Contents`. Press ENTER.

6. Choose Numbered List from the drop-down Format menu (see Figure 12-4).

7. Type in the items in the table of contents. Notice that the numbers are automatically put in for you. You will make each item in the table of contents a hot spot as additional pages are added to the Web. This can be seen in Figure 12-13, which shows the top half of the GardenClub page.

8. To insert a Search form so users can search for a particular keyword, select Insert | WebBot Component. This will bring up the Insert WebBot Components dialog box.

9. Select Search, then click on OK. This brings up the Search Bot Properties dialog box.

10. Accept all defaults, then click on OK. This will place the Search form into your page. Visitors will now be able to search your entire Web (except the discussion group) for a specific topic. Figure 12-14 shows the rest of these features in the bottom half of the GardenClub page.

11. Save your work.

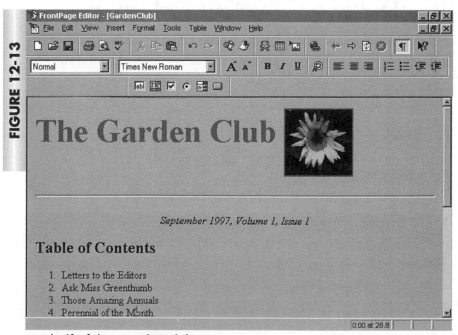

FIGURE 12-13

Top half of the GardenClub page

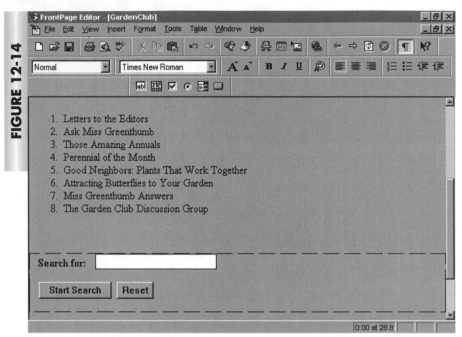

FIGURE 12-14

Bottom half of the GardenClub page

Lesson 8: Creating a Page with a Scrolling Text Box

The first page you will make in the GardenClub Web is the Letters to the Editors page. Subscribers will use a scrolling text box to enter comments and suggestions addressed to the editors of the magazine. Beneath the form, selected letters from the previous month will be displayed for all subscribers to view.

1. In FP Explorer, open the GardenClub Web (if it is not already open).

2. Go to FP Editor, then select File | New. This brings up the New Page dialog box.

3. Select Normal page, then click OK. This opens up a new page.

4. Select File | Save As, then type in Letters, then click on OK. Figure 12-15 shows the Save As dialog box. Now you have a new Web page called Letters.

5. Select Heading 1 from the drop-down Format menu, then select the Centering icon in the toolbar. Type Letters to the Editors.

6. Place your cursor below the heading. Make sure you are in Normal in the drop-down Format menu and left-justified. Type in some brief instructions.

FIGURE 12-15

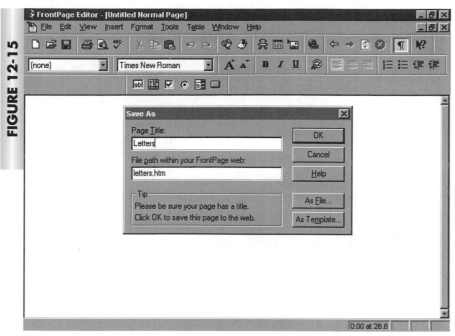

Save As dialog box

7. To insert a form, place your cursor to the immediate right of the last sentence of instructions.

8. Select Insert | Form Field | Scrolling Text Box. This places the form field in your page.

9. Click on the form field to select it, then choose Edit | Form Field Properties. This brings up the Scrolling Text Box Properties dialog box.

10. Enter Letters in the Name field. Adjust Width in characters to 60 and Number of lines to 6. Figure 12-16 shows the Scrolling Text Box Properties dialog box.

11. Click on OK.

12. To add a Submit button, press [ENTER] to place your cursor below the text box. Choose Insert | Form Field | Push Button. This places the push button into your page. You don't need to edit this button so leave it as is.

13. Follow the same procedure to insert a Reset button, except you will have to edit this button.

14. Click on the button to select it, then choose Edit | Form Field Properties. This brings up the Push Button Properties dialog box. Type in Reset in the Value/Label field and select Reset as the Button type. Figure 12-17 shows the Push Button Properties dialog box. Figure 12-18 shows the Letters to the Editors page. Beneath the form is a section in which selected letters from the past month will be displayed.

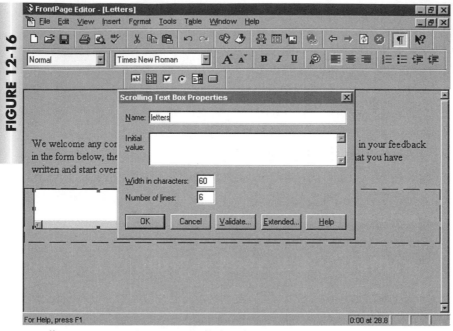

Scrolling Text Box Properties dialog box

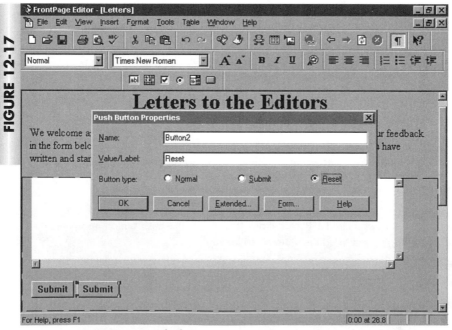

Push Button Properties dialog box

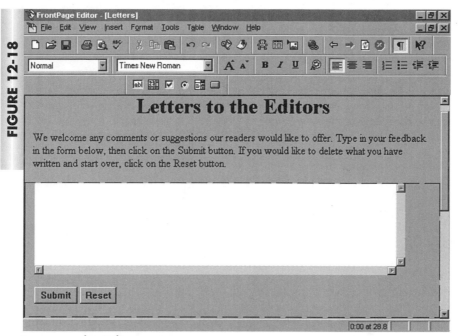

Letters to the Editors page

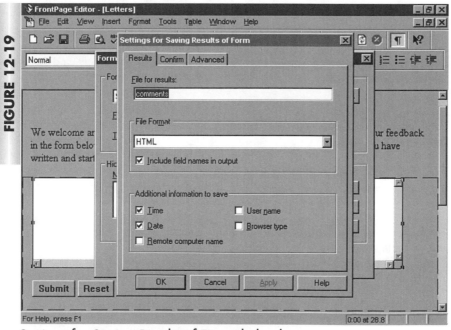

Settings for Saving Results of Form dialog box

15. To save visitor feedback in its own special file, select the Submit button by double-clicking on it. This brings up the Push Button Properties dialog box.

16. Click on the Form button. This brings up the Form Properties dialog box.

17. Select the Save Results WebBot Component from the Form Handler window (click the down arrow to scroll), then click on Settings.

18. In the File For Results field, enter Comments as the file name. Select Time and Date in the Additional information to save box. Figure 12-19 shows the Settings for Saving Results of Form dialog box.

19. Click on OK to exit the dialog boxes, then save and close this page.

Lesson 9: Creating a Page with a Table

One of the feature articles in the magazine is entitled "Good Neighbors: Plants that Work Together." This article will have a table that lists plants that should be grown together.

1. In FP Editor, open a new page in your Web. Make sure GardenClub is still open in FP Explorer because this new page will be a part of the GardenClub Web.

2. Type in the title using Heading 1 in the drop-down Format menu. Type in some introductory text.

3. To insert a table, select Table | Insert Table. This brings up the Insert Table dialog box.

4. Change Rows to 10, Columns to 2, Alignment to Center, and Border Size to 4.

5. Change Cell Padding, which is the space between the contents of the cells and the inside edges of cells, to 3.

6. Change Width, which is how much of the window the table will span, to 80%. Figure 12-20 shows the Insert Table dialog box.

7. Click on OK. This inserts the table into your page.

8. Type in the text of the table, including column heads.

9. To bold the column heads, place your cursor inside the row, then select Table | Select Row.

10. Now click on the B icon in the toolbar to bold the column heads. Figure 12-21 shows the table created in the new page.

11. Save this new page as GoodNeighbors.

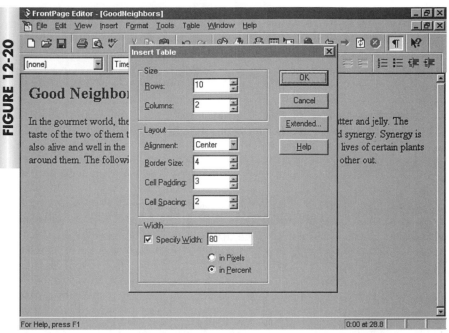

Insert Table dialog box

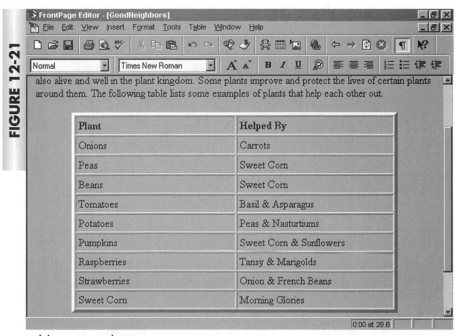

Table in a Web page

Lesson 10: Linking Pages into the Table of Contents

The two pages created so far, Letters and GoodNeighbors, need to be linked to the table of contents in the GardenClub page. To do this, take the following steps:

1. In FP Explorer, open the GardenClub Web (if it is not already open). Figure 12-22 shows the FrontPage Explorer view of this Web before any hyperlinks are made.

2. Double-click on GardenClub in the Hyperlinks for 'GardenClub' view to bring up the GardenClub page in FP Editor.

3. Select the phrase `Letters to the Editors` in the table of contents.

4. Choose Edit | Hyperlink. This brings up the Create Hyperlink dialog box.

5. Choose the Current FrontPage Web tab, then click on Browse. This will bring up a list of your current Web pages.

6. Select Letters, then click on OK. Click OK again to exit the Create Hyperlink dialog box. Now the `Letters to the Editors` phrase in the table of contents is a hot spot. It is underlined and has changed color, signifying the link.

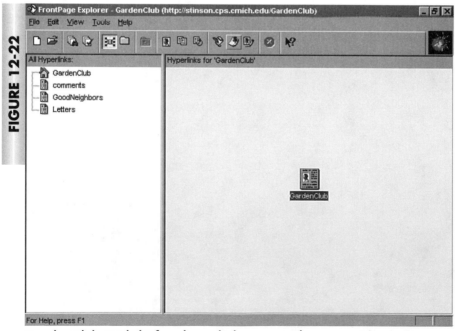

FIGURE 12-22

GardenClub Web before hyperlinks are made

Tip

To test a link, place your cursor on the hot spot, then select Tools: Follow Hyperlink. This will transport you to the target of the link.

7. Now follow Steps 1 through 5 to link the GoodNeighbors page to the table of contents in the GardenClub Web.

8. Save your work.

Figure 12-23 shows the two underlined links (or hotspots) in the table of contents. Figure 12-24 shows the FrontPage Explorer view of GardenClub with its two hyperlinks. Notice in the All Hyperlinks view in Figure 12-24 that Letters and GoodNeighbors are now linked underneath the GardenClub Web instead of outside it.

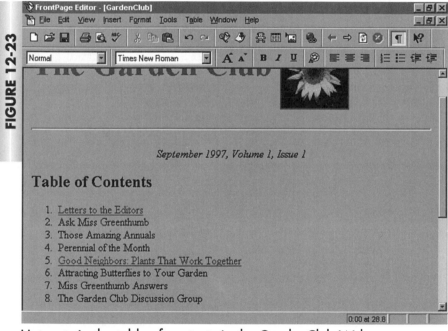

FIGURE 12-23

Hotspots in the table of contents in the GardenClub Web

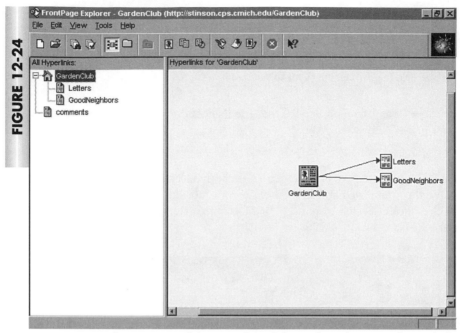

FrontPage Explorer view of the GardenClub Web with its two hyperlinks

Lesson 11: Creating a Page with Frames

The regular monthly article entitled "Amazing Annuals" will provide information about three different annuals. Frames will be used so the reader can click on a picture of a particular flower, then go directly to information about that annual. Bookmarks will also be used to mark the targets of the links.

1. With GardenClub still open in FP Explorer, go to FP Editor and select File | New. This brings up the New Page dialog box.

2. Select Frames Wizard, then click on OK.

3. In the Choose Technique screen, select Pick a Template, then click on Next.

4. In the Pick Template Layout screen, select Simple Table of Contents from the Layout list. The layout display on the left will show your selection. At this point it is important to make a note of your target frames which are *contents* and *main*. Figure 12-25 shows the Frames Wizard–Pick Template Layout box. Click on Next.

5. In the Choose Alternate Content screen, no alternate page is chosen at this time (this page would be displayed by browsers that don't support frames).

6. In the Save Page screen, type `Anframe` (for Annuals frame) in the Title field. Type `Anframe.htm` in the URL field. Click on Finish.

7. Go to FP Explorer to see the view of the Anframe page, as shown in Figure 12-26. Notice that the page has two parts: the table of contents and the Main frame.

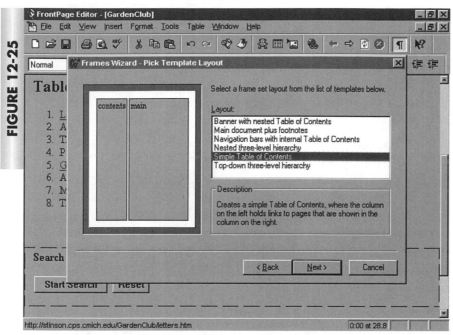

Frames Wizard–Pick Template Layout dialog box

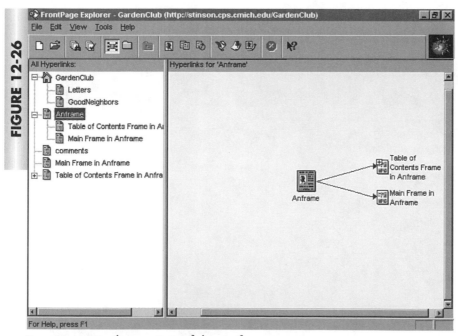

FrontPage Explorer view of the Anframe page

8. Double-click on the Table of Contents frame. This brings it up in FP Editor.

9. Read the supplied text, then delete it.

10. Select Heading 3 from the drop-down Format menu, then type `This Month's Amazing Annuals`.

11. Underneath the title, type in some instructions (be sure you're in Normal in the drop-down Format menu).

12. To insert an image that you have in your system, place the cursor at the insertion point.

13. Select Insert | Image. This brings up the Image dialog box.

14. Select From File. Click on Browse. Select My Computer.

15. Choose the appropriate image file, then click on Open. Now the image, in this case a sunflower, is displayed in the Table of Contents frame. (See Chapter 11 for details on placing images in your computer.)

16. Type in a name to the right of the image.

17. Repeat Steps 11 through 15 to insert the pansy and marigold images.

18. To center the names of the images, click on an image, then go to Edit | Properties. This brings up the Image Properties dialog box.

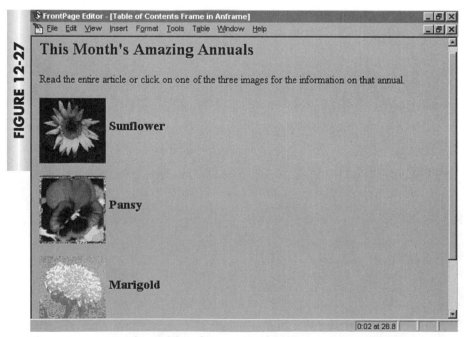

FIGURE 12-27

Three images in the Table of Contents frame

19. In the Appearance tab, choose Absmiddle in the Alignment field. Figure 12-27 shows the three images with the aligned titles in the Table of Contents frame.

20. Save this frame using File | Save.

21. Go back to FP Explorer and double-click on Main Frame in Anframe in the Hyperlinks for Anframe view. This brings up the Main Frame file in FP Editor.

22. Read the supplied text, then delete the text and the heading.

23. Type in three paragraphs, one on sunflowers, one on pansies, and one on marigolds.

24. Save your work.

Lesson 12: Using Bookmarks

Bookmarks and links will be used to connect the images in the Table of Contents frame with the information in the Main frame. Bookmarks mark specific areas or words within a page that are targets of links. This allows you to link to positions farther down your current page or to particular spots on other pages.

1. In the Main frame, select the bolded word Sunflowers in the first paragraph.

2. Select Edit | Bookmark. This brings up the Bookmark dialog box. The Bookmark Name defaults to Sunflowers. Click on OK. A dashed line appears under the word, indicating a bookmark.

3. Use this same procedure to insert bookmarks at Pansies and Marigolds in the second and third paragraphs. Figure 12-28 shows the Bookmark dialog box.

4. Save Main frame. Next you will create the hyperlinks that go with the bookmarks.

5. Go back to FP Explorer and double-click on the Table of Contents frame. This brings it up in FP Editor.

6. Select the sunflower image by clicking on the Rectangle in the Image toolbar, then dragging the "pencil" from the upper-left to lower-right corner of the image. This creates a hot spot and brings up the Create Hyperlink dialog box.

7. In the Open Pages tab, select Main frame in Anframe.

8. In the Bookmark field, click on the down arrow to display the bookmarks you just created. Select Sunflowers. Figure 12-29 shows the Create Hyperlink dialog box.

 Tip

Note the URL at the bottom of the Edit Link dialog box. It gives the page and the word that define the bookmark.

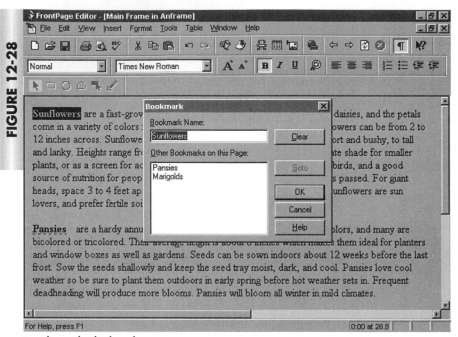

Bookmark dialog box

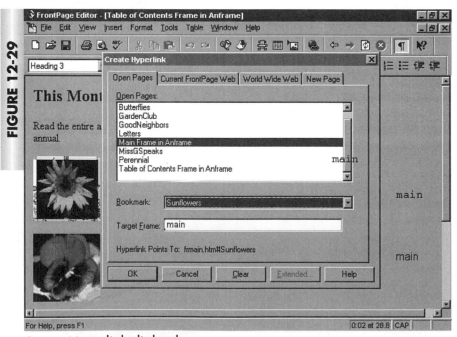

Create Hyperlink dialog box

9. In the Target Frame window, type in `main` (this is one of the target frames you made note of in Lesson 11).

10. Click on OK to create the hyperlink.

11. Follow Steps 1 through 9 to make the other two images hot spots and link them to their respective bookmarks.

12. Save the Table of Contents frame.

13. Follow Steps 1 through 6 in Lesson 10 to link the Anframe file into the table of contents in the GardenClub Web. Amazing Annuals will be the hot spot in the table of contents, and Anframe will be the name of the file you select in the Current Web tab of the Create Hyperlink dialog box.

A back link has also been added from GardenClub to your original home page, `index.htm`. Lesson 14 explains Back to links. Figure 12-30 shows the FrontPage Explorer view of the current structure of the GardenClub Web.

FIGURE 12-30

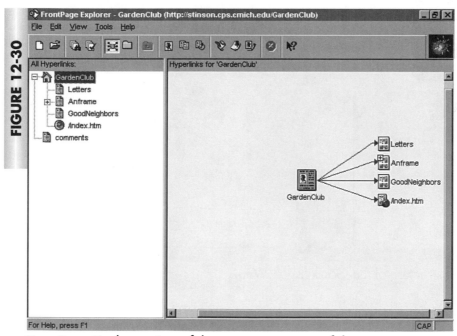

FrontPage Explorer view of the current structure of the GardenClub Web

Lesson 13: Creating the Remaining Pages

To complete the GardenClub Web, the rest of the magazine's pages need to be created and linked into the table of contents. The remaining pages will be articles with the following titles: Perennial of the Month, Attracting Butterflies to Your Garden, Ask Miss Greenthumb, and Miss Greenthumb Answers. The page titled Ask Miss Greenthumb will have a scrolling text box form like the one in Lesson 8. The other three pages will be filled with text and images. To link these pages to the table of contents, follow the same process used in Lesson 10. Figure 12-31 shows the structure of the GardenClub Web after these pages have been added. Figure 12-32 shows the GardenClub page in FP Editor with the links in the table of contents.

FIGURE 12-31

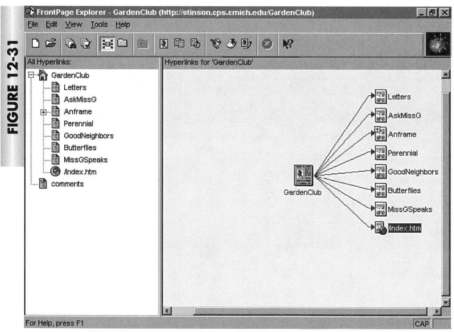

Current structure of the GardenClub Web

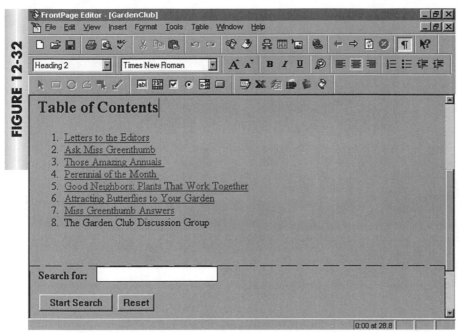

FIGURE 12-32

GardenClub page with links in the table of contents

Lesson 14: Back to Links

A Back to link transports the user back to a specified target page.

After all the pages in the GardenClub Web are in place, Ned points out that some browsers are not equipped with Back buttons. Therefore, he creates a Back to link for each page. Ned links the GardenClub page back to the home page, then he links all the magazine pages back to the GardenClub page, which houses the table of contents. These links can be at either the top or the bottom of pages; Ned chooses to put them at the bottom. For example:

1. With GardenClub open in FP Explorer, open the Letters page in FP Editor.

2. Type in `Back to Table of Contents Page` at the bottom of the Letters page.

3. Select this phrase, then select Edit | Hyperlink. This brings up the Edit Hyperlink dialog box.

4. Choose the WebOpen Pages tab.

5. Select GardenClub and click on OK. This creates the Back to link.

Figure 12-33 shows the Back to link at the bottom of the Letters page. Figure 12-34 shows the FrontPage Explorer view of the Back to link. Notice in both views that GardenClub is linked to Letters, which is also linked to GardenClub. Figure 12-35 shows the GardenClub Web structure with all the Back to links added.

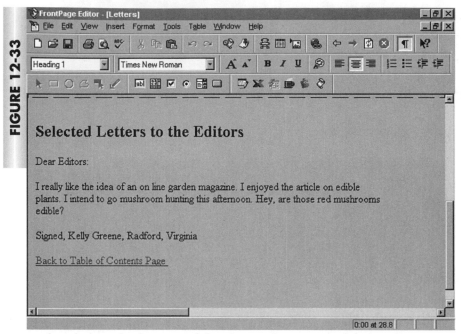

FIGURE 12-33

Back to link at the bottom of the Letters page

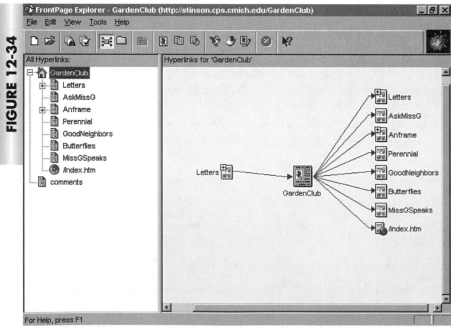

FIGURE 12-34

FrontPage Explorer view showing the Back to link from Letters to GardenClub

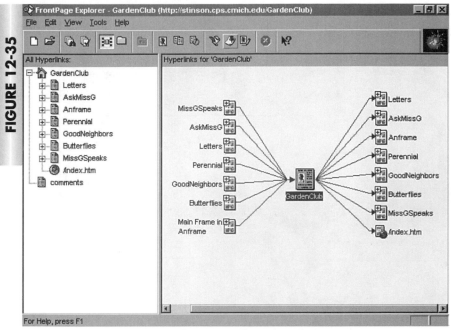

FIGURE 12-35

FrontPage Explorer view showing all Back to links

Lesson 15: Using the To Do List

Because the discussion group still needs to be completed, this task is placed in a To Do List as a reminder. (See Lesson 13 in Chapter 16, "Forms and Security" for instructions for a discussion group.) Follow these steps to create a To Do List:

1. In FP Editor or Explorer, click on the To Do List button in the toolbar. This brings up the FrontPage To Do List dialog box.

2. Click on Add. This brings up the Add To Do Task dialog box.

3. Type in the task name, who it is assigned to, the priority, and the task's description. For this lesson, type in Discussion Group, assigned to Ned, and high priority. The description is Develop the discussion group Web.

4. Click on OK to exit the Add To Do Task dialog box.

5. Use Add to add more tasks, or click on Close to exit the To Do List. Figure 12-36 shows the To Do List for GardenClub.

FIGURE 12-36

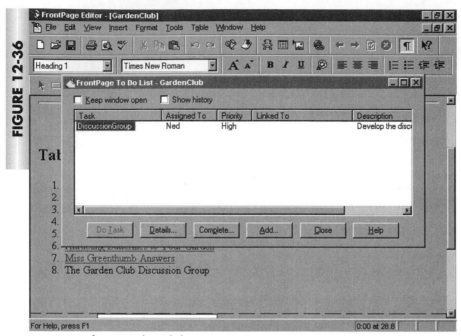

To Do List for GardenClub

Lesson 16: Using the Search Form in a Browser

To test the Search form located below the table of contents in the GardenClub page, go into Netscape Navigator to view the Web site, then follow these steps:

1. In the browser, type in the URL of the GardenClub Web. (The URL is displayed across the top of the screen when working in FrontPage.)

2. In the browser (in this case, Netscape Navigator) at the bottom of the GardenClub page, type Sunflowers into the Search form field, then click on Start Search. Figure 12-37 shows the Search form.

3. A security screen will come up; select Continue. The computer will think for a minute, then the search results will appear below the form. The three document titles are hot spots that will transport you to the articles with the keyword Sunflowers. Figure 12-38 shows the results of the search.

You won't be able to see the frame set of the Anframe file in FrontPage. If you view the Web site in Netscape Navigator, you will see how the Anframe page will appear to users. In the GardenClub page in Netscape Navigator, click on the Amazing Annuals hot spot. Figure 12-39 shows the Netscape Navigator view.

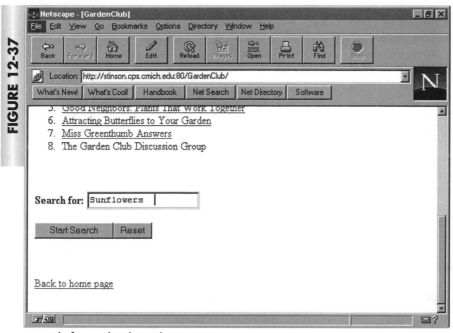

Search form displayed in Netscape Navigator

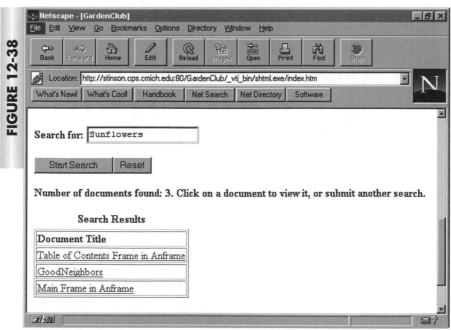

Results of the search

Netscape Navigator view of frame set

Web Summary

The lessons in this chapter demonstrate the usefulness and efficiency of FrontPage in the creation of a Web site.

Steve, Jane, and Ned are very pleased with the look and structure of their site. If, however, they need to change their Web's structure at some point, FrontPage is flexible enough to accomplish this with ease.

Possible future additions to their Web site include advertising, which would turn their hobby into a money-making business. Also, they would like to add links from their GardenClub home page to Jane, Steve, and Ned's personal home pages. Whatever modifications they choose, FrontPage will be invaluable in implementing them.

FrontPage Software Developer's Kit

13

In this chapter you will learn:

The Components that Make Up the FrontPage Software Developer's Kit

The Special Files and Directories that Tell FrontPage How to Build Wizards and Templates

How to Create Your Own Page and Web Templates

The Elements Required to Build Your Own Wizards

The OLE Automation Interfaces Provided by FrontPage

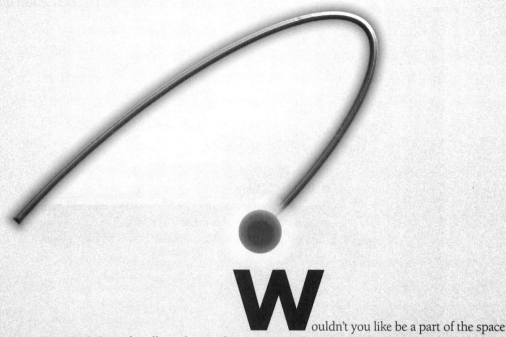

Wouldn't you like be a part of the space program? Consider all you know about space exploration. You may understand how the solar system is structured and how space shuttles take off, orbit the earth, and return to earth. You may even understand some of the lunar formations or be interested in taking your favorite pet to space. But what if you could build you own space shuttle? What if someone provided you with all the necessary tools, an unlimited budget, and resources to perform your own space exploration? Unfortunately, NASA probably won't be knocking on your door anytime soon, but you can perform the next best version of space exploration—cyberspace travel using the FrontPage Developer's Kit. Although you may not consider customizing FrontPage as extraordinary as being in the NASA space program, you'll feel like you've been to the moon when you see everything the developer's kit places at your disposal.

Components

The FrontPage Software Developer's Kit (SDK) is a collection of documentation and examples that will allow you to build your own FrontPage templates and wizards. This means you can perform such feats as creating a template Web for your entire intranet. Consider how much time and effort would be saved with multiple groups creating their own Webs in a corporate intranet. You could create a basic Web and then clone all other Webs from this original. In fact, you could even write your own wizard to automate some of the additional customization steps required at your site (is your motor revved yet?)! You will find the following components in the SDK:

◁ Templates

◁ Wizards

◁ Utility programs

◁ CGI scripts

These components are covered in more detail in the following lessons.

FrontPage Templates

You will often find that you reuse many elements among your Web pages. In fact, some pages may differ by only a few lines. Wouldn't it be nice if you could create new pages based on existing pages or predefined formats? FrontPage rushes to the rescue by offering page templates. Templates consist of one or more Web pages and their associated settings that can be used to generate new pages. FrontPage includes a number of standard templates:

◁ Normal page

◁ Bibliography

◁ Confirmation form

◁ Directory of press releases

◁ Employee directory

◁ Employment opportunities

◁ Feedback form

◁ Fequently asked questions

◁ Glossary of terms

◁ Guest book

◁ Hot list

◁ Hyperdocument page

◁ Lecture abstract

◁ Meeting agenda

◁ Office directory

◁ Press release

◁ Product description

◁ Product or event registration

◁ Search page

◁   Seminar schedule

◁   Software data sheet

◁   Survey form

◁   User registration

◁   What's new

These page templates allow you to incorporate many common elements found in Web pages. However, there are times when you may wish to use your own pages as templates. In addition, you may wish to clone your entire Web site and use it as a template for future projects. Using FrontPage and the FrontPage SDK, you can clone pages and Webs to your heart's content.

Template Directory

For a page or Web to be recognized by FrontPage as a template, it must conform to naming conventions. All page or Web templates must be located in a directory that contains a `.TEM` extension (for example, `MyWeb.TEM`). This directory must then be placed into the FrontPage `Webs` or `Pages` directory, depending on whether the template contains Web or page content.

Locate Your FrontPage Directory

Although you may designate the name of your template directory, you may be wondering where your FrontPage directory is located. Take a look in your Windows directory (for example, `C:\Windows`) and locate a file called `FRONTPG.INI`. If you open this file, you will find the location of the FrontPage directory listed as follows:

```
[FrontPage 2.0]
FrontPageRoot=C:\Microsoft FrontPage
```

The Information File

FrontPage relies on most of its customization information being within an information file. This file follows the Microsoft INI file format. What is the INI file format? It is a text file that is composed of sections, keys, and values. Let's look at a sample `.INI` file.

```
[FrontPage 2.0]
FrontPageRoot=C:\Program Files\Microsoft FrontPage
PWSRoot=C:\Webs\Front Page
FrontPageLangID=0x0409
FrontPageLexicon=C:\Program Files\Microsoft FrontPage\bin\mssp2_en.lex
FrontPageSpellEngine=C:\Program Files\Microsoft FrontPage\bin\mssp232.dll
CheckedHostName=w78zpa15
```

continued on next page

continued from previous page
```
[Port 80]
servertype=frontpage
```

Within an `.INI` file, each section is surrounded by angle brackets (for example, `[Section]`). Under each section, one or more keys and their values are specified, following a `key=value` format.

To specify your own templates, you need to inform FrontPage of your template. To track your template, your template pages must be located in a `*.TEM` directory and you must include an information file whose name matches the `*.TEM` directory and contains an `.INF` extension. Figure 13-1 contains an illustration of the FrontPage Customer Support Web template directory. Notice how the `CUSTSUPP.INF` information file name must match the `CUSTSUPP.TEM` template directory name. In addition, Listing 13-1 contains the contents of the `CUSTSUPP.INF` file.

FIGURE 13-1

The Customer Support Web Template directory and `.INF` file

Listing 13-1 Contents of **CUSTSUPP.INF** information file

```
[info]
title=Customer Support Web
description=Create a web to improve your customer support services,
particularly for software companies.
[FileList]
buglist.htm=
bugrep.htm=
cusuaftr.htm=
cusuahdr.htm=
cusucfrm.htm=
cusufoot.htm=
cusuhead.htm=
cusupost.htm=
cususrch.htm=
cusutoc.htm=
discuss.htm=
download.htm=
faq.htm=
feedback.htm=
footer.htm=
header.htm=
images\scrnshot.gif=images/scrnshot.gif
images\undercon.gif=images/undercon.gif
index.htm=
search.htm=
suggest.htm=
tn-001.htm=
whatsnew.htm=
```

The information file is critical for proper handling of your template. Within your **.INF** file, you may include the following optional sections:

◁ **[info]** section

◁ **[MetaInfo]** section

◁ **[TaskList]** section

Although the FrontPage Editor does not read these sections when reading page templates, these sections will be used by the explorer when it uploads a Web template to a server.

The **[info]** Section

Let's take a look at the Template or Wizard dialog boxes that the FrontPage Editor and Explorer present to you (see Figure 13-2). You may be wondering how FrontPage knows the titles of the wizards and templates (and how it will know about your additions)! Ah, the secret is in the sauce—rather, in the **.INF** file.

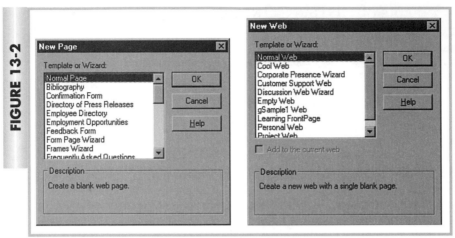

The FrontPage Template or Wizard dialog boxes

Upon closer examination of the **CUSTSUPP.INF** file's **[info]** section (see Listing 13-2), you will discover the secret to the message in the dialog boxes.

Listing 13-2 The **[info]** section of the **CUSTSUPP.INF** file

```
[info]
title=Customer Support Web
description=Create a web to improve your customer support services,
particularly for software companies.
```

 Note

The description line is wrapped onto the next line. There is no line break.

FrontPage reads the title and description keys from the **[info]** section of an **.INF** file. To prevent runtime errors, FrontPage will determine whether or not the file or **[info]** section exists. If one or the other is missing, FrontPage will fill in the dialog box with the name of the base template directory.

The **[FileList]** Section

The **[FileList]** section allows you to specify exactly which HTML files make up your Web, as well as the Uniform Resource Locators (URLs) for these pages. This is a particularly flexible section, enabling you to use pages from other subdirectories and giving you the control to dictate which pages will be included in your template. As in Listing 13-3, the **[FileList]** section contains zero or more lines that specify **filename=URL**.

Listing 13-3 Excerpt from the `CUSTSUPP.INF` `[FileList]` section

```
[FileList]
cusupost.htm=
cususrch.htm=
cusutoc.htm=
images\scrnshot.gif=images/scrnshot.gif
images\undercon.gif=images/undercon.gif
whatsnew.htm=
```

Because the `[FileList]` section is optional, FrontPage needs to know how to handle your template if either this section or the file is missing. In this event, FrontPage will include all files that are located in your template directory and load them as part of your template. In addition, it will take all GIF, JPG, and JPEG graphic images and upload them into the images directory within the Web. Note that you now do not have a choice about which files can be included in the template, and FrontPage will not process any subdirectories within your template directory. If you want more control or would like to keep test pages in your template directory, you should designate the appropriate files in the `[FileList]` section.

One of the powerful features of this section is the ability to specify a remote URL as the source for a particular Web page. However, you may be wondering how to designate a local versus a remote file. To keep the process simple, follow the `key=name` convention, but leave the name portion blank. To clarify things, let's look at the example in Listing 13-4. Here FrontPage will read each line and determine that the file should be located in the same directory. If you designated a URL, then FrontPage would go off and retrieve the corresponding page.

Listing 13-4 Designating local file within the `[FileList]` section

```
[FileList]
whatsnew.htm=
```

In addition, if you wish to specify a template subdirectory within your `[FileList]` section, you should specify this only if the page resides in `images`, `private,` or `cgi-bin` and if you follow the subdirectory name with a forward slash (for example, `images\mypage.htm=images/mypage.htm`). These directories will be created automatically when a new Web is created using FrontPage Explorer.

`[MetaInfo]` Section

On certain occasions, you will want to be able to pass information on to a page template or to the Substitution WebBot (it replaces strings in page) in a generic manner. To address this issue, you may specify variables (not case sensitive) within the `[MetaInfo]` section of your `.INF` file. Although this is an optional section, it allows you to generate tailored pages for the Web user. Consider the `[MetaInfo]` section in Listing 13-5. Using this information in conjunction with the Substitution WebBot will enable the page to incorporate these items and tailor your Web for the user. One caveat—although you may freely use any variable name you desire, Microsoft reserves names beginning with `_vti` for Web administration.

Listing 13-5 Sample `[MetaInfo]` section

```
[MetaInfo]
Age=32
Address=123 Milky Way
```

`[TaskList]` Section

Group collaboration is an important element of many of today's Web sites. Webs are big enough that it may take a number of individuals to put together various components of the Web. When designing your Web template, you can identify various tasks ahead of time, which will make it easier for the Web developers to separate the work. You can accomplish this by designating tasks in the optional `[TaskList]` section of the `.INF` file. In the context of FrontPage, a task consists of the attributes listed in Table 13-1.

Table 13-1 Task attributes within the `[TaskList]` section

Task Attribute	Description	Comments
TaskName	A short phrase stating the task	Typically three or four words
Priority	An integer value	1=High 2=Medium 3=Low
CreatedBy	The name of the template creating the task	String
URL	The path to the page or image to which the task refers	Uniform Resource Locator (for example, `http://www.myweb.com`)
Cookie	An additional target point within the target URL	An HTML bookmark designated by `#bookmark`
Comment	Short sentence describing the task in detail	Cannot contain newline characters

Within each line of the `[TaskList]` section, the task attributes are encoded as follows:

`TaskNum=TaskName | Priority | CreatedBy | URL | Cookie | Comment`

where TaskNum is a unique key, such as `Task01`, and each task attribute is separated by a vertical bar character (|).

Storage Layout

When designing your templates, it will be important for you to decide whether or not you will be creating a page or a Web template. Page templates serve as foundations for individual pages, are used by the editor, and must contain all their images and HTML files within the same directory. As such, the FrontPage Editor will rewrite links within a page whenever it is saved to a Web or a disk file.

In contrast, a Web template contains the structure of a complete Web, is referenced by the FrontPage Explorer, and includes a subdirectory for images. Images have their own directory so that references in the template Web will use the same relative path both within the template and within the generated Web.

When designing your Web template, keep in mind that you will need to create an images directory and place all your graphic images into this subdirectory. In addition, if you update the [FileList] section of the .INF file, you will need to specify the relative path of each image (for example, images/mypic.gif).

Home Page Management

When designing your Web template, you may consider adding a home page. A home page is the default page that is returned by the Web server when you connect to a site. This page will then be resolved, by the Web server, to a directory on the server. If you include a home page in your Web template, the FrontPage Explorer will perform special handling for the URL index.htm. When loading your Web template, the FrontPage Explorer template loader will determine the correct index name (default page) for your Web and rename any URL called index.htm with the correct index name. For example, this would allow you to call your index page Welcome.htm and have FrontPage correctly identify this page as the index. If you wish to use this functionality, you need to ensure that any of your pages that refer to the index are directed to the link, ./ (dot-slash). By doing this, you will force the server to locate the proper home page and redirect the browser to it.

However, you may decide that you do not wish to enable this behavior; you can toggle its action by making an entry in the [info] section of your template's .INF file as follows (1=True, 0=False):

```
NoIndexRenaming=1
```

How to Create Page Templates

Creating a page template is as simple as clicking a menu option. This is a good opportunity for you to follow along with the procedure. The steps for creating a page template are as follows:

1. Launch the FrontPage Editor, either standalone or from the explorer.

2. Use the editor to create the page layout that you desire.

3. Choose the File | Save As menu option to open the Save As dialog box (see Figure 13-3).

FIGURE 13-3

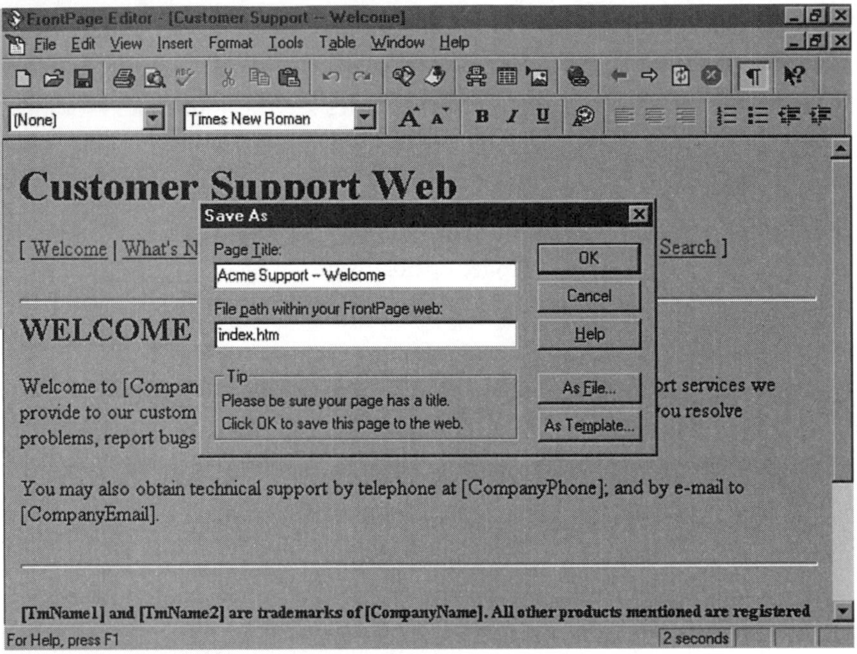

Choosing the File | Save As menu option

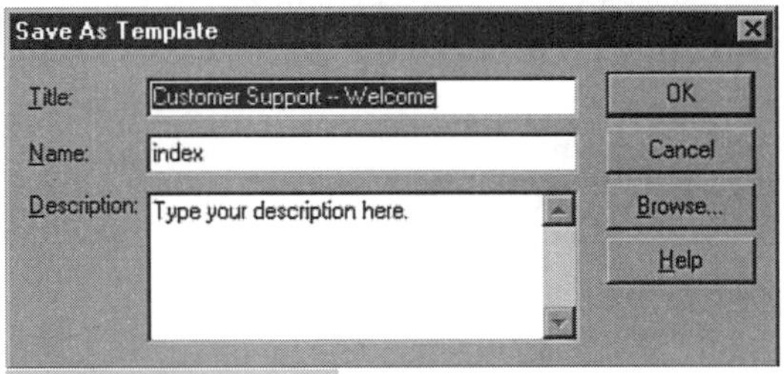

FIGURE 13-4 Save As Template dialog box

4. Specifiy an appropriate page title and URL for your page.

5. Click the As Template button to invoke the Save As Template dialog box (see Figure 13-4).

6. Specify the Title, Name, and Description for your page template. If you want to know the names of existing templates, you can click the Browse button.

7. Click the OK button to save your template.

After you have created your page template, you should be able to look into the **Pages** directory within your FrontPage installation directory and see the new directory that has been created as **<your_template>.TEM**. Further investigation of this directory will show you that FrontPage created both initial HTM and INF files for you.

How to Create Web Templates

Although creating a page template can be automated using the FrontPage Editor, the process for creating a Web template is a little more involved. There are two basic methods for creating a Web template—the manual method and the automatic method. You probably would love to jump right into the automated method and make your life easier, right? Well, because Web templates are so much fun and you *really* want to understand the work that happens behind the scenes (yes, this a Jedi mind trick), you'll be exposed to the manual method first. However, before giving you the keys, let's cover some Web template driving basics.

◁ The FrontPage **Content** directory contains the Web contents for all Webs that you create. By default, this is a directory under **c:\FrontPage Webs\Content**. For example, if your Web is called MyWeb, then the Web content is located within **c:\FrontPage Webs\Content\MyWeb**. You will need to determine the name of your **Content** directory before proceeding with manual Web template creation.

◁ The **images** subdirectory of your Web will contain the **.GIF** and **.JPG** images that you will be using in your Web pages.

◁ Pages that contain WebBots (bots) are saved to the Web in two versions, one with the bot in source form as a list of name-value pairs and one with the bot expanded into HTML. The source version will take precedence over the expanded version of a page with WebBots. Consider the source page as the source code that will be compiled into the expanded version when it is interpreted by the FrontPage Server Extensions. The browser will always read the expanded version of a page stored in the main Web directory, although the source will be stored in the **_vti_shm** directory of the main Web directory.

Manual Web Templates—Using the Stickshift

For FrontPage to recognize your Web as a template, you need to prepare your Web for the replication. Following is a manual procedure to create a sample Web template called CoolWeb:

1. Create a new Web or copy an existing Web using the FrontPage Explorer and name it SampWeb (see Figure 13-5).

2. Open Windows Explorer and create a directory, **CoolWeb.tem**, under the FrontPage **Webs** directory.

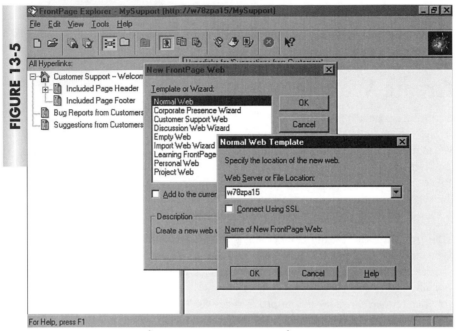

FIGURE 13-5

Creating a new Web using FrontPage Explorer

3. Using Windows Explorer, locate the directory containing your Web (SampWeb) content.

4. Copy the Web images directory into the CoolWeb.tem directory that you previously created.

The next phase is to copy the pages into your new **CoolWeb.tem** template as follows:

1. Copy the static pages in the main Web directory (C:\FrontPage Webs\Content \SampWeb) into CoolWeb.tem. Do not copy the access control files, such as #haccess.ctl.

2. Copy the Web's WebBot pages (C:\FrontPage Webs\Content\SampWeb_vti_shm) into CoolWeb.tem. You may replace any existing files.

3. Use a text editor, such as Notepad.exe, to create a CoolWeb.INF file in the CoolWeb.tem directory.

4. Within CoolWeb.INF, create the following sections (add tasks and metainfo if you desire):

```
[info]
title=Cool Web
description=A cool web created from a template using the FPDK
```

5. If you have any content in any of your `SampWeb` subdirectories (such as `private`, `cgi-bin`), copy the pages and/or code into their respective subdirectories under the `CoolWeb.tem` directory.

If your Web includes any content in subdirectories, you will need to create a `[FileList]` section in your `.INF` file as described above to ensure that those files get loaded properly by the explorer.

Automated Web Templates—Using Web Template Maker

As you may have guessed, the automated method of creating a Web template is much easier than the manual method. However, it doesn't hurt to understand the process, does it? In any case, you can automate the creation of a Web template by using the FrontPage Web Template Maker. This program is included in the `Utility\Webtmpl` directory of your development kit directory as `WEBTMPL.EXE` (see Figure 13-6).

Following is an automated procedure to create a sample Web template, CoolWeb, using the Web Template Maker:

1. Create a new Web or copy an existing Web using the FrontPage Explorer and name it `SampWeb`.

2. Locate your FrontPage Developer's Kit directory and run the utility `<kit-path>\Utility\Webtmpl\WEBTMPL.EXE`.

FIGURE 13-6

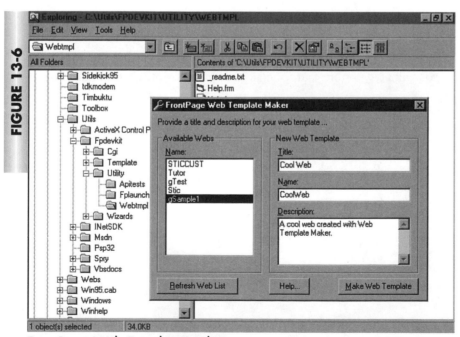

FrontPage Web Template Maker

3. Select your source Web (SampWeb) from the list of available Webs.

4. Type in a Title, Name, and Description for your new Web template as follows:

```
Title=Cool Web
Name=CoolWeb
Description=A cool web created from a template using the FPDK
```

5. Click the Make New Template button to generate your new Web template.

If you investigate the results of this action, you will find that the Wizard Template Maker created the proper template directory, generated an **.INF** file, and copied all the necessary source files for you. This will save you considerable time in creating future Web templates.

Frameset Templates

One of the most popular Web page components is frameset pages. With FrontPage, support for framesets has been provided via the Frames Wizard (see Figure 13-7). The Frames Wizard is used for creating and editing HTML frameset pages. In case you are wondering, a frameset page divides a page into independent scrollable regions that can each contain a separate Web page. This allows the reader to perceive navigation through your Web from one central page. When creating these pages, Web authors can cause documents to be loaded into individual frame regions by using a special Target attribute that can be attached to a link.

Storage Conventions

The Frames Wizard provides the option of creating an entire frameset, including component pages, from one of several templates. If you wish to create your own frameset templates, you will need to store your templates within the FrontPage **pages** directory.

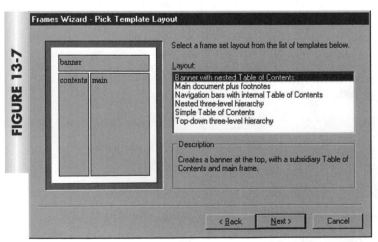

FIGURE 13-7

FrontPage Frames Wizard

In contrast with page and Web templates, frameset templates are stored differently. Each frameset template is stored in a file with an extension of `.FRM`. The `.FRM` file is stored in Microsoft INI file format processing by the Frames Wizard. Listing 13-6 illustrates the structure of an `.FRM` file.

Listing 13-6 Structure of a Frames Wizard `.FRM` file

```
[info]
title=name of frameset as it will appear in the wizard
description=long description of the purpose of the wizard
noframesURL=ignored; alternate page is assigned by wizard
layout=specification of frameset geometry using compact notation


[frame name 1...N]
title=name of frame as it will appear in the page title
description=long description of what the frame should contain
URL=ignored; page URL for frame is assigned dynamically by wizard
marginWidth=width of margin; default is 1
marginHeight=height of margin; default is 1
scrolling=how scrollbars are displayed; default is _auto
noresize=turns off scrolling; default is _False
target=name of default target frame for this page
```

The first section of the `.INF` file should contain an `[info]` section, which describes the main frameset page, whereas the subsequent section describes component pages. The section names must match the frame names, which are derived from the following frameset layout specification in the `[info]` section:

```
layout=[R(15%,85%)F("banner",[C(35%,65%)F("contents","main")])]
```

A frameset can be recursive, which allows a frameset to include subsequent framesets. You should surround each frameset with square brackets (`[]`). Within each frameset, you need to specify a row or column (R or C), followed by a list of frames. If defining a row, use an R followed by a comma-separated list of frames. Each row entry needs to be expressed as a percentage of the total available height. If you define a column, you should follow the same convention as for a row, except that a C denotes a column, whereas an R denotes a row. Denote each frame list with an F, followed by a comma-separated list including each item (inside double quotes) or a full frameset designation (inside square brackets).

Using the layout string given above, the meaning can be deciphered as follows. The frameset consists of two main rows—a short one (banner), 15% of window height, and a long one, the remaining 85% of window height. The long row is subdivided into two columns, a first frame (1/3 window width), called *contents*; and a second frame (2/3 of window width), called *main*.

The Frames Wizard is programmed to read this frameset information from within any files containing an extension `.FRM`. It will then process the layout string and display a graphical image that conforms to these attributes. This assists the users in customizing their framesets.

Once the user has chosen customization options, the wizard generates the frameset page and its companion pages into the current Web or the editor. Within the generated page, an Annotation WebBot is added to document the frame's purpose, owner, default targets, and editing options.

FrontPage Wizards

In the course of creating a Web, sometimes you may desire to perform tasks, both simple and complex, to allow customization of the Web. Wizards are miniprograms that prompt you for information and choices to design your pages or Web as you wish. The wizards prompt you by using one or more dialog boxes for you to enter information and communicates with FrontPage using OLE Automation. The beauty of a wizard lies in its ability to generate one or more pages to get you started in your customization. This will potentially save you many hours of development time. As such, FrontPage includes a number of standard wizards:

◁ Corporate Presence Wizard, which generates a Web site for your company or organization

◁ Discussion Web Wizard, which builds a threaded discussion group into a new or existing Web

◁ Personal Home Page Wizard, which creates a single page just for you

◁ Frames Wizard, which allows you to create a form that implements HTML framesets

◁ Form Page Wizard, which   allows you to build and customize a form to gather user input

Like a template, a wizard is stored in a subdirectory under the FrontPage directory. A wizard directory must end in **.wiz** (for example, **CoolWeb.wiz**) and must be located in the FrontPage Webs or pages directory, depending on the type of wizard to be employed. If you are not sure where your FrontPage directory is located, look in your Windows directory in the file **FRONTPG.INI** (see Listing 13-7).

Listing 13-7 **FRONTPG.INI** file contents

```
[FrontPage 2.0]
FrontPageRoot=C:\Program Files\Microsoft FrontPage
PWSRoot=C:\Webs\Front Page
FrontPageLangID=0x0409
FrontPageLexicon=C:\Program Files\Microsoft FrontPage\bin\mssp2_en.lex
FrontPageSpellEngine=C:\Program Files\Microsoft FrontPage\bin\mssp232.dll
CheckedHostName=w78zpa15

[Port 80]
servertype=frontpage
```

The Information File

Like templates, wizards also use an information file (`*.INF`), as shown in Listing 13-8. The `[info]` section contains the name and title keys of your wizard for use in the FrontPage Wizard dialog boxes.

Listing 13-8 Sample wizard `.INF` file

```
[info]
title=Frames Wizard
description=Create a page divided into tiled areas called frames. Each frame
contains another page or image.
editor=1
```

If the wizard executable will be different from the directory name, you should include a key named **exename** whose value will be the name of the wizard executable. In addition, if the wizard can be invoked as both an editor and a generator, you should include the editor key and set its value to 1.

Types of Wizards

In the world of FrontPage, there are two types of wizards—page wizards and Web wizards. In general, a page wizard is used to generate a single Web page, whereas a Web wizard will enable you to design all or a portion of an entire Web. Although this distinction exists, it is not rigidly enforced. Like a good Samaritan, FrontPage will not discriminate a wizard based upon its type—that's your job. However, it is important for you to recognize this difference because FrontPage will launch a page wizard only from the editor, whereas Web wizards are always launched from the explorer.

In case you haven't seen a page wizard in action, Figure 13-8 illustrates the Frames Wizard in all its glory. A page wizard's use is pretty clear because it presents the user with a series

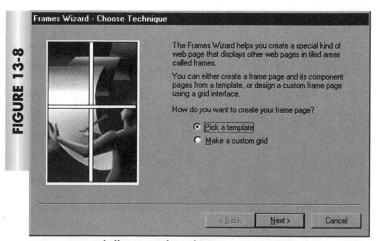

FIGURE 13-8

Page wizard illustrated in the Frames Wizard

of dialog boxes to gather input and/or customization options and then generates a single HTML page into the FrontPage temp directory (typically, `C:\Microsoft FrontPage\temp`). From here, the page is loaded into the editor transparently. In other words, this appears seamlessly while the copying and loading happens in the background.

If the actions of the page wizard aren't quite enough excitement for you, let's look at a Web wizard. Figure 13-9 shows the Corporate Presence Wizard in action. Because this wizard will generate a complete Web for you, it requires a lot of customization. You're probably wondering what the magic is behind the Web wizards, so let's get into it. Like its page counterpart, the Web wizard presents the user with a series of dialogs to collect input for site customization. It then generates one or more HTML pages into the FrontPage `temp` directory. These pages are uploaded into the current Web, along with any resources, such as images stored in the wizard directory. If the user elects to create a new Web rather than add to the current one, FrontPage Explorer will create the new Web prior to beginning the Web wizard.

Passing Parameters

One of the powerful features of a FrontPage wizard is the communication possible between the user, FrontPage, and the wizard itself. You may be wondering how such communication occurs. Although the user will interact with the dialogs the wizard presents, the FrontPage and wizard intercommunication happens within a parameter file. The parameter file is quite important in this symbiotic relationship because it will tell both FrontPage and the wizard how to react to particular events. All wizards are launched with a single argument. Ths argument contains the path to a temporary file (in `.INI` format, of course)

FIGURE 13-9

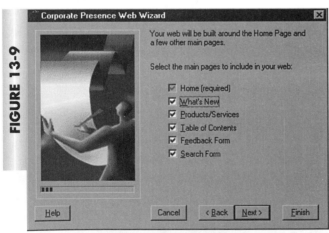

Web wizard illustrated in the Corporate Presence Wizard

containing a number of sections, keys, and values. It is possible to invoke a wizard without this parameter file, such as if the executable is launched from Windows Explorer or Windows File Manager. In this case, either your page wizard will load a page into the FrontPage Editor or your Web wizard will load multiple pages into the current Web.

Listing 13-9 shows the format of a wizard's parameter file. Careful observation reveals that three sections must exist in the parameter file. These sections are [Input], [Environment], and [Output]. The [Input] section contains all required and optional wizard parameters. The [Environment] section contains a current snapshot of the parent's environment variables. The [Output] section is initially empty, but this is where the wizard can write variables that can be read and processed by the calling program (chiefly, FrontPage) under particular circumstances.

Listing 13-9 Format of a wizard's parameter file

```
[Input]
arg1=value1
arg2=value2
[Environment]
var1=value1
var2=value2
[Output]
```

Input Parameters

When a wizard is invoked by FrontPage, the parameter file will contain the following entries in the [Input] section:

◁ Dir: Contains the absolute path to the wizard directory.

◁ Inf: Contains the absolute path to the wizard's .INF file.

◁ Blocking: This will have a value of 1 or 0, depending upon whether the caller is blocked or not. If a wizard is launched with blocking=0 (default), it should delete the parameter file mentioned in the command line upon exit. This avoids unnecessary files in the temporary directory. However, if the wizard is launched with blocking=1, the launching program expects to be able to retrieve output variables from the wizard. In this case, the launching program will process the [Output] section and delete the parameter file after the wizard exits.

◁ Editing: If the wizard is being invoked as an editor, this parameter will contain a value of 1. Otherwise, it will be set to 0. If this wizard can be invoked as an editor, you need to ensure that the editor=1 key is specified in the .INF file's [info] section.

In the case of page wizards, some additional parameters may be specified:

◁ Destination: Contains editor, Web, or disk. If the value contains editor, the generate file should be loaded into the FrontPage Editor using OLE automation (more about this later). If the value contains Web, then the file should be loaded into the current Web using OLE automation. If the value contains disk, the wizard is expected to generate its output into temporary files and return a list of file name and URL variables within the [Output] section.

◁ PageURL: This will contain a Web-relative path to the page being created. For example, you could specify welcome.htm.

◁ PageTitle: This will be the name of the page that is to be created, such as My Funny Page.

◁ PageFile: This contains an absolute path to the file being edited, which has typically been downloaded by the explorer. This parameter will be set only if the Editing key is set to the value of 1.

In addition to the aforementioned [Input] parameters, FrontPage may also pass additional parameters for backward compatibility for Version 1.0 wizard support. These parameters are passed by the FrontPage Explorer, but should not be processed by your wizards because future support is not guaranteed: WebName, ServerName, Proxy, User.

Output Parameters

When your wizard is complete and the Blocking=1 [Input] parameter is set, you should fill the [Output] section with the following parameters:

◁ ExitStatus: This will contain one of the text strings error, cancel, or ok. This enables the launching program to handle the termination of your wizard properly. If you do not return a value for this parameter, FrontPage will assume an error occurred in your wizard.

◁ FileCount: If the [Input] section parameter Destination=disk is set, then your wizard should provide the count of files that will be listed under keys FileN and URLN.

◁ FileN: Contains the absolute path to a file generated by your wizard. If FileCount is greater than 0, then you should include one of these keys for each file generated. It is important to note that File1 will be the main HTML file generated by a page wizard.

◁ URLN: Contains the target URL to a file generated by your wizard. If FileCount is greater than 0, then you should include one of these keys for each file generated.

Sample Parameter File

Listing 13-10 contains a sample parameter file that Microsoft includes with the FrontPage SDK.

Listing 13-10 Sample wizard parameter file

```
[Input]
PageURL=test.htm
PageTitle=Test Page
Dir=E:\FrontPage\pages\vtiform.wiz
Inf=E:\FrontPage\pages\vtiform.wiz\vtiform.inf
Blocking=0
Editing=0
[Environment]
COMPUTERNAME=ARBUS
ComSpec=E:\WINNT35\system32\cmd.exe
HOMEDRIVE=E:
HOMEPATH=\users\default
MSINPUT=E:\MSINPUT
OS=Windows_NT
Os2LibPath=E:\WINNT35\system32\os2\dll;
Path=E:\WINNT35\system32;E:\WINNT35
PROCESSOR_ARCHITECTURE=x86
PROCESSOR_IDENTIFIER=x86 Family 5 Model 2 Stepping 11, GenuineIntel
PROCESSOR_LEVEL=5
PROCESSOR_REVISION=020b
SystemRoot=E:\WINNT35
SystemDrive=E:
temp=E:\temp
tmp=E:\temp
USERDOMAIN=EMINENT
USERNAME=rsasnett
windir=E:\WINNT35
[Output]
```

Wizard User Interface Considerations

When designing your wizards, it recommended that you follow Windows' user interface guidelines for wizards. This will not only simplify and standardize your interface, it will ensure that your wizard's interface is consistent with the FrontPage and Windows wizards. Figure 13-10 illustrates the components of a wizard dialog box.

A FrontPage wizard should look like a Windows dialog box but will contain a number of buttons for the user to navigate between dialog pages. The Back, Next, and Cancel buttons should be on all pages, except on the final page, where you should substitute Finish for the Next button. If you think users may need additional assistance while using your wizard, you may also include a Help button. When clicked, the Help button should launch a Windows Help (*.HLP) file. In addition, your buttons should always be visible and accessible at the bottom of the wizard's dialog box. Again, users will expect a consistent user interface

FIGURE 13-10

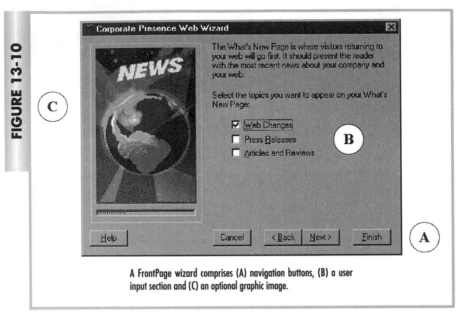

A FrontPage wizard comprises (A) navigation buttons, (B) a user
input section and (C) an optional graphic image.

Components of a FrontPage wizard

and will expect your buttons to be in this location. One of the more aesthetically pleasing features of some wizards is an image or graphical output area. If you choose to use an
image on your dialog page, it should appear to the left of the dialog page but above the
navigation buttons. Additionally, it is beneficial to the user if your images either reflect a
graphical representation of the step being performed or illustrate the result of selected options.
Figure 13-11 illustrates some sample graphical images used in wizards.

Data File Settings

In certain cases, you may decide that you want your wizard to store data for future invo-
cations. For example, you may wish to store the names and addresses entered in a
Mailing List Wizard. Although you can pass this information within a parameter file, this
will eventually be deleted by either FrontPage or your wizard. To save your data, you may
store this information in an `.INI` file. Within your `.INI` file, you can store whatever data
you desire. However, you will need to keep a couple of issues in mind.

◁   The name of your `.INI` file should be the same as the base name of your wizard executable program, but must include the `.INI` file extension.

◁   The location of your `.INI` file must be in the data subdirectory of the
FrontPage installation directory. Your `.INI` file is separated from your wizard
directory because your wizard directory could be placed on a read-only disk
drive, network drive, or CD-ROM drive. This is also why your wizards must
write to the FrontPage `temp` directory.

FIGURE 13-11

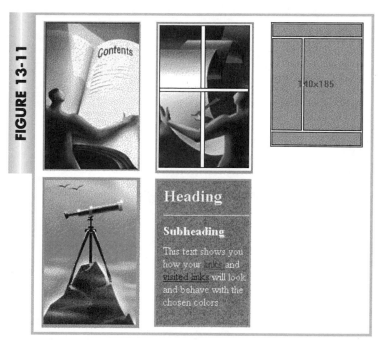

Sample FrontPage wizard images

Changing Location of FrontPage Directories

If you wish to change the location of the FrontPage Webs and pages directories, you can modify the FRONTPG.INI file, which is located in your Windows directory. The following keys denote these directories:

```
[FrontPage 2.0]
WebWizardsDir=<insert your directory here>
PageWizardsDir=<insert your directory here>
```

Naming Conventions

Because all FrontPage wizards are located within the **Webs** and **pages** directories, each wizard name must be unique within that particular directory. In addition, your wizard directory name should include the name of your wizard with the extension **.wiz** for FrontPage to recognize this as a wizard directory.

FrontPage Communication

All communication performed between FrontPage and your wizards will be peformed via OLE automation. If you wish to observe the OLE Application Programming Interfaces (APIs), please consult the FrontPage SDK documentation.

FrontPage OLE Automation

This section provides a bird's-eye look at the FrontPage OLE automation interfaces available to you. If you are not familiar with OLE or need a refresher, refer to Kraig Brockschmidt's *Inside OLE*, Second Edition (Microsoft Press, 1996), which is the definitive reference guide for OLE and the Microsoft Common Object Model. This book is not an OLE tutorial, so it is assumed that you have had plenty of exposure to OLE.

FrontPage performs most of its communication through OLE automation. Three main components in FrontPage can be controlled externally through OLE automation. If you examine the Windows registry (under key **\HKEY_CLASSES_ROOT**), you will find that the FrontPage Explorer, Editor, and To Do List all contain OLE identifiers. For FrontPage version 2.0, the OLE identifiers are listed as **FrontPage.Explorer.2.0**, **FrontPage.Editor.2.0**, and **FrontPage.ToDoList.2.0** for the explorer, editor, and to do list, respectively. If you wish to communicate with the generic, release-independent identifiers, you may address **FrontPage.Explorer**, **FrontPage.Editor**, and **FrontPage.ToDoList** as necessary.

Evolving OLE Interfaces

Microsoft ensures that the FrontPage OLE interfaces correspond appropriately to the release of FrontPage. The names of the interfaces as well as the functionality available may change in subsequent releases. It is recommended that you write your wizard code so that you communicate with the interfaces in localized code. This will save you time in making enhancements for later releases.

Explorer Interface

The central component for FrontPage communication is the FrontPage Explorer. This is the main interface for OLE automation. The explorer interface is responsible for operating on Web-level objects, which make up the pages within a URL directory accessible through a Web server running the FrontPage Server Extensions. Using this approach, FrontPage can administer and author in the root Web and any subsequent Webs that you have created. The following Web components can be addressed via the FrontPage Explorer interface:

◁ Security attributes

◁ Metainfo variables

Using the Explorer OLE interface, you can create or delete a Web, move documents between the local file system and the Web server, remove documents from the Web server, store and retrieve metainfo variables, read page metainfo variables, retrieve a list of files or images in the current Web, process the To Do List, and retrieve the URL and title of the current Web.

Security Attributes

Within a Web, there are designated security roles or attributes for administrators, Web authors, and users. The explorer interface allows administrators to create and delete Webs and set other permissions. Authors and users are permitted to maintain Web pages, set user permissions, and browse the Web.

Metainfo Variables

Within your Web and your Web pages, you may define metainfo variables, which contain additional information to be used by your Web or wizards. These variables are stored in configuration files within the Web. You are free to use any metainfo variable names except ones that begin with **vti_**, because these are reserved by Microsoft.

Editor Interface

The FrontPage Editor allows you to edit HTML pages in a WYSIWYG editor. These files are then stored on the Web server as **.HTM** or **.HTML** files for processing by the server. The editor allows you to open, create, edit, and save these files into the current Web, viewed by the FrontPage Explorer, or to the local system.

Unfortunately, the FrontPage Editor OLE interface does not allow page content (for operations to be performed outside of the FrontPage program itself). However, you may use this interface to create a new empty page, open an existing page, and determine whether or not a particular page is currently being edited.

To Do List Interface

FrontPage includes a To Do List to help you manage the tasks for your Web completion, using a grid-like object that manages and displays a list of tasks to be performed on the current Web opened by the explorer. Some of the features included with the To Do List follow:

◁ Detailed column listing of critical items such as task name, priority, and name

◁ Sorting by category

◁ Task reassigning

◁ Clicking the task moves you to the point of your page that requires work

◁ Automatic prompting for completed tasks

◁ Detecting authors trying to perform same task

◁ Historical viewing of completed tasks

◁ Deleting tasks as they are completed

The To Do List OLE interface allows you to add new tasks and to hide or display the To Do List interface.

Programming Considerations

Before you invoke an OLE method, you need to establish a connection to the automation server's exported object interfaces. You can invoke the server's OLE methods by calling them from the client side of the OLE connection. When you have finished using the calling method, you need to close the connection to the OLE automation server. An additional concern involves the lifetime of the connection. It is highly recommended that you open and close the OLE connection inside a single function to minimize the lifetime of the connection. If the user chooses to exit FrontPage while you are connected to the OLE automation server, your connection will fail, so it is a good idea to minimize this connection time.

Programming Examples

Listings 13-11 and 13-12 demonstrate OLE automation from both Visual Basic and Visual C++.

Listing 13-11 OLE automation from Visual Basic

```
Function btnSomeEvent_Click()
{
Dim explorer as Object

        Set explorer = CreateObject("FrontPage.Explorer.2.0")
        explorer.vtiRefreshWebFromServer
        Set explorer = Nothing
        ' NOTE: it is important to set the OLE object variable
        ' to Nothing so that the OLE connection is released
}
```

Listing 13-12 OLE automation from Visual C++

```
#include "webber.h"

void OnSomeEvent()
{
IWebber explorer;
COleException error;

        if(!explorer.CreateDispatch("FrontPage.Explorer.2.0",&error))
        {
                AfxMessageBox("Error connecting to FrontPage Explorer.");
```

```
        return;
    }
    explorer.vtiRefreshWebFromServer();
    explorer.ReleaseDispatch();
}
```

In the above listings, based upon an event (**btnEvent_Click** in the Visual Basic example), the code attempts to allocate a FrontPage Explorer object. Upon successful allocation, FrontPage Explorer is opened and the Web is reloaded. After completion, the FrontPage Explorer object is deallocated and closed.

OLE Automation Methods Supported by FrontPage

Although you will find more detail within the FrontPage SDK, the following tables provide a listing of the OLE automation methods supported by the FrontPage components.

Explorer Automation Methods

Table 13-2 is a list of the OLE automation methods supported by the FrontPage Explorer within the OLE identifier **FrontPage.Explorer.2.0**.

Table 13-2 OLE automation methods supported by **FrontPage.Explorer.2.0**

Method	Description
long vtiCreateWeb(LPCTSTR szServerURL, LPCTSTR szWebName);	Creates a new Web on the Web server
void vtiRefreshWebFromServer();	Refreshes all views of the current Web
long vtiPutDocument(LPCTSTR szFileName, LPCTSTR szURL, BOOL bBlockingRequest);	Uploads a local file to current Web
long vtiPutWebMetaInfo(LPCTSTR szNameValuePairs);	Establishes metainfo variables for Web documents
void vtiSetWebRecalcDependencies(BOOL bRecalcOn);	Toggles document dependency
BSTR vtiGetWebPageMetaInfo(LPCTSTR szURL, LPCTSTR szKeyName);	Looks up value of a metainfo variable
void vtiBringToTop();	Brings explorer to top of all application windows
BSTR vtiGetWebTitle();	Returns title of current Web
BSTR vtiGetWebURL();	Returns full URL of current Web
void vtiPromptOpenWeb();	Displays Open Web dialog box

continued on next page

continued from previous page

Method	Description
`long vtiRemoveWeb(LPCTSTR szWebName);`	Removes Web from Web server, if authorized
`BOOL vtiIsPageInWeb(LPCTSTR szURL);`	Checks for document existence in current Web
`BSTR vtiGetWebMetaInfo(LPCTSTR szKey);`	Looks up value of read-only metainfo key
`BSTR vtiGetPageList(long lType);`	Returns list of documents of a given type
`BOOL vtiPutDocuments(LPCTSTR szFileList, LPCTSTR szUrlList);`	Uploads multiple documents to current Web
`void vtiCancelRequests();`	Interrupts any pending explorer requests
`BOOL vtiOpenWeb(LPCTSTR pszServer, LPCTSTR pszWebName, LPCTSTR pszUser);`	Begins open of a given Web on HTTP server
`long vtiEditWebPage(LPCTSTR pszPageURL);`	Loads a Web into a given editor
`long vtiPutWebPageMetaInfo(LPCTSTR pszURL, LPCTSTR pszNameValuePairs);`	Sets one or more metainfo variables for a page
`long vtiGetDocToFile(LPCTSTR pszURL, LPCTSTR pszFilename);`	Saves a Web document to local file

Editor Automation Methods

Table 13-3 is a list of the OLE automation methods supported by the FrontPage Editor within the OLE identifier `FrontPage.Editor.2.0`.

Table 13-3 OLE automation methods supported by `FrontPage.Editor.2.0`

Method	Description
`LPDISPATCH vtiOpenWebPage(LPCTSTR szFileName, LPCTSTR szURL, LPCTSTR szWebURL, LPCTSTR szWebTitle);`	Opens an existing Web page from a local file
`long vtiQueryWebPage(LPCTSTR szURL, LPCTSTR szWebURL);`	Determines if the editor is editing a given page
`void vtiBringToTop();`	Brings the editor to top of application windows
`LPDISPATCH vtiNewWebPage(LPCTSTR szURL, LPCTSTR szWebURL, LPCTSTR szWebTitle);`	Creates a new page with default URL and Web info

To Do List Automation Methods

Table 13-4 is a list of the OLE automation methods supported by the FrontPage To Do List within the OLE indentifier `FrontPage.ToDoList.2.0`.

Table 13-4 OLE automation methods supported by `FrontPage.ToDoList.2.0`

Method	Description
`void vtiShow();`	Displays To Do List
`void vtiHide();`	Hides To Do List
`BOOL vtiAddTask(LPCTSTR taskName, short priority, LPCTSTR createdBy, LPCTSTR url, LPCTSTR cookie, LPCTSTR comment);`	Creates a new task in To Do List
`long vtiGetActiveCount();`	Returns number of To Do List tasks
`BOOL vtiCompletedTaskByUrl(LPCTSTR url, LPCTSTR cookie);`	Marks task matching URL and rremoves from list
`BOOL vtiWorkedOnTaskByUrl(LPCTSTR url, LPCTSTR cookie);`	Adds a notation that the current user updated task
`BOOL vtiAddTaskAskUser(LPCTSTR taskName, short priority, LPCTSTR createdBy, LPCTSTR url, LPCTSTR cookie, LPCTSTR comment);`	Adds a new task and assigns a new user

Examples

Bundled with the FrontPage SDK are numerous examples that illustrate how to create your own wizards and templates for FrontPage. In addition, there are examples and documentation for creating custom Common Gateway Interface (CGI) programs and other utilities for interacting with the FrontPage Server Extensions and OLE automation APIs. This section outlines the files that are included with the FrontPage SDK.

Documentation

An extensive documentation file is provided in both DOC and RTF format. Included is an extensive technical breakdown of the FrontPage components, similar to the content of this chapter.

Templates

These files are actual templates created with either FrontPage or the SDK. The files included are shown in Table 13-5.

Table 13-5 Templates included in the FrontPage SDK

Directory\File	Description
pages\tablepag.tem	A page template containing a table; created with the Save As Template command in the FrontPage Editor
webs\testcorp.tem	A Web template containing documents from the FrontPage Corporate Presence Web Wizard; created with the Web Template Maker utility
frames\sample.frm	A frameset template with recursive frames and multiple targets

Wizards

The wizards shown in Table 13-6 were created using Visual Basic 4.0. Take a look at the included source code to create your own wizards.

Table 13-6 Wizards included with the FrontPage SDK

Directory\File	Description
pages\hello.wiz	A very simple page wizard
pages\calendar.wiz	A page wizard that creates a calendar for a selected month and year using an HTML table
webs\helloweb.wiz	A very simple Web wizard
webs\realest.wiz	A Web wizard that creates a small Web of interconnected pages about real estate

Utility Programs

The examples shown in Table 13-7 allow you to explore the FrontPage OLE automation APIs. The code has been written so that you can copy the methods with only slight modifications within your code.

Table 13-7 Sample programs included with the FrontPage SDK

Utility Program	Description
APITests	A program that exercises all the automation interfaces to the FrontPage tools; includes a lot of reusable code for common tasks
FPlaunch	A helper application that opens a Web and starts editing a page when the user follows a link; uses a parameter file stored on the Web server
WebTmpl	A program that creates Web template directories for FrontPage 2.0 based on a current Web managed by a local FrontPage Personal Web Server

CGI Scripts

The SDK includes a number of sample CGI scripts to illustrate interaction with your Web server. These scripts are listed in Table 13-8.

Table 13-8 CGI scripts in the FrontPage SDK

CGI Script	Description
hello	A very simple example showing how to create a CGI program in C using the standard I/O (stdio) interface
cgiwin32	A gateway between the stdio CGI interface and the CGI-WIN interface; written in C
olecgi	A gateway between the stdio CGI interface and OLE server DLLs created with Visual Basic 4.0; written in C
olecgivb	Example CGI handler objects and utility classes for use with olecgi; written in Microsoft Visual Basic 4.0

Where to Go from Here?

You now have seen many of the components that make up the FrontPage SDK, which truly opens up the FrontPage interface and will enable you to create your own wizards and templates. Now that you have been exposed to this toolkit, it is your turn to take this information to build your own shuttle to travel the light-years of cyberspace!

Scripting—Easy as 1...VB

14

In this chapter you will learn:

The Background and Definition of Visual Basic Scripting
Edition (VBScript)

How to Incorporate VBScript into Your Web Pages

How to Use the Language Elements Available Within
VBScript

How to Include and Interact with ActiveX Control Objects

Responding to Form and Control Events

Designing Validation Forms

How to Troubleshoot Your Code

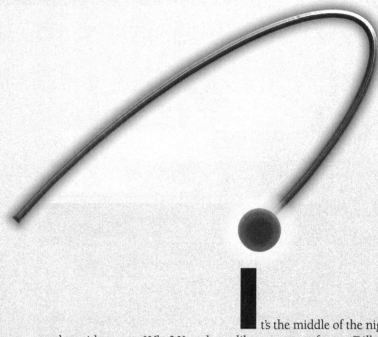

It's the middle of the night and you are one tired and trepid person. Why? Your boss, like a manager from a Dilbert cartoon, had the urge to torture some poor soul and you happened to walk by. You have been assigned to design a Web page that is fast, flexible, can interact with Java and ActiveX controls, and can perform data validation. Thinking this daunting task was impossible, you fled the office. Then, on the ledge of the Empire State Building, the answer comes to you—Visual Basic Scripting Edition!

What Is VBScript?

"What is VBScript?" has been a burning question for both professional Webmasters and novices. Everyone wants to know what this language is, how it compares to existing languages, and how they can use it spruce up their Web pages. This section addresses some of these issues to help you understand what VBScript is and how you can use FrontPage to add fuel to your hot site.

The Newest Member of the VB Family

Visual Basic Scripting Edition (VBScript) is Microsoft's latest addition to its development toolset. Based on the widely used Visual Basic language, VBScript is the third member of this powerful family, following in the footsteps of Visual Basic for Applications (VBA) and Visual Basic (VB). This language offers existing VB developers an opportunity to leverage their skills in the Internet arena and provides neophyte programmers the foundation to expand their knowledge upward through the Visual Basic hierarchy, as shown in Figure 14-1.

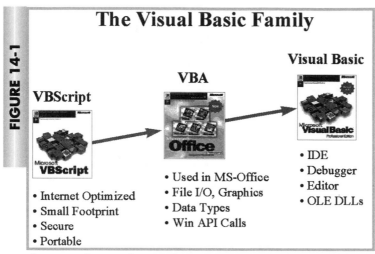

The Visual Basic hierarchy

VBScript Is a Scripting Language

You may ask, "What is a scripting language?" A smart-aleck author might answer, "Why, VBScript, of course!" Well, to be honest, that wouldn't be a totally accurate answer. In reality, a scripting language is similar to a programming language in that it, too, involves preparing a set of instructions for the computer to execute. However, a scripting language is meant to be implemented on a smaller scale and perform smaller, yet powerful tasks. For example, you would probably use a large programming language, such as C++, to create FrontPage, whereas you could use some sort of scripting language to automate various FrontPage commands. VBScript falls into the scripting language category. But don't let the scripting taste fool you, because you can use VBScript to perform some very powerful tasks. In fact, VBScript will allow you to perform many tasks that have traditionally been performed on the server via CGI.

VBScript Is an Extension to HTML

VBScript is embedded within HTML code. Therefore, you need to be familiar with the basics of HTML. You may wonder why you need to know HTML when FrontPage does so much for you. Consider the purpose of VBScript—to add functionality and automation to your pages. FrontPage will do a lot for you, but when you need to really extend your page, maybe by adding something like calculator functionality, you will want to use VBScript to accomplish this in a programmatic manner.

VBScript Can Interact with Objects

Much of the power of current and future Web pages will reside in the use of objects (such as charts, graphs, documents, and videos). VBScript is powerful enough to interact with both ActiveX controls and Java classes as well. This object interaction will enable Web pages to exploit functionality over the Web that previously existed only on the desktop.

VBScript in HTML: The `<SCRIPT>` Tag

Let's take a look at a general example:

```
...
<SCRIPT LANGUAGE=VBSCRIPT>
<!--
    Function SayHelloWorld()
        MsgBox "Hello World", 0, "My First Hello Program"
    End Function
-->
</SCRIPT>
...
```

What Is HTML?

If you have never seen HTML code before, then this may look like Greek to you. If so, then you will want to review Chapter 4, "HTML Made Easy," for an HTML refresher. If this seems old hat, then let's continue.

Notice the use of the `<SCRIPT>` tag. All VBScript code will reside in your HTML between paired `<SCRIPT>` tags. It doesn't really matter where in the code you put the `<SCRIPT>` tag, but you want to use it *somewhere* if you want to add VBScript code and have a VBScript-enabled browser read it.

Now let's take a look at the additional entry on the `<SCRIPT>` tag. Because Internet Explorer allows multiple scripting languages to exist in code, you need to specify which language is to be used via the `LANGUAGE=VBSCRIPT` line. Also notice that the VBScript code is enclosed within comment blocks to allow incompatible browsers to view this code as comments. One last consideration involves the placement of the code and tags. VBScript can be used anywhere within your HTML page, although the general convention is to place all functions in the `<HEAD>` section to centralize the code.

Scripting Languages and the `<SCRIPT>` Tag

At the time of this writing, the only two scripting languages available are Visual Basic Scripting Edition (Microsoft) and JavaScript (Netscape). However, because both companies are working with the World Wide Web Consortium (W3C), they have agreed to use the HTML standard `<SCRIPT>` tag which is designed to support future scripting languages, if necessary.

VBScript and the FrontPage Editor

Okay. You now have an idea what VBScript is, but in order to learn it, it is best that you follow along with the examples in this chapter to learn the basics (so to speak). You will need to learn how to add VBScript code to your Web pages using the FrontPage Editor. To aid you in achieving your scripting desires, the FrontPage Editor now includes the Script Editor and the Scripting Wizard (see Figure 14-2).

Invoking the Script Editor

For the purposes of this chapter, invoke the Script Editor and enter your code in the editor window as follows:

1. Choose menu option Insert | Script.

2. When presented with the editing window (see Figure 14-3), ensure that the VBScript option is marked.

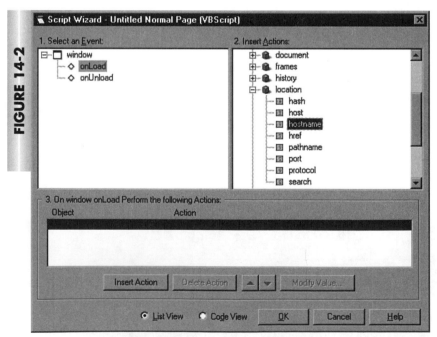

FIGURE 14-2

Figure 14-2 The FrontPage Scripting Wizard

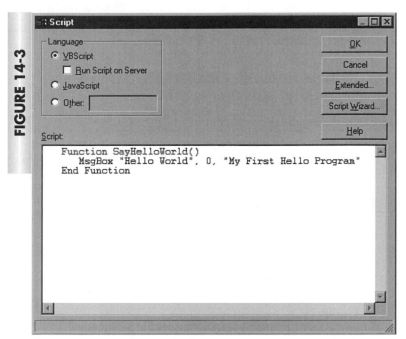

The editing window with the VBScript option marked

3. Begin typing in the editing window. As you grow bolder in your endeavors, you can use the Scripting Wizard button and manipulate various objects and events (covered later).

4. When you are ready to return to the page, press the OK button.

Data Types

Although other languages may use numerous data types, VBScript allows the use of a single data type—a *variant*. What is a variant? Well, a variant is a special data type that can store various types of information. Think of a variant as a chameleon that can change depending on its environment or storage value. In the context of data types, the variant can emulate other types. For example, a variant can be a number, a string, or even a date! Because only one data type is needed, the programmer is freed from having to declare various data types and the footprint of the VBScript runtime is decreased. Table 14-1 lists the common categories of data types that can be stored within the variant data type.

Table 14-1 Subtypes supported by the VBScript variant type

Type	Description
Boolean	Value of True or False
Byte	Integer in the range from 0 to 255
Date (Time)	A number representing a date between January 1, 1900, and December 31, 9999
Double	A double-precision, floating-point number in the range from -1.79769313486232E308 to -4.94065645841247E-324 for negative values; -4.94065645841247E-324 to 1.79769313486232E308 for positive values
Empty	Uninitialized value; strings are set to "" and numbers are set to 0
Error	An error number
Integer	Integer number in the range from -32,768 to 32,767
Long	Integer number in the range from -2,147,483,648 to 2,147,483,647
Null	No valid data value
Object	An OLE automation object
Single	A single-precision, floating-point number in the range -3.402823E38 to -1.401298E-45 for negative values; 1.401298E-45 to 3.402823E38 for positive values
String	A variable-length string that may be up to approximately 2 billion characters in length

Working with Variables

To get anything useful done in a program, you will usually incorporate variables into your program. This section covers the following topics:

◁ What is a variable?

◁ Variable declaration

◁ Naming restrictions

◁ Assigning values

◁ Scope and lifetime

◁ Handling arrays and vectors

What Is a Variable?

Consider the many roles you may play throughout your life. One day you go out onto the basketball court as a basketball player and at other times you are a student. To your parents, you are their child and to your friends, you are a buddy. No matter what role you take on, you are still one thing—a human. In fact, you could say that your basic label is *human*, yet you can take on different meanings (values) to other people.

This concept is tantamount to a variable. What is a variable? In techno-speak, a variable is a symbolic label that represents a storage location. Clear as mud? Let's clarify this. Think back to those days in algebra class where X=1. In this example, X is a variable that holds the value of 1. By using X, you can write a generic formula, such as X=X+2. Although you could have stated 3=1+2, any time you wanted to change the initial number, you would have had to rewrite your formula. It is much easier to use the variable, X, and change its value and leave your formula intact. Given the following formula, which would you rather change, X or the formula?

```
X = 5
X = (sin(x) + sqrt(x)) * (X*3200) / arc(x+82) - 5
```

Figure 14-4 illustrates how a variable is represented in computer memory.

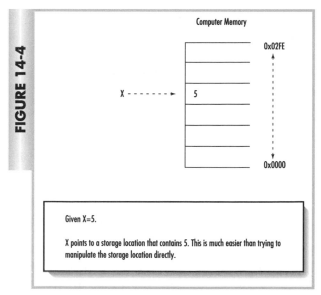

FIGURE 14-4

Computer Memory

X - - - - - - - → 5

0x02FE

0x0000

Given X=5.

X points to a storage location that contains 5. This is much easier than trying to manipulate the storage location directly.

A variable represented in computer memory

Declaration

Now that you are ready to add variables to your code, you may be wondering how to accomplish this in VBScript code. This is performed using the **Dim** (short for Dimensioning) statement. An example follows:

```
<SCRIPT LANGUAGE=VBSCRIPT>
<!--
    Dim PizzaCost
-->
</SCRIPT>
```

Note that all you have to do is specify the **Dim** statement, followed by one or more variable names. If you wish to add more variable names, you can either concatenate them on the same line or provide them on their own lines, as follows:

```
<SCRIPT LANGUAGE=VBSCRIPT>
<!--
    Dim PizzaCost, CheesePrice, ButteredCrust
    Dim Salad
-->
</SCRIPT>
```

Dim and Visual Basic Syntax

If you are a Visual Basic programmer, you will quickly notice that there is no
Dim As Type used in variable declaration. Because VBScript has only one
data type, variant, there is no need to specify a type in the declaration
statement.

Don't Worry—Be Explicit

Another feature of VBScript is the ability to define a variable implicitly by using its name within your code. Although this is a nice feature, it is good programming practice to declare all your variables before using them. By not declaring your variables, you are prone to making variable spelling errors that may be hard to track down. As such, VBScript includes an additional statement to force you to declare your variables. This statement is called **Option Explicit**.

The **Option Explicit** statement should be the first statement inside your **<SCRIPT>** tag. The purpose of this statement is to force you to declare your variables explictly (hence the name) before using them. This may seem like a restriction, but if you misspell the name of your variable, you will receive a runtime error telling you that you have an undeclared variable. This is much easier to fix than a hidden spelling error that may throw off your calculations. Let's examine what happens when you omit or use the **Option Explicit** statement.

```
<SCRIPT LANGUAGE=VBSCRIPT>
<!--
```

```
'-----------------------------------------------------
' Here we declare "myvar" but DO NOT declare "myvar2"
' No runtime error produced.
'-----------------------------------------------------
    dim myvar
    Sub Button1_OnClick
        dim myvar
        myvar = "I love VBScript."
        myvar2 = "Don't You?"
        MsgBox myvar & myvar2
End Sub
-->
</SCRIPT>

<SCRIPT LANGUAGE=VBSCRIPT>
<!--
 Option Explicit
'-----------------------------------------------------
' Because we used "Option Explicit" we MUST declare
' all variables. Assignment of "myvar2" will fail.
' Runtime error produced.
'-----------------------------------------------------
    dim myvar
    Sub Button1_OnClick
        dim myvar
        myvar = "I love VBScript."
        myvar2 = "Don't You?"
        MsgBox myvar & myvar2
End Sub
-->
</SCRIPT>
```

In the first example, the code will run successfully because of the lack of the **Option Explicit** statement. It is quite probable that misspelled variable names would not be caught during the execution of the code. In the second example, the VBScript interpreter (browser) will recognize that all variables *must* be declared (via **Dim**) before their actual use. Failure to do so will produce a runtime error by the browser.

Naming Restrictions

As you get ready to declare your variables, you are probably wondering, "What's the catch?" Indeed, there are some restrictions to declaring variables in VBScript.

◁ Variable names must begin with an alphabetic character. This means you cannot begin a variable with a number or some other nonalphabetic character.

◁ Variable names cannot contain an embedded period. As you'll see when you get into advanced VBScript topics, the period is used to access object properties. If you used a variable with a period, the browser would get quite confused.

◁ Variable names must not exceed 255 characters. 255 characters should be plenty for a variable name. An excessively lengthy variable name will hinder readability of your code.

◁ The variable must be unique within the scope in which it is declared (more about scope in a moment). For example, if you declare a variable in a function or procedure, then you can't define another variable with the same name within that same function or procedure.

◁ A variable name cannot be the same as a reserved VBScript word. For example, you cannot declare a variable named `Dim` because this is a VBScript keyword.

Assigning Values

It is very easy to assign a value to a variable. The basic format for assignment is as follows:

```
variable = expression
```

The variable is on the left side of the expression, and the value you want to assign is on the right, as shown in the following example:

```
<SCRIPT LANGUAGE=VBSCRIPT>
<!--
   Rate = 34
-->
</SCRIPT>
```

Scope and Lifetime

Let's look at a simple code segment:

```
<SCRIPT LANGUAGE=VBSCRIPT>
<!--
   Function Increment(num)
      Dim tempnum
      tempnum = num + 1
      Increment = tempnum
   End Function
-->
</SCRIPT>
```

In this example, notice the use of the variable `tempnum`. This variable is declared with the function and will exist only until the function is terminated. In other words, the *scope* or *lifetime* of this variable is within the `Increment` function. Scope is essentially the period for which a variable is activated. In the context of computer language, scope and lifetime are synonymous. You will see references to each throughout computer documentation.

Procedure-Level Variables

Tempnum, in the previous example, would be defined as a procedure-level variable or a variable having a procedure-level scope. This means that this variable exists only for the period that the function or procedure is running. Note, however, that each time the function or procedure is invoked, a new copy of the variable is created and will exist until the function terminates.

Script-Level Variables

Conversely, a script-level variable is one that exists during the lifetime of the script.

```
<SCRIPT LANGUAGE=VBSCRIPT>
<!--
    Function Increment(num)
        Dim tempnum
        tempnum = num + 1
        Increment = tempnum
    End Function

    Dim myVar
-->
</SCRIPT>
```

Without getting into the details of the code, notice that **myVar** is declared within the script, yet outside of the function. Because **myVar** has a script-level scope, it will continue to exist until the script is concluded.

Static Tricks

Suppose you want to declare a procedure-level variable that retains its value between calls to the procedure. One solution would be to use a script-level variable, but you want this to be a procedure variable. Is this possible? Yes. VBScript includes the **Static** statement for this purpose.

```
<SCRIPT LANGUAGE=VBSCRIPT>
<!--
    Sub toggle
        static f_switch =0
        f_switch = 1 - f_switch
    End Sub
-->
</SCRIPT>
```

In the above example, **f_switch** can retain a value over subsequent calls to the toggle procedure. This approach allows you to define the variable once and then change its value within the procedure.

Arrays

Suppose you want to keep track of 100 items, called Apple, in your code. How would you address this? Your first thought might be to use 100 individual variables, as follows:

```
Dim Apple1, Apple2, ..., Apple100
```

Although this approach would solve your problem, it also introduces potential limitations to your program. If you wanted to use **Apple** as a single entity with individual apples, this would not be possible with the previous example. However, this can be solved with the use of an *array*. Arrays allow you to address a series of variables (same data type) as one name and to use a number to identify each one explictly. Arrays allow you to write generic loops that can be used to access each array element rather than requiring numerous repetitive lines.

Zero-Based Arrays

VBScript arrays are called *zero-based arrays*. This means that the first element in the array is indexed with zero. As such, the following statement implies that there are actually 20 elements in the **MyList** array:

```
<SCRIPT LANGUAGE=VBSCRIPT>
<!--
'---------------------------------------------
' Print out first five values of array MyList
'---------------------------------------------
  Dim MyList(20)
  Dim j
  MyList(0) = 32
  MyList(1) = 64
  MyList(2) = 128
  MyList(3) = 256
  MyList(4) = 512
  For j= 0 to 4
     MsgBox "Value(" & j & ") = " & MyList(j)
  Next
-->
</SCRIPT>
```

Static and Dynamic Arrays

You may or may not know the number of elements that are going to be stored in an array. How do you declare arrays that will meet either criteria? Fortunately, VBScript provides you with the ability to achieve both scenarios with *static* and *dynamic* arrays.

A static array is one in which you already know the maximum number of elements your array will need to hold, whereas a dynamic array is one that can be resized during runtime to accommodate your needs. You have already seen a static array in the previous example. However, you can resize the array by redeclaring it using the **ReDim** keyword. Let's take a look at an example:

```
<SCRIPT LANGUAGE=VBSCRIPT>
<!--
' First, declare a 100 element array
    Dim MyArray(100)
' Next, resize that array to hold 200 elements
    ReDim Preserve MyArray(200)
-->
</SCRIPT>
```

You may notice a couple of things from this example. The first observation is that you need to use **ReDim**, rather than **Dim**, to resize the array to hold 200 elements. You may also notice the use of the **Preserve** keyword. **Preserve** allows you to save the elements in your current array when you resize it. This implies that if you omit this keyword, your existing data will be lost when the array is resized. One other word of warning—if you decrease the size of an existing array, then you will lose the data that is in the eliminated elements.

Constants

Often you will find that you have variables that never change throughout your code. Such variables may include formulas or values, such as pi. Although you may not have known it, you were using constant variables. A *constant* is a variable that represents a value and never changes. This is very useful because you can rely on this variable containing the same value, no matter where you use it in your code.

Declaring Constants

You declare a constant just as you would any other variable, with the **Dim** statement. In fact, because you declare constants just like ordinary variables, it may be difficult to tell them apart from other variables. As such, you will probably want to use some type of naming convention for your constant variables. For example, you may want to only use uppercase characters to represent constants. VBScript uses its own naming convention: All VBScript constants are prefixed with the characters **vb**. Sample constant declarations follow:

```
<SCRIPT LANGUAGE=VBSCRIPT>
<!--
  Option Explicit
'-------------------------------------------------------
' This code uses a constant TAX_DAY and determines whether
' the tax payer is early or needs to pay a late fee.
'-------------------------------------------------------
  Dim TAX_DAY
  Dim cur_day, rate
  TAX_DAY = 15
  cur_day = InputBox("Which day of the month is this?")
  if cur_day > TAX_DAY then
      rate = (cur_day - TAX_DAY) * 200
      msgbox "Penalty time. You owe us " & rate & " dollars."
  Else
```

```
        msgbox "You still have time to file."
    End if


-->
</SCRIPT>
```

Note that if you wished to expand on this script, you could use **TAX_DAY** throughout your program consistently (that is, as a constant).

VBScript Constants

VBScript provides many useful constants that you can place in your code and that VBScript itself uses in many function calls. Table 14-2 illustrates just a few of the VBScript constants at your disposal.

Table 14-2 Sample VBScript constants

Constant	Description
vbCr	Carriage return character
vbCrLf	Carriage return and line feed characters (useful for terminating text strings)
vbFalse	Boolean value of zero (0)
vbLf	Line feed character
vbTrue	Boolean value of one (1)

Hello, Operator?

Wouldn't it be nice if you had some way to perform calculations, assignments, or comparisons in your code? Don't think so? Well, if you didn't perform at least one of those functions in your code, you probably would have a useless program! VBScript allows you to build robust programs and thus includes a full suite of operators, including arithmetic operators, comparison operators, concatenation operators, and logical operators.

Unary Versus Binary Operators

Although there are many types of operators, they all fall into one of two categories: *unary* or *binary*. A unary operator is one that takes only one operand, whereas a binary operator takes two operands, one on the left and one on the right of the operator. The following example illustrates the use of both operator types:

```
<SCRIPT LANGUAGE=VBSCRIPT>
<!--
' The '=' operator is binary (left and right side)
```

```
    x = 5
-->
</SCRIPT>

<SCRIPT LANGUAGE=VBSCRIPT>
<!--
   'The NOT operator is unary (left side only)
   x = Not y
-->
</SCRIPT>
```

Operator Precedence

Just like math operators, VBScript operators follow an order of precedence. In other words, the sequence in which the operators are ordered may influence the resulting value of the operation. If you wish to override the order of precedence, you may use parentheses to force the enclosing operation to be performed first. However, please note that within the parentheses, the normal operator precedence still follows.

Sometimes you may combine operators from more than one category. In this case, there is still an order of precedence. Arithmetic operators are evaluated first, with comparison operators and logical operators evaluated successively. All comparison operators have equal precedence that allows evaluation from left to right. Table 14-3 illustrates the operator categories and the order of precedence.

Table 14-3 VBScript operator precedence

Symbol	Description	Category
^	Exponentiation	Arithmetic (x ^ 2 equals "x squared")
-	Unary negation	-x + y
*	Multiplication	x * y
/	Division	x /y
\	Integer division	x\y
Mod	Modulo arithmetic	Mod(y)
+	Addition	x + y
-	Subtraction	x - y
&	String concatenation	(not arithmetic, but evaluated before comparison operators) "Hello " & x & ". How are you?"

continued on next page

continued from previous page

Symbol	Description	Category
=	Equality	Comparison x = y
<>	Inequality	x <> y
<	Less than	x < y
>	Greater than	x > y
<=	Less than or equal to	x <= y
>=	Greater than or equal to	x >= y
Is	Object equivalence	x Is object
Not	Logical negation	Logical Not(y)
AND	Logical conjunction	(x AND y)
OR	Logical disjunction	(x OR y)
XOR	Logical exclusion	x = XOR(y)
Eqv	Logical equivalence	x Eqv y
Imp	Logical implication	x Imp y

Controlling Program Flow

You are well on your way to learning the secrets of VBScript and can now add some basic functionality into your code, but how do you incorporate logic or repetition into your code? Computer people tend to use the terms *conditional statements* and *control structures* to refer to handling conditions and loops. Quite simple, isn't it?

if...then...else Statements

The `if...then...else` statement is one of the easiest language elements to understand because it completely follows logical thinking (as shown below).

```
if (true condition)  then (do 1 or more statements) <Else do 1 or more
statements>
```

Let's explore some basic elements of this statement. First, it is important to understand that the condition must always evaluate to True or False. If your condition does not result in one of these two values, then you will receive a syntax error. The following example illustrates the basic `if...then` single-line syntax:

```
<SCRIPT LANGUAGE="VBSCRIPT">
<!--
   Dim myName
   myName = "Joe"
   If myName = "Joe" then myName = "Joe Cool"
-->
</SCRIPT>
```

In particular situations, you may prefer to execute multiple lines when the condition is True. As such, you may employ the multiple-line syntax. However, note that this format requires the use of the **end if** statement, so that VBScript knows which lines belong to your condition. An example follows:

```
<SCRIPT LANGUAGE="VBSCRIPT">
<!--
   Dim myName
   Dim myAddress
   myName = "Joe"
   If myName = "Joe" then
      myName = "Joe Cool"
      myAddress = "123 Cool Avenue"
   End If
-->
</SCRIPT>
```

If you wish to run one set of statements when a condition is True and then run another set of statements when the condition is False, you should use the full **if...then...else** statement, as shown in the following example:

```
<SCRIPT LANGUAGE="VBSCRIPT">
<!--
   Dim myName
   Dim myAddress
   If myName = "Joe" then
      myName = "Joe Cool"
      myAddress = "123 Cool Avenue"
   Else
      myName = "John Doe"
      myAddress = "Nowhere Lane"
   End If
-->
</SCRIPT>
```

Round and Round Again

It may be sad to say, but much of life is repetition. Think of the many times you have to repeat the same thing over and over again. You start off each day by waking up, eating, performing some daily activities, and then going back to sleep. Sounds pretty mundane, doesn't it? You will find, however, that this looping nature allows you to accomplish a lot each day. Fortunately, you can also perform some pretty useful tasks using loops in programming languages. VBScript provides the **do...** loop, **while...wend**, **for...next**, and **for...each** statements to assist in your looping needs.

do... Loop

The **do...** loop is simple, yet flexible. It is used to perform a statement or set of statements while a condition is True or becomes True. Let's take a look at an example:

```
<SCRIPT LANGUAGE="VBSCRIPT">
<!--
   Dim LoopCounter, maxReps
   maxReps = 5
   LoopCounter = 0
   Do While LoopCounter < maxReps
      LoopCounter = LoopCounter + 1
   Loop
   MsgBox "My loop was processed " & LoopCounter & " times."
-->
</SCRIPT>
```

How Many Times MUST Your Loop Execute?

Within the do... loop, the while keyword can be used to force your code to execute zero or more times. For example, if you place the while condition with the do keyword, the inner statements will be executed *only* if this condition is True. In contrast, if you place the while keyword after the Loop keyword, then you will guarantee that the inner loop statements are executed at least once.

In the above example, a terminating condition is established with the **while** keyword. If this condition is True, then the loop will continue. Although this is a basic example, it does not mask the flexibility of the **do...** loop. The **while** keyword can also be placed after the **loop** keyword, allowing your statements to be executed before the terminating condition is terminated. The following examples illustrate how both versions can be used:

```
<SCRIPT LANGUAGE="VBScript">
<!--
Sub PreSheepCounter()
   dim sheep
   dim sheepcount
   sheep = 0
   sheepcount = 75
'-------------------------------------------------
' If the following statement were not true, this
' loop would never execute.
'-------------------------------------------------
   Do While sheepcount > 50
        sheep = sheep + 1
        sheepcount = sheepcount - 1
   Loop
   msgbox "Early sheep = " & sheep
End Sub
```

```
-->
</SCRIPT>

<SCRIPT LANGUAGE="VBScript">
<!--
Sub PostSheepCounter()
   dim sheep
   dim sheepcount
   sheep = 0
   sheepcount = 49
'------------------------------------------------------------
' Even though the WHILE condition is FALSE, this
' loop will execute at least ONCE because the check does
' not happen until AFTER the loop contents are processed
'------------------------------------------------------------
   Do
        sheep = sheep + 1
        sheepcount = sheepcount - 1
   Loop While sheepcount > 50
   msgbox "Late sheep = " & sheep
End Sub
-->
</SCRIPT>
```

Using the until Keyword

Suppose you want to peform your loop until a certain condition becomes True. You could accomplish this using the `while` keyword, but VBScript also provides another means, the `until` keyword. In the following examples and Figures 14-5 and 14-6, the loop will begin and continue until the condition becomes True. (That would make sense, wouldn't it?)

```
<SCRIPT LANGUAGE="VBScript">
<!--
   Dim loopCounter, maxReps, internal
      maxReps = 5
      loopCounter = 5
      internal = 0
'------------------------------------------------------------
' Perform conditional check BEFORE going into loop.
' The loop contents will NOT be executed because
' the condition evaluates to TRUE.
'------------------------------------------------------------
   Do Until loopCounter = maxReps
      loopCounter = loopCounter + 1
      internal=internal+1
   Loop
   MsgBox "Pre-My loop was processed " & internal & " times."
-->
</SCRIPT>
```

continued on next page

continued from previous page

```
<SCRIPT LANGUAGE="VBScript">
<!--
Sub PostLoop()
    Dim LoopCounter, maxReps, internal
        maxReps = 5
        LoopCounter = 5
        internal = 0
    '------------------------------------------------
    ' Perform conditional check AFTER going into loop.
    ' The loop contents will be executed at least once
    ' because there is no initial comparison.
     '------------------------------------------------
    Do
        LoopCounter = LoopCounter + 1
        internal = internal+1
    Loop Until LoopCounter >= maxReps
    MsgBox "Post-My loop was processed " & internal & " times."
End Sub
-->
</SCRIPT>
```

Exiting a `Do...` Loop Statement Within the Loop Body

In some cases, you may want to exit out of your loop. For example, if your loop is infinite (keeps going on and on), you want to offer a way out so the rest of your program can execute. This can be accomplished with the **exit do** statement. This statement is usually called as a result from an **if...then...else** statement.

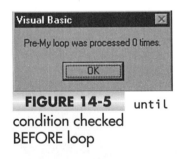

FIGURE 14-5 `until` condition checked BEFORE loop

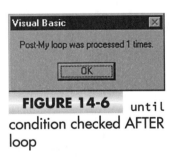

FIGURE 14-6 `until` condition checked AFTER loop

In Listing 14-1 (results in Figure 14-7), the user is prompted for information until he or she enters an exit value. This exit value will be the terminating condition for the loop.

Listing 14-1 Using **exit...do** to leave a code segment

```
<SCRIPT LANGUAGE="VBScript">
<!--
   Dim myResult, userValue
   myResult = 0
'----------------------------------------------------------
' The user will be repeatedly prompted for numbers until a
' zero (0) is entered. After which, execution will drop
' out of the Do...Loop and the message will be displayed.
'----------------------------------------------------------
   Do
      userValue = InputBox("Please enter a number to add (0 = quit): ")
      if userValue = 0 then Exit Do
      myResult = myResult + userValue
   Loop
   MsgBox "The sum of your entries is " & myResult & "."
-->
</SCRIPT>
```

Interacting with the User

There are times when you may want to interact with the user. VBScript provides you with two built-in functions, InputBox and MsgBox. InputBox is used to gather input (such as entering a value or pressing a button) from the user. MsgBox is used to provide the user with information and then provide the program with a value corresponding to the button that was pressed by the user. InputBox and MsgBox are covered in greater detail in the Function-Procedures section of this chapter.

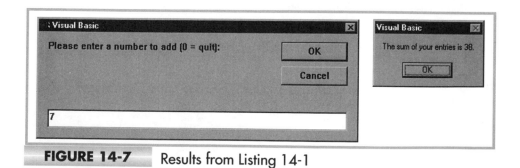

FIGURE 14-7   Results from Listing 14-1

while...wend

Think of the `while...wend` statement as your basic `do...` loop without the glitz. This statement is a carry-over from Visual Basic. However, Microsoft recommends that you use the `do...` loop because the `while...wend` statement does not have the flexibility of an `exit...do` statement to terminate execution. An example of the `while...wend` statement follows:

```
<SCRIPT LANGUAGE="VBSCRIPT">
<!--
    Dim loopCounter, maxReps
    maxReps = 5
    loopCounter = 0
    While loopCounter < maxReps
        loopCounter = loopCounter + 1
    Wend
    MsgBox "My loop was processed " & loopCounter & " times."
-->
</SCRIPT>
```

for...next

The `do...` loop is flexible enough to allow you to run a block a number of times, but the termination logic is your responsibility. In fact, if you aren't careful, you could inadvertently allow your loop to execute more times than you expect. The `for...next` loop addresses this situation. With the `do...` and `for...next` statements, a block of statements can be executed a number of times while the `for...next` manages a counter variable that is increased or decreased with each repetition of the loop.

If you were writing code that deals cards to a player, you would probably want to simulate the dealing of a certain number of cards. Let's look at an example.

```
<SCRIPT LANGUAGE="VBSCRIPT">
<!--
    Dim cardHand, loopCounter
    cardHand = 5
    For loopCounter = 1 to cardHand
        DealCard
    Next
-->
</SCRIPT>
```

In this example, the player would be dealt five cards. Notice that the `for...next` statement manages the value of the `loopCounter` variable. All that is required in the `for...next` statement are initial and ending values for the `counter` variable.

For added flexibility, you can increase or decrease the value of the `counter` variable using the `step` keyword. In the following example, the player is dealt only an even number of cards because the value of `loopCounter` will be incremented by 2.

```
<SCRIPT LANGUAGE="VBSCRIPT">
<!--
    Dim cardHand, loopCounter
```

```
        cardHand = 10
        For LoopCounter = 2 to cardHand Step 2
            DealCard
        Next
    -->
    </SCRIPT>
```

for each...next

The **for each...next** statement is similar to **for...next**, but the **for each...next** state-ment allows you to repeat a set of statements based upon each object in a collection. In this case, VBScript will set and maintain an object variable during the lifetime of your loop. Continuing with the dealer example, the **for each...next** statement is used to process each card in the deck.

```
<SCRIPT LANGUAGE="VBSCRIPT">
<!--
    For Each myCard in MyDeck
        If myCard.value > 10 Then
            myCard.Caption = "Face Card"
        End If
    Next
-->
</SCRIPT>
```

Exiting for Loops

You can exit both **for...next** statements and **for each...next** statements by using the **exit for** statement. This statement is useful when you need to exit the loop before the terminating condition is True. In both of the following examples, a set of cards is read until the right card is found or no more cards are left in the hand (in some circles, this is called cheating).

```
<SCRIPT LANGUAGE="VBSCRIPT">
<!--
    Dim LoopCounter, tgtCard
    tgtCard = SpyOnUserCard
    For LoopCounter = 1 to 10
        if LoopCounter = tgtCard then
            StoreUserCard(LoopCounter)
            Exit For
        End If
    Next
-->
</SCRIPT>

<SCRIPT LANGUAGE="VBSCRIPT">
<!--
    Dim LoopCounter, tgtCard
    tgtCard = SpyOnUserCard
    For Each myCard in myHand
```

continued on next page

continued from previous page

```
            if myCard.Value = tgtCard then
                StoreUserCard(tgtCard)
                Exit For
            End If
        Next
    -->
    </SCRIPT>
```

Procedures

Procedures are very powerful language components. They can be considered programs within programs. They can be called from within various parts of your program. Why use procedures? If you needed to perform a common function, such as display a message box with a message, you normally would write this code every time you need to perform this action. If the code for a message box consisted of 100 lines, then you would have to include all 100 lines each time you wanted to display the message box. Procedures allow you the capability to call the code whenever you need it. This helps make your program readable and flexible.

How Procedures Work

There will probably be times when you have tasks that need to be performed multiple times throughout your program. It is good programming practice to create code that can be reused repeatedly. In technical terms, this is called *modularization*. By modularizing your program, you not only build common code segments but you also make your program easier to read. You may be wondering just how a procedure does its job. Let's look at a code sample to see a procedure declaration and invocation in effect.

```
<SCRIPT LANGUAGE="VBSCRIPT">
<!--
'--------------------------------------------
' This procedure will display a message along
' with the name it receives.
'--------------------------------------------
    Sub SayHello(name)
        MsgBox "Hello " & name
    End Sub

    Dim name
    dim myloop
'--------------------------------------------
' Prompt user for 3 names and display 3
' separate messages with the input name.
'--------------------------------------------
    for myloop=1 to 3
        name = InputBox("Please enter a name: ")
        SayHello(name)
    next
-->
</SCRIPT>
```

Figure 14-8 shows the sample code in action.

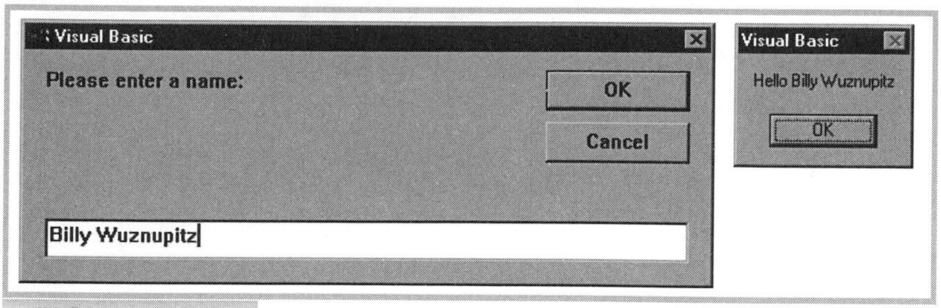

FIGURE 14-8 The SayHello() example in action

By using a procedure, the VBScript interpreter would jump to the definition of the SayHello() procedure, process the statement, and then return to the for...next loop. A number of issues are raised by this sample code. First, you declare a SayHello() procedure. Then, in your loop, you can repeatedly call the SayHello() procedure to display your message. If there were no procedure, you would have to display the message in the loop. In this example, it may seem that this was not an efficient use of a procedure. However, if this program contained numerous places where it needed to display the Hello... message, then the display would have to be specified in every location it was needed. This also raises another issue, concerning modularization. By using the procedure, the Hello... functionality is located in only one piece of code. If the programmer later decides to expand or change the message to Top 'o the morning to you, the change would need to be made only within the procedure itself. In the latter scenario, the programmer would have to change the line in every piece of code where the Hello... string was mentioned.

Declaring Procedures

All procedures need to be defined before they can be used. This also implies that one procedure (P1) cannot call another procedure (P2) before it (P2) has been declared. It is recommended that you put all procedure declarations at the beginning of the <HEAD> section of your HTML page in the order in which they will be needed. Some programmers also place the rest of their code in the <HEAD> section as well, but this is not mandatory. Also, keep in mind that all VBScript code needs to be located between paired <SCRIPT> and comment (< ! --and -->) tags.

Types of Procedures

VBScript provides two types of procedures: the Sub procedure and the Function procedure. A Sub procedure follows the form

```
Sub name [(arglist)]
    [statements]
    [Exit Sub]
    [statements]
End Sub
```

where **name** is any string that follows variable naming requirements, **arglist** represents zero or more parameters, **statements** are any code segments to be executed within the body of the **Sub** procedure, and **Exit Sub** will immediately terminate the procedure.

In contrast, the **Function** procedure is defined as

```
Sub name [(arglist)]
    [statements]
    [name = expression]
    [Exit Function]
    [statements]
    [name = expression]
End Sub
```

where **name** is any string that follows variable naming requirements, **arglist** represents zero or more parameters, **statements** are any code segments to be executed within the body of the **Function** procedure, **name=expression** returns a value to the calling program, and **Exit Function** will immediately terminate the procedure.

Sub *Procedures*

A **Sub** procedure is a series of statements, enclosed by the **Sub** and **End Sub** statements, that does not return a value. This does not mean that you can't manipulate global variables, but rather that your procedure won't pass any values back directly. **Sub** procedures allow you to pass arguments (more about this in a bit). All arguments must be enclosed within parentheses. Even if you have no arguments, you must still use a set of empty parentheses. The example below shows a sample **Sub** procedure:

```
<SCRIPT LANGUAGE="VBSCRIPT">
<!--
'--------------------------
' Sub procedure declaration
' Display a string.
'--------------------------
    Sub HelloWorld(strMessage)
        MsgBox strMessage
    End Sub

    Dim mymsg
    mymsg = "Hello World. It is a lovely day."
'------------------------------------------
' Call the procedure to display the string
'------------------------------------------
    HelloWorld(mymsg)
-->
</SCRIPT>
```

Function *Procedures*

A **Function** procedure is a series of statements, enclosed by the **Function** and **End Function** statements, that returns a value. Functions are very useful for performing operations on values but may be used very similarly to **Sub** procedures. As with **Sub** procedures, you may pass arguments into your function but they must be enclosed within parentheses. (Yes. Empty arguments still get parentheses.) The example below shows a sample **Function** procedure.

```
<SCRIPT LANGUAGE="VBSCRIPT">
<!--
'----------------------------------------------
' Function Declaration:
' This function returns the cube of a number.
'----------------------------------------------

    Function Cubed(intValue)
        Cubed = intValue * intValue * intValue
    End Function

    Dim intCubeVal
'----------------------------------------------
' Call the Cubed() function.
' Notice that functions ALWAYS return a value
'----------------------------------------------
    intCubedVal = Cubed(5)
    MsgBox "5 Cubed is " & intCubedVal & "."
-->
</SCRIPT>
```

Passing the Buck—Er, Arguments

An *argument is* data that you pass into your procedures. Arguments are the values that you want your procedure to use as input. They do not have to be in any order, but you must include them within parentheses. Even an empty set of arguments must be enclosed in parentheses. Also, keep in mind that you will need to use a **Function** procedure if you wish to return a variable to the caller.

Pass by Value and Pass by Reference

By default, when a variable is passed to a procedure, it is *passed by reference*, meaning that the actual variable is passed to it. This implies that any changes made to the variable during the lifetime of the procedure will result in changes to the global variable, as well. However, this activity can be overridden with the **ByVal** keyword in the **Sub** statement. **ByVal** enables the calling program to pass a copy of the variable to the procedure. This allows the procedure to perform any manipulation to the variable copy without harming the contents of the original variable.

FIGURE 14-9 The `InputBox` and `MsgBox` function procedures

User Interaction—`InputBox()` and `MsgBox()`

Occasionally, you will find that you wish to interact with the users of your Web page. Within VBScript, two functions help to achieve this purpose—the `InputBox` and `MsgBox` functions (see Figure 14-9). The `InputBox` function is used to gather input from the user, whereas the `MsgBox` function is used to display messages. Although you've seen these functions in previous examples, let's examine the syntax of these functions.

The `InputBox` function follows the form of

```
InputBox(prompt[, title][, default][, xpos][, ypos][, helpfile, context])
```

where the following are defined:

◁ `prompt` is a string displayed as the message in the dialog box. The maximum length of `prompt` is approximately 1024 characters, depending on the width of the characters used. If you wish to separate the prompt into multiple lines, you can separate it using either a carriage return character (`Chr(13)`), a line feed character (`Chr(10)`), or a combination of both (for example, VBScript constant `vbCrLf`).

◁ `title` (optional) is a string expression displayed in the title bar of the dialog box. If you omit `title`, the application name is placed in the title bar.

◁ `default` (optional) is a string representing the default response, should the user enter no input. If this field is omitted, the default value is empty.

◁ `xpos` (optional) represents (in twips) the horizontal distance of the left edge of the box from the left edge of the screen. If this field is omitted, the box will be centered.

◁ `ypos` (optional) represents (in twips) the vertical distance of the top of the box from the top of the screen. If this field is omitted, the box will be placed approximately one-third of the way down on the screen.

◁ helpfile (optional) is a string that identifies the Help file to use to provide context-sensitive help for the dialog box. If helpfile is provided, context must also be provided. When the field is specified, the user can press F1 to invoke help against that particular dialog box.

◁ context (optional) is a number that is the Help context number the Help author assigned to the appropriate Help topic. If context is provided, helpfile must also be provided.

If the user chooses OK or presses ENTER, the **InputBox** function returns the string that is located in the text box. If the user chooses Cancel, the function returns an empty string ("").

The **MsgBox** function follows the form of

```
MsgBox(prompt[, buttons][, title][, helpfile, context])
```

where the following are defined:

◁ prompt is a string displayed as the message in the dialog box. The maximum length of prompt is approximately 1024 characters, depending on the width of the characters used. If you wish to separate the prompt into multiple lines, you can separate it using either a carriage return character (Chr(13)), a line feed character (Chr(10)), or a combination of both (for example, VBScript constant vbCrLf).

◁ buttons (optional) is a number representing the sum of values specifying the number and type of buttons to display, the icon style to use, the identity of the Default button, and the modality of the message box. If omitted, the default value for buttons is 0. See Table 14-4 for a list of possible button values.

◁ title (optional) is a string displayed in the title bar of the dialog box. If you omit title, the application name is placed in the title bar.

◁ helpfile (optional) is a string that identifies the Help file to use to provide context-sensitive help for the dialog box. If helpfile is provided, context must also be provided. When the field is specified, the user can press F1 to invoke help against that particular dialog box.

◁ context (optional) is a number that is the Help context number the Help author assigned to the appropriate Help topic. If context is provided, helpfile must also be provided.

Table 14-4 MsgBox button values

Value	Description	Group Type
0	Display OK button only	Button
1	Display OK and Cancel buttons	Button
2	Display Abort, Retry, and Ignore buttons	Button
3	Display Yes, No, and Cancel buttons	Button
4	Display Yes and No buttons	Button
5	Display Retry and Cancel buttons	Button
16	Display Critical Message icon	Icon
32	Display Warning Query icon	Icon
48	Display Warning Message icon	Icon
64	Display Information Message icon	Icon
0	First button is default	Default Button
256	Second button is default	Default Button
512	Third button is default	Default Button
768	Fourth button is default	Default Button
0	Application modal; the user must respond to the message box before continuing work in the current application	Modality
4096	System modal; all applications are suspended until the user responds to the message box	Modality

Table 14-5 illustrates the possible return values from the **MsgBox** function.

Table 14-5 MsgBox return values

Value	Button Chosen
1	OK
2	Cancel
3	Abort
4	Retry

Value	Button Chosen
5	Ignore
6	Yes
7	No

As you can see, the **MsgBox** and **InputBox** functions will provide you with some flexibility in your interaction with the user.

The Object of Your Desire

Objects is one of the most important concepts within the VBScript language. A VBScript object can be considered as a base representation with a set of variables and procedures attached to it. These variables can be considered attributes or details that constitute the object, whereas the attached procedure provides the operations that are performed against that object. Without getting too in-depth, let's take a look at a scenario. Consider the pants that you are wearing (shorts, skirts, and kilts count, too). Your pants have a size, length, color, and style. In computer terms, your pants would be considered an object, and the size, length, color, and style would represent the pants' properties or attributes. For a closer example, let's examine your browser. If you consider your browser an object, then you can associate properties, such as buttons, default colors, network preferences, and window size, with it. In addition, you can determine the procedures that can be performed with your browser, such as opening a document or downloading a file.

Objects are all the rave in VBScript. Almost everything you interact with is an object and has properties. In the world of the Web, you may be confronted with all types of objects, including buttons, text boxes, ActiveX controls, and Java objects. An object and its property may be referenced as

```
object.property
```

Let's take a look at a **Button** object, which you typically see on Web forms. A **Button** object has properties such as name and value. In addition, a **Button** object also has a **click** method (essentially, a procedure). In code, you would refer to the **Button** object as

```
button.name
button.value
button.Click()
```

To set an object's properties, manipulate it like any other variable with the exception that you must use the **object.property** convention. The following example illustrates how to set various properties.

```
Label.text = "Hello World."
Button.name = "btnHello"
pants.size = 32
```

Much like procedures, an object's methods can also be invoked simply by using the **object.method** calling convention. Keep in mind that an object's method can be coded as a `Function` procedure, enabling the method to return a value to the caller. Below are some sample object method calls.

```
btnHello.Click()
rate = StateTax.GetRate("MI")
Index.SetTemp(95)
```

The next section takes a closer look at objects and controls and sees how these fit into the scope of VBScript and your Web pages.

 ## ActiveX Controls

Microsoft has created a Windows object technology known as Object Linking and Embedding (OLE), which is based on a Common Object Model (COM). Object controls (.OCX) that use this technology were known as OLE controls until Microsoft renamed these to ActiveX controls. Microsoft is working with the W3C to have ActiveX controls adapted as the standard objects for WWW use.

ActiveX Control Objects (formerly OLE Controls)

To use ActiveX (or Java) control objects in your HTML pages, include an object using `<OBJECT>` tags and set its initial property values using `<PARAM>` tags. Note that using the `<PARAM>` tags is just like setting initial properties for a control on a form. The following example illustrates how to set the `<OBJECT>` and `<PARAM>` tags to the ActiveX Label control for a page.

```
<OBJECT
        classid="clsid:99B42120-6EC7-11CF-A6C7-00AA00A47DD2"
        id=lblSample
        width=250
        height=250
        align=left
        hspace=20
        vspace=0
>
<PARAM NAME="Angle" VALUE="360">
<PARAM NAME="Alignment" VALUE="2">
<PARAM NAME="BackStyle" VALUE="0">
<PARAM NAME="Caption" VALUE="A Sample Label">
<PARAM NAME="FontName" VALUE="Arial">
<PARAM NAME="FontSize" VALUE="20">
<PARAM NAME="FontBold" VALUE="1">
<PARAM NAME="FrColor" VALUE="0">
</OBJECT>
```

If you take a closer look at this example, `classid` tells the browser the identity of the `Label` control. This numeric identity will be stored on the user's machine within the Windows system registry key `/HKEY_CLASSES_ROOT`. If the label control did not exist on the user's machine, this code would not work. An additional `<OBJECT>` field called `codebase` identifies the source of the control. By specifying a **codebase**, as follows, the browser would automatically download the control from the URL listed in the **codebase** field:

```
codebase="http://www.microsoft.com"
```

Another important field is the **id**. The **id** identifies the object with your form so that the **control** object (with its properties and methods) can be referenced with the HTML or code. The other fields further specify how the control is to be drawn on the form.

The **<PARAM>** tags are used to set various properties of the control. By setting these properties, it is possible to set default values for the control.

In addition, you can retrieve and set control properties and invoke methods just as with any of the form controls. The following code, for example, includes **<FORM>** controls you can use to manipulate two of the Label control's properties:

```
<FORM NAME="LabelControls">
<INPUT TYPE="TEXT" NAME="txtNewText" SIZE=25>
<INPUT TYPE="BUTTON" NAME="cmdChangeIt" VALUE="Change Text">
<INPUT TYPE="BUTTON" NAME="cmdRotate" VALUE="Rotate Label">
</FORM>
```

Once the form is defined, you can create a VBScript event procedure to change the label text in response to the **cmdChangeIt** button click event. (Events are covered in more detail later.)

```
<SCRIPT LANGUAGE="VBScript">
<!--
Sub cmdChangeIt_onClick
        Dim TheForm
        Set TheForm = Document.LabelControls
        lblSample.Caption = TheForm.txtNewText.Value
End Sub
-->
</SCRIPT>
```

Figure 14-10 illustrates the use of the previous examples to create and interact with various controls on a page.

Locating Valid CLASSIDs and PROGIDs

At the time of this writing, one of the main criticisms of object declaration was locating (and typing) the correct CLASSID in HTML code. Before the release of Internet Explorer 3.0, Microsoft attempted to ease the frustration with the release of the program **ACLIST.EXE**. Figure 14-11 shows ACLIST in action.

ACLIST is a handy utility that reads through your Windows Registry and finds all valid ActiveX control names, CLASSIDs, and PROGIDs (like a CLASSID, but a text identifier). You then may select a control from the list to copy the **<OBJECT>** tag syntax to the Windows clipboard for pasting into your page.

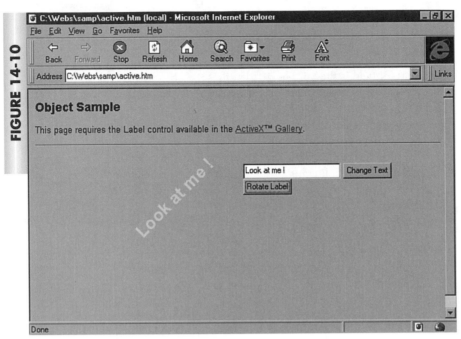

FIGURE 14-10

Using the Label control on an HTML page

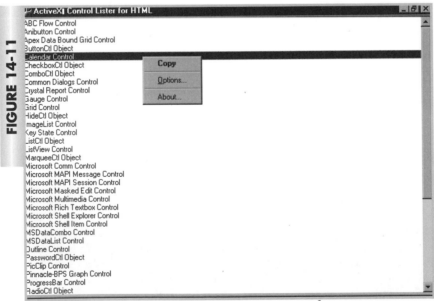

FIGURE 14-11

Microsoft `ACLIST.EXE` generates `<OBJECT>` tags for ActiveX controls

Welcome to the Main Event

So you think you've discovered all the power of VBScript? Hold on to your hats—you have only skimmed the surface! A VBScript program that does a calculation is a nice program, but think about your interaction with most programs. Many applications include interactivity. Consider your Web browser. Most of its actions are in response to your mouse movements or menu commands. Although this might appear to be done with smoke and mirrors, these applications are actually responding to events. An *event* is something that happens that could be used to trigger your VBScript code. Much of the power of VBScript lies in the ability to wait on specific events and launch your appropriate code segments.

Common Types of Events

You're probably wondering to yourself, "Events are fine and dandy. But how do I know what to wait for?" Rather than just telling you about events, let's take a look at some common ones and how they are used.

◁ The `Click` event is triggered when a user clicks the mouse button on either a link or some other object (such as a button or check box).

◁ The `Focus` event occurs when the user either clicks on an object or presses the `TAB` key to activate the control. Most `Focus` objects are enclosed by a thin black rectangle.

◁ The `Blur` event is triggered when the focus is removed from the currently in-focus object to another object. This can be triggered by the user either moving the mouse to another location on the page or pressing the `TAB` key to activate another object.

◁ The `Change` event occurs after a user has modified the input of a form object and then shifted the focus away from the current object. Examples of `Change` include the user selecting an item from a list box and typing text into a text box.

◁ The `MouseOver` event occurs after the user has moved the mouse pointer over a link or object on the page. This event is useful for providing additional information to the user, such as displaying the URL address of a hypertext link.

◁ A `Select` event occurs after the user has selected text in a text box.

◁ A `Submit` event occurs after a user clicks the Submit button. Because this event occurs *before* the form is submitted, you can include VBScript code to validate fields or perform calculations as well as to determine whether or not the form should be submitted.

Looking Out for Events

To act on events, you need to tell your code to watch out for these events. This is accomplished by naming your controls and then coding the corresponding event handling procedures. Suppose you define a button, named **BtnHello**, as follows:

```
<INPUT TYPE=BUTTON VALUE="Click Me" NAME="BtnHello">
```

In this example, the **TYPE** field identifies to the browser the type of control object to be used for input (in this case a **BUTTON**). The **VALUE** field is used to specify the button's caption and the **NAME** field identifies the button so that the form, other controls on the page, or code can interact and respond to events generated by the button.

To process events that involve **BtnHello**, code the event handling procedure as follows:

```
Sub BtnHello_OnEvent()

    Code goes here

End Sub
```

where you name the procedure **object_Event**. In this example, you must specify the name of the object (**btnHello**) you want to trap (**_OnClick**). To process the **Click** event, you would code your procedure as follows (see Figure 14-12 for output):

```
'---------------------------------------
' The code will be invoked when the user
' clicks the btnHello button. Here we
' will display a message to the user.
'---------------------------------------
Sub BtnHello_OnClick()
   MsgBox "Thanks for clicking me!"
End Sub
```

If you again look at the common event types, their associated event handler would be as follows:

◁ object_OnClick

◁ object_OnFocus

◁ object_OnBlur

◁ object_OnChange

◁ object_OnMouseOver

◁ object_OnSelect

◁ object_OnSubmit

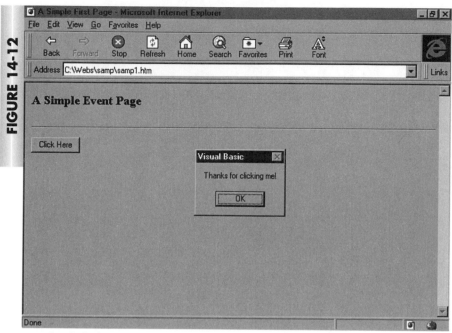

FIGURE 14-12

Result of clicking BtnHello button

Common Events

Now that you have been exposed to events, know how to react to them, and have even seen the onClick event in action, let's take a look at several more common events to illustrate how an event is handled and how the browser reacts to these events.

onFocus

In this case, you will plant an event trigger that will occur if the user moves the page focus to one of the objects on the form. Our form consists of two text boxes that prompt for arbitrary data. When focus is placed on either of these elements, an associated VBScript statement will be invoked.

```
<INPUT NAME=quote TYPE="" ROWS=1 SIZE="15" onFocus="window.status='I feel a ⇐
quote...'">Please leave a Quote
        <INPUT NAME=mynum TYPE="" ROWS=1 SIZE="3" onFocus="window.status= ⇐
'Pick any number...'">Type a number
```

Note that the code watches for and triggers the proper event. However, rather than calling a VBScript function, an explicit VBScript statement is executed. Figure 14-13 shows a form with the above elements. If you click in either text box, thus changing the focus, the message in the status line will change accordingly.

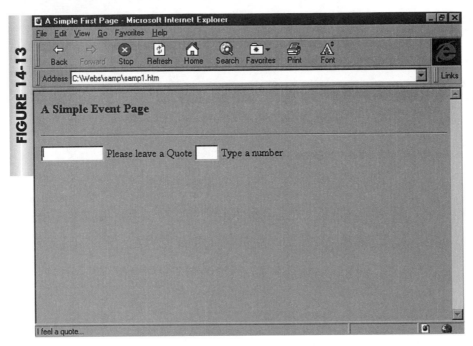

Responding to the onFocus event

onSubmit

In this example, you will watch for the user attempting to submit a form. In this case, you present the user with a text box to enter a user ID. After entering the ID, the user must then press the Submit button. You could then write an event handler to validate the userid, but, instead, focus on the event triggered when the user submits the form (see Figure 14-14 for output).

```
<SCRIPT LANGUAGE='VBScript'
<!--
'----------------------------------------
' Event Handler: Display 'Pass' message
'----------------------------------------
Sub validate_ID()
   MsgBox "Pass"
End Sub
-->
</SCRIPT>

<FORM onSubmit="validate_ID()">
       <INPUT NAME=userid TYPE="" ROWS=1 SIZE="15" >Enter User ID
       <INPUT NAME=submit TYPE="submit">
       <INPUT NAME=reset TYPE="reset">
</FORM>
```

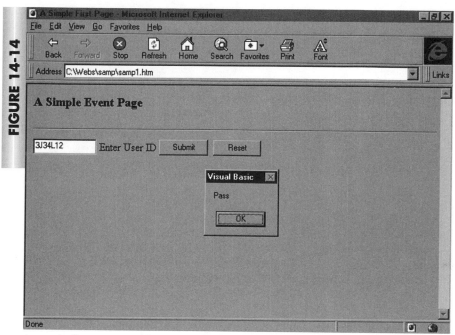

FIGURE 14-14

Sample form using the `onSubmit` event

In this example, the user is presented with a text box and two buttons, Submit and Reset. In the `<FORM>` tag, you tell the browser to keep a watch for the `onSubmit` event. When the user presses the Submit button, the `onSubmit` event is triggered and the `validate_ID()` event handler is invoked.

Working with Forms

Although the use of forms is covered elsewhere, let's take a moment to examine how VBScript can be used in a form. In the traditional Web form:

1. The user is prompted for some information.

2. After the user provides the information, the click of a button or link will send the form's data to the server.

3. A Common Gateway Interface (CGI) program on the server then validates the data.

4. If the data is valid, the server performs some action. Otherwise, an error is raised and the user is either denied or prompted again for valid data.

This approach has worked well over the years. However, it is a costly procedure in terms of network traffic and the time spent waiting for the server to validate the data. Enter VBScript.

VBScript allows *client-side* processing. This means that all programming functions take place right on the page and the server has to get involved only when the time is right, which reduces the amount of network traffic. Per the previous scenario, form validation can take place on the page, before the data is sent to the server. This allows the page designer to ensure that the data is correct *before* the server program is invoked. Let's examine a code sample (see Figure 14-15 for output):

```
<HTML>
<HEAD><TITLE>Joes Insurance Company</TITLE>
<SCRIPT LANGUAGE=VBSCRIPT>
<!--
'-------------------------------------------
' Process the number and display a message
'-------------------------------------------
  Sub Submit_OnClick()
'-------------------------------------------
' Must declare the form so we can access
' its controls (i.e. Text1)
'-------------------------------------------
  Dim myForm
  Set myForm = Document.InsuranceForm
  If IsNumeric(myForm.Text1.Value) Then
      if myForm.Text1.Value > 1 and myForm.Text1.Value < 26 then
         msgbox "Oh. We are going to sock it to you good!"
      else
         msgbox "We want to sock it to you, but you avoided us -- THIS TIME"
      end if
    else
       msgbox "Come on. Please enter a REAL age."
    end if
  end sub
-->
</SCRIPT>
</HEAD>
<BODY>
<FORM NAME="InsuranceForm" Action="">
Please enter your age for Insurance Processing:
  <INPUT NAME="Text1"
         TYPE= "TEXT"
         SIZE="3">
  <INPUT NAME="Submit"
         TYPE="BUTTON"
         VALUE="Submit">
</FORM>
</BODY>
</HTML>
```

In this example, a form is presented to the user that prompts for his or her age. When the user presses the Submit button, an event is triggered and the VBScript validation routine (`Submit_onClick`) is invoked to validate the age and display a message to the user. Note that the server does not have to be involved during the interaction with the user. In a more complex example, it would be efficient to do most (if not all) data entry validation within your VBScript code. This cuts down on network traffic and allows the user quicker response time.

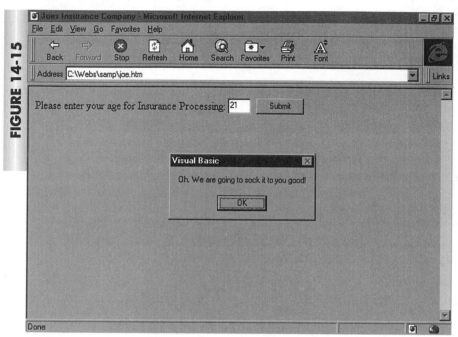

FIGURE 14-15

Sample validation form

Troubleshooting

As with most any other endeavor, programs don't always work the first time around. You will no doubt experience the joy of troubleshooting your VBScript programs. In computer lingo, this troubleshooting is termed *debugging*. In other words, you will be trying to eradicate the bugs (er, errors) from your program.

Like any good exterminator, you will need to understand what you're seeking and the tools that you have at your disposal. Due to its youth, VBScript is limited in its error messages, but it does provide you with a starting point when things go wrong.

Error Messages

Syntax errors, as in Figure 14-16, are introduced into your code either when you enter (inadvertently, of course) unknown statements or when you omit parameters from keywords or functions.

In many cases, VBScript will provide you with error messages. However, the message descriptions are sometimes cryptic at best.

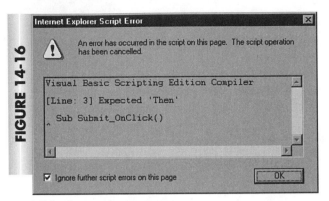

VBScript error message

The Coal Miner Approach

Sometimes your code just won't work the way you intended. This is the time to get out your coal miner's hat and begin digging into your code. This is often the hardest part of debugging your code. There is one sure-fire way to track down that erroneous code:

◁ Locate the code where you think the problem may reside.

◁]Trace the program logic (see box Debugging Tip: Write It Out) and ensure that it does what it is *supposed* to do—not what you *think* it should do.

Fortunately, a number of resources are at your disposal to aid you in your problem resolution.

Debugging Tip: Write it Out

Often, one of the easiest ways to locate where your code is awry is to put in some code that provides a status. Many programmers use the MsgBox() function or document.write() to write out a message to let the user know which part of code is being accessed. In most circumstances, you will be able to home in on your problem code within a few lines by using this popular technique.

Where to Go from Here?

Visual Basic Script Edition will continue to gain in popularity. With this increase in fame, the Web will be filled with resources on VBScript. Here are a few of the many valuable Web sites with precious information:

◁ http://www.microsoft.com/vbscript—This is the premier location for all VBScript releases and product documentation. Microsoft provides updates, examples, and links to other valuable VBScript-related material.

◁ http://www.gamelan.com—This Web site is exclusively dedicated to Java and JavaScript. This site provides a wealth of information because VBScript can interact with Java classes and many excellent JavaScript examples can be ported to VBScript.

◁ http://www.inquiry.com/vbscentral—At the time of this writing, this site is bidding to become the gamelan of VBScript. Here you will find numerous VBScript and ActiveX examples.

◁ Appendix B, "Visual Basic Script Reference"—This appendix includes language features, data types, object references, variable naming conventions, and object naming conventions.

Plenty more resources are available, but part of the fun is in the search! Now that you are armed with the essentials, unleash the power of VBScript!

Brewing Java and JavaScript

15

In this chapter you will learn:

The Differences Between Java, JavaScript, and HotJava

The Difference Between a Java Applet and a Java Program

How to Add Java Applets to Your Webs

How to Use the ImageMap and Animator Java Demo Applets Provided with This Book

How to Add JavaScript Code to Your Webs

How to Write Simple JavaScript Applications

How to Use JavaScript to Check a Form and Dynamically Change the Content of a Web Page or Frame in a Page

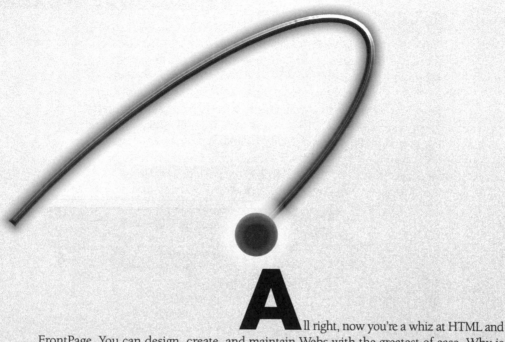

All right, now you're a whiz at HTML and FrontPage. You can design, create, and maintain Webs with the greatest of ease. Why is it, then, that every time you pick up a magazine about the Internet, you find an article about Java? What's all the hoopla? You've got a great site and you never had to deal with Java! Is this some plan by the Colombians to rule the Internet? Are you doomed because you prefer your Java in a cup and not a net? No. Java is something very new and potentially very powerful.

Java is an interpreted language, and Java interpreters are being created for many different kinds of computers and platforms. Huh? OK, that was a mouthful, but it's not all that bad. It works something like this: Suppose someone put a calculator in front of you and said, "Add the numbers 32 and 45 together and tell me their sum." Then they took that calculator away, gave you a different one, and told you, "Add 32 and 45 and tell me their sum." Despite the fact that the calculators are different, you could probably figure out how to add 32 and 45. In this analogy, "Add the numbers 32 and 45 and tell me their sum," is the program, you are the interpreter, and the calculators are the computers. Java works the same way. A Java program is a series of generic instructions, and it's up to the interpreter for that machine to figure out what buttons to push to execute those instructions. As of this writing, there are Java interpreters for MS Windows 95, MS Windows NT, Sun's Solaris, the Macintosh, and the Power PC. This means you could write a Java program and it would run on all these systems without any special changes or effort on your part! How's that for sharing information and cross-platform development?

Note

Because Java programs need an interpreter to be executed, some extra overhead is associated with them. This means that, like all interpreted languages, Java programs normally run slower than native code programs. The creators of Java knew this when they created Java: They designed it to minimize the overhead involved, making Java relatively fast for an interpreted language and still keeping the benefits of portability. Additionally, the speed of Java programs can be improved by making better interpreters or creating special compilers that change Java bytecode into native instructions for particular platforms. Additionally, Sun has announced that it is licensing Java technologies to many companies that produce operating systems, and you can expect Java interpreters to be included in future operating systems.

Java, JavaScript, HotJava...You're Javan' Me Crazy!

As with anything that comes to fame overnight, there's some confusion about Java. It seems that everyone is trying to get into the act, as if anything with the word Java attached to it is bound to turn to gold.

◁ Java is a programming language developed by Sun Microsystems. Java is used for two main purposes: writing applets for the World Wide Web (WWW or Web) and writing platform-independent programs. Why is it called Java? There's some debate about that issue. It's been hypothesized that Java stands for "Just Another Vague Acronym," but this has been denied by Sun. Sun claims the name Java is just a marketing decision. Given the popularity of coffee and other caffeine supplements among programmers, Java probably contributed more to the project than just its name.

◁ JavaScript is not Java. It is a scripting language loosely based on Java. It was first introduced by Netscape under the code name Mocha. It is not used to write standalone programs, but rather to add functionality to HTML documents. The code for a JavaScript program is part of the HTML document itself (though there are plans to enable the code to be stored in special `.js` files that will be loaded with a special HTML tag, but these plans were not implemented at this writing). JavaScript code is not compiled and is interpreted by the browser in a manner similar to the rest of the HTML document. It does not operate outside the browser's environment. JavaScript is still under development, but at the rate the Internet is developing, it will probably be commonplace by the time you read this book.

◁ HotJava is more than just a cup of Joe, it's also the name of a WWW browser from Sun Microsystems. It was written using the Java programming language to demonstrate the language's power. The first Java applets (written
using the alpha version of Java) ran only on this browser. Now many
browsers support Java applets, including Microsoft's Internet Explorer and
Netscape Navigator.

Java isn't something that we just spill on the keyboard anymore. It represents a new way
of programming. It allows a developer to reach a very broad audience quickly and easily.
The syntax used by Java is very similar to the popular programming languages C and C++,
so developers find it easy to learn. Java was designed to be a small, portable, and secure
programming language. For these reasons and others, it is quickly becoming the language
of choice for Intranet and Internet applications and applets.

Java is a topic too deep for full coverage in this volume. You won't learn how to write
Java code in this book—there wouldn't be room for FrontPage! Instead, you'll get the nick-
el tour of Java. You'll see some of the capabilities of Java and how to incorporate Java applets
into your Web. You don't need to be a programmer or have any special expertise to use Java
applets. The examples should give you a glimpse of Java's potential and help jazz up your
Webs without making your head spin.

What Can Java Do?

Java comes in two basic flavors. The first is a program. Java programs are like any other
program you've ever encountered and shouldn't present any real confusion. The second
Java flavor is the applet. Applets are a very special kind of program, written expressly for
HTML pages and the WWW and run by your Web browser.

Programs

Java programs are standalone. The word processor you use could be written in Java (if it
were, you would never know unless you asked). These programs don't have a large bear-
ing on Web development, so there's no real reason to get too deep into them, but you should
be aware that a Java program is not necessarily the same as the applets you will be
embedding in your Webs.

The life cycle of a Java program is outlined in Figure 15-1. First, a text file is created
that holds the Java source code. This code is then compiled into Java *bytecode* using a Java
compiler. Bytecode is a series of binary instructions that represent the code. Think of bytecode as shorthand for the source code: It's smaller, more efficiently organized, and quicker
for the computer. Additionally, the bytecode is the same no matter what system it's compiled on: The bytecode from a program compiled on a PowerPC will look the same as if
the program had been compiled on a Windows or UNIX system. This bytecode is the Java
program and it can be distributed to many other platforms. When the bytecode is executed
(the program is run), it is sent to an interpreter. The interpreter reads the instructions encoded in the bytecode and performs them, running the program. Interpreters are being
written for many different platforms, and any machine with a Java interpreter can run a
Java program. All interpreters are made to execute the Java bytecode in a similar fashion,
making the Java program behave the same no matter on what platform.

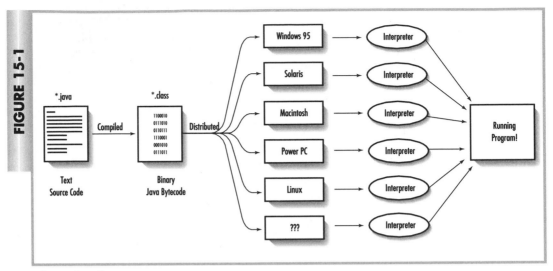

Life cycle of a Java program

Note

The Java bytecodes were originally designed to run on a virtual machine. The designers basically said, "A typical computer could work like this...." They then wrote compilers to produce bytecode that would run on this imaginary system. Interpreters simulate this virtual machine, enabling the bytecode to be executed on many platforms. Because of Java's huge growth and popularity, Sun Microsystems has announced that it will produce Java chips. Java chips are processors that use Java bytecode as their native instruction set, which means that Java programs will execute very fast on them because there won't be a need for an interpreter. This is truly unique; in the past, hardware systems were created first, then compilers to make programs for the platform were created, and then, if the platform were really popular, interpreter programs were written so programs written for the platform could run on other systems. In Java's case, the compilers and interpreters came first and now hardware is coming second—a real role reversal.

Applets

Applets are a potent spice you add to your Web. They enable you to do such things as animations, sounds, interactivity, games, databases, spreadsheets, and word processing—the list could go on for miles. Applets embedded in Webs are safe to use and add excitement and functionality in a way not possible with ordinary HTML or scripts. Java applets have many security features built in. These rules prevent applets from harming anyone's system or invading anyone's privacy. Applets cannot access anyone's hard disk (other than the one on which they reside) and cannot execute programs on the client's machine. They do not have direct access to the user's memory, so they cannot probe the user's system. This means that they're safe to use on the Web. It all boils down to this: Java applets embedded on other people's home pages cannot harm your computer, and applets you put on your Webs cannot harm others.

The life of a Java applet is outlined in Figure 15-2. As you can see, it is very similar to the way a Java program works. The code is created and compiled in the same manner. Note, however, that it might work only as a program or only as an applet, or it might (although not normally) run either way. After being compiled, the applet is designated by a special tag in an HTML document (covered later). Distribution occurs when someone browses the HTML document on the Web and his browser gets the Java applet named in the HTML code. The browser contains a special interpreter for applets, which it uses to run the byte-code—causing the applet to do its thing.

FrontPage 97 Web Designer's Guide has no space to teach you how to write an applet, but examples are provided on the disk included with this book in the folder named **Chap15**. Examples of applet use are included as well. You can easily add these applets to your Web pages without a deep knowledge of how they work internally, just as you can use a program without knowing what's going on behind the scenes.

What Do Java Applets Look Like in the HTML?

Well, Java in an HTML document is a little more than a coffee spot, but not much more difficult to make. If you can add images to your Web pages, you can add Java applets. An HTML document with an embedded Java applet is illustrated in Listing 15-1.

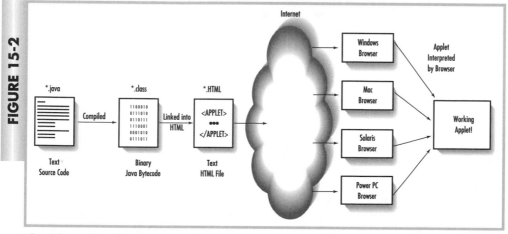

FIGURE 15-2

The life cycle of a Java applet

Listing 15-1 Sample HTML template containing a Java applet

```
<HTML>
<HEAD>
</HEAD>
<BODY>
  <APPLET CODE="TheProgramURL.class" WIDTH=150 HEIGHT=25>
    <PARAM NAME="Parameter1Name" VALUE="Parameter1Value">
    <PARAM NAME="Parameter2Name" VALUE="Parameter2Value">
  </APPLET>
</BODY>
</HTML>
```

Inserting an applet into your document is just like any other HTML addition, you just insert the appropriate tag (in this case the **<APPLET>** tag). Inside the applet tag, you would use **CODE=** to specify the name of the Java applet. All Java applets end with the extension **.class**. You set the size of the window the applet runs in with the **WIDTH=** and **HEIGHT=** modifiers, though some Java applets are able to size themselves dynamically in your document. The **<PARAM>** tag is used to provide information to the applet. If you've ever used DOS or UNIX programs, you'll find that these parameters are similar to command-line arguments. They provide information to the Java applets, which can then adjust their behavior accordingly. The **NAME=** modifier specifies the name of the characteristic or value you want to modify, and the **VALUE=** modifier is the value or data you want to give that parameter.

Note

Because Java was designed with modern operating systems in mind, it does not include much support (at this time) for older file systems. This means there is no 8.3 format for Java code. Java was made to work with 32-bit systems that support long file names, and no three-character DOS equivalent extensions for .class and .java exist at this time.

The best part about adding applets is that now the FrontPage Editor has built-in support for them!

Lesson 1: Inserting Java Applets into Your Web

To add a Java applet to your Web, first open the Web with the FrontPage Explorer. You learned how to do this in Chapter 9. Then import the Java program's **.java** files. Once those files are imported, open the document to which you want to add the applet with the FrontPage Editor. Position the cursor where you would like the applet to be inserted, then select Insert | Other Components > Java Applet from the menu bar. This brings up the Java Applet Properties window, as shown in Figure 15-3.

In this dialog, you enter the data for your applet. It is really just a fill in the blank form for the applet tag that we described above. The Applet Source box corresponds to the name of the Java applet. This file ends with a **.class** extension. The Applet Base URL field is the relative URL where all the class files are stored. Often times, you'll put all of your Java applets

FIGURE 15-3

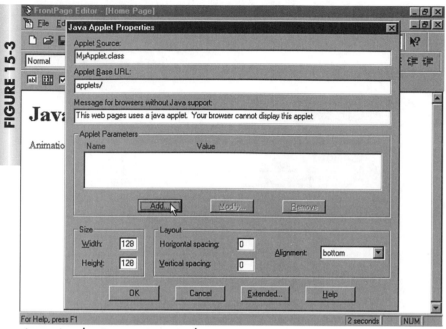

Java Applet Properties window

into one directory: that's the base URL. For example, if I put all my `.class` files into a folder called applets in my Web, then the base URL is `applets/`. You also have the option of displaying a text message in place of the Java applet for those people who don't use a Java-enabled browser. The size and layout options for the applet behave similarly to the corresponding fields for an image. They allow you to specify the width and height of the applet, provide a spacing buffer, and specify how text should align with the applet.

Tip

Java is case sensitive, even in the naming of its class files. It is important that you keep this in mind when entering the applet source. If you don't capitalize the name correctly, your applet may not work!

The applet parameters are values passed to the applet, and are used to specify how the applet should behave. The parameters accepted vary from applet to applet. These parameters are specified in HTML with the `<Param>` tag, as we described above. To add a parameter, just click the Add button, and fill in the Name and Value fields of the Set Attribute Value dialog shown in Figure 15-4.

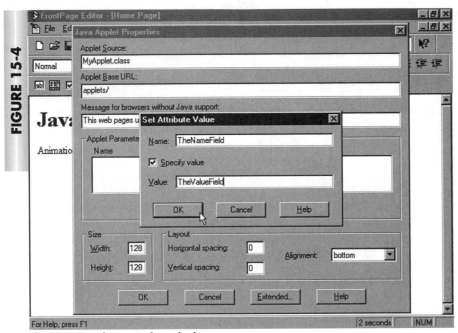

FIGURE 15-4

The Set Attribute Value dialog

When you're finished entering the data for your applet, FrontPage will put a placemarker in your document, as shown in Figure 15-5. The FrontPage Editor will not run your applet, but the placemarker will help you keep the feel of your Web page by marking off the area where the applet will be.

Tip

If you want to see how the applet looks while running in your page, select File | Preview in Browser from the menu bar of the FrontPage Explorer. This will allow you to load the current page right into the browser of your choice, without any extra steps.

Samples

These examples are publicly available on the Internet from JavaSoft—the spinoff from Sun Microsystems created to promote Java. They are all available without cost to the public, so you can use them freely in your Webs. Other applets provided on the CD-ROM are not discussed in this book. You may want to explore them as well. They are in the **Chap15** folder.

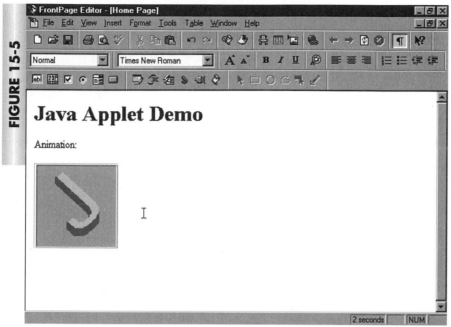

The Java Applet component as represented in the FrontPage Editor

Lesson 2: The Animator Applet

The Animator applet is used to display animations and simultaneously play sounds. It has many parameters you can configure to customize its effects. Clicking on the applet will cause it to cease its activities, giving visitors to your Web the ability to stop the animations and sounds if they find them annoying. Listing 15-2 gives an HTML template for this applet's use in a Web page, and Table 15-1 provides a complete explanation of the parameters for the Animator applet and their functions. You can use the example on the CD-ROM as a template for inserting this applet into a FrontPage document.

Listing 15-2 Template for adding the Animator applet to an HTML document

```
<APPLET CLASS="Animator" HEIGHT=100 WIDTH=50>
 <PARAM NAME="IMAGESOURCE" VALUE="DirectoryURL">
 <PARAM NAME="STARTUP"     VALUE="URLtoImage">
 <PARAM NAME="BACKGROUND"  VALUE="URLtoImage">
 <PARAM NAME="STARTIMAGE"  VALUE="ImageNumber">
 <PARAM NAME="ENDIMAGE"    VALUE="ImageNumber">
 <PARAM NAME="IMAGES"      VALUE="1|2|3|4|3|2|5">
 <PARAM NAME="POSITIONS"   VALUE="100@50|||50@100|||50@50|">
 <PARAM NAME="PAUSE"       VALUE="100">
```

continued on next page

continued from previous page

```
        <PARAM NAME="PAUSES"       VALUE="1000|2000||500|||1000">
        <PARAM NAME="REPEAT"       VALUE="TRUE">
        <PARAM NAME="SOUNDSOURCE"  VALUE="DirectoryURL">
        <PARAM NAME="SOUNDTRACK"   VALUE="URLtoSound">
        <PARAM NAME="SOUNDS"       VALUE="SoundURL1|||SoundURL2|||">
    </APPLET>395
```

Table 15-1 Parameters and their functions for the Animator applet

Parameter	Function
IMAGESOURCE	The directory where the images are found. The images must be in JPG or CompuServe's GIF format, and named T1.gif, T2.gif, T3.gif, and so on. The number ending the name is used to reference the images.
STARTUP	This is the image that should be displayed while the other resources are loading. It is always loaded and displayed first.
BACKGROUND	This is the background image that you want displayed in the window. If the other images are saved as transparent GIFs, this background will show through.
BACKGROUNDCOLOR	This is the hexadecimal representation of a background color in RRGGBB hexadecimal format.
STARTIMAGE	This is the number of the first image that is to be displayed. The animator will then display images sequentially until the value specified by the ENDIMAGE parameter is reached. This parameter is overridden by the IMAGES parameter.
ENDIMAGE	This is the last image that should be displayed. This parameter is overridden by the IMAGES parameter.
IMAGES	This allows you to specify the order in which the frames are displayed, allowing you to play your frames out of order. If this parameter is set, it will override the STARTIMAGE and ENDIMAGE parameters. The image numbers to be displayed are separated by the pipe symbol: |. If nothing is between the pipes, no image is displayed. The next image is displayed after each pause, the duration of which can be specified with the PAUSE and PAUSES parameters.
POSITIONS	This parameter is the coordinates that the image should display inside the applet's window in (X,Y) fashion. The horizontal and vertical values are separated with an @ symbol. Each X,Y pair is separated with a pipe symbol: |. If no value is specified between the pipes, then the last value entered (or 0,0) is used.

Parameter	Function
PAUSE	This is the number of milliseconds that the animator should wait between displaying images. This parameter is the default if the PAUSES parameter is also specified. If no value is specified, it defaults to 1000 (1 second).
PAUSES	If you'd like, you can specify pauses between the display of each image. The duration of each pause is separated by the pipe symbol. If no value is specified, the value specified by the PAUSE parameter is used.
REPEAT	If this value is set to True or not specified, the images and sound will loop continuously. If it is not set or set to False, the sequence will display only once.
SOUNDSOURCE	This is the directory that contains the sound files. Note that this applet plays only Sun/NeXT AU format sound files sampled at 8000 Hz and saved with 8 bit mLog encoding.
SOUNDTRACK	This is the audio file that is to be played in the background throughout the animation. It loops continuously until the applet stops.
SOUNDS	This allows you to specify individual sounds that should play as each image is loaded, which occurs after each pause is finished. The sound files are separated with the pipe symbol: |. If no file is specified, no sound is played for that frame.

OK, seeing this information is a good start, but an example will make it easier for you to integrate this very clever applet into your Webs. First, go to the FrontPage Explorer and create a new normal Web. The next step is to import the files needed for the demo. From the FrontPage Explorer, select File | Import. Then click the Add folder button. Now browse through the CD-ROM provided with this book and select the audio, applets, and images folders in the **d:source\chap15\animator** directory. These folders contain the applet and resources we need to make it work.

Once you've finished importing these folders, load the empty normal page into the FrontPage Editor. Type a heading and set up the page so it looks something like Figure 15-6.

You are going to use a Java component as described in Lesson 1, so position the cursor as shown in Figure 15-6. Now select Insert | Other Component > Java Applet from the menu bar. This will bring up the Java Applet Properties window. We're going to fill it out so our applet will run. In the Applet Source text box type **Animator.class**, and remember to watch your capitalization. For the base URL, enter **applets/**. Set the width to 200, and the height to 100. Now, you need to add a lot of parameters. Start by clicking the Add button in the Applet Parameters area. In the Set Attributes dialog, enter **startimage** as the name, and **1** as the value. Then click OK. Repeat this process until all the names and values from Table 15-2 are entered.

FIGURE 15-6

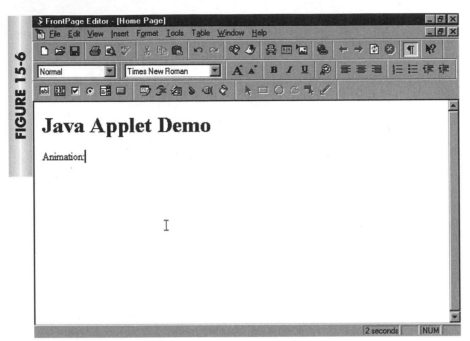

First steps in creating the Animator example

Note

The pauses and sounds parameters in Table 15-2 have values that contain a special character called a pipe symbol. It usually looks like a vertical bar, or a colon made with small vertical bars instead of dots. Make sure you enter these correctly, because they are used to separate data in the parameters.

Table 15-2 Parameters and values for the Animator Applet Demo

Name	Value
startimage	1
endimage	13
repeat	false
pause	1000
pauses	||||||100|100|100|100|100|100|100|

Name	Value
soundsource	audio
sounds	ding.au|ding.au|ding.au|ding.au|ding.au|ding.au|explosion.au|||||
imagesource	images

After you've entered all the parameters, double-check that they're correct. The Applet properties dialog should look like Figure 15-7. Click the OK button when you're finished. This applet is configured to display a series of GIF images representing a countdown. The clock beeps as it counts down. When the count gets to zero, the clock display explodes, and an exploding sound can be heard. Figure 15-8 shows what the applet looks like in a browser.

If you have problems with this lesson, open the **d:\source\chap15\animator** as a Web. It contains a working example of this lesson. Because this same applet can be configured in many different ways, it can be used for many things—not necessarily anything like the example presented here. Browse the CD-ROM that comes with this book for the source code and an example of using this applet.

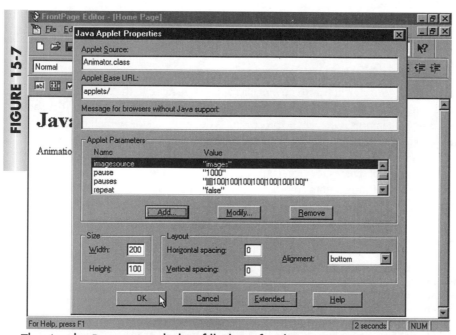

FIGURE 15-7

The Applet Properties dialog filled out for the animation demonstration

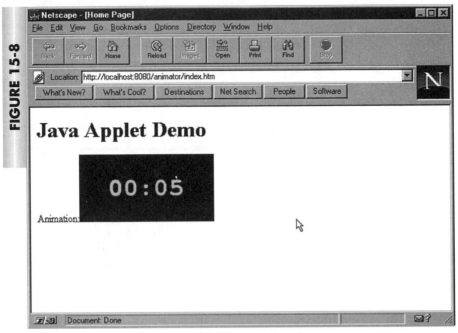

FIGURE 15-8

The Animator applet example as viewed with Netscape 3.0

Lesson 3: The ImageMap Applet

The ImageMap applet is a great way to present clickable image maps to the user. These image maps behave much the same way as the ones you can make with FrontPage, but there are some important differences. First, all the processing is done client-side, which means using these image maps places no processing responsibilities on your server. Second, this image map is able to convey more information to the user about its functions. Traditional image maps must have visual queues to suggest the meaning of each link they contain, but the Java ImageMap applet can contain sound, text, and highlighting to convey that information as well. An HTML outline for the use of the ImageMap applet is given in Listing 15-3.

Listing 15-3 An HTML template for the ImageMap applet example

```
<APPLET CODE="ImageMap" WIDTH=100 HEIGHT=100>
    <PARAM NAME=IMG VALUE="ImageURL">
    <PARAM NAME=highlight VALUE="brighter40">
    <PARAM NAME=area1 VALUE="ClickArea,0,0,100,100">
    <PARAM NAME=area2 VALUE="HighlightArea,10,10,10,10">
    <PARAM NAME=area3 VALUE="NameArea,10,10,10,10,Text1">
    <PARAM NAME=area4 VALUE="SoundArea,10,10,10,10,SoundURL">
    <PARAM NAME=area7 VALUE="HrefButtonArea,25,25,50,50,URL">
    <PARAM NAME=area9 VALUE="RoundHrefButtonArea,75,75,25,25,URL">
</APPLET>
```

As you can see, this applet passes information using the same format as the Animator applet, but it uses a different technique. Rather than having a lot of predefined variables to configure, this applet allows you to define as many areas as you need, each with its own properties. Table 15-3 contains a description of the parameters the ImageMap applet accepts, and the different kinds of areas you can define.

Table 15-3 The parameters and values for the ImageMap applet

Parameter	Function
MG	The value of this parameter is a URL to the image that is to be used for the map.
Highlight	This value is always `brighter` followed by some number. This number represents how much the image map should be brightened when creating the highlights for the buttons or lightening the highlight areas.
area#	There can be many of these parameters, all ending with numbers increasing by 1. The value of these parameters represents the type of area, the X coordinate, the Y coordinate, the width, the height, and URL or text (if needed), respectively, as represented by that area. The values are separated by commas, and the whole value should be enclosed in quotes.

Table 15-4 Description of the area types

Area Type	Properties
ClickArea	This is a region of the image that "watches" the mouse cursor. Make this your first area and size it so that it covers your whole image.
HighlightArea	This is a rectangular region on the image. When the mouse is over this area, it lightens up as specified by the `Highlight` parameter.
NameArea	This is a rectangular region on the image. When the mouse is over this area, the text specified is displayed in the status bar (usually along the bottom of the browser).
SoundArea	This is a rectangular region on the image. When the mouse enters this area, the sound specified is played. Note that the sound should be in the Sun/NeXT AU format, saved in 8-bit mLog format and sampled at 8000Hz.
HrefButtonArea	This is a rectangular area. Highlighting occurs around the border of this region when the mouse enters it, giving it a raised button look. When this area is clicked (that is, the button is pushed) with the mouse, the browser is sent to the URL specified in a manner similar to other image maps.

continued on next page

continued from previous page

Area Type	Properties
RoundHrefButtonArea	This defines an elliptical area similar to the HrefButtonArea. The border is created in a similar manner, and clicking the button takes the user to the specified URL.

To use this applet in your FrontPage Webs, you will use the same techniques outlined for the Animator applet example. First, open the FrontPage Explorer and create a new normal Web. From the FrontPage Explorer, select File | Import, and then click the Folder button. From the CD-ROM provided with this book, select the audio, applets, and images folders in the **d:source\chap15\imagemap** directory. Click the OK button when you're done and import the files. Then open the Normal page with the FrontPage Editor. Edit the document so it looks similar to Figure 15-9.

Move the cursor so it's under the `ImageMap Applet Demo` line in the document, as shown in Figure 15-9. Then, from the menu bar, select Insert | Other component | Java Applet. Set up the Java Applet by entering the information as shown in Figure 15-10. Don't forget the size attributes.

Once that is done, you'll need to specify parameters for this applet. This demo has eight parameters, and they are listed in Table 15-5. Enter them the same way you did for the previous lesson: Click the Add button, enter the information, then click OK. Continue adding all the parameters to your Web page, double-checking for accuracy.

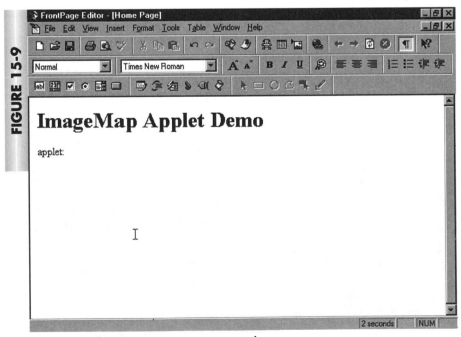

FIGURE 15-9

Setup step for the ImageMap example

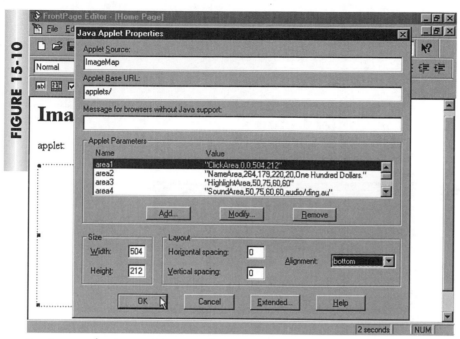

Setting up the ImageMap applet

Table 15-5 ImageMap parameters for the demonstration page

Name	Value
img	images/100.jpg
Highlight	brighter40
area1	ClickArea,0,0,504,212
area2	NameArea,264,179,220,20,One Hundred Dollars
area3	HighlightArea,50,75,60,60
area4	SoundArea,50,75,60,60,audio/ding.au
area5	HrefButtonArea,264,179,220,20,http://www.ustreas.gov/treasury/whatsnew/newcur/
area6	RoundHrefButtonArea,130,10,180,195,http://www.teachersoft.com/Library/nonfict/biog/franklin/contents.htm

When you have added all the parameters, save the page. Congratulations. If everything was done correctly, you should have created a working image map! It appears like Figure 15-11 in Netscape Navigator 3.0. If you'd like to see a working example without creating

FIGURE 15-11

The ImageMap applet as viewed with Netscape 3.0

it yourself, open the sample Web provided on the CD-ROM. It contains a working example of this demonstration.

Note

If you'd like more information on Java, or are interested in learning to program Java, try these WWW sites:

```
http://www.javasoft.com
http://www.gamelan.com
http://www.javaworld.com
http://www.teamjava.com
http://users.aol.com/thingtone/workshop
```

JavaScript

JavaScript is a small programming language that resembles Java in context, which means it looks a little like Java on the outside, but doesn't work the same on the inside.

JavaScripts are placed directly inside the HTML code of a Web page. JavaScript is not truly object oriented, but it has some built-in objects that you can use. JavaScript variables are dynamically typed. This means a JavaScript variable can hold any data you want, be it a number, a string, or an object. JavaScripts can be used to respond to events that occur during the viewing and use of a Web page. This means that JavaScripts can actively respond to the viewers of the document.

If that seems a little technical, don't worry. You will cover all this in detail in the upcoming pages. Just know that JavaScript is a safe, simple language that should be easy to learn and use.

Because of new additions and changes to the JavaScript language, some of the examples may not work exactly as shown. The examples are pretty basic, so they should be stable—but it's not guaranteed. This language is still evolving and may change.

Why Use JavaScript?

Suppose your HTML page needs to react in a nonstandard way to a user: It needs to display a special graphic based on user input (such as the Make a Smiley example you'll encounter in Lesson 9). In the past, Common Gateway Interface (CGI) scripts did this. CGI scripts are programs that run on the server and are able to respond to input sent to them over the Internet. To display this special graphic, the user's machine (called the *client*) fetches the Web page containing the form the user needs to fill out. The user inputs data into the form and then sends this information back across the Internet to the server. The server then analyzes the input and produces a document that the client has to fetch. In this arrangement, information needs to be sent across the Internet three times (twice to the client, once to the server). Communication is slow compared to the speed at which most computers operate, so anything you can do to reduce the amount of communicating that takes place can improve performance. Additionally, the server is responsible for processing the client's requests. If there are many requests, this can dramatically slow the performance of the server, and everyone suffers.

By using a JavaScript, you can send instructions along with your original input form. This system (called client-side processing) works like this: The client fetches the page that contains both the form and the program for dealing with the input. The user inputs the data, and the client's computer does the calculations to determine what it needs. It then fetches the appropriate data from the server. This system involves only two communications between the client and server, and no special processing burden is placed on the server. That's what makes JavaScript (and Java) so valuable.

What Does JavaScript Look Like in HTML?

Just like anything else you would put into your HTML documents, JavaScripts are added using special tags that tell the browser what to expect. Listing 15-4 shows the format for an HTML document containing a JavaScript.

Listing 15-4 Sample HTML template for including JavaScript code

```
<HTML>
<HEAD>
    <SCRIPT LANGUAGE="JavaScript"><!--
        //JavaScript Code Here
    //--></SCRIPT>
</HEAD>
<BODY>
</BODY>
</HTML>
```

To insert a script, just enclose the code with the **<SCRIPT LANGUAGE="JavaScript">** and **</SCRIPT>** tags. Just in case you forgot, anything between the **<!--** and **-->** tags is commented out. Some old browsers don't support JavaScript, so they don't know what to do with the code between the **<SCRIPT>** tags. To prevent them from displaying the JavaScript code along with the rest of the document, the code is placed inside commenting tags. Also, notice that there's a pair of slashes before the final **-->** tag. These two slashes are used to make comments in the JavaScript language. Whatever comes after them is ignored as far as JavaScript is concerned. For example, without those two slashes in front of the line **JavaScript Code Here**, an error would be produced when the page is loaded. The same goes for the **-->** tag; if it weren't commented out, it would produce an error. By using this format, old browsers won't display your code, your programs will still run, and everything is peachy. Pretty clever, eh?

All the other parts of the HTML document remain the same, regardless of the fact that JavaScript code is present. Notice that the script is inside the **<HEAD>** tags and not the **<BODY>** tags in the example. That's because it's very important to keep the JavaScript code near the top of the HTML document. The script could be placed anywhere in the **<BODY>** portion, but there are good reasons to keep it in the **<HEAD>** portion. You'll learn about those later. Inserting JavaScript code into your FrontPage documents is virtually the same as inserting Java applets.

Writing JavaScripts

Now that you know the tags to use to insert JavaScript code, you're halfway to writing a program! But beware, programming is not something that most people pick up overnight. It's something that can require a long time and a lot of work to master. A complete explanation of JavaScript would be beyond the scope of this book. However, you can gain a great deal of utility from just a little understanding, so take a slow, guided survey of the subject. If you had a programming class in high school or college, know what a variable is and how to use it, understand simple logic structures (**if...then**, **for** loops, and so on), and understand functions, you should have no problems with this section. After you master this little bit, a great deal of power will be at your fingertips.

Lesson 4: A Simple Hello World Wide Web Program

Note

For all of these lessons, you will be working in plain HTML. The reason for this is that it exposes you more to the underlying structure of your document. If you don't understand what's going on behind the scenes with the HTML, you will have a very difficult time learning JavaScript. Working with the HTML directly will help you see what's going on each step of the way.

For an example HTML document for your first JavaScript program, see Listing 15-5.

Listing 15-5 Simplest HTML document containing a Hello World program

```
<HTML>
<HEAD>
</HEAD>
<BODY>
<SCRIPT LANGUAGE="JavaScript"><!--
    document.write("Hello World Wide Web!<BR>")
 //--></SCRIPT>
</BODY>
</HTML>
```

To create this document with FrontPage, open a new normal Web with the Explorer. Then edit the Normal page with the Editor. You don't need to add any text, just go right to View | HTML. Then enter text to make the document look like Listing 15-6.

Listing 15-6 The Hello World JavaScript program

```
<SCRIPT LANGUAGE="JavaScript"><!--
  document.write("Hello World Wide Web!<BR>")
//--></SCRIPT>
```

Figure 15-12 shows the FrontPage Edit HTML dialog with the JavaScript program added. Once the data is entered, click the OK button. The page is now complete, and after you save it, you can view it with your favorite JavaScript-capable browser, as shown in Figure 15-13.

A very important concept is at work in this example: objects. What is an object? An object can be just about anything, but most important, it's a way of thinking. Using objects to program has become very popular; the reasons are a little abstract, but it's important that you understand the basics.

In this case, the object document is told to do something: It's being told to write **Hello World Wide Web**. This command, **write**, is called a method. Objects can have many methods associated with them. For example, you can use a hammer to pound, pry, pull, or crack. Every one of these actions would be called a method, and the hammer would be called an

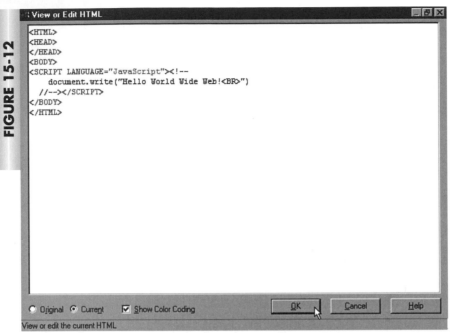

FIGURE 15-12

Entering the JavaScript code directly into the HTML

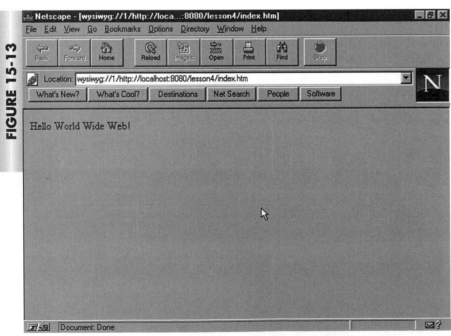

FIGURE 15-13

The Hello World script as viewed with Netscape 3.0

object. In the example program, the document is writing in the same way a hammer can pound or a bird can sing. Don't worry if this seems a little confusing; it will become more understandable as you work with it.

You can see that the line `document.write("Hello World Wide Web<BR>")` caused that message to be printed on the screen by the browser. Take note that the `<BR>` tag was included in the text. That's because the output is treated exactly as if it were part of the HTML document! Without the `<BR>` tag, the line following the message (if there were one) would run onto the end of the message.

One more important item to keep in mind is that JavaScript is case sensitive. This means that `document.write("MyMessage")` is not the same as `document.Write("MyMessage")`, because the W is capitalized! Be sure to watch your capitalization for mistakes like that. As a general rule, most JavaScript objects and keywords are all lowercase. There are exceptions that you'll have to pick up on as you go along. Don't worry, it's a pretty easy mistake to find and fix, as long as you know to look for it.

Lesson 5: Changing the Hello World Program

Now you need to make some changes in the document. Just select View | HTML from the menu bar, then edit its contents so it contains Listing 15-7.

Your FrontPage Editor's View HTML window should look like Figure 15-14. Click the OK button when you've finished.

FIGURE 15-14

```
<HTML>
<HEAD>
</HEAD>
<BODY onLoad="WriteHello()">
<SCRIPT LANGUAGE="JavaScript"><!--
    function WriteHello() {
        document.write("Hello World Wide Web!<BR>")
    }
//--></SCRIPT>
</BODY>
</HTML>
```

The editor after editing in the new Write Hello function

Listing 15-7 HTML containing a Hello World function

```
<HTML>
<HEAD>
</HEAD>
<BODY onLoad="WriteHello()">
<SCRIPT LANGUAGE="JavaScript"><!--
    function WriteHello() {
       document.write("Hello World Wide Web!<BR>")
    }
  //--></SCRIPT>
</BODY>
</HTML>
```

Yikes, that's a lot of changes, but the output is exactly the same! What's going on here? Well, you created a function called `WriteHello()` that writes your message for you. A function can be thought of as a miniprogram. It contains a set of instructions that are related in that they work together to achieve a relatively simple goal, in this case writing `Hello World Wide Web!` in the browser. This function is being called when the `<BODY>` of the document is loaded.

Look closely at how the function is set up. First, you state that you want to create a function. You do this by using the keyword `function`. That's simple enough. Then you provide the name of the function, in this case `WriteHello()`. Then you have to write the code for the function, which is the same as the previous example. Notice that the code for the function is enclosed in brackets: `{` and `}`. The code for all functions must be enclosed in brackets.

Another big change is the addition of `onLoad="WriteHello()"` to the beginning `<BODY>` tag. This is called an event handler, and working with events to execute your code is called event-driven programming. It's similar to hiring a phone service to answer your calls and take messages. When the phone rings, the service answers it and does the work. In this analogy, the phone ringing would be the event, and the answering service would be the function assigned to handle that event. In the case of your program, the `<BODY>` tag loading is the event, and the `WriteHello()` function is responsible for dealing with it, which it does by printing the message. Many different kinds of events can occur during the viewing of your page, and you can pick and choose which events you feel need special treatment and assign specialfunctions to each of them.

If you think back, you'll remember a suggestion about keeping your JavaScripts near the top of the page. That's because most of the things you do with JavaScript are event driven, and you'll get an error if you try to call a function before it's available. For example,you've probably sat through the slow, painful download of a large Web page once or twice. If you have, you're aware that parts of the document are often displayed before the whole page is loaded. If the `onLoad` event called the function `WriteHello()` before it had a chance to load, there would be problems and an error would result. For this reason, it's good practice to keep the scripts at the top of the page, because the top of the page is downloaded first. This way these scripts will be available when events occur that may call them.

Lesson 6: Getting Crazy Saying Hello

Examine some other ways to say hello, by creating a document with FrontPage that is similar to Listing 15-8.

Listing 15-8 HTML document containing several Hello World functions called by various events

```
<HTML>
<HEAD>
</HEAD>
<BODY>
  <SCRIPT LANGUAGE="JavaScript"><!--
    // This puts our message in the browser's status bar...
    function StateHello() {
      window.status="Hello World Wide Web!"
    }
    // This produces a message window...
    function PopHello() {
      window.alert("Hello World Wide Web!")
    }
  //--></SCRIPT>
  <A HREF="/" onMouseOver="StateHello(); return true">
    Bring the mouse here.</A>
  <BR>
  <!--Remember previous discussions about forms?-->
  <FORM>
    <INPUT TYPE="button" NAME="button1" VALUE="Click Here"
      onClick="PopHello()">
  </FORM>
  <P>Clicking the button causes a Message Box to be brought up with our
message.  Putting the mouse over the link causes our message to be displayed
in the status bar.
</BODY>
</HTML>
To create this document, you'll use the same method as before.  Select View |
HTML, and then edit the text so that it is the same as as Listing 15-8. You'll
use this same technique in all of the other examples as well.
```

Figure 15-15 shows what this document looks like when viewed with a browser, and Figure 15-16 shows the message box produced by clicking on the button.

Take a look again at Listing 15-8 and compare it to the previous HTML document you created (see Listing 15-7). With this example, you can see two new events: **onMouseOver** and **onClick**. These events are also associated with different objects. What triggers these events is pretty self-explanatory: Clicking the button causes an **onClick** event, and moving the mouse over the link causes an **onMouseOver** event. These events cause the **PopHello()** and **StateHello()** functions to be called. These functions work with the window object. The window object has its own set of methods associated with it. Two of the most useful, **alert()** and **status**, are demonstrated in this example.

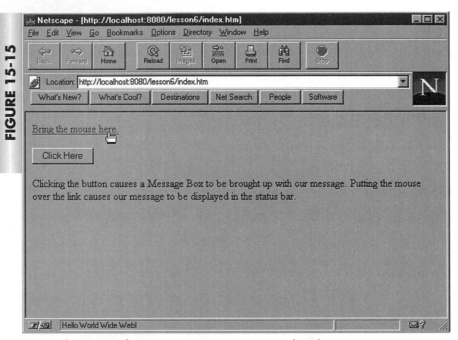

HTML document from Listing 15-8 as viewed with Netscape 3.0

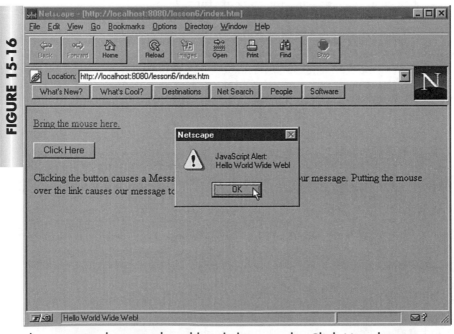

The message box produced by clicking on the Click Here button shown in Figure 15-15

Did you notice the unusual syntax in the `StateHello()` function? It looks like this: `window.status="Hello World Wide Web!"`. This format is different from the `window.alert()` and `document.write()` formats because `window.status` is not a method, it's a property. This brings you to the second lesson concerning objects: They can have properties as well as methods. Working with the hammer analogy, you can name a number of properties associated with hammers. A hammer has a weight, a manufacturer, and an age. You use these properties to describe the hammer, whereas you use methods to describe the functions of a hammer. The window has a status the same way a hammer has a certain weight and a bird is a certain color. If you wanted to tell the hammer to pound, you would say `hammer.pound()`, and if you wanted to know how much it weighed, you would look at `hammer.weight`. The line `window.status="Hello World Wide Web"` sets the status property to your message. The status of the browser is usually displayed at the bottom of the window. You can see your message there in Figure 15-24.

Lesson 7: The Permission Button Script

Now that you've covered some of the basics, you can begin doing some truly useful programs. This demonstration will illustrate a couple of new techniques. The first is checking the status of fields in a form, and the second is moving the user to other documents. FrontPage already has some validation techniques built into each form control, but for truly useful form validation, you'll have to write your own validation routine with JavaScript. The HTML code for the Permission Button example is given in Listing 15-9. This HTML document, when viewed with Netscape Navigator 2.0, looks like Figure 15-17.

Listing 15-9 HTML document demonstrating use of JavaScript to check the state of a Form element

```
<HTML>
<HEAD>
</HEAD>
<BODY>
  <SCRIPT LANGUAGE="JavaScript"><!--
    // This goes to the "previous" page...
    function GoBack() {
      this.location="previous.html"
    }
    // This produces a message window...
    function CheckPermission() {
      if (document.Form1.PermissionBox.checked) {
        this.location="next.html"
      }
      else {
        var msg;
        msg = "You are not eligible to continue.  "
              + "Please click the \"back\" button."
        window.alert(msg)
      }
    }
```

continued on next page

continued from previous page

```
   //--></SCRIPT>
<FORM NAME="Form1">
   <INPUT TYPE="checkbox" NAME="PermissionBox">
   Check here if you are eligible to continue.
   <BR><BR>
   <INPUT TYPE="button" NAME="BackBtn"
    VALUE="   Back    "
    onClick="GoBack()">
   <INPUT TYPE="button" NAME="ContinueBtn"
    VALUE="Continue" onClick="CheckPermission()">
   <BR>
</FORM>
<P>Clicking the &quot;Continue&quot; button will without checking the check-
box will cause a message box to appear stating that you do not have permission
to continue.  Clicking the &quot;Continue&quot; button with the checkbox
marked will take the user to the URL &quot;next.html&quot;.  Pressing the back
button will take the user to the URL &quot;previous.html&quot;.
</BODY>
</HTML>
```

Let's discuss some of the new concepts. The **if** statement is used here for the first time. This statement allows you to selectively execute certain parts of your code. This should seem familiar if you've ever done any programming before. The **if** statement has been a staple of most programming languages for a long time. The JavaScript syntax for an **if** statement looks like Listing 15-10.

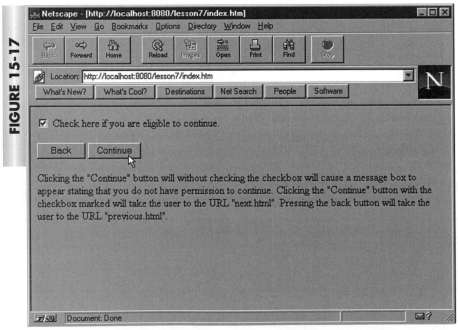

View of the Permission Button JavaScript HTML document

Listing 15-10 General format for the **if** statement in JavaScript

(Note: Bold items are required, nonbold are optional.)

```
if ( conditions ) {
  statements
} else {
  more statements
}
```

Another point of interest is the condition used to evaluate the **if** statement: **document.Form1.PermissionBox.checked**. Here, you are trying to find out if the check box is marked in your form. This style of referencing is just like that you were doing before, but there's more of it. It is similar to determining whether the handle of the hammer in the toolbox is varnished, which could look like this: **toolbox.hammer.handle.varnished**. You're being very specific about what you reference, which is often necessary. If you hadn't specified what hammer owned the handle, how would you know which hammer handle? If you had just used **handle.varnished**, you couldn't tell if if it were a popsicle handle or a door handle. Long references help remove ambiguity.

You used the keyword **this** for the first time in this example. It is a very special reference. The term **this** refers to the object that is currently active. The line **this.location="previous.html"** causes the browser to load the page called **previous.html**. That's because the currently active object is the window, and one of the properties of the window is location. A browser window's location property refers to the URL currently being viewed. By changing this value to **previous.html**, you caused a new page to be loaded. You had to use the keyword **this** because there is some ambiguity associated with a line such as **window.location="previous.html"**. If several windows were open, how would you know which window? The keyword **this** removes the confusion; it is a very powerful tool indeed!

Notice how you declared the variable **msg**? Inside the **else** statement is **var msg**; this declares **msg** to be a variable. Unlike other languages, JavaScript does not require you to specify what kind of value this variable holds. Variables are dynamically typed, which means you can put anything you want in them. You can assign numbers, strings (as you have done), and objects to the same variable, but not all at once. In the perfectly valid example shown in Listing 15-11, **MyVariable** is holding many different kinds of values at different times.

Listing 15-11 Demonstration of dynamic variable typing by JavaScript

```
var MyVariable = 7
MyVariable = "Seven"
MyVariable = true
MyVariable = document.form.text1.value
MyVariable = document.form
```

Remember how you added on to the end of the **msg** string. You did this using the + sign. Strings can be concatenated in this manner. Take a look at Listing 15-12 to get a feel for how this works.

Listing 15-12 Demonstration of simple string manipulation using JavaScript

```
var MyVar1 = "five "
var MyVar2 = "six "
MyVar1 = MyVar1 + MyVar2
// MyVar1 now holds the value "five six "
MyVar2 = 7
MyVar1 = MyVar1 + MyVar2
// MyVar1 now hold
the value "five six 7"
MyVar1 = MyVar2 + 1
// MyVar1 now equals 8
```

You can use a number of arithmetic operators to manipulate data. A quick summary of some of the basic ones is found in Table 15-6.

Table 15-6 Common arithmetic operators and their functions

Operator	Function
+	Addition, string concatenation
-	Subtraction
*	Multiplication
/	Division
%	Modulus division (returns remainder)
++	Increment (adds 1)
--	Decrement (subtracts 1)

Lesson 8: Checking Forms

This program checks all the fields in a form to make sure that they're filled in and have reasonable data. It does a little formatting as well. This application of JavaScript is a very good
• way to validate information before sending it to the server, which removes that burden from the server and prevents the excess communication required if it wasn't filled out properly in the first place.

The HTML code is given in Listing 15-13. There is quite a bit there, but that makes for a good example. To create this document, you're going to use the same technique as before. Open a new document and edit the HTML directly.

Listing 15-13 HTML document containing JavaScript code to verify proper input in a form

```
<HTML>
<HEAD>
```

```
</HEAD>
<BODY>
  <SCRIPT LANGUAGE="JavaScript"><!--
    //****************************************************
    // This function coverts the value of a field to all
    // uppercase letters.
    function ConvertToCaps(Field) {
      Field.value = Field.value.toUpperCase()
    }
    //****************************************************
    // This is a supporting function that counts the
    // number of digits there are in a control...
    function CountDigits(Field) {
      var NumDigits = 0
      for(var i=0; i<Field.value.length; i=i+1) {
        var Char = Field.value.substring(i, i+1)
        if (Char == "0" || Char == "1" || Char == "2" ||
            Char == "3" || Char == "4" || Char == "5" ||
            Char == "6" || Char == "7" || Char == "8" ||
            Char == "9") {
          NumDigits = NumDigits + 1
        }
      } // close the for loop
      // now I'll just return the number of digits I
      // counted in that loop...
      return NumDigits
    } // end function
    //****************************************************
    // This returns true if the Field is empty,
    // and false if it is not....
    function IsEmpty(Field)
    {
      if(Field.value.length == 0) {
        return true
      }
      else {
        return false
      }
    } // end function
    //****************************************************
    // This checks the form...
    function ValidateForm(Form) {
      // first I'll check that the name fields are
      // both filled in...
      if(IsEmpty(Form.Name1) || IsEmpty(Form.Name2)) {
        window.alert("Please enter your name.")
        return false
      }
      // Then I'll check that the first address field
      // is filled in...
      if(IsEmpty(Form.Address1)) {
        window.alert("Please fill in your street address.")
```

continued on next page

continued from previous page

```
            return false
        }
        // Now I'll look at the City field...
        if(IsEmpty(Form.City)) {
          window.alert("Please fill in your city.")
          return false
        }
        // Then I'll check that they used a two
        // letter abbreviation for their state...
        if(Form.State.value.length != 2) {
          var msg = "Please enter your two letter "
                    + "State abbreviation."
          window.alert(msg)
          return false
        }
        // I'll check that the Zipcode has either
        // 5 or 11 digits.
        if(CountDigits(Form.Zip) != 5  &&
                    CountDigits(Form.Zip) != 11) {
          var msg = "Please make sure your Zipcode "
                    + "is correctly filled in."
          window.alert(msg)
          return false
        }
        // Last, I'll check that all 11 digits
        // are present in the phone number.
        if(CountDigits(Form.Phone) != 10) {
          var msg = "Please enter your full phone number, "
                    + "including your area code."
          window.alert(msg)
          return false
        }
        // If got this far without hitting a return
        // statement, everything must be OK, so we'll
        // go ahead and let them know that...
        document.open()
        document.write("<HTML><HEAD></HEAD><BODY>")
        document.write("<H2>OK... Thank-you..</H2>")
        document.write("</BODY></HTML>")
        document.close()
        return true
      } // end function
    //--></SCRIPT>
<H3>Please fill in the following:</H3>
  <FORM NAME="Form1">
    <TT>
    First Name:.......
    <INPUT TYPE="text" NAME="Name1" SIZE=20>
    <BR>
    Last Name:........
    <INPUT TYPE="text" NAME="Name2" SIZE=20>
    <BR>
```

```
      Street Address(1):
      <INPUT TYPE="text" NAME="Address1" SIZE=40>
      <BR>
      Street Address(2):
      <INPUT TYPE="text" NAME="Address2" SIZE=40>
      <BR>
      City:............
      <INPUT TYPE="text" NAME="City" SIZE=20>
      <BR>
      State:...........
      <INPUT TYPE="text" NAME="State" SIZE=5
       onBlur="ConvertToCaps(this.form.State)">
      <BR>
      ZipCode:..........
      <INPUT TYPE="text" NAME="Zip" SIZE=12>
      <BR>
      Phone:............
      <INPUT TYPE="text" NAME="Phone" SIZE=20>
      <BR>
      </TT>
      <BR><BR>
      <INPUT TYPE="button" NAME="ContinueBtn" VALUE="Continue"
       onClick="ValidateForm(this.form)">
      <BR>
    </FORM>
  </BODY>
</HTML>
```

FIGURE 15-18

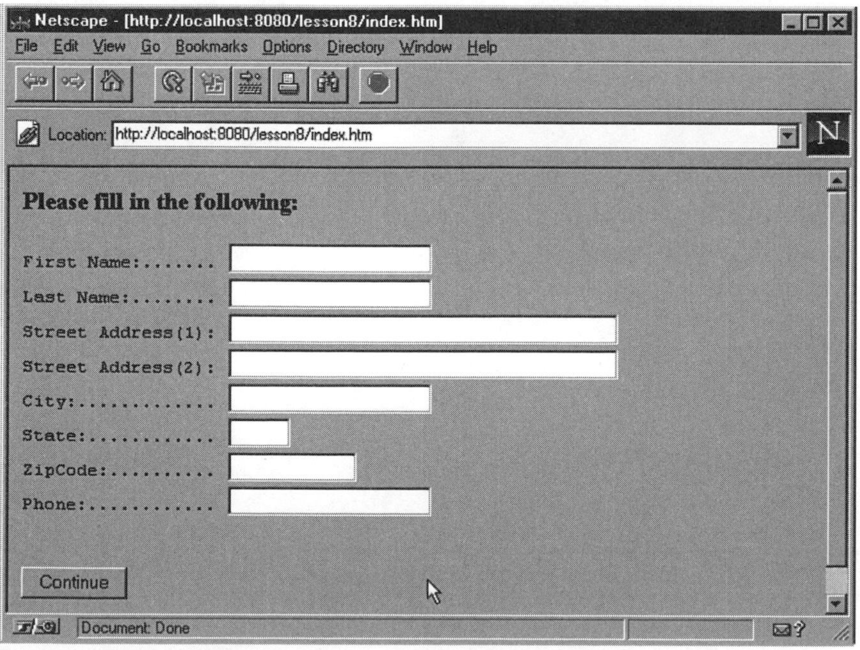

Browser view of the Check Forms HTML document

Something new in this program is a `for` loop. It's used in the `CountDigits` function. The generalized format of a `for` loop in JavaScript is shown in Listing 15-14.

Listing 15-14 General format of `for` loops in JavaScript

(Note: Bold items are required, nonbold are optional.)

```
for(initialization; condition; increment/decrement) {
    statements
}
```

The `for` loop works by executing the code it contains until a certain condition is met. In JavaScript, this often involves declaring a **counter** variable (in this case, i), and then adding or subtracting from that counter until it meets a certain condition. In this example, you start i at zero and then increment it until it is larger than the number of characters in the field. Between each increment, the code inside the `for` loop is executed. This allows you to look at each character, determine if it's a digit, and keep track of the number of digits in the field.

You've initialized variables before, so that should not be a problem. The increment/decrement portion is often done with one of two unary operators: ++ or --. Unary operators take only one operand and act only upon it. For example, **count++** would increase the value of count by 1, whereas **count--** would decrease the value of count by 1. The position of these operators determines their precedence. If one of these operators is placed after the operand (called *postfix*), it affects the variable after other instructions are executed. If the operator precedes the operand (called *prefix*), it takes effect before that operand is used in that statement. Examine Listing 15-15 for a better understanding.

Listing 15-15 Demonstration of the unary operators ++ and --

```
var x = 1
var y = 2
x++          //(x=x+1)
// x now equals 2
x = y++      //(x=y),(y=Y+1)
// x now equals 2, y equals 3
y = --x      //(x=x-1),(y=x)
// x and y are both 1
```

You're also using comparison operators in this example. Comparisons are really simple, but they get more complex when you add them together. Table 15-7 shows some important logical and comparison operators.

Table 15-7 Common relational operators and their functions

Operator	Function
>	Greater than
<	Less than

Operator	Function
==	Equal
>=	Greater than or equal
<=	Less than or equal
!=	Not equal
&&	Logical and
||	Logical or

Notice also that the functions have a new statement: `return`. This statement causes the function to terminate immediately and to return the value specified. For example, a line that reads `return 1;` would cause the function to return the value 1. Functions that do not specify a value with their `return` statements or that don't have `return` statements return a null value.

You'll discover another event in this example as well. Notice that the text input element for `state` responds to an `onBlur` event. The `onBlur` event occurs when the focus moves off that element. If you type in this box, nothing exceptional happens, but when you tab to the next field, the text in the box gets changed to all capital letters. That's because the `ConvertToCaps` function is being called, and it's changing the input to capital letters.

Lesson 9: Make a Smiley Example

This program demonstrates the use of JavaScript in conjunction with frames. This demonstration removes all processing responsibilities from the server and places them on the client's computer. It allows the user to select the eyes and mouth of a smiley face from list box elements in a form. Hitting the Build Now button will cause a series of `.GIF` files to be loaded in the bottom frame, which represent the selections made by the user.

The base HTML document that loads the frames is shown in Listing 15-16.

Listing 15-16 HTML document that contains the Make a Smiley example

(It loads the HTML documents `TopFrame.html` and `BottomFrame.html` into two separate frames.)

```
<HTML>
<HEAD>
  <TITLE>Build Your Own Smiley</TITLE>
</HEAD>
  <FRAMESET ROWS="50%,50%">
    <FRAME SRC="TopFrame.html" NAME="TopFrame" SCROLLING="auto">
    <FRAME SRC="BottomFrame.html" NAME="BottomFrame" SCROLLING="auto">
  </FRAMESET>
<BODY>
  <NOFRAMES>
    <H3><BLINK>Your browser does not support frames!</BLINK></H3>
```

continued on next page

continued from previous page

```
        <P>This example will not work.
      </NOFRAMES>
    </BODY>
  </HTML>
```

The upper frame contains the HTML document that holds the JavaScript code. This code is capable of manipulating the bottom frame based on user input. This document is shown in Listing 15-17.

Listing 15-17 HTML document that is loaded into the top frame in the Make a Smiley example

```
<HTML>
<HEAD>
  <SCRIPT LANGUAGE="JavaScript"><!--

    //******************************************************
    // This function returns the location of the current
    // "directory".  It accepts a string representing an
    // URL, and returns the "Path" to that URL.
    function GetPath(URL) {
      var LastSlashPosition = URL.lastIndexOf("/")
      var PathToURL = URL.substring(0, (LastSlashPosition + 1))
      return PathToURL

    }

    //******************************************************
    // This function accepts a selection control as a
    // parameter, and returns the text value of the
    // selected item in that control.
    function GetSelection(SelectField) {
      var SelectNum = SelectField.selectedIndex
      var SelectText = SelectField.options[SelectNum].text
      return SelectText
    }

    //******************************************************
    // This function is called when the user clicks the
    // "Build Now" button.  It accepts a form object, and
    // writes an HTML document to the bottom frame based
    // on the information expressed in the form.
    function DisplaySmiley(Form) {
      var PicPath  = GetPath(this.document.location)
                     + "images/"
      var eyeref   = PicPath + GetSelection(Form.Eyes)
                     + ".gif"
      var mouthref = PicPath + GetSelection(Form.Mouth)
                     + ".gif"
```

```
        var newframe = "<HTML><HEAD></HEAD><BODY>"
                     + "<H3>Here's your smiley:</H3>"
                     + "<IMG SRC='" + eyeref + "' "
                     + "WIDTH=150 HEIGHT=80><BR>"
                     + "<IMG SRC='" + mouthref + "' "
                     + "WIDTH=150 HEIGHT=70><BR>"
                     + "</BODY></HTML>"
        parent.BottomFrame.document.write(newframe)
        parent.BottomFrame.document.close()
      }

  //--></SCRIPT>
</HEAD>
<BODY>
  <FORM NAME="Form1">
    <TT>
    Eyes......
    </TT>

    <SELECT NAME="Eyes">
      <OPTION>big
      <OPTION>glasses
      <OPTION>closed
    </SELECT>
    <BR>
    <TT>
    Mouth.....
    </TT>
    <SELECT NAME="Mouth">
      <OPTION>frown
      <OPTION>smile
      <OPTION>poker
    </SELECT>
    <BR><BR>
    <INPUT TYPE="button" NAME="BuildNow" VALUE="Build Now"
      onClick="DisplaySmiley(this.form)">
  </FORM>
</BODY>
</HTML>
```

The bottom frame will be overwritten when the button in the top frame is pushed. The code for the bottom frame is shown in Listing 15-18.

Listing 15-18 Initial HTML document loaded into the bottom frame in the Make a Smiley example

(This is replaced when the user clicks the Build Now button in the top frame.)

```
<HTML>
<HEAD>
```

continued on next page

continued from previous page

```
</HEAD>
<BODY>
  <H3>Building your own Smiley!</H3>
  <P>To build your smiley, just select the head, face, and body from the list
boxes in the frame above.  Then click the &quot;Build Now&quot; button.  This
frame will be overwritten with your new creation.
</BODY>
</HTML>
```

Figure 15-19 shows the document as viewed with Netscape Navigator 2.0, and Figure 15-20 shows what the document looks like after clicking the Build Now button.

Despite the fact that this example is quite different from the previous examples, it introduces only three new concepts. The first concept is arrays, the second is the <SELECT> object and its corresponding properties, and the third is the **parent** keyword. The <SELECT> form element object and the **parent** keyword are very similar to concepts covered before and shouldn't present much difficulty.

The first new object is the <SELECTION> element of a form. The <SELECTION> element is not much different from the <INPUT> elements you encountered before. The first property you reference belonging to it is the **selectedIndex** property. The **selectedIndex** property

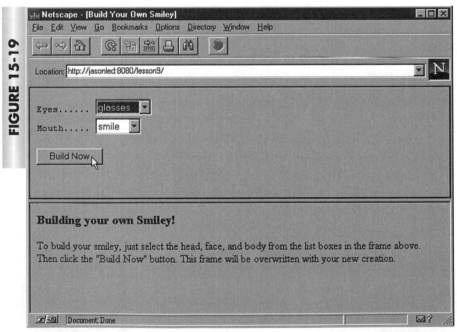

FIGURE 15-19

The Make a Smiley example with Netscape Navigator 2.02 before clicking the Build Now button in the top frame

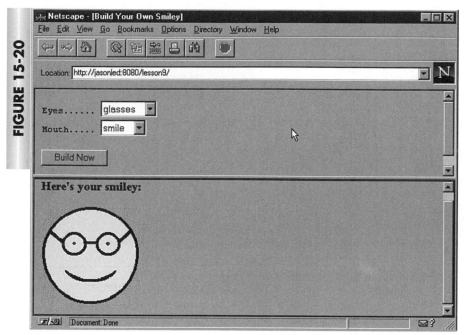

The Make a Smiley example in Netscape Navigator 2.02 after clicking the Build Now button in the top frame

of a **<SELECTION>** object is the number of the **<OPTION>** that was chosen from the **<SELECTION>** form element. This may seem a little confusing, but don't worry, read on.

Did you notice that every **<SELECTION>** element contains several **<OPTION>** elements within it? Many elements contain a **NAME=** property you can use to reference them, but how do you distinguish the different **<OPTION>** elements from one another? The answer is with an array.

Arrays work hand in hand with the **<SELECTION>** element. That's because the **<SELECTION>** element contains an array of **<OPTION>**s. Referencing arrays in JavaScript is very similar to referencing arrays in most other languages. Each element of an array can be referenced with a number. Just to confuse everyone, the first element is numbered 0, the second element is numbered 1, the third element is numbered 2, and so on. Examine Listing 15-19 to gain a better understanding of how arrays work in JavaScript.

Listing 15-19 Demonstration of array manipulation using JavaScript

```
var MyArray[]        // declares MyArray to be an array
MyArray[0] = "One "
MyArray[1] = "Two "
MyArray[2] = "Three"
var Count = MyArray[0] + MyArray[1] + MyArray[2]
// Count now equals "One Two Three"
```

```
var Highest = 2
var Lowest =  0
// MyArray[Highest] equals "Three"
// MyArray[Lowest] equals "One "
```

This example pulls double duty, because at the same time it demonstrates arrays for the first time, it introduces the `<SELECTION>` form element. Examine two properties of the `<SELECTION>` element: the `selectedIndex` and the `option` array. The `selectedIndex` property returns the number (or *index*) of the currently selected `<OPTION>` element. This allows you to identify the user's selection. For example, the `Eyes` `<SELECTION>` element contains an array of four `<OPTION>`s: `Lopsided`, `Closed`, `Glasses`, and `Glazed`. The phrase `document.Form1.Eyes.option[0].text` would refer to the value `Lopsided`, whereas the phrase `document.Form1.Head.option[2].text` would refer to the value `Glasses`. If the value `Closed` were selected by the user, the `document.Form1.Head.selectedIndex` property would be equal to 1.

To identify the user's selection in the example, you first looked at the index of the selected element with the line `var Index = SelectField.selectedIndex`. You then used that value to find the text stored in the selected option with the line `var StringValue = SelectField.options[Index].text`. This value was used to help determine the proper URL for the image you wished to load.

Another new concept is the keyword `parent`. This refers to the object owning the current document. If you look at the example, you'll see that the top and bottom frames are loaded by a completely separate HTML document, which doesn't display anything at all (unless your browser does not support frames). This document is the parent of each of the two frames, because it resides on the imaginary level above them and controls them.

Therefore, the line `parent.BottomFrame.document.write(newframe)` causes `NewFrame`'s value to replace the document currently displayed in the frame named `BottomFrame`. As you can see, the keyword `parent` is a concept similar to that of the keyword `this`. The term `parent` refers to the document calling and controlling the frame of the current document.

The Script Wizard

In all the examples we've done, you've edited the HTML directly. This helps you understand the basics of JavaScript. Once you become proficient, you'll want to find the quickest way possible to create JavaScripts. FrontPage includes an excellent tool to help you build these scripts. It's called the Script Wizard.

To access the Script Wizard, simply select Insert | Script from the FrontPage Editor Menus, then click the Script Wizard button. The Script Wizard is shown in Figure 15-21.

In the left side of the Script Wizard is a hierarchical listing of all possible events for your page. In the right side is a list of properties and methods you can manipulate or call. The bottom text area represents the code for each event. If you've never worked with an event-driven code editor like this before, it can be a little confusing. Once you get the hang of it, you'll find yourself much more productive, since all of your tools will be right at your fingertips.

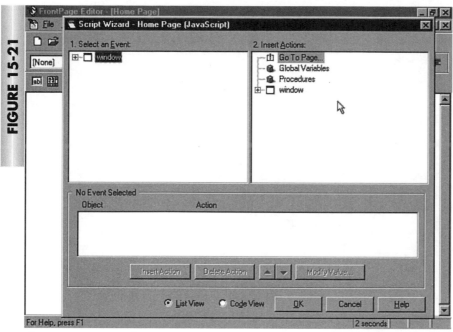

FIGURE 15-21

The Script Wizard

Lesson 10: Using the Script Wizard

To demonstrate this tool, we're going to effectively re-create the program in Lesson 5 (Listing 15-7). This is just a simple demonstration to give you a feel for the Script Wizard.

First, open a new Web. Then open the default document associated with it. Then Click Insert | Script. In the Script dialog, click the Script Wizard button (make sure you have JavaScript selected as the scripting language). This brings up the Script Wizard dialog.

The event pane lists the objects in your page and the window object, as well as their associated events. For example, the window object has an `onload` event. Expand the window tree, then click the `onload` event. Click the Radio button representing code view at the bottom of the dialog. This will allow us to edit code for the event right in the bottom portion of the window, and expose more methods in the action area.

Now, we'll add some code to execute when the `onload` event occurs. If you remember, we just wrote "Hello World Wide Web!" to the document. To accomplish this with the Script Wizard, expand the window tree in the actions panel. Then go down to document, and expand its methods as well. Notice that `write` is one of the methods listed. That's what we want to use, so double-click it. You should notice that the code appears in the lower panel, as shown in Figure 15-22.

This code is a template for the method. It's filled out with the default variable `psarray` to help remind you how the method is used. In this case, we want to replace `psarray` with `Hello World Wide Web!<BR>`. Do that, then click OK and embed the script into your page. When you're finished, it should look like Figure 15-23.

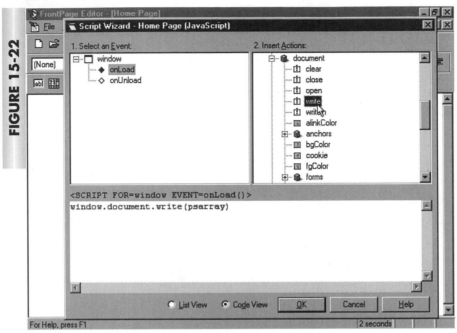

Results of adding a `write` method to the `onload` event

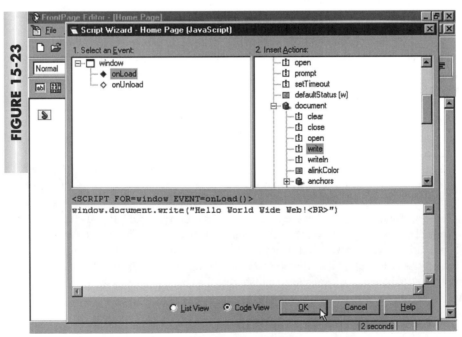

Editing the code in the code view

Save your work, then view the page with your favorite JavaScript-enabled browser. It should appear like Figure 15-14, since it does essentially the same thing. Some of these concepts of scripting languages are difficult to grasp, but the more you work with them, the easier they become. This model of programming is confusing at first, but you'll find yourself making fewer mistakes in the long run.

If you made it this far, you've reached a considerable level of accomplishment using JavaScript. You can validate forms before submitting them to your Webs or CGI scripts, you can react to user events as they occur during the viewing of your Web for true interactivity, and you can dynamically create forms and display them in frames without wasting bandwidth or server processing power.

Note

Many of the most useful JavaScript objects and their characteristics can be found in Appendix C of this book. For more up-to-date information on JavaScript and more tutorials on JavaScript programming, try these WWW sites:

```
http://www.netscape.com/eng/mozilla/Gold/
handbook/javascript
http://www.gamelan.com
http://www.c2.org/~andreww/javascript
http://www.freqgrafx.com/411
```

Forms and Security

16

In this chapter you will learn:

Form Functions
How to Create Various Forms in FrontPage
Form Bots
Security Concerns on the Internet
Public-Key Cryptography
SSL and S-HTTP Security Protocols

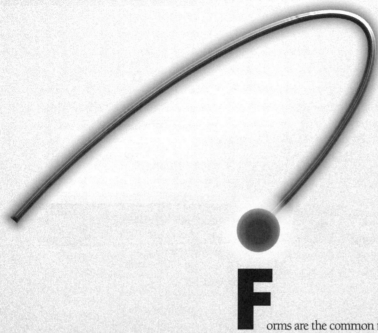

Forms are the common method for allowing users to submit data to a World Wide Web (WWW or Web) server. Forms have a variety of uses on the Web, including registering for services, obtaining memberships in clubs, searching databases, and shopping online.

As the number and variety of online transactions continues to expand, individual users have become concerned about sending personal information on forms out into cyberspace. Addresses, phone numbers, and credit card numbers can be stolen by bogus companies and dishonest hackers. Government and businesses are also concerned for similar reasons. This chapter presents an overview of forms and some lessons on creating forms in FrontPage and then discusses types of Web security.

Form Functions

Forms allow users to send a variety of information to WWW servers. Submitting forms lets users interact with the Web in the following ways:

◁ Shopping online

◁ Searching databases

◁ Registering for organizations or services

◁ Requesting a user-defined action

◁ Collecting demographics

◁ Distance learning

Online Shopping

Online shopping involves buying goods, as well as requesting brochures, catalogs, and services. You are usually required to fill out an order form with your name, address, and credit card information. Many Web sites give you a "shopping cart" that allows you to collect the specific goods or services you want as you browse through the site. At the check out, your selections are totaled and you are given your bill.

 Tip

Check out the All-Internet Shopping Directory at http://www.webcom.com/~tbrown/.

Searching Databases

If you need information on a specific topic, forms let you search the many online databases that exist on the Web. These databases act as indexes of Web sites. Yahoo! is an example of an online database that can help you quickly find a particular Web site. All you need to do is type your keywords into a one-line form located at the top of the Yahoo! home page, then click on the Search button. Yahoo! then builds a custom index of entries containing your keywords.

 Tip

Check out Yahoo! at http://www.yahoo.com.

Registering for Organizations or Services

Forms allow you to sign up for the thousands of offers and services on the Web, such as discussion groups, clubs, contests, and credit cards. Registration forms ask you to supply general information such as your name, street address, phone number, and e-mail address. Many Web sites require you to be registered before they let you explore any deeper into their site.

Requesting a User-Defined Action

Forms let you request a server to run a specific program for you. The types of programs you can request depend on the capabilities of the particular server you are dealing with. For example, Earth Viewer can display a current satellite view of the earth based on latitude and longitude coordinates that you specify on a form.

Tip

Check out Earth Viewer at `http://www.fourmilab.ch/earthview/vplanet.html`.

Collecting Demographics

Business, consumer research, and marketing agencies use forms to collect data about certain groups of users. This data can include level of education, job, age, and product satisfaction. This information keeps these agencies in touch with customer preferences and up to date on the characteristics of specific consumer markets. You may also want to collect information from users who visit your Web site. For example, you could ask how visitors discovered your site or for suggestions on how to improve your site.

Distance Learning

Distance learning is a new educational direction that includes a *virtual* classroom with lectures on a virtual chalkboard. Some browsers have voice capability that allows lectures and student responses to be heard by the entire classroom. In this virtual environment, electronic forms are needed to test students. Fill-in-the-blank, true-false, multiple choice, and essay questions easily lend themselves to the form format.

Form Facts

You've probably filled out thousands of forms in your lifetime. Forms allow collection, processing, and response to data. If you put a form in your Web site, you will have a truly interactive relationship with the users who view your page and complete the form.

Uses for forms, especially in electronic commerce, are seemingly endless. They allow users to order products and services, obtain memberships in clubs and organizations, and submit data for market research.

Forms are supported by most browsers and are easily inserted into a Web page using FrontPage. Forms have several components, including check boxes, text-input boxes, pull-down menus, clickable buttons, and clickable images. Regular text and images can also be placed inside forms to give users directions as to how to complete the form. After a form is filled out, the user submits it to the information provider's server by clicking on a special button or pressing the ENTER key.

A form consists of a series of fields designed to collect information from users. The following lessons demonstrate how FrontPage allows you to include forms in your Web site.

Lesson 1: FrontPage Form Fields

Table 16-1 lists the form fields FrontPage can insert into your Web page. These form fields can be quickly accessed from the Forms toolbar. To display the Forms toolbar, select View | Forms Toolbar. Figure 16-1 shows the Forms toolbar.

Table 16-1 FrontPage form field inserts for Web pages

Form Field	Explanation
Check box	Allows the user to choose something by clicking on a box
Drop-down menu	Allows the user to choose from items in a menu
One-line text box	Allows the user to type text into a one-line field
Push button	Allows the user either to submit a form or to reset the form to its original state
Radio button	Allows the user to choose something by clicking on a button
Scrolling text box	Allows the user to type text into a multiline field

Each form field has its own parameters, such as its name, value, type, initial state, and width. You can input or alter these specifications by accessing a form field's properties dialog box. This process is demonstrated in the following lessons.

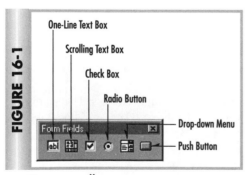

FIGURE 16-1

Forms toolbar

Lesson 2: Creating a Form

You're humming along in FrontPage Editor (FP Editor), creating your Web site, when you come to a spot where you would like some user feedback. You would like to place a scrolling text box at this insertion point. An *insertion point* is where the cursor is placed and where you will insert a form or form field. It is often to the immediate right of the last line of text.

1. In a new page in FP Editor, type User Feedback. Highlight these words, then select Heading 2 from the Change Style window.

2. Place your cursor at the insertion point, which is to the immediate right of User Feedback.

3. As shown in Figure 16-2, choose Insert, then Form Field, then Scrolling Text Box. This inserts the form into your page.

4. Now you must set the field's properties. Select the form field by clicking on it, then select Edit | Form Field Properties. This brings up the Scrolling Text Box Properties dialog box. The name of the field defaults to Scrolling Text1, but you can change the name if necessary. When the Initial Value box is left blank, this means that the form field will initially be blank, so leave this box empty. Adjust Width in characters to 60 and Number of lines to 6. Figure 16-3 illustrates all this input.

5. Click OK to exit the Text Box Properties dialog box.

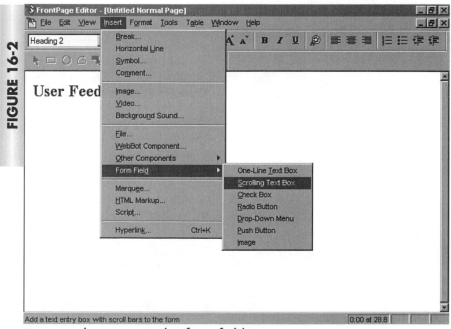

FIGURE 16-2

How to select a particular form field

6. Place your cursor at the immediate left of the top of the text box, then press ENTER to create a line on top. Type in the question, If you had a million dollars, how would you spend it?

7. To add additional text underneath the form field, place the cursor to the immediate right of the form field, then press ENTER to create a new line. Figure 16-4 shows the final form displayed in your Web page.

Form fields can be inserted on either the inside or the outside of forms. In this case, a field was placed outside any existing forms, so FrontPage created a new form with the single form field inside it. The dashed border indicates the form. Within this form, you can add other form fields, text, images, and extra white space, just as you would if you were typing in a regular page.

Lesson 3: Adding a Submit Button

You've just added a form to your Web page. Now you would like to add a Submit button to the form so the user can send in the information to be processed.

1. Place the cursor to the right of the last line of text in your form.

2. Press ENTER to create a new line in the form. Now the insertion point is on this new line.

3. Choose Insert, then Form Field, then Push Button. A Submit button is automatically placed into the page.

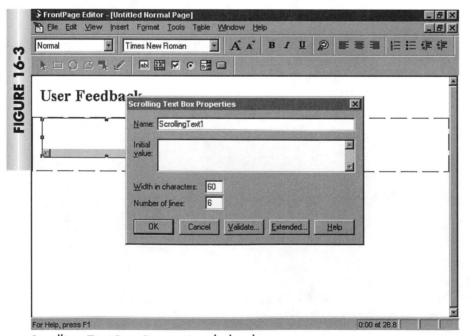

FIGURE 16-3

Scrolling Text Box Properties dialog box

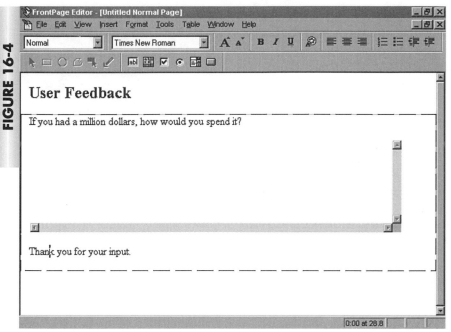

FIGURE 16-4

Form with a scrolling text box

Tip

The Forms toolbar has an icon for each type of form field. Therefore, you can click on the Push Button icon in the toolbar instead of using the Insert menu. Figure 16-1 shows the Forms toolbar.

4. The Value/Label for the button defaults to Submit. If you would like to create a more specific label such as Submit Reply, click on the button to select it, then select Edit | Form Field Properties. This brings up the Push Button Properties dialog box. In the Value/Label field, type Submit Reply. The Button type defaults to Submit, so leave it as is.

5. Click OK to exit the Push Button Properties dialog box.

6. Push Buttons can also be used to reset or clear a form. Insert another button next to the Submit Reply button by clicking on the Push Button icon in the Forms toolbar. In the Push Button Properties dialog box, set the Button type to Reset.

7. Click OK.

Figure 16-5 shows the final form with the two added push buttons.

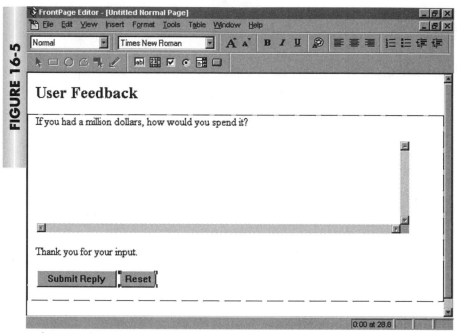

A form with a scrolling text box, a Submit button, and a Reset button

Lesson 4: A Form with Check Boxes

Suppose you want users to choose one or more items in a list of items. Inserting a series of check box form fields makes this possible. The following steps show you how to add check boxes to a form.

1. From your Web page in FrontPage Editor, click on the Check Box icon in the Forms toolbar. This inserts a check box into your page.

2. To set the parameters for the check box, click on it, then press ALT + ENTER. This brings up the Check Box Properties dialog box.

3. Accept the default Name and Value.

4. The Initial state option defaults to Not Checked, so leave it as is because you don't want the box to be checked initially. Figure 16-6 shows the Check Box Properties dialog box.

5. Click OK to exit the Check Box Properties dialog box.

6. Now type in the label Superior to the right of the check box.

7. Press ENTER to move to the next line. This is your next insertion point.

8. Repeat Steps 1 through 7 to insert three more check boxes labeled Above average, Fair, and Poor.

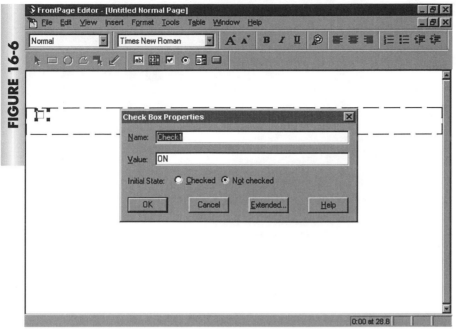

FIGURE 16-6

Check Box Properties dialog box

9. Now place your cursor to the immediate left of the first check box. Press ENTER to create a line at the top for your question. Type in How would you rate your writing skills?. Figure 16-7 shows the final form displayed in your Web page.

Lesson 5: A Form with a Drop-Down Menu

If you would like users to choose one or more items from a long list of choices, you may want to use a drop-down menu. The following steps illustrate how to insert a drop-down menu form field.

1. Place your cursor at the insertion point.

2. Click on the Drop-Down Menu icon in the Forms toolbar. This inserts a drop-down menu into your page.

3. To list items in your drop-down menu, click on it, then select Edit I Form Field Properties. This brings up the Drop-Down Menu Properties dialog box.

4. Click on Add. This will bring up the Add Choice dialog box.

5. Enter the first choice in the list, Labrador Retriever. The Initial State option will default to Not Selected, which is what you want, so leave it as is. Unless you click on the Specify Value box, the Value will default to the choice name. Figure 16-8 shows the Add Choice dialog box.

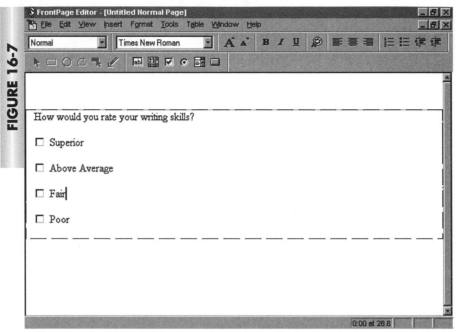

A form with check boxes

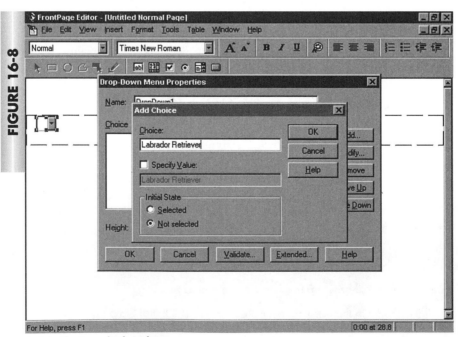

Add Choice dialog box

6. Click OK to add this choice to your drop-down menu. The Add Choice dialog box will disappear and `Labrador Retriever` will show up in the Drop-Down Menu dialog box as the first item in your list. Figure 16-9 shows the Drop-Down Menu dialog box at this point.

7. Repeat Steps 4 through 6 to add more choices to your drop-down menu.

8. In the Height window in the Drop-Down Menu Properties dialog box, change the height of the menu to 5 so more than one choice can be displayed in your menu.

9. Click OK to exit the Drop-Down Menu dialog box.

10. In your Web page, place the cursor to the immediate left of the top of the menu and press `ENTER` to create a line at the top for your question. Type in `Which dog in the following list would you like to have as a pet? Click on your selection`. Figure 16-10 shows the final form in your Web page.

You may wish to use additional commands in the Drop-Down Menu dialog box. After clicking on or highlighting a menu choice, you can change it by clicking Modify, which will send you to the Add Choice dialog box. Remove will delete this menu choice. Move Up will move your highlighted field up the menu. Move Down will move your highlighted field down the menu. A Yes for the Allow multiple selections option allows users to select more than one menu item. A No will limit users to only one selection.

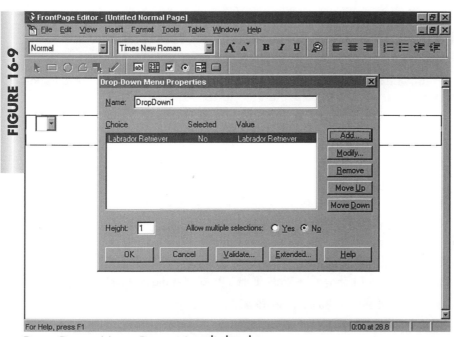

FIGURE 16-9

Drop-Down Menu Properties dialog box

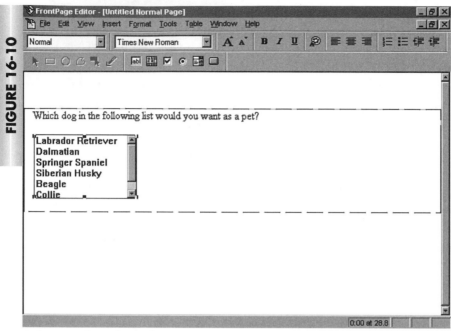

A form with a drop-down menu

Lesson 6: A Form with Radio Buttons

Radio buttons allow users to select one choice from a short list of items. Suppose you are creating a quiz with a series of multiple choice questions and you want the first question to be an example. The following steps illustrate the use of radio buttons.

1. Place the cursor at the insertion point.

2. Click on the Radio Button icon in the Forms toolbar. This inserts a radio button into your page.

3. To set the parameters for this button, click on it, then select Edit | Form Field Properties. This brings up the Radio Button Properties dialog box.

4. You can change the Group Name or accept the default (the group name will not show up in your page). The Value defaults to Choice 1. Accept this default.

5. The Initial State of the radio button defaults to Selected. Change this option to Not Selected. Figure 16-11 shows the Radio Button Properties dialog box.

6. Click OK to exit the Radio Button Properties dialog box.

7. One radio button should now appear in your Web page. Now type the label Seagull next to it.

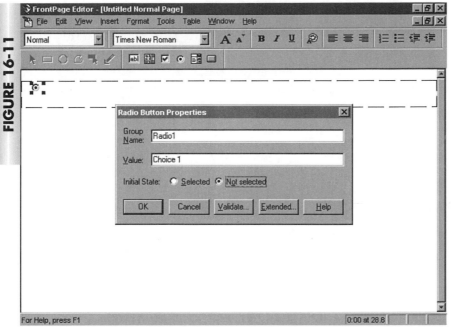

FIGURE 16-11

Radio Button Properties dialog box

8. Press ENTER to go to the next insertion point on the line below.

9. Repeat Steps 1 through 8 to insert two more radio buttons labeled Albatross and Sandpiper. Because this first question is an example, you want the answer already selected. Therefore, when you are adding the Albatross radio button, its Initial State will be Selected.

10. After you have finished inserting the three radio buttons, place your cursor to the left of the first button, then press ENTER to create space at the top for a caption and a question.

11. Type in Reading Comprehension Quiz. Highlight this line, then select Heading 2 from the Style Change window.

12. On the next line, type Read the Rhyme of the Ancient Mariner, then answer the questions. The first question is an example.. Figure 16-12 shows the final form in your Web page.

Tip

If you would like to delete a form, delete every object inside the form. Then, in the empty form, use the Backspace or Delete key to delete it.

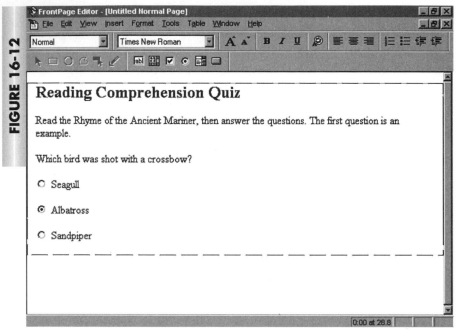

FIGURE 16-12

Form with radio buttons

Lesson 7: Form Handlers and Form Bots

A *form handler* is a program on your server that processes forms after they are submitted by users. Each form field's name and value are sent to the form handler as a name-value pair.

Like form fields, entire forms also have certain properties. One of these properties is the particular form handler you give the form. One type of form handler is called Custom Common Gateway Interface (CGI) script. This is a user-defined form handler that requires programming skills.

Luckily, FrontPage has given you some shortcuts when it comes to form handlers. These shortcuts are called *Form Bots*. Form Bots are types of form handlers that execute common form-handling tasks. Form Bots make creating your own scripts unnecessary in most cases.

Lesson 8: Configuring a Form

In this lesson, you will learn how to assign a certain form handler (Form Bot) to a form, then you will configure that form handler. In this case, the form handler is the Save Results Bot, which stores a form's data in a particular file and in a specified format.

1. Place your cursor inside a form. Click on the right mouse button, then select Form Properties. This will bring up the Form Properties dialog box.

2. Click in the Form Handler box. A drop-down menu will list all available WebBot Components.

3. Choose the Save Results WebBot Component. Figure 16-13 shows the filled-in Form Properties dialog box.

5. Click on Settings. This will bring up the Settings for Saving Results of Form dialog box. This dialog box has a Results tab, a Confirm tab, and an Advanced tab. In the Results tab, type `comments.htm` into the File for Results window. This is the file where the bot will save the response data from your form.

6. The File Format option defaults to HTML. This format will be acceptable in most cases, so leave it as is. Other options can be accessed by clicking the down arrow of the File Format window, and include HTML definition list, HTML bulleted list, text, and text database format. Figure 16-14 shows the filled-in Results tab of the Settings For Saving Results of Form dialog box.

7. Click on OK to exit the Settings For Saving Results of Form dialog box.

8. Click on OK to exit the Form Properties dialog box.

Now you have assigned the Save Results Bot form handler to your form. You also set up a file (`comments.htm`) in which the results will be saved.

Tip

See Chapter 8, "WebBot Components," for more information.

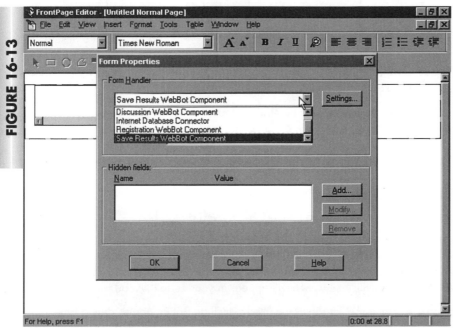

FIGURE 16-13

Form Properties dialog box

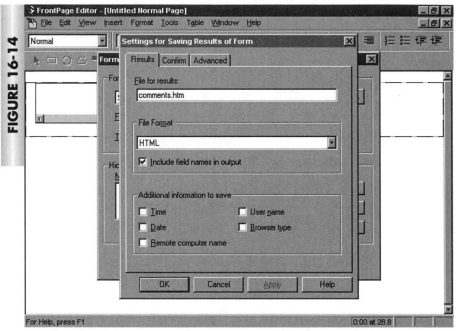

FIGURE 16-14

Results tab of the Settings for Saving Results of Form dialog box

Lesson 9: Inserting an Include Bot

When you insert an Include Bot in your Web page, it is replaced by data or a design element from a specified file on the same Web. This bot is useful when you want the same element to look uniform in multiple Web pages. For example, suppose you want to insert a starred line at the top of all of your Web pages.

1. Place your cursor at the insertion point at the top of your first Web page.

2. Choose Insert | WebBot Component. This will bring up the WebBot Components dialog box.

3. Select Include from the Select a Component box, then click on OK. This will bring up the Include Bot Properties dialog box.

4. Click on Browse. This will bring up the Current Web dialog box.

5. Select the file stars.htm. (While your Web is open, you can create the stars.htm file by selecting File | New; then, select Normal Page and click OK, type in a line of stars, choose Save As and type stars in the Page Title field; then click OK. Now the file stars.htm will appear in your current Web.)

6. Click on OK. Figure 16-15 shows the filled-in Include Bot Properties dialog box.

7. Click on OK to exit the Include Bot Properties dialog box.

8. Repeat steps 1 through 7 to insert this bot in the rest of your Web pages.

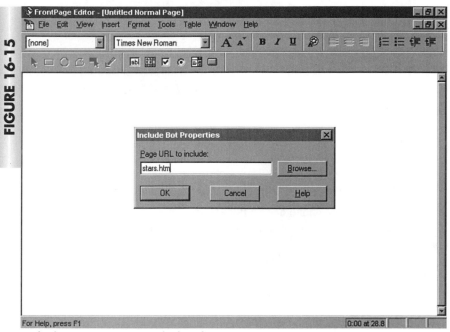

Include Bot Properties dialog box

When you have inserted this bot in all your Web pages, a single starred line will appear at the top of all the pages.

Tip

A special robot cursor is used to identify a bot on a Web page. When your regular cursor changes to a robot cursor, you can open the properties dialog box of that bot by clicking the left mouse button. A single click on the right mouse button displays further editing choices.

Lesson 10: Creating a Search Form

If you have multiple Web pages, you may want to include a Search form on your first Web page. A Search form allows users to locate topics of interest to them without having to browse through your entire Web. Users simply enter a particular word in the Search form and click on a push button; then, they are transported to a page containing that word. FrontPage lets you create Search forms in the following way:

1. In your Web page in FP Editor, place your cursor at the insertion point.

2. Select Insert | WebBot Component. This will bring up the WebBot Components dialog box.

3. Select Search, then click on OK. This brings up the Search Bot Properties dialog box. (The Search Bot will create a One-Line Text Box form field for user input.)

4. Type in a label for the One-Line Text Box in the Label for Input field (you can also accept the default).

5. Type in the width of the input field in the Width in Characters field (you can also accept the default).

6. Type in the label for the push button that will start the search in the Label for Start Search button field (you can also accept the default).

7. Type in the label for the push button that will clear the form in the Label for "Clear" Button field (you can also accept the default).

8. Select which part of your Web the Search Bot will search for users' topics in the Word List to Search field. You can choose All, which means your entire Web, except discussion groups, will be searched, or you can enter a directory for a particular discussion group. The three check boxes at the bottom allow you to display further information such as Score (closeness of match), File Date, and File Size found. Figure 16-16 shows the Search Bot Properties dialog box.

9. Click on OK to exit the Insert Bot dialog box. Figure 16-17 shows the final form in your home page.

FIGURE 16-16

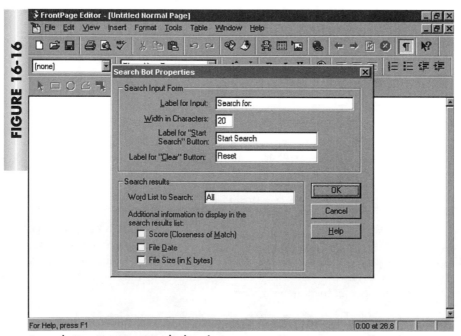

Search Bot Properties dialog box

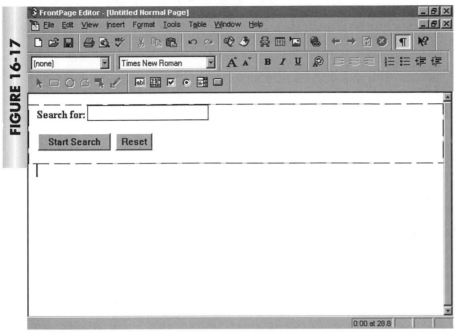

A Search form

Lesson 11: Creating a User Registration Form

If you would like to have users register at your Web site, FrontPage can help you create a User Registration form. Alwaysregister users from the root Web because it is your main Web (see Figure 16-18 for a diagram of a root Web and child Webs). Child Webs are smaller, offshoot Webs of the root Web.

To create a User Registration form, follow these steps:

1. In FrontPage Explorer, open up the Web where you would like users to register. This is also called the *target Web* . This will be a child Web of the root Web. For this example, we will refer to it as Testweb.

2. Select Tools I Permissions. This will bring up the Permissions dialog box for Testweb.

3. In the Settings tab (this is the default tab, so you don't have to choose it), choose Use Unique Permissions For This Web, then click on Apply.

4. Click on the Users tab. Choose Only registered users have browse access, then click on OK. Figure 16-19 shows the Users tab of the Permissions dialog box for Testweb.

5. Close Testweb.

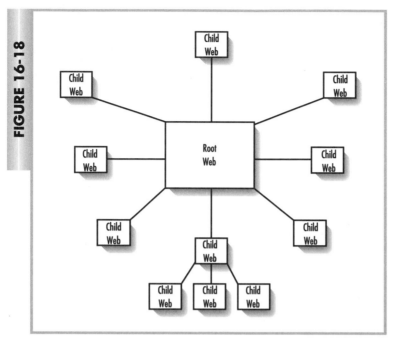

FIGURE 16-18

Root Web and child Webs

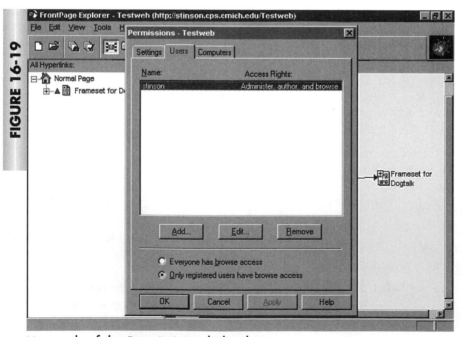

FIGURE 16-19

Users tab of the Permissions dialog box

6. Open the root Web in FrontPage Explorer.

7. From the root Web, click on the Editor button in the toolbar to open FP Editor.

8. Choose File | New. This will bring up the New Page dialog box.

9. Choose User Registration, then click on OK. FrontPage will now create a new page with a User Registration form and text.

10. In the new form, click on any form field to select it. Click on the right mouse button, then choose Form Properties. This will bring up the Form Properties dialog box.

11. Click on Settings. This will bring up the Settings For Registration Form Handler dialog box.

12. In the Registration tab (this is the default tab, so you don't have to choose it), in the Web Name field, type in the name of the Web where you want to register users; in this case, it is Testweb. Figure 16-20 shows the filled-in Registration tab of the Settings For Registration Form Handler dialog box.

13. Click on OK to exit the Settings For Registration Form Handler dialog box.

14. Click on OK to exit the Form Properties dialog box. Figure 16-21 shows the final User Registration form.

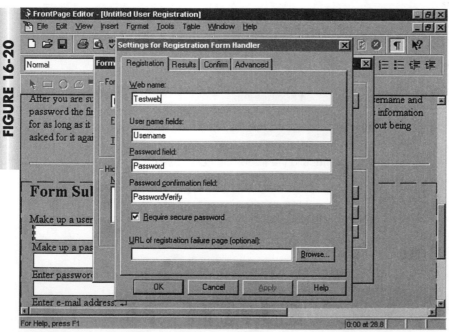

FIGURE 16-20

Registration tab of the Settings For Registration Form Handler dialog box

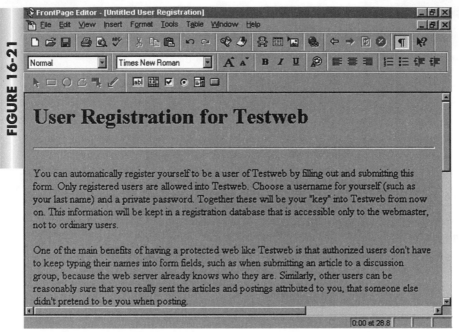

FIGURE 16-21

User Registration form

15. Now edit the Registration form. Begin by deleting the top two paragraphs of instructions.

16. To find and replace [Other Web] on your page with Testweb, select Edit | Replace. Type [Other Web] into the Find What field. Type Testweb into the Replace With field, then click on Replace All.

18. Now you can edit your text to conform to your particular site.

19. Select File | Save As. Choose a name for your Registration form, such as Testreg (for test registration), type that into the Page Title field, then click on OK.

This form allows you to identify and count the number of visitors to your Web. This number will also be the number of people registered at your site. You will find that some visitors will make repeat trips to your site to see what is new and interesting. This may encourage you to form discussion groups for interested individuals.

Lesson 12: Creating a Discussion Group

A discussion group allows users to discuss certain topics in an open forum. Users can search for discussion topics by entering a word or phrase in a Search form. The table of contents also directs users to particular topics.

A discussion group Web can be linked to any page in a Web that already exists, or it can stand alone. In this lesson, you will create a discussion Web and link it to a page in an existing Web. To create a discussion group Web, complete the following steps:

1. In FrontPage Explorer, open the Web to which you will add a discussion group. (If your Web has multiple pages, decide to which one you will link your discussion Web.) If you have not created any Webs yet, open a new Web by selecting File | New Web, then choose Normal Web. Call your new Web Webtest in the New Web From Template dialog box, then click on OK. This brings up the FrontPage Explorer view of your Normal Page.

2. To create a discussion group Web, choose File | New Web. This will bring up the New FrontPage Web dialog box.

3. Check the Add to the Current Web box. (You can add the discussion Web to the current Web because you opened your current Web in step 1.)

4. Choose Discussion Web Wizard, then click on OK. This will bring up the first screen of the Discussion Web Wizard.

5. Read the directions, then click on Next.

6. In the second screen of the Discussion Web Wizard, choose the discussion group features you would like from the list:

   ◁ Table of contents

   ◁ Search form—allows users to search discussion topics

   ◁ Threaded replies—allows users to enter new topics for discussion or to reply to current topics

   ◁ Confirmation page—confirms a user's discussion entry

7. Click on Next.

   Figure 16-22 shows the main feature checklist in the Discussion Web Wizard. After you have chosen your features, click on Next.

8. Type in a specific title for the discussion group. For this lesson, the title will be Dogtalk. The title should relate to the purpose of the discussion group. Click on Next.

9. Choose the fields that will be on the form where the user will submit topics. You are required to choose subject and comments, but you may also include categories or products. Click on Next.

10. Choose whether or not users will be required to register for this Web. If you decide to register users, a Registration form will be created and opened in FrontPage Editor. Make sure to transfer the Registration form to your root Web. Click on Next.

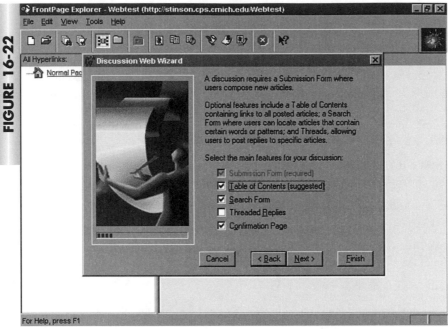

FIGURE 16-22

Main feature checklist of Discussion Web Wizard

11. Choose the order for the sort in the table of contents, either oldest to newest or vice versa. Click on Next.

12. Select whether you want the table of contents to replace your home page. If you choose Yes, the discussion group table of contents will overwrite the home page in your current Web, called Webtest. If you choose No, the table of contents will be on its own page. For this lesson, choose No. (If your discussion group Web is going to stand alone, you will always choose Yes for this option.) Click on Next.

13. Decide on the options for the Search form, such as size, date, and a relevance value called score. Click on Next.

14. Choose the color settings for the pages and links in the discussion group Web. Click on Next.

15. You have the option to choose a frameset to display the discussion group. Chapter 12, "A FrontPage Project," Lesson 11, "Creating a Page with Frames," discusses frames. Because most browsers support frames, it is fairly safe to choose this option. Click on Next.

16. Click on Finish to exit the Discussion Web Wizard. FrontPage Explorer will now display the FrontPage Explorer view of your discussion group Web. Note that so many pages are generated. The most important pages you will deal with are Frameset for Dogtalk and Dogtalk Submission form.

17. In FrontPage Explorer, open the page you wish to link the discussion group to in FP Editor. In this case, this page is called Normal page. Type in the words Dogtalk Discussion or a phrase that is appropriate. Highlight the phrase and choose Edit | Hyperlink.

18. This brings up the Create Hyperlink dialog box. Choose the Current FrontPage Web tab and click on browse.

19. Select Frameset for Dogtalk if you have chosen a frameset. Otherwise, choose Dogtalk TOC (Table of Contents). Click on OK. This links this page to the discussion group. Figure 16-23 shows the Current Web dialog box.

20. Click on OK to exit the Create Link dialog box.

21. Now save the Normal page using File | Save.

22. You may now edit or customize the discussion group pages created by the Discussion Web Wizard by first going back to FrontPage Explorer, then opening up particular pages. Figure 16-24 shows the link between the Normal page and the Frameset for Dogtalk.

23. Use your browser to test your discussion group Web and see how it works. To obtain the address of your page, place the cursor on the page and press the right

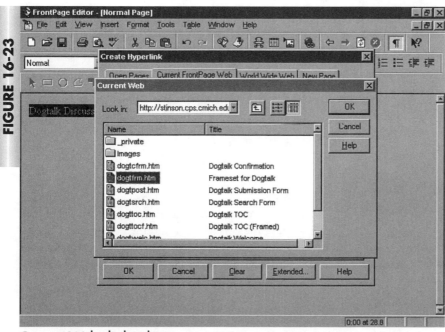

FIGURE 16-23

Current Web dialog box

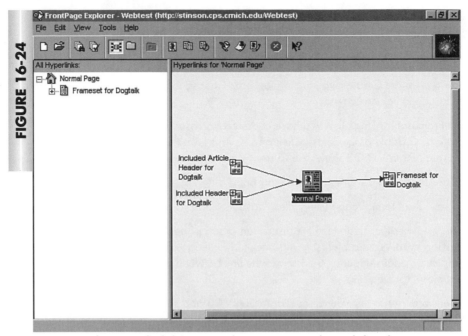

FIGURE 16-24

Structure showing link between the current Web and the discussion group Web

mouse button. From this list, choose Properties. From the Properties dialog box, copy the URL of your home page. When you bring up your browser, place the URL in the location box.

Security

Users in government, education, and business, as well as individual users, need to consider the possible security risks of operating on the Internet. Although crime on the Net is relatively low compared to other types of crime, viruses, hackers, and fraudulent companies do exist and are expected to increase in number with the rapid growth of the Internet. There are two kinds of Internet criminals: the curious user and the hard-core thief. The curious user doesn't steal or cause damage, but seeks to learn as much as possible by exploring and seeing how far he or she can go before getting caught. The hard-core thief wants to profit illegally from the Internet and does so by swiping software and information. Both the curious user and the hard-core thief may cause damage to data or equipment. Table 16-2 is a list of terms describing computer criminals.

Table 16-2 Terms used to describe computer criminals

Term	Definition
Hacker	Anyone who is good with computers; not necessarily a computer criminal
Cracker	Breaks into computer systems by guessing or bypassing passwords; can gain access to credit card numbers and other personal data
Phreak	Hacks phone systems to steal long distance time or voice mail accounts; tampers with phone switch capability
Phracker	Combination of a cracker and a phreak: Destroys networks by breaking into both computer and phone systems
Pirate	Steals proprietary software and downloads it to a special site so friends and clients may use it

When you submit a form with information such as your credit card number, the chances of it being stolen are slim due to the transaction security strategies that exist on the Net. The rest of this chapter is devoted to these strategies, as well as to other aspects of security that users should be concerned about, such as

◁ The security of your own computer

◁ The security of your server

◁ The security of the connection between your computer and your server

Figure 16-25 shows the major security concerns on the Internet, and the following paragraphs explain these concerns.

Your Computer

The way you set up your computer can greatly increase or decrease the chance of a security breach. The way you configure software applications such as Microsoft Word can sometimes pick up mischievous auto-exec macros while you are surfing the Web. Trouble-making macros and viruses can also be hidden in games on the Web that you download for free. Anything you download off the Web can contain hidden gremlins that may damage your computer.

You may want to consider purchasing software that allows you to avoid many of the viruses that may haunt the WWW. Check out all software thoroughly and be sure to get software that can be updated periodically. You may want to search the Web using keywords such as `virus protection` and `software`. Two major companies that have excellent reputations in this area are Symantec (Norton) and McAfee. You can find more information about these companies at `http://www.nha.com/navint.html` and `http://www.mcafee.com/mstore/mstore.html`.

FIGURE 16-25

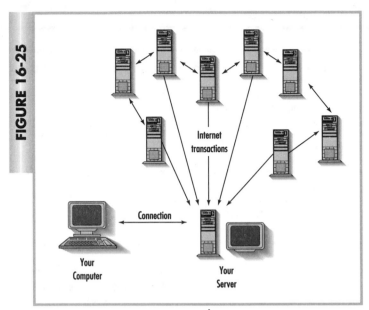

Major security concerns on the Internet

How you pick and handle your passwords can also affect you computer's security. You may have a password for access to a network and other passwords to access various Web sites. Important points to remember regarding passwords include the following:

◁ Select passwords that can't be easily figured out. Names of spouses, children, and pets are the first passwords crackers try.

◁ Use a combination of numbers and letters.

◁ Longer passwords are harder to crack.

◁ Memorize your password.

◁ If you write your password down, hide the piece of paper so no one can find it but you.

◁ Don't tell anyone your password.

◁ Change your password often.

◁ Don't use a password you use on your own computer when registering at a site on the Internet. If you do, owners of that site will know your personal password.

> **Tip**
>
> The safest passwords are eight or more characters long, combine letters and numbers, and contain no words that can be found in a dictionary.

Your Server

If your server isn't managed properly, it can be a security risk to the system. Probably the most important defense a server can have is a good firewall. A *firewall* is a way of protecting one network from another risky network. In this case, firewalls protect your server's network (which includes your computer) from the Internet. A firewall is like a traffic cop that blocks some traffic out while letting other traffic in. Some firewalls concentrate on blocking traffic, and others emphasize letting traffic flow. For example, some may allow only e-mail communication, whereas others allow full Internet access. Firewalls have two important functions.

1. Authentication of users—Firewalls prevent unauthorized users from gaining access to resources on a network and prevent the unauthorized downloading of proprietary information.

2. Logging of access—In case a security breach does occur, a detailed log records what happened.

Search the Internet using the keywords `firewall` and `Internet`. This will give you a great number of references (more than 50). To select the right software, you can study a number of the frequently asked question (FAQ) documents on this subject. If you are part of a group that uses a LAN, you may wish to check out the WinGate home page at `http://nz.com/NZ/Commerce/creative-cqi/special/qbik/wingate.htm`.

Your Computer-Server Connection

Many other computers may make up the chain between your computer and your Web server. The more computers in this network, the higher the chances of a transmission breach. This type of connection security risk is usually unavoidable, but you can minimize the risk by safeguarding your own computer, as discussed in the above section.

 > **Tip**
>
> If you would like to know more about credit card transactions on the Web, go to `http://www.netscape.com/newsref/std/credit.html`.

Transaction Security

Transaction security includes cash transactions over the Net, as well as the transfer of private data. The security strategy most often employed for these transactions is called *encryption,* which is a way of hiding data so that unauthorized users can't get to it. Basically, encryption puts data into a code that needs a *key* to be read. For example, *candy* could be encrypted into *dboez* where each letter in *candy* is moved up to the next letter. This is called a *Caesar 1 cipher*, because the letters are shifted by one position. *Candy* could also be encrypted as 0 3011 40 42 5. The key to this code would be to place the numbers in pairs, then match them to the letters of the alphabet.

03 01 14 04 25

C A N D Y

You can also add meaningless letters in between the numbers, like this:

0RV30YJG11US40KLNM42WSDF25NBV

This would look like a menacing code if you didn't know to ignore the letters.

An encryption method (or algorithm) can be based on a secret keyword. For example, if the key to an encrypted message is the word *cat*, this means that the first letter in the message has been moved up three letters (because *c* is third in the alphabet), the second letter has been moved up one letter (because *a* is first in the alphabet), and the third letter has been moved up 20 letters (because *t* is the 20th letter). The fourth letter would start over with *c* and be moved up three letters, and so on. Therefore, the coded message

PBEHJNVP

with the *cat* key would be decoded to

MAKEITSO or MAKE IT SO

This kind of encryption is called the *Vigunere cipher*. Both the sender and the receiver of the message have to know the same key, so this is called *symmetric-key cryptography*. If the receiver doesn't know the key, the sender has to send the key, then the message. A third party could intercept both transmissions and easily decode the message. The solution to this problem is discussed below.

RSA Public-Key Cryptography

Most Web security strategies begin with Rivest-Shamir-Adleman (RSA) *public-key* encryption technology. Unlike symmetric-key cryptography, where both sender and receiver use the same key to code and decode messages, public-key cryptography has two different keys. One is a public key that is used by the sender to code a message. The other is a private key that is used by the receiver to decode the message.

Each participant has a set of two keys. Each set contains a public key that is located on a public database where anyone can see it, and a private key that is kept secret. If Jack wants to send an encrypted message to Jill, Jack finds Jill's public key on the public database, codes the message, and sends it. The beauty of this scheme is that only Jill's private key can decode the message. If Jill wants to respond to Jack's message, Jill uses her private key to code the message. Her message can be decoded only by her public key. This lets Jack verify that the response is definitely coming from Jill because only Jill's public key can decipher messages coded with her private key. To summarize:

◁ If Jack wants to send Jill a message only Jill can read, Jack uses Jill's public key to encrypt the message.

◁ If Jack receives a response that he decrypts with Jill's public key, the message must have come from Jill.

In responding to Jack's initial message with a private-key encryption, Jill has created a digital signature. A *digital signature* guarantees a user's identity (assuming the private key stays private).

Tip

RSA, Inc. provides a product for Windows called RSA Secure that is integrated into the file manager. It provides RSA coding for the Windows file system. For more information, go to http://www.rsa.com.

Table 16-3 summarizes the important cryptography terms discussed so far.

Table 16-3 A summary of cryptography terms

Term	Definition
Encryption algorithm	A method of encrypting a message
Secret key	Used to code and decode a message in symmetric-key encryption
Public key	Needed to send a user a message that only that user can read; needs to be made public
Private key	Needed to decode a message that has been coded using a public key; kept secret
Digital signature	Created when a private key is used to code a message; guarantees a user's identity

PGP

Pretty Good Privacy (PGP) is another popular public-key encryption program. It was developed at MIT and is similar to the RSA encryption scheme except it uses smaller key numbers than RSA. Though PGP is not as secure as RSA, it is considered "pretty good privacy."

Tip

You can download the latest version of PGP from `ftp://net-dist.mit.edu/pub/PGP`. For more information about PGP and public-key cryptography, go to `http://bs.mit.edu:8001/pgp-form.html`.

SSL and S-HTTP

Secure Sockets Layer (SSL) and Secure-HyperText Transfer Protocol (S-HTTP) are the two most widely used transaction security standards. Both are based on public-key cryptography.

The SSL protocol is Netscape's version of a transaction security strategy. SSL provides security for HTTP, FTP, Gopher, and Telnet by being located between these protocols and TCP/IP. SSL allows a user on a Netscape browser to transfer credit card or other information securely to the Netscape Commerce server. With SSL incorporated into both the browser and the server, information transmitted over the Internet is securely encrypted.

S-HTTP was designed by Enterprise Integration Technologies. S-HTTP adds public-key encryption and support for digital signatures to the HTTP Web standard. Generally, non-S-HTTP browsers and servers should be able to interface with S-HTTP. With S-HTTP, users do not need their own public keys to participate in secure transactions.

These two protocols are competing to become the universal standard for commerce on the Internet. Recently, SSL and S-HTTP were integrated into a single development package. This allows users to communicate easily and securely no matter which protocol is on their browser. This common approach also makes it easier for information providers to provide secure information on the Web. A dual-protocol security kit containing both SSL and S-HTTP is also in development.

The commercial growth of the Internet has been hindered by competing and incompatible security protocols. The Net needs a universal integrated security standard that will help build and maintain a mass market for electronic transactions.

Tip

If you would like to learn more about Web security issues, go to `http://www-genome.wi.mit.edu/WWW/faqs/www-security-faq.html`.

FrontPage Security

FrontPage security includes three main areas:

1. Access to the Web

2. Proxy support

3. Encryption

Access

The FrontPage Server Extensions allow three levels of access to your Web: end-user, author, and administrator. The end-user has permission only to browse, or look at, your Web. The author can, in addition to browsing, update as well as add pages or new information to the Web. The administrator has the highest level of access. In addition to the other permissions, the administrator can set the permissions of individuals that use the Web.

Proxy

Many Webs use a firewall to between the client and the server. This provides security when the user is not directly at the Intranet site of the server. The encryption method is unique to FrontPage. It guards against the casual snooper, but not the hard-core cracker. FrontPage 97 additionally supports the stronger encryption standard of Secure Sockets Layer (SSL).

Encryption

FrontPage encrypts all communication between the client and the server. This provides security when the user is not directly at the Intranet site of the server. The encryption method is unique to FrontPage. It guards against the casual snooper, but not the hard-core cracker. FrontPage 97 additionally supports the stronger encryption standard of Secure Sockets Layer (SSL).

Summary

Whether you are filling out forms in Web sites, downloading information, or playing games on the Net, you must always keep the security of your computer system in mind. FrontPage offers a security precaution called a Registration form that lets you keep track of visitors to your Web site. The best defense against the abuse of your computer by outside invaders is your own good sense and watchfulness. Use other information in this chapter to help safeguard your Internet transactions, and search the Net for more information on security. Ask your ISP about the security precautions already built into your server.

CGI Overview

17

In this chapter you will learn:

What a CGI Script Is, and Some Uses for Them

A General Overview for What Happens When
a CGI Script Is Called

Points to Consider Regarding the Server When
Implementing CGI Scripts

Suitability of Popular Programming Languages Used
to Create CGI Scripts

How CGI Scripts and WebBots Relate

How to Add a Hit Counter to a Web Page Using FrontPage

How to Set Up a Custom CGI Script to Handle Form Input

A Brief Overview of Technologies That Are Replacing CGI

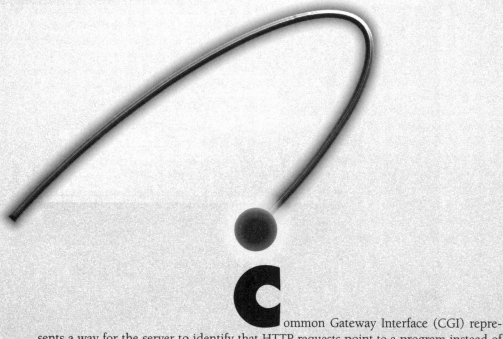

Common Gateway Interface (CGI) represents a way for the server to identify that HTTP requests point to a program instead of to a static document. CGI scripts are, therefore, programs run by the Web server at the request of your Web browser. This mechanism allows a Web server to communicate with the client dynamically, adjusting or recording output according to variables passed from the client. CGI scripts are most commonly used to make page-hit counters, to implement image maps, to process form input, to perform searches, and to create dynamic content.

 Note

CGI programs are commonly called *scripts*. They were originally UNIX scripts—files containing UNIX commands—executed by the server. These scripts are comparable to DOS batch files. Today, CGI scripts are often full-fledged programs, but the term *script* has stuck.

FrontPage has prepackaged many of the most common CGI script functions in WebBots: WebBots are CGI scripts in sheep's clothing. They are easy to use and simple to implement in Webs. You don't have to be a techie to use a WebBot, but using CGI requires a little more knowledge, and creating WebBots often requires good programming skills.

Perhaps you have already established a Web and want to move that Web to FrontPage so you can enjoy FrontPage's easy editing features. You'll be happy to know that you can still use your old CGI scripts. The FrontPage Personal Server has full support for CGI standards (although not for WinCGI), and the server extension won't mess up your other server's configurations. The FrontPage Editor won't recognize your scripts or treat them specially (as it does WebBots), but it will allow you to add your scripts to your documents with special effort.

The good news is that the most common functions of CGI scripts are already captured in FrontPage through WebBots, and you might never need to deal with CGI. The bad news is that WebBots can't do everything, and there are times when CGI scripts might be the best (and possibly the only) way to solve a problem or achieve a desired effect. Potential uses for CGI scripts include interfacing with databases or other information services, storing information on the server in a format not supported by a WebBot, creating dynamic content for the client based on information from the client, and performing other nonstandard tasks.

Despite their complexity and inefficiencies, CGI scripts solve a lot of problems, add a lot of capabilities, and have a large enough installation base that they will be with us for a long time.

How Does CGI Work?

To understand how CGI works, take a look at what happens when you load an HTML page with a browser. The client (browser) sends a request to your server for a document. Most often this document is an HTML document. The server receives this request, locates the document, sends it on its way across the Internet, and then terminates the connection. Upon receipt of this document, the browser looks at the document and (assuming it's an HTML document) says, "Ah, here's an `<IMG>` tag...I'll need that image." It then sends out a request for the image located at the URL specified by the tag and displays it as it's received. This continues until all the items in the page have been loaded. The process looks something like Figure 17-1. The most important concepts are there, albeit somewhat simplified.

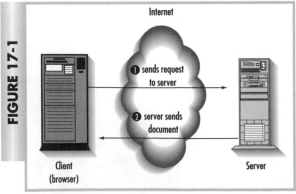

FIGURE 17-1

Outline of document retrieval

If a CGI script is specified by the browser's request, the server has extra steps to go through. First, the HTTP server recognizes that the document requested is, in fact, a program, not a file. The server then starts that program and passes what it knows to it. The server waits while the program (a CGI script) executes. When the script is finished, it passes its output to the server, which has been politely waiting the whole time. The server then passes the information across the Net to the client. This process is outlined in Figure 17-2.

As you can see, there is more involved when using a script instead of a document. CGI scripts place more demands on the server than static Web pages and are often higher in maintenance.

Considerations When Using CGI Scripts

Three main factors to consider when deciding on whether or not to use a CGI script are server horsepower, security, and technical issues. If the server can't supply the horsepower to run scripts effectively, you don't anticipate having the appropriate technical skills to support a set of scripts properly, or your site requires exceptional security measures, you might want to find alternatives to custom CGI programs. These considerations apply to WebBots as well. Remember, WebBots are really CGI scripts in disguise.

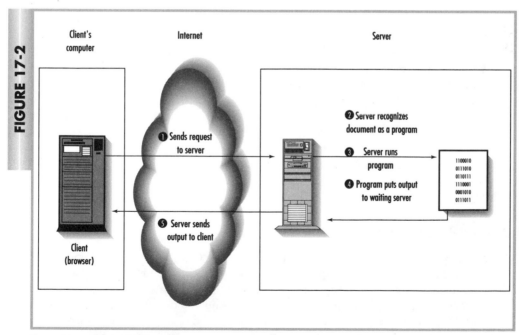

FIGURE 17-2

Execution of a CGI script

Server Horsepower

CGI scripts can place a great strain on a server, especially for very busy sites. If your site is visited often, each visitor is going to request that the script embedded in your site be run. This could lead to many copies of the script running simultaneously. If the script is large, computationally intensive, or performs a lot of disk accesses, it could cripple server performance.

Additionally, overhead is associated with the way CGI works regardless of how efficient or insignificant a script is. Every time a request is made, the CGI script must be opened and loaded. Granted, most scripts are small, but if you're writing an interface to a database that loads several large controls and connections to many resources, the script might take several seconds just to load, even before beginning to do any processing. Additionally, the program must reload for every use, because it terminates when it finishes a task. Also, the server must have a mechanism for waiting for the input; the server can use several possible mechanisms to do this, but they all involve additional resources. That could be a lot of overhead to incur every time someone accesses a page, especially if several people access pages containing CGI scripts at the same time. Your system could be crushed merely by the amount of memory needed to load so many programs at once, not to mention the processing it must provide.

If your site supports a database, there could be problems with disk space as the database grows, not to mention the horrid access speeds (relative to memory, which can be accessed thousands of times more quickly) experienced with hard disks.

Security

The original CGI scripts contained operating system directives. Crackers could send information to these scripts that would cause unintended results. Obviously, this kind of security hole is not acceptable. Fortunately, a CGI programmer and Webmaster can take some simple steps to prevent this sort of mischief, although that's a topic for another book.

Don't forget that CGI scripts are programs, and just like any other program they have access to your system. They could cause damage, which is why you should be very careful when downloading scripts from the Internet to use with your Webs. In addition to the security hazard these scripts present, privacy issues are also involved. These scripts could be used to convey information about your system or your visitors to other sources on the Internet.

Technical Issues

Creating CGI scripts requires programming skills; using CGI scripts does not. If you need a CGI script and don't have the expertise to write one yourself, you might need to hire someone to do so or find a script that suits your needs from some other source. Freeware and shareware CGI scripts are available on the Internet, and you may find one that suits your needs. Of course, security issues need consideration when going this route. Also, a time may come when changes need to be made in the script, and you'll need to find sources for that as well.

Writing a CGI script is always a possibility. CGI scripts are often much simpler to write than other programs, because there is practically no user interface to be concerned with. On the other hand, you have to deal with more issues. Suppose you're writing a simple page-hit counter. Your CGI script would open a file that contains the number of hits your site received, increment that number by one, and then save the result. Simple. But what if two users open your page at the same time, starting your script twice? How would the script handle access to a file if that file is already in use by another copy of the script? CGI scripts need to be especially robust, because they are by nature meant to run autonomously. This means extra care in programming.

Choosing CGI Scripts

Whole books have been written about CGI programming; you won't learn the right way to create a script yourself in just one chapter. Rather, here you are presented the advantages and disadvantages of certain kinds of scripts and how to incorporate them into your FrontPage Webs. The biggest variable in scripts is their source code. The language that was used to create them says a lot about the kinds of capabilities they have and the demands they'll place on your server and staff. Table 17-1 shows a list of the most common CGI programming languages and a cursory summary of their characteristics.

Table 17-1 Summary of common CGI languages and their features

Language	Speed	Ease of Use	String Manipulation	Security	Portability
Visual Basic	Very slow	Simple	Easy	Secure	None
C/C++	Fast	Difficult	Complex	Secure	Possible
Perl	Average	Simple	Easy	Hazardous	Easy
Java	Average	Difficult	Average	Secure	Easy
Shell	Average	Simple	Complex	Hazardous	None

Visual Basic

Visual Basic (VB) is a programming language introduced by Microsoft as an easy way to program Windows applications. It became amazingly popular, and Microsoft leveraged that popularity by using it as the basis for macrolanguages for many of its popular applications, such as Word, Excel, and Access. Visual Basic is also the basis upon which VBScript is built.

Because VB is very easy to learn and has a large following, it's natural that it became a very popular CGI tool. It has good string manipulation features, which are important to CGI programmers who are creating dynamic HTML documents. It's compiled to p-code (a concept similar to Java bytecode), so there is some measure of security. Additionally, VB has a lot of tools available to it for interfacing with existing databases, and there is no shortage of VB programmers. VB could represent a very easy way to interface an existing database with your Web.

The biggest disadvantage of VB is its execution speed. Granted, it doesn't run much slower than any other interpreted language (such as Perl or Java), but VB programs incur a lot of overhead just to load and get running. Running a VB program is like running any other Windows program: Your system must do a lot of work just because of the overhead involved. Even the simplest VB applications take a second or two (and a lot of processor muscle and disk accesses) to get up and running, all before doing even simple calculations. Other interpreted languages don't face this overhead because they are command-line based, not based in the Windows environment like VB. If your system is not high powered or you anticipate that the script you desire will be called often, you may want to choose a different tool to create your CGI script.

Because VB is a Microsoft Windows programming tool, programs written in it are not usable in other environments. If your server is a Windows NT or Windows 95 machine, VB may be an option. If your server is a UNIX or Macintosh machine or if you plan on moving to one of these machines in the future, VB is probably not a good choice.

C/C++

C and C++ are the speed demons of CGI programming. Because they compile to native instructions, they have the fastest execution speed, the lowest potential overhead, and the most secure executables. If your concern is responsiveness, C or C++ should be your first choice.

There are disadvantages to these languages, though. String manipulation is disastrous in C and only slightly better in C++. If you want to create documents on-the-fly and don't want to deal with a lot of code, another language might be a better option, unless speed is a critical factor. Portability may also be an issue. Well-written C/C++ source codes can be designed for portability from one system to another. Of course, the programs will have to be recompiled on the new system, but C and C++ compilers are created for just about every imaginable platform. These languages are also very popular, and it shouldn't be difficult to find people to support these scripts.

Perl

Perl stands for Practical Extraction and Report Language; it was designed for reporting data. This means it has outstanding string manipulation functions, and that's great for generating HTML documents on-the-fly. Perl is an interpreted language, and versions of it have been ported to many different systems, including most flavors of UNIX and DOS. Ports have been made to Windows machines, and both Perl4 and Perl5 programs can run on Windows 95 and Windows NT, as long as they are configured correctly. Perl is also very easy to learn and use. It's not a tough language and it has few abstract concepts to learn. Perl is probably the most popular choice for programmers creating CGI scripts.

The downside of Perl is the fact that its code is not compiled in any manner. The file is run as is. This means that if a clever hacker is able to get ahold of your source, he or she may be able to find and exploit security flaws in it. Another disadvantage is that there aren't a lot of Perl programmers around, but their numbers are growing. Of course, the language is pretty easy to learn and use.

Java

Most people think of Java for its applets that are embedded in HTML documents. Java can also be used to make standalone programs that are not dependent on the browser. Many operating system vendors are licensing Java technology and will probably include Java interpreters in their operating systems in the future. This means Java may become the language to use client-side in the form of applets and server-side in the form of CGI scripts (or their equivalent). If you want to use one language to do it all, Java is it.

Java, though modeled after C and C++, has even more support for strings. Java interpreters are available for many different systems, and it seems Java is becoming the first choice for parties interested in cross-platform development because of its wide acceptance. Because Java is compiled to bytecode, there is some measure of security, though Java dissemblers are freely available.

The biggest disadvantage of Java as a CGI scripting language is the difficulty associated with learning it. Java is a nearly pure object-oriented language, a programming paradigm many find hard to adjust to. Additionally, although it's new and very popular, there aren't very many Java programmers around yet, and existing Java programmers are commanding a high premium. If the language continues to grow in popularity, that may change.

UNIX Shell

If you're running a UNIX machine as your server and you are familiar with UNIX commands, shell scripts are the easiest to work with. If you know how to use the operating system, you're well on your way to creating scripts. You just call programs to do your work from a file that resembles a DOS batch program.

The disadvantages are the potential lack of security and the lack of a true programming language. Scripts are not really meant to replace programs; rather, they should be thought of as macros to ease complex tasks. As such, they don't have most of the features a true programming language provides. Shell scripts are also a great potential for security problems. If the input from a script isn't checked properly, a cracker might insert control codes instead of the expected input, which are then passed to variables in your script, which are then appended to script commands in the form of command-line arguments. Those arguments could contain directives harmful to your system.

WebBots

A great amount of the functionality you will want with CGI scripts has already been covered with WebBots. These don't require any programming skills on your part, are easy to use, and are well documented. Additionally, developers can produce custom bots for you to use in your Webs. You can use these bots much more easily than CGI scripts. In short, fewer technical skills are needed by the end user.

CGI Scripts with FrontPage

Placing a CGI script in a FrontPage Web is very easy. All you need to do is make the URL of the CGI script the modifier that points to the resource in the HTML tag. You'll also need to import the CGI script and supporting resources into your Web. That sounds a little daunting, but you'll discover how to do all this in Lesson 1. One of the most common uses for CGI is to handle form input. Using CGI scripts to handle forms involves setting the handler for the Form Bot to your CGI script; that's covered in depth in Lesson 2.

Normally, CGI scripts live in a special directory called `cgi-bin`. This directory is found underneath the folder where most of the content for that Web is stored. The reason for the special location is security. Normally, you want to provide mechanisms for restricting access to certain files, and executable CGI scripts are something that should be controlled. Placing all the scripts in one directory is a method of damage control. The `cgi-bin` directory has become the standard location for scripts, although there is no reason that you can't place your scripts in a different location. When you create a new Web with FrontPage, the `cgi-bin` directory is automatically created for you.

Lesson 1: Adding a Page-Hit Counter to Your Web

One of the most common uses of CGI is for a page-hit counter. This utility tells the world how many times the page has been loaded and is often used to show off the popularity of asite. Surprisingly, FrontPage does not come with a WebBot encapsulating this functionality, so you'll have the opportunity to use it as an example—gaining new capabilities with FrontPage. The example is an executable program that can create an image or series of digits representing the hit count for an HTML page. It was written using C and compiled to run on a Windows machine. If you are using the Personal Web Server, this example should work fine. If you are working with a different server, check to make sure the machine it's running on is a Windows-based machine.

A page-hit counter works like this: Every time a page is loaded, the browser goes out and fetches the CGI script. The server, realizing that a script has been requested and that it is not a static document, runs the script. This script then opens a file that contains a number representing how many times that script has been called. This script increments that number by one and then saves it back to that file. Now, the script loads a series of GIFs that represent the digits in the number. It strings these GIFs together to make one long GIF, which it returns to the server. The server passes this image, which represents the number of hits, on to the client, which displays it. This sequence is outlined in Figure 17-3.

To start, open a new normal Web with FrontPage Explorer. You need to import the script and supporting resources to this Web. From the menu bar, select File, then Import. Click the Add File... button in the Import File to Web dialog that appears. Make sure the compact disc (CD-ROM) that came with this book is in your CD-ROM drive. In the Add File to Import List window, go to the CD-ROM and find the directory containing the files

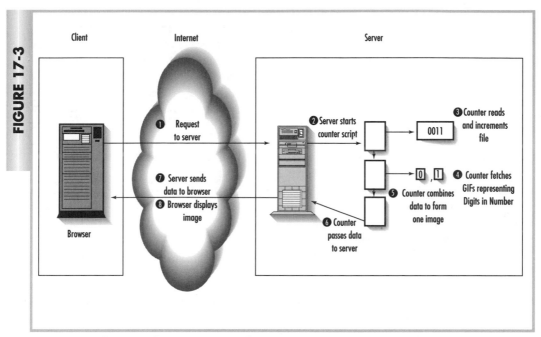

How a simple page-hit counter works

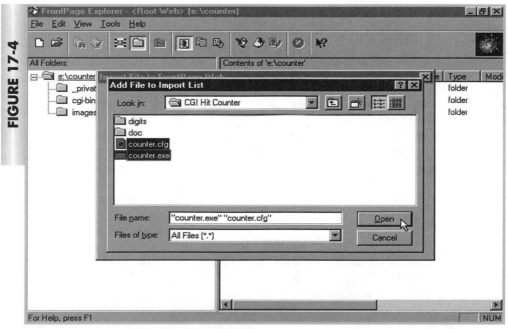

Selecting files to import to your Web

for this example (it should be in **d:\source\chap17\counter**). You'll need to change the Files of type: option in the window to All Files (*.*) to be able to see the files in their folder. Select only the files named **counter.cfg** and **counter.exe**; then click the Open button, as shown in Figure 17-4. You can select multiple files by holding down the **<CTRL>** key while single-clicking on them with the mouse.

Now you need to add some supporting files for the script, namely the GIF files that represent the digits. Click the Add File... button again. Then go into the **d:\source\chap17\ counter\digits\odometer** folder on the CD-ROM. From inside this directory, select the 10 GIFs named **0.gif** through **9.gif**, and then click the Open button. You may need to change the file type selection to view these files. Your Import File to FrontPage Web window should look something like Figure 17-5.

Click the OK button as shown in Figure 17-5. You'll need to change the view on the FrontPage Explorer to the folder view so you can more easily move these files around on the server. Because the counter is a CGI script and it is customary to place CGI scripts in the **cgi-bin** directory, you are going to move it there. Additionally, the CGI script needs to access the images you've just imported, and it expects them to be in a certain location, so you'll have to move them as well.

First, let's create the **cgi-bin** directory. This is done by selecting the topmost folder by clicking on it. Then, click on File | New > Folder, as shown in Figure 17-6. This creates a folder named **New_Folder**. Right-click on this folder, and then choose Rename from the popup menu. Change the name of the folder to **cgi-bin**.

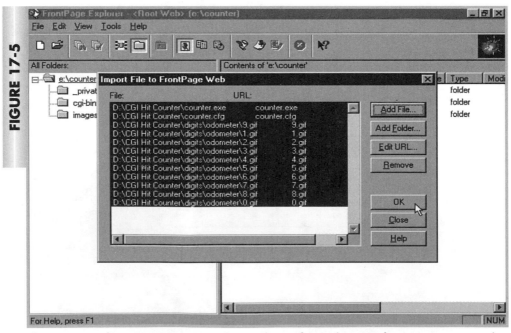

FIGURE 17-5

The Import File to FrontPage Web window after selecting the resources needed for the page-hit counter CGI script

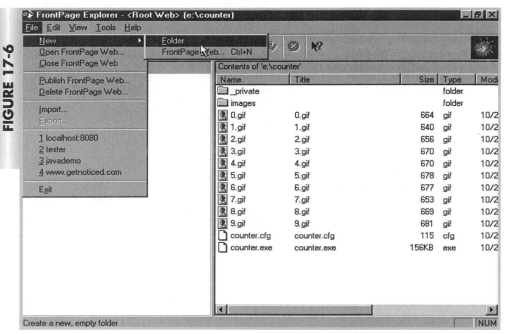

FIGURE 17-6

Creating a new folder in the Web

Now you're going to move the files into this folder. Simply highlight the `counter.exe`, `counter.cfg`, `0.gif`, `1.gif`, ... `9.gif` files by holding down the (CTRL) key and clicking on them one at a time in the contents (right) side of the FrontPage Explorer. Then click and drag the files into the `cgi-bin` folder we just created.

Because the script is a program, you'll need to set up the server to allow the program to run. This is an extra security measure taken to guard against unwanted code being placed into your Webs and executed. To allow scripts to run inside a certain folder, right-click on the folder (in this case the `cgi-bin` folder), and select properties from the pop-up menu. In the properties dialog, make sure the `Allow scripts or programs to be run` option is checked then click OK.

Now that you've got the scripts in place, it's time to move the `gif` files it needs to the appropriate location. To do this, click the `cgi-bin` directory to open it. Then select File | New > Folder from the menu bar, just as before. The `new_folder` will be under the `cgi-bin` directory. Rename it `digits`. Then create a sub-folder under this one called odometer, using the same technique. Next, select the image files (`0.gif` through `9.gif`) and move them into the new directory by clicking and dragging. After the rename dialog goes away, your images should be in `/cgi-bin/digits/odometer/`, and your FrontPage Explorer should look like Figure 17-7.

Note

The `counter.cfg` file is a configuration file for the counter script. By editing it, you can prevent the counter from being incremented when certain machines, like your own, view that open page. You can also specify which hosts have the right to access your counter. The practice of counterterrorism on the Net necessitates this additional feature. Some less-than-scrupulous individuals put tags for this CGI script into their Webs and point them to the counter program on someone else's host. That surrogate host then has the unwanted responsibility of keeping track of hits for these parasitic Web pages. For more information on configuring this script, see the documentation on the CD-ROM (`d:\source\chap17\counter\docs\`). Please note: This counter is a donation-ware utility. If you use it in a published Web, please send the requested gratuity to the script's author, as described in the documentation.

Now that all the resources are in place, you will edit the document that will use them. Start this process by opening the Normal page with the FrontPage Editor. Set up the document so it looks something like Figure 17-8.

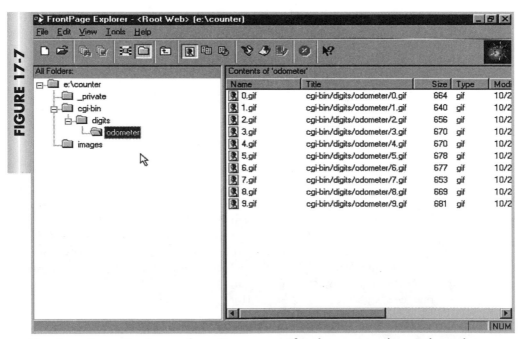

FIGURE 17-7

The FrontPage Explorer after all resources for the counter lesson have been moved to their proper homes

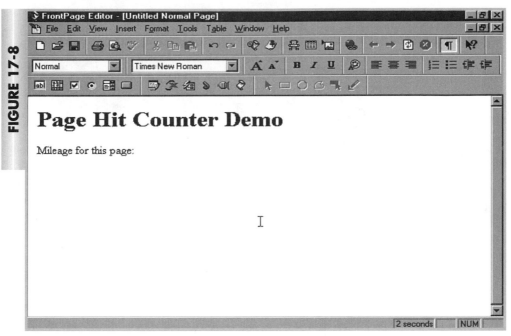

FIGURE 17-8

The beginnings of the page-hit counter example

Position the cursor at the end of the line `Mileage for this page:`, as shown in Figure 17-8. Select Insert from the menu, then Image. In the Insert Image window, click the Other Location tab. Now you are going to enter the URL where the CGI script can be located. Select the From Location option and type in the text area `"cgi-bin/counter.exe? link=NormalPage&style=odometer"`. Then click the OK button, as shown in Figure 17-9.

The `?` denotes that the information following it is for the script and is followed by a list of variables and their values, separated with `=` and `&` symbols, respectively. The general format for this type of notation is: `TheScriptsURL?Variable1=Value1&Variable2=Value2&...` and so on. FrontPage will run the script and display the resulting image right in its Editor. You can even manipulate the image by right-clicking on it and selecting properties. From the Image properties dialog you can specify height and width tags, text alignment, spacing, border thickness—essentially any of the attributes you could specify with a plain image.

Save your work; if everything was done properly, you should have a working script on your hands. The resulting page, viewed with the Netscape Navigator 3.0 browser, is shown in Figure 17-10.

For more information on the counter script and its notations, uses, and configurations, see the documentation provided on the CD-ROM.

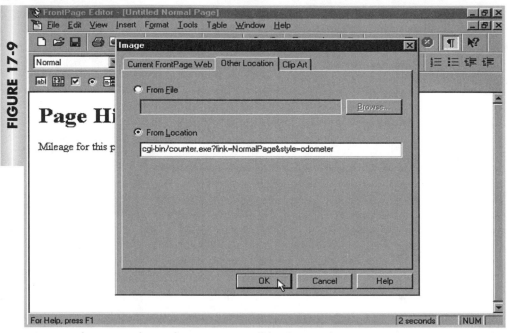

FIGURE 17-9

Entering the URL where the counter will be located

FIGURE 17-10

Browser's view of the counter script in action

Lesson 2: Using a Custom CGI Script to Handle Form Input

The most common uses for form handlers are covered in Chapter 8, "WebBot Components." You might want to review their functionality before deciding whether you need to create a custom script to handle your input. If you must use a script, this lesson shows you how.

First, use the FrontPage Explorer to open the Web in which you wish to add the script. Then open the page holding the form with the FrontPage Editor. Create the form by inserting form fields as needed for your CGI script. Don't forget to name the fields the same way the CGI script expects. These values will depend on the script you are using, so be sure to consult with the script's author for this information.

After creating the form, right-click on the Form Bot and select Form Properties from the popup menu. In the Form Handler drop-down list box, make sure that Custom ISAPI, NSAPI, or CGI Script is selected. Then click the Settings button.

This brings up the SettingsFor Custom Form Handler dialog. In the Action text area, enter the absolute URL of the CGI script you wish to use. Select the appropriate method. The method depends on how the script was written and explaining it is beyond the scope of this book. Consult with the script's author if you need help. If the communication is to be encoded, enter the encoding method in the Encoding Type text area.

If the script you're going to use is to be kept in your Web, you'll need to import it. Do this in the same manner that you imported the `counter.exe` file in the previous lesson. In FrontPage Explorer, select Import from the File menu. Then click the Add File button and select the CGI script you wish to import. If you need other supporting resources, import them as well (see the script's author for this information). You may need to change the URLs of the documents, just as you did in Lesson 1. When you've done all this, you should have a working script to handle your form input.

The Future of CGI

CGI is finding itself in competition with other client/server models. Many new technologies are emerging that tend to move the processing responsibility from the server to the client. This should help increase the performance of the Web as a whole, because the server machine can concentrate on distributing information rather than processing it.

Examples of these client-side technologies include Java, plug-ins, ActiveX, VBScript, and JavaScript. Java, VBScript, and JavaScript are discussed throughout this book, so you should be aware of their capabilities. Plug-ins are helper applications that are called on by the browser to handle certain data. The concept of plug-ins and their implementation was developed by Netscape. Examples of plug-ins include Shockwave for multimedia presentations, Adobe Amber for document distribution, and RealAudio for sound transmissions. If you've been around the Web for a little while, these names should sound familiar. Plug-ins modify the capabilities of the client so that it can handle information in new ways. Of course, many plug-ins provide features that require augmentation of the server as well, often meaning CGI scripts.

Netscape, starting with Netscape Navigator version 3.0, has begun providing methods by which Java applets, plug-ins, JavaScripts, and other browser objects can communicate with one another. This technology, called LiveConnect, allows Java applets (and other browser objects) capabilities not previously possible for security reasons. These objects can communicate with each other and conceivably with special plug-ins that allow disk access to the client's machine, access to supporting utilities, and other valuable capabilities. Microsoft has introduced its own interfacing technology, called ActiveX. ActiveX builds on the history and code library formerly known as OLE.

Of course, tremendous security issues remain with both of these schemes.

Another direction for CGI involves a change in the mechanism CGI uses. When the server recognizes that a request is directed at a CGI script, it must execute that script and wait for the output. Startinganother program and waiting for output involve a lot of overhead. Process Software (creators of the Purveyor Web server) and Microsoft are championing a new way of dealing with scripts called the Internet Server Application Programming Interface (ISAPI). Through ISAPI, the server calls a library function provided to it, rather than starting a whole new program. This is much more desirable because less overhead is required. The library function that replaces the traditional CGI script is also capable of taking control of the connection from the server, eliminating the server from the middle position and allowing easy expansion to the capabilities of the server. In short, ISAPI causes the CGI script to live inside the server, rather than independently of it.

Netscape has also proposed a similar mechanism to add functionality to Web servers called NSAPI. In the case of both ISAPI and NSAPI, CGI scripts remain usable by creating wrappers to start the scripts through the ISAPI or NSAPI interfaces. New scripts using the ISAPI or NSAPI technologies will benefit greatly from the reduced overhead and extended capabilities these technologies offer. These tools will allow the direct extension of the server and offer performance benefits not possible with CGI scripts alone.

Note

The Microsoft Internet Information Server, Process Software's Purveyor Web servers, and others offer the ISAPI technologies. Netscape offers servers supporting the NSAPI technology. It is uncertain which will become the de facto standard over time, but ISAPI seems to be catching on quicker.

Summary

You should now have a large enough understanding of CGI technology to integrate CGI scripts into your Webs effectively. You should also be aware of the different technologies associated with CGI and be able to make reasonable decisions on what tools best match your needs. You have also learned general guidelines for evaluating the relative server performance needed to run different CGI scripts and WebBots.

Certainly, you've learned a lot about FrontPage and the Web by now. You are probably curious about what the future holds. Seeing the future of the Web is very difficult because computing technology moves very fast. It's common to hear the phrase "the speed of the Internet" used to refer to the breakneck pace of development. Not to be left flat-footed, the next chapter covers some of these emerging technologies.

The Road Ahead

18

In this chapter you will learn:

New Possibilities Provided by the Web and the Internet
Problems the Web and the Internet Face
Challenges Currently Being Addressed

What does the future hold for the World Wide Web? Many people speculate on that very subject. Those that make good guesses and act on their hunches are likely to be very successful financially. It's hard to predict with certainty where the Web and the information highway will go, but some things are readily apparent. It's safe to say that any industry that is experiencing a 1000-percent annual growth rate has more than a fair chance of success. With that growth comes incredible opportunity, growing pains, and some hard knocks: After all, the information superhighway is still under construction.

The Good

What does it offer? The Web has the potential to change the fundamental methods people use to communicate, especially when it comes to accessing information. The Web, or its future derivative, may shape the lives of the next generation of children the same way the printing press and telephone shaped the one before. The Web is about communication, especially communicating ideas and information. It provides a method for accessing information from around the globe without the barriers of travel and format. It allows the exchange of easily updated data in a timely fashion. With the Web, you can spread your message quickly to anyone who is listening for a relatively low cost.

A side effect of this increased communication is the potential for a huge new market of the more traditional definition: a place where goods are sold and traded. The Web provides the potential for a free market much larger than has ever existed before. Imagine being able to gather information about products that interest you, find the lowest-cost suppliers of those products, review other people's experiences with those suppliers, and place an order for the product you want from the supplier you've chosen based on that research, all from the comfort of your home. Additionally, the supplier may be located nearly anywhere in the world! The Web is not quite there yet, but the potential certainly exists.

Note

Because of the new potential for trade, some entrepreneurs use the Web to sell stock in their companies instead of selling through one of the major exchanges such as NASDAQ or NYSE. This allows them to avoid having fees imposed on transactions involving their stocks. An example of this (and possibly the first company to do so) is Spring Street Brewing Company, Inc. This company uses a bulletin-board type trading system called Wit-Trade to facilitate the trade of its stocks. Check out `http://plaza.interport.net/witbeer/` to see Wit-Trade in action.

The Web has brought forth new technologies. Businesses are springing up everywhere to provide services that allow new and innovative uses for the Internet and the Web. Large companies are realizing the potential of the Web and are redesigning customer service departments, sometimes reorienting the whole company itself, to take advantage of the potential provided by the Internet. Businesses recognize the communication improvements possible with the Web and are eager to capitalize on it. Even if the Web does not fulfill its promises, the technologies that make it work will retain a role in corporate intranets for years to come.

The Bad

Of course, with the rampant growth of the Web and Internet, mistakes will be made. Some issues are not pleasant, but must be dealt with. For example, current phone systems are not designed to deal with the exchange of digital information. And the lack of bandwidth relative to the amount of information exchanging hands can cause the whole Internet to slow. The people on the East Coast of the United States can tell when those on the West Coast show up for work and start logging in because of the slow-down of the Internet. If the Internet continues to grow at a phenomenal rate, it will certainly be challenged to meet user demand. The growth is not only in the number of users; each user is now asking for more than ever before. When the Internet was young, text-based computing such as FTP and e-mail was sufficient. Now that the Web is coming of age, most people want graphics, multimedia, lively applets, and teleconferencing. All this means more bandwidth from an already pressed system. Of course, solutions are in the works, but there are so many loaves in the oven that it's hard to tell whether the next standard connection will be integrated services digital network (ISDN), cable modems, satellite links, Asynchronous Transfer Mode communications (ATM), or something not yet known. Rapid advances in these technologies make it difficult to invest wisely in new equipment and technologies, which slows the growth and performance of the Internet. Current favorites are ISDN modems as a quick fix, but most technology experts pick ATM as the next long-lasting communication standard. Of course, with all these technologies in flux, selecting a standard is often little more than guesswork, and no one wants to make such an expensive bet and lose.

Another disappointment is that people are finding that the Web is not as lucrative a venture as they had anticipated. Remember, the Internet was spawned on the idea of the *free* exchange of information. Many of the people who started the Internet resent today's efforts at commercialization. Additionally, businesses on the Web apply traditional marketing techniques: They sell advertising billboards on their sites to make a couple of bucks and try to generate traditional marketing data to justify their prices. Unfortunately, the Web as a medium does not lend itself well to these techniques. The Web is still young; a better system will evolve as the Web matures and new ways to manage and capitalize on this medium emerge. In the meantime, a small number of sites attract the majority of the advertising dollars spent on the Web, leaving many would-bes disappointed and out of luck.

Another disappointment with the Web is the lack of quality content. Cyberspace is cheap, so everyone's buying a piece. Unfortunately, the Web is so new that few people know how to develop content for it, and those who do are very busy. Much of the Web is under construction. That perturbs people new to computing and the Web who have unreasonably high expectations of a medium that allows anyone to publish a document and have it distributed worldwide for twenty dollars or less a month. Over time, as more quality content is created, the Web will become more useful and valuable.

The Ugly

Among other issues concerning the Web, perhaps the biggest is security. Security on the Internet is a hot topic today because there seems to be no easy way to ensure private communication, system security for the host, and privacy for the surfer. These issues become especially important as programs are distributed over the Internet. Plug-ins, ActiveX technologies, and even Java have the potential to cause users harm. Until security can be guaranteed, true commercialism probably will not be a big part of the Web. Fortunately, many people are working on this issue, and, despite the difficulties, a solution can be anticipated down the line.

Another problem is the difficulty in regulating the Web. Because the Web is not centralized, it is difficult to monitor and control. How is something that spans national borders regulated? Who decides what is and is not appropriate for the Internet? Worse yet, who will be responsible for enforcing those decisions and what authority will they have? No matter what laws the U.S. government passes in an attempt to restrict what can be placed on the Internet, the 40 percent (at this time) of the Internet that lies outside the United States will remain unaffected. This issue has received much media attention lately, although it escaped notice in the past, when the Internet was small enough that it could regulate itself.

Much of the concern over the safety of the Internet is based on a lack of knowledge about how it works and what it really is. Many of us have an initial fear of technologies we don't understand and that, frankly, intimidate us. The Internet is a case study of this phenomenon. Consider the fear most people have about making purchases over the Internet. How many times have you given your credit card to a store clerk you actually knew? That clerk, a perfect stranger, not only has your card number and expiration date, but also your signature! How many times have you given out your credit card number over the phone to an unknown operator? Sure, someone with expertise could hijack unprotected transmissions from the Net, and possibly nab your card number without your consent. But compared to the day-to-day lackadaisical attitude we take in securing such valuable information, this risk is really insignificant. Besides, most credit card companies are very cooperative with their customers when it comes to identifying rogue transactions. I'm not aware of any instance where credit card fraud was committed using information gathered by Internet "packet-sniffing."

Another common misconception of the Internet is that it is a lair for pornography. We are bombarded by the press with stories about how a pornography ring was using an on-line service for trading illegal wares. Everyone frowns upon that service, and manages to place some blame on it for the activity of its users. The public is highly critical of technology, and it's reflected in this type of reporting. After all, no one got upset with the U.S. Post Office when bombs were sent through the mail. No one expects the U.S. Postal Service to check and make sure that what's inside those brown-wrapper packages is deemed "decent." No one hounds package delivery services when they unknowingly deliver illegal goods. But the double standard does exist for Internet exchanges.

Perhaps as all the newbies to the Internet gain experience and the press becomes more familiar with the technology, people will learn how to deal with the dark side of the Internet. They might even realize that the Internet is no more insecure than a postal letter, and no more based on pornography than the television they watch or the magazines they read. In the meantime, regulation will remain a sticky issue.

Another difficulty is the challenge of standardization. It's not easy to create lots of translators that allow devices that speak different languages to communicate. Invariably, these translators slow system performance, add expense, and reduce the number of features that can be used easily. Therefore, it is important that people agree on the best ways to communicate. Disagreement on what e-mail protocols to use, how binary information should be exchanged, or the best format for exchanging documents will generate more problems to solve in the future.

How fast and how much current standards are to be extended offers another problem. Inventing the next greatest set of HTML tags isn't useful if no one else supports them. It's hard to set aside great ideas until they can be standardized. The Internet is growing outrageously fast, and everyone is trying to get noticed and outpace the competition with inventive technologies. Ultimately, the mad dash to establish leadership will cause confusion among consumers and will do more harm than good.

Identifying the best standard and sticking with it is another difficulty. Consumers are notorious for not standardizing the proposals with the most usefulness or potential. The standards that catch on do so because of superior marketing or other bias. Computers and computer technology often stimulate debate that parallels a religious discussion, in which everyone believes his or her opinion to be correct and the hapless consumer, in desperation, selects the product perceived to be the most popular. Unbiased opinion as the basis for selection of standards is desirable, but not commonly used. Standardizing will be a big challenge as the Web grows.

The Better

Surviving the bad and working through the ugly makes the good seem that much better. In the meantime, the Web remains an extraordinary means of communication with the potential to change lives radically. The information highway has already made a lot of progress, although it has a long way to go. Important decisions are being made and new technologies are being developed that will affect the future of the Web. FrontPage makes it easy to make a contribution to the information highway and help decide the course of the road ahead.

Appendix A: HTML TAGS

A

The ANCHOR element links documents and indicates a hypertext portal that can be entered by clicking on a word or phrase called a hotspot (Syntax: `<A> characters . . . </A>`). This element has several attributes:

◁ Href—Identifies the location or Uniform Resource Locator (URL) of the hypertext document. It's where you will travel when you click on a hotspot.

◁ Name—Creates a name for the anchor that can be referred to within or outside the document. Adding a name to the anchored text turns it into a hypertext destination to which users can leap within your document.

◁ Title—Defines a title for the document indicated in the Href attribute.

◁ Rel—Defines the relationship from your document to the Href document (see Rel attribute under LINK element).

◁ Rev—Defines the relationship from the Href document to your document (see Rev attribute under LINK element).

◁ Urn—Establishes the Uniform Resource Name of the Href document.

◁ Methods—Gives information on the functions that can be performed on the Href document.

ADDRESS

Shows authorship of a document and is usually placed at the end of a Web page. Personal information such as an e-mail address, home address, or office address can be placed between ADDRESS tags. Every Web page should have an e-mail address at the bottom. Syntax: `<ADDRESS>characters . . . </ADDRESS>`

APPLET

Allows you to insert a Java program within an HTML document (Netscape 2.0+ only). PARAM elements embedded within this element define parameters of the APPLET. Syntax: `<APPLET></APPLET>`

B

BOLD; dictates the appearance of text. Characters placed between B tags will be bolded. Syntax: `<B> characters . . . </B>`

BASE

Identifies the URL of other documents used in your Web page. If a document has been moved from its original location, it is important to indicate its original source. This will make the loading of hypertext links more accurate. The BASE element has one attribute, Href, which identifies the URL of other resources. Syntax: `<BASE Href= " . . . " >`

BASEFONT SIZE

Changes the BASEFONT or default font (which defaults to 3) that all relative font changes are based on. Values range from 1 to 7. (HTML Version 2.0) Syntax: `<BASEFONT SIZE = value>`

BIG

BIG PRINT; dictates the appearance of text. Enclosed text between BIG tags will have a big font compared with normal text. (HTML Version 3.0) Syntax: `<BIG> characters . . . </BIG>`

BLOCKQUOTE

Separates a section of text, such as a quote, from the rest of the document. The text is usually indented on both sides and centered. Syntax: `<BLOCKQUOTE></BLOCKQUOTE>`

BODY

Marks the portion of your Web page that will be displayed by the Web browser. Unlike HEAD elements, elements within the BODY tags will affect the look and style of your final document. The **Background** attribute (HTML Version 3.0) can be used here to specify an image that you want in the background of the document. Syntax: `<BODY> characters . . . </BODY>`

BR

LINE BREAK; allows you to control the amount of text on specific lines. This element comes in handy when writing postal addresses or poems. Syntax: `<BR>`

CAPTION

CAPTION for a table; should appear inside TABLE tags, but not inside TR or TD tags (HTML Version 3.0). Captions are centered relative to the table. Syntax:

`<CAPTION></CAPTION>`

CENTER

Centers text between left and right margins. (HTML Version 2.0) Syntax:

`<CENTER> characters . . . </CENTER>`

CITE

Marks the citation of a book or another type of document. Syntax:

`<CITE> characters . . . </CITE>`

CODE

Indicates computer code usually displayed in a fixed-width font. Syntax:

`<CODE> characters . . . </CODE>`

DD

Definition description embedded within the DL element. Syntax:

`<DD> characters . . .`

DIR

Allows the creation of a list of short words or phrases that the Web browser organizes into columns. Each word or phrase should be less than 20 characters. The Compact attribute can be used with this element to tell the Web browser to closely group the items. Syntax:

`<DIR></DIR>`

DL

DEFINITION LIST or glossary. DT and DD elements are embedded within this element. For example:

`<DL>`
`<DT>` term to be defined
`<DD>` definition of term
`<DT>` second term to be defined
`<DD>` definition of second term
`</DL>`

Can include the Compact attribute. Syntax: `<DL></DL>`

DT

DEFINITION TERM embedded within the DL element. Syntax: `<DT> characters . . .`

EM

For emphasis; usually displayed in italics. Syntax: `<EM> characters . . . </EM>`

FONT SIZE

Changes the font size in a document relative to the default font which is 3. Values range from 1 to 7. (HTML Version 2.0) Syntax: `<FONT SIZE = value> characters . . . </FONT>`

FORM

Defines a form to be filled out within an HTML document. The user fills out the form and then sends it back to the information provider. INPUT, SELECT, OPTION, and TEXTAREA may be embedded elements within this element. (HTML Version 2.0) Syntax: `<FORM></FORM>`

H1, H2, H3, H4, H5, H6

Creates headers which decrease in font size from H1 to H6. H5 and H6 are rarely used because of their tiny size. HEADERS are placed within the `BODY` and `BLOCKQUOTE` tags. Syntax: `<H1> characters . . . </H1>`

HEAD

Contains properties that apply to the entire document such as the title and additional indexing information. Components of the HEAD element are not displayed by the Web browser, but are used by the browser in a number of ways. There may be links that signal connections with another document and a URL which is the address of that other document. Syntax: `<HEAD> characters . . . </HEAD>`

HR

Creates a horizontal line in your Web page. Horizontal lines are often used before and after the main body of text or underneath an image. Syntax: `<HR>`

HTML

All-encompassing element that defines the document as an HTML document. It is the first and last element in an HTML document. Syntax: `<HTML></HTML>`

I

ITALICIZE; controls the appearance of text. Characters placed between the I tags will be italicized. Syntax: `<I> characters . . . </I>`

IMG

Allows you to place graphical images in your document where this element tag is located. (Syntax: `<IMG Src= " . . ." >`) This element has several attributes:

◁ Src—Identifies the source file of the image.

◁ Alt—Describes a string of characters that will be displayed in nongraphical browsers.

◁ Align—Sets the position of the graphic relative to the text. Align has the following parameters:

```
top text following the graphic is aligned with the top of the graphic
middle text following the graphic is aligned with the middle of the
graphic
bottom text following the graphic is aligned with the bottom of the
graphic
```

INPUT

Defines a field in a form where a user is supposed to enter information. (HTML Version 2.0) Syntax: `<INPUT>`

ISINDEX

Signals the Web browser that a document listed in the BASE element can be searched. The server where the file is located must be able to support a search. This element can also be found in other parts of the HTML format such as the BODY, BLOCKQUOTE, and LI. Syntax: `<ISINDEX>`

KBD

Tags text or commands that the user is directed to type into the keyboard. Syntax: `<KBD> characters . . . </KBD>`

LI

Marks each item of a list, and causes these items to be indented in the final document. This element is embedded within the UL, OL, MENU, and DIR elements. Syntax: `<LI> characters . . .`

LINK

Gives details on the relationship between your current document and other documents or objects. (Syntax: `<LINK Href= " . . . ">`) This element has several attributes:

◁ Href—Gives the name of the document the link describes.

◁ Name—Names this link so it can be used as a possible hypertext destination.

◁ Rel—Describes the relationship defined by this link according to the HTML Registration Authority's list of relationships. Example: `Rel= "made"` means that the URL given in the Href is the author of the document.

◁ Rev—Similar but opposite to Rel. Example: `Rev= "made"` means that the current document is the author of the URL given in the Href.

◁ Urn—Indicates the document's Uniform Resource Name.

◁ Methods—Describes the HTTP methods the object in the Href of the link element supports.

MARQUEE

Creates a scrolling text marquee (Microsoft Internet Explorer 2.0 only). The Align attribute is used with this element to specify the position of the scrolling text. Syntax:
`<MARQUEE Align = "top, middle, or bottom " </MARQUEE>`

MENU

Creates a list that is very similar to an unordered list except the rendered MENU list will appear smaller and tighter. ibute can be used with this element to tell the Web browser to closely group the items. Syntax: `<MENU></MENU>`

META

Provides meta-information, that is, information about information in the current document. (Syntax: `<META Content= " . . . ">`) This element has several attributes:

◁ Http-equiv—Connects the meta element to a particular protocol which is created by the HTTP server of the document.

◁ Name—Classifies the information in the document. (Name does not indicate the title of the document.)

◁ Content—A name for the content that accompanies the given name.

NEXTID

Similar to an identification code. Used by HTML editors and Web browsers to keep track of pages. This element is usually composed of two letters and two numbers such as CD23. Its only attribute, N, is used to define the next ID code. Syntax:
`<NEXTID N=" . . . ">`

NOBR

NO BREAK; signals the browser that all text within the start and end **NOBR** tags will have no line breaks. (HTML Version 2.0) Syntax:`<NOBR></NOBR>`

OL

ORDERED LIST; each item in a series is given a number. The LI element is also used here to tag and indent the items. The Compact attribute can be used with this element to tell the Web browser to closely group the items. Syntax: `<OL></OL>`

OPTION

Embedded within the SELECT element in a form. Tags each component of a SELECT list. (HTML Version 2.0) Syntax: `<OPTION>`

P

Separates individual paragraphs by placing a blank line between them. Some Web browsers require only one P to be used either at the beginning or end of a paragraph. If there are end `</P>` tags, they will be ignored by browsers that don't require them. Syntax: `<P></P>`

PRE

Starts a new line and makes the font monospaced. Allows you to preformat a block of text. That is, if you want a poem or a chart to show up on your Web page exactly as you have typed and spaced it, this element signals the Web browser to render it exactly as is. PRE has one attribute, Width, which allows you to specify the number of characters that can be typed on a line before it will automatically wrap to the next line. The default is 80 characters. Syntax: `<PRE> characters . . . </PRE>`

SAMP

For an example of literal characters; denotes a string of characters that is to be rendered as it is; monospaced. Syntax: `<SAMP> characters . . . </SAMP>`

SELECT

Defines a set of items from which the user must pick in a form. Requires an OPTION element for each item in the list. (HTML Version 2.0) Syntax: `<SELECT></SELECT>`

SMALL

SMALL PRINT; dictates the appearance of text. Characters between SMALL tags will have a small font compared to normal text. (HTML Version 3.0) Syntax: `<SMALL> characters . . . </SMALL>`

STRONG

Similar to the BOLD element. It is used to give strong emphasis to a word or phrase which is usually bold. Syntax: `<STRONG> characters . . . </STRONG>`

SUB

SUBSCRIPT; characters between SUB tags will be displayed as subscript in a smaller font. (HTML Version 3.0) Syntax: `<SUB> characters . . . </SUB>`

SUP

SUPERSCRIPT; characters between SUP tags will be displayed as superscript in a smaller font. (HTML Version 3.0) Syntax: `<SUP> characters . . . </SUP>`

TABLE

Allows you to create tables in your document (HTML Version 3.0). The TR, TD, TH, and CAPTION elements are embedded within this element. (Syntax: `<TABLE></TABLE>`) This element has the following attributes:

- ◁ Align—If inside a CAPTION element, it can have values of top or bottom, and places the caption to the top or bottom of the table. If inside a TR, TH, or TD element, it can have values of left, center, or right, and determines where text will be horizontally placed within the cells.

- ◁ Border—If inside the TABLE element, a border will be placed around all table cells.

- ◁ Colspan—Can be placed inside TH or TD elements, and determines how many columns a table cell will span. The default is 1.

- ◁ Nowrap—Can be placed inside TH or TD elements, and specifies that lines within cells cannot be broken to fit the width of the cells.

- ◁ Rowspan—Can be placed inside TH or TD elements, and determines how many rows of a table a cell will span. The default is 1.

◁ Valign—Can be placed inside TR, TH, or TD elements, and determines where text will be vertically placed within the cells. It has values of top, middle, bottom, or baseline.

TD

TABLE DATA; defines the size of a table data cell (HTML Version 3.0). Table data cells only appear in table rows. Syntax: `<TD></TD>`

TEXTAREA

Defines a rectangular field in a form where the user may enter information. (HTML Version 2.0) Syntax: `<TEXTAREA></TEXTAREA>`

TH

TABLE HEADER; similar to data cells except that header cells are bold and centered (HTML Version 3.0). Syntax: `<TH></TH>`

TITLE

The most important type of header in that it helps other users identify and track your Web page (especially when using hotlists, bookmarks, and spiders). Usually the Web browser will print the TITLE in the title bar of the browser. It must be descriptive, less than 50 characters, and cannot contain other HTML formatting elements or attributes. Syntax: `<TITLE> characters . . . </TITLE>`

TR

TABLE ROW; tags each row in a table (HTML Version 3.0). Syntax: `<TR></TR>`

TT

Creates typewriter fixed-width font text. Syntax: `<TT> characters . . . </TT>`

U

UNDERLINE; dictates the appearance of text. Characters placed between the U tags will be underlined. Syntax: `<U> characters . . . </U>`

UL

Allows you to make an unordered list. An unordered list is similar to an ordered list except the items are bulleted instead of numbered. The Compact attribute can be used with this element to tell the Web browser to closely group the items. Syntax: `<UL></UL>`

VAR

Used to indicate a variable in computer code. Usually the user is directed to fill this in with an appropriate parameter. Syntax: `<VAR> characters . . . </VAR>`

WBR

WORD BREAK. Tells the browser where a word can be broken, but does not create a line break. (HTML Version 2.0) Syntax: `<WBR>`

Appendix B: Visual Basic Script Reference

So, now that you have all of the power to create the world's best Web pages, you want to go one step further and infuse your pages with VBScript. Have no fear, as we aim to assist you in your quest for the sacred Web design. Although fully covering Visual Basic Script is beyond the scope of this book, we have included some handy reference material so that you can begin adding VBScript code into your Web pages today!

Language Features

Although numerous language features are available within the Visual Basic family, only a subset of these is available within VBScript for portability, security, speed, and size of the language runtime. Table B-1 highlights the various language features that are available within VBScript.

Table B-1 VBScript language features

Category	Sub-Category	Feature
Assignment		=
		Let
		Set
Comments		REM
Control Flow		Do...Loop
		For...Next
		For Each...Next
		While...Wend
		If...Then...Else

continued on next page

continued from previous page

Category	Sub-Category	Feature
Error Trapping		On Error Resume Next Err Object
Literals		Empty Nothing Null True, False Numerics Strings Based Integers
Operators	Arithmetic	+, -, *, /, \, ^, Mod, Negation (-), String concatenation (&)
	Comparison	=, <>, <, >, <=, >=, Is
	Logical	Not, And, Or, Xor, Eqv, Imp
Procedures	Declaring	Function, Sub
	Calling	Call
	Exiting	Exit Function, Exit Sub
Variables	Procedure Scope	Dim <variable>

VBScript Data Types

Although other languages may use numerous data types, VBScript only allows the use of one data type, a Variant. What is a Variant? Well, a Variant is a special data type that can store various types of information. Table B-2 lists the common categories of data types that can be stored within the Variant data type:

Table B-2 Subtypes supported by the VBScript variant type

Type	Description
Boolean	Value of TRUE or FALSE
Byte	Integer in the range from 0 to 255

Type	Description
Date (Time)	A number representing a date between January 1, 1900 and December 31, 9999
Double	A double-precision, floating-point number in the range -1.79769313486232E308 to -4.94065645841247E-324 for negative values; -4.94065645841247E-324 to 1.79769313486232E308 for positive values
Empty	Uninitialized value. Strings are set to "" and numbers are set to 0
Error	An error number
Integer	Integer number in the range from -32,768 to 32,767
Long	Integer number in the range from -2,147,483,648 to 2,147,483,647
Null	No valid data value
Object	An OLE automation object
Single	A single-precision, floating-point number in the range -3.402823E38 to -1.401298E-45 for negative values; 1.401298E-45 to 3.402823E38 for positive values
String	A variable-length string that may be up to approximately 2 billion characters in length

VBScript Objects

One of the most powerful features of VBScript is the ability to manipulate objects. By using objects, you will be able to exploit functionality and properties without having to program these features in your code. The following sections highlight some common objects that you may wish to use in your code.

The **document** Object

Table B-3 shows various properties, methods, and events used by the **document** object.

Table B-3 Characteristics of the **document** object

Name	Category	Description
alinkColor	Property	Active link color
anchors.length	Property	Total number of anchors in current page
anchors[]	Property	Array of named locations (in sequence) within current page
bgColor	Property	Background color
fgColor	Property	Foreground color
forms.length	Property	Number of forms listed in forms[]
forms[]	Property	Array of forms
lastModified	Property	Last modification date
linkColor	Property	Color of link that has not been visited or clicked
links.length	Property	Total number of links in current page
links[]	Property	Array of links (in sequence) within current page
loadedDate	Property	Date the page was loaded
location	Property	The URL of the current page
title	Property	Title of document
vlinkColor	Property	Color of link which has been visited
clear()	Method	Clears display window
close()	Method	Closes the window
write("string")	Method	Writes an HTML string to the window
writeln("string")	Method	Writes an HTML string to the window (with newline)
Load	Event	Page has been loaded
Unload	Event	Page has been unloaded

The **history** Object

Did you ever wish you could go back in time? Well, in VBScript, you can programmatically accomplish this feat by manipulating the **history** object. The **history** object is maintained by your Web browser: It contains a list of the Uniform Resource Locators (URLs) that the user has visited. Within your code, you can interact with the history object and send the user to a designated URL. Table B-4 shows various properties, methods, and events used by the **history** object.

Table B-4 Characteristics of the `history` object

Name	Category	Description
length	Property	Length of the history list
back()	Method	Moves user back to previous URL in the history list
forward()	Method	Moves user forward to next URL in the history list
go("string")	Method	Go to "string" URL in the history list
go(X)	Method	Go to URL X in the history list

The **Form** Object

Each pair of corresponding **FORM** tags with an HTML page has a **FORM** object. You can interact with this object to gather data for a CGI program or to validate user information. Table B-5 shows various properties, methods, and events used by the **FORM** object.

Table B-5 Characteristics of the **FORM** object

Name	Category	Description
action	Property	String value of the <FORM> ACTION attribute
elements[x]	Property	An array of the objects within your current form
method	Property	Value of the <FORM> METHOD attribute(0=Get,1=Post)
name	Property	String value of the <FORM> NAME attribute
target	Property	Target window for response after form is submitted
submit()	Method	Submits the form
Submit	Event	Form has been submitted

Variable Naming Conventions

Use the following self-descriptive variable naming prefixes, as shown in Table B-6, to enhance readability of your VBScript code.

Table B-6 Variable naming conventions

Variant	TypePrefix	Example
Boolean	bln	blnExists
Byte	byt	bytSmall
Date (Time)	dtm	dtmDateBegin
Double	dbl	dblVelocity
Error	err	errPhoneEntry
Integer	int	intCount
Long	lng	lngLightYears
Object	obj	objCar
Single	sng	sngRate
String	str	strAddress

Object Naming Conventions

Use the following self-descriptive object naming prefixes, as shown in Table B-7, to enhance readability of your VBScript code.

Table B-7 Object naming conventions

Object	Prefix	Example
3D Panel	pnl	pnlRecords
Animated Button	ani	aniFlag
Check Box	chk	chkSendMail
Combo Box, Drop-down list box	cbo	cboDirectory
Command Button	cmd	cmdSubmit
Frame	fra	fraTableOfContents
Horizontal Scroll Bar	hsb	hsbIntensity
Image	img	imgLogo
Label	lbl	lblDescription
Line	lin	linConnector

Object	Prefix	Example
List Box	lst	lstFiles
Spin Button	spn	spnDays
Text Box	txt	txtEmployer
Vertical Scroll Bar	vsb	vsbVolume
Slider	sld	sldSpeed

Appendix C: JavaScript Keys

This appendix provides a listing of some of the most useful JavaScript objects and their associated properties, methods, and events. This is not a complete list, but it contains the most commonly used features of the JavaScript language. For full documentation of the JavaScript language, see `http://www.netscape.com/eng/mozilla/Gold/handbook/javascript`.

Form Objects

Form

```
<FORM name="form1" TARGET="windowname" ACTION="URL" METHOD=POST> </FORM>
```

Properties

◁ `elements.length`—Number of elements (fields) in the form

◁ `elements[index]`—A specific field in the form

◁ `target`—Value of the Target attribute (`"windowname"` as above)

Methods

◁ `submit`—Submits the form. Functionally equivalent to pushing the Submit button.

Events

◁ `onSubmit`—Occurs when the user clicks the Submit button or the `submit` method is executed.

Button

```
<INPUT TYPE="button"  name="button1" VALUE="text">
```

Properties

◁ name—Value of the Name attribute ("button1" above)

Events

◁ onClick—Occurs when the user clicks the Form button

Checkbox

```
<INPUT TYPE="checkbox"  name="check1">
```

Properties

◁ name—The value of the Name attribute ("check1" above)

◁ checked—True (nonzero) value if the box is marked; False if it is not

Events

◁ onClick—Occurs when the user clicks on the element

Password

```
<INPUT TYPE="password"  name="password1" SIZE=20>
```

Properties

◁ name—Value of the Name attribute ("password1" above)

◁ value—String entered into the text area of the element

Radio

```
<INPUT TYPE="radio"  name="radiogroup1">
```

Properties

◁ name—Value of the Name attribute ("radiogroup1" above). All buttons in the same group should have the same name.

◁ checked—Returns True if a specific element is selected, False if that element is not (usage: "radiogroup1[index].checked")

◁ `index`—Returns the index number of the radio button currently selected

◁ `length`—Number of radio buttons in the group (all radio buttons with the same Name attribute are in the same group)

Events

◁ `onClick`—Occurs when the user clicks on the element

Select

```
<SELECT name="select1"> <OPTION>choice1</SELECT>
```

Properties

◁ `name`—Value of the Name attribute (`"select1"` above)

◁ `length`—Number of options contained in the element

◁ `selectedIndex`—Index of the currently selected option

◁ `options.text`—Text representing the option (usage: `"select1.options[index].text"`, `"choice1"` above)

Events

◁ `onChange`—Occurs whenever a different option is chosen

Text

```
<INPUT TYPE="text"  name="text1" SIZE=20>
```

Properties

◁ `name`—Value of the Name attribute (`"text1"` above)

◁ `value`—String representing the text entered into the element

Events

◁ `onBlur`—Occurs when the cursor is removed from the text box (named for when the element loses focus)

◁ `onChange`—Occurs whenever changes are made to the text inside the text box

TextArea

```
<TEXTAREA name="textarea1"  ROWS=10 COLS=20> </TEXTAREA>
```

Properties

◁ name—The value of the Name attribute ("textarea1" above)

◁ value—String representing the contents of the text area

Events

◁ onBlur—Occurs when the cursor is removed from the text area (named for when the element loses focus)

◁ onChange—Occurs whenever changes are made to the text inside the text area

Browser and Document Objects

Document

```
<BODY  BACKGROUND="ImageURL" BGCOLOR="color" FGCOLOR="color" LINK="color"
VLINK="color"></BODY>
```

Properties

◁ linkColor—RGB triplet (RRGGBB) representing the color of hypertext links

◁ alinkColor—RGB triplet representing the color of a hypertext link in the process of being selected

◁ vlinkColor—RGB triplet representing the color of a hypertext link that leads to a previously visited resource

◁ bgColor—RGB triplet representing the color of the background of the document

◁ fgColor—RGB triplet representing the color of the text (foreground)

◁ location—String representing the complete URL of the document

◁ forms—Array of form objects in the order they appear in the document (usage: document.forms[index]")

◁ links—Array of link objects in the order they appear in the document (usage: "document.links[index]")

◁ frames—Array of objects corresponding to each frame of a document

◁ referrer—Returns the URL of the calling document

Methods

◁ clear—Clears the document (removes all HTML). Often requires that the close method be used to update the display

◁ close—Forces the contents of the document to be displayed

◁ write—Writes the string passed to it to the HTML of the document (usage: "document.write("string")")

◁ writeln—Same as the write method, only adds a new-line character to the end of the string (usage: "document.write("string")")

Events

◁ onLoad—Occurs when the page is finished loading

Frame

```
<FRAMESET ROWS=values   COLS=values><FRAME SRC="URL" name="frame1">
</FRAMESET>
```

Properties

◁ parent—Parent document responsible for the current frame

◁ name—Name of the frame ("frame1" above)

Note

A frame also has the properties of a document and window.

Methods

Note

A frame also can perform the methods for a document or window.

Link

```
<A name="Link1" HREF="URL"  TARGET="window"></A>
```

Properties

◁ `target`—Window or frame that should display the results of the hyperlink

Events

◁ `onClick`—Occurs when the hyperlink is selected

◁ `onMouseOver`—Occurs when the mouse pointer is over the hyperlink

Window (Top-Level)

Properties

◁ `frames`—Array of frame objects contained in that window

Methods

◁ `alert`—Causes a message box to appear. The message must be supplied (usage: `"window.alert("TheMessage")"`).

◁ `close`—Closes the current browser.

◁ `open`—Causes a new browser window to be spawned on the client. Requires a URL and window name be passed to it (usage: `"window.open("URL", "windowname")`).

◁ `prompt`—Displays a dialog box that can receive client input. You must specify the message (usage: `"prompt("Enter The Answer")"`).

Abstract Objects

Date

◁ `getDate`—Returns the day of the month (1 to 31) of the date object (usage: `"date.getDate()"`)

◁ `getDay`—Returns an integer representing the day of the week (1=Sunday, 2=Monday, and so forth)

◁ `getHours`—Returns the hour of the day in 24-hour clock format (0=12:00 AM, 1 = 1:00 AM, 23= 11:00 PM)

◁ `getMinutes`—Returns the minutes of the hour of the date object (0-59)

◁ `getSeconds`—Returns the seconds of the minute of the date object (0-59)

◁ `getTime`—Returns the number of milliseconds since January 1, 1970 00:00:00

◁ `getTimeZoneoffset`—Returns the time zone offset for the client's location, if properly set on that system

◁ `getYear`—Returns the last two digits of the year (96)

◁ `toGMTstring`—Converts the time to GMT format

◁ `toLocalString`—Converts the date to a date and time string using the local conventions. ("1/9/96 12:00:00" in USA, and "9/1/96 12:00:00" in the UK.)

Math

Properties

◁ `E`—Euler's constant (base of natural logs, approximately 2.718)

◁ `LN10`—Natural Log of 10 (approximately 2.302)

◁ `LN2`—Natural Log of 2 (approximately .693)

◁ `PI`—Constant, ratio of the circumference of a circle to its diameter (approximately 3.1415)

Methods

◁ `random`—Returns a (pseudo) random number between 0 and 1

◁ `sin`—Returns the sign of a number represented in radians (usage: "`Math.sin(1.3)`")

◁ `cos`—Returns the sign of a number represented in radians

◁ `tan`—Returns the tangent of a number represented in radians

◁ `sqrt`—Returns the square root of a number (usage: "`Math.sqrt(9)`")

◁ `exp`—Returns Euler's constant to the given power ("`Math.exp(2)`" is equivalent to e^2)

◁ `pow`—Returns one number to the other's power ("`Math.pow (2, 3)`" is equivalent to 2^3)

◁   `abs`—Returns the absolute value of a number

◁   R—Returns a number rounded to its nearest integer ("`Math.round(2.5)`" yields the value 3)

String

Properties

◁   `length`—Number of characters in the string. (The highest index is one less than the length, because the index starts numbering from 0, but the length starts with 1.)

String Methods

◁   `indexOf`—The index of the first character of a matching substring. (The last index equals "`string.length-1`".) You may supply a starting point for the search: "`string.indexOf("searchstring", index)`" will search for "`searchstring`" inside the string object starting at the value of index.

◁   `lastIndexOf`—Similar to `indexOf()`, but returns the last occurrence of a string, rather than the first.

◁   `substring`—Returns a portion of the string starting with the lowest parameter and ending before the greater parameter: "`string.substring(index1, index2)`" would return the substring starting with the character at *index1* and ending with the character at *index2* -1, assuming *index1<index2*.

◁   `toLowerCase`—Converts the string to lowercase characters.

◁   `toUpperCase`—Converts the string to uppercase characters.

Appendix D: Additional Resources

This is a brief compilation of some useful Internet resources. These locations should provide you with resources to help you in your Web development.

CGI Resources

◁ `http://www2.eff.org/~erict/Scripts`—Collection of freeware scripts, very nice looking site

◁ `http://worldwidemart.com/scripts`—Another free script archive

◁ `http://solo.dc3.com/white/extending.html`—White paper comparing CGI, SSI, and server API-ISAs; a little technical

FrontPage Resources

◁ `http://www.microsoft.com/frontpage`—The home page for FrontPage

◁ `http://www.microsoft.com/frontpage/ispinfo/isplist.htm`—List of hosts that support the FrontPage Server Extensions for your Webs

◁ `microsoft.public.frontpage.*`—Series of news groups dealing with FrontPage

Graphics Resources

◁ `http://www.stars.com/Vlib/Providers/Images_and_Icons.html`—Index of sites supplying images and icons

◁ `http://fsinfo.cs.uni-sb.de/~leo/trans.html`—Archive of more than 3MB of icons

◁ `http://www.ip.pt/webground/front.htm`—Lots of textures and so forth for backgrounds

◁ `http://www.mccannas.com`—Site belonging to Laurie McCanna, an author, consultant, and graphics guru

◁ `http://www.lynda.com`—Site belonging to Lynda Weinman, another graphics guru

◁ `http://www.publishersdepot.com`—Sells clip art, fonts, and other media online

HTML Resources

◁ `http://www.w3.org/pub/WWW/MarkUp`—HTML guides straight from the World Wide Web Consortium

◁ `http://info.med.yale.edu/caim/StyleManual_Top.html`—A great document on the principles of design for the Web

◁ `http://www.cs.cmu.edu/~tilt/cgh`—Guide to composing good HTML

◁ `http://sdcc8.ucsd.edu/~m1wilson/htmlref.html`—Listing of the most popular HTML tags

Internet Access Providers

◁ `http://thelist.iworld.com`—List of ISPs maintained by the folks from iworld, who bring you *Internet World*, *Web Week*, and *Web Developer* magazines

◁ `http://www.att.com/worldnet`—AT&T's offering of ISP services at good rates and Web hosting services that use FrontPage

◁ `http://www.earthlink.net`—ISP

◁ `http://www.usonline.com`—Sells a CD that can help you identify an ISP to meet your needs

◁ `http://www.psi.net`—ISP, also known as Pipeline and InterRamp

◁ http://www.sprynet.com—ISP

◁ http://www.concentric.net—ISP

Java Resources

◁ http://java.sun.com—Java right from the source, Sun Microsystems

◁ http://www.gamelan.com—The mother of all Java-related sources

◁ http://www.javaworld.com—Home of IDG's *JavaWorld* magazine

◁ http://www.digitalfocus.com/digitalfocus/faq—Specializes in technologies such as Java and provides some advanced resources

◁ http://users.aol.com/thingtone/workshop—Thingtone's Java Workshop, an excellent source for Java beginners

◁ http://www.nebulex.com/URN/devel.html—Index of Java and JavaScript resources

JavaScript Resources

◁ http://www.ipst.com/docs.htm—Your chance to download the JavaScript manuals in PDF format

◁ http://www.freqgrafx.com/411—Excellent resource for tutorials and more

◁ http://gmccomb.com/javascript—Plenty of JavaScript sample code

◁ http://www.c2.org/~andreww/javascript—Good all-around source for JavaScript info

◁ http://www.dannyg.com/javascript—Yet more examples

◁ http://www.netscape.com/eng/mozilla/Gold/handbook/javascript—The JavaScript guide straight from the horse's mouth

VBScript Resources

◁ http://www.microsoft.com/vbscript—The VBScript home page, straight from its mom—Microsoft

Web Presence Providers

◁ `http://thelist.iworld.com`—List of ISPs maintained by the folks from iworld, who bring you *Internet World*, *Web Week*, and *Web Developer* magazines

◁ `http://www.att.com/worldnet`—Phone company turned Web host, includes FrontPage extensions in some packages

◁ `http://rawspace.net`—Net hosting, good prices

◁ `http://www.microsoft.com/frontpage/ispinfo/isplist.htm`—List of hosts that support the FrontPage Server Extensions for your Webs

General Web Development Resources

◁ `http://rs.internic.net`—Register new domain names here

◁ `http://gagme.wwa.com/~boba/masters1.html`—The Webmaster's home page, an excellent starting place to find all kinds of resources

◁ `http://home.netscape.com/home/how-to-create-web-services.html`—The Netscape guide to Web development

◁ `http://www.stars.com`—The Web Developer's Virtual Library, a plethora of information and useful links

◁ `http://www.microsoft.com/sitebuilder`—Microsoft's forum for Web developers, lots of information on Microsoft products and technologies

◁ `comp.infosystems.www.authoring.*`—Series of Internet news groups that contain much discussion about Web development

Miscellaneous and of Interest

◁ `http://www.lies.com/feb96/021496.html`—Interesting e-zine article about ISPs, politics, and service

◁ `http://www.eff.org/blueribbon.html`—Blue-ribbon campaign in support of second amendment rights to free speech in the United States

◁ `http://www.genmagic.com/internet/trends`—Internet trends

◁ `http://www.nielsenmedia.com/demo.htm`—Nielsen interactive Internet surveys

◁ `http://www.ora.com/research`—Information about conducting business on the Internet presented by O'Reilly and Associates

Index

D

I

M

N

O

R

U

W

X - Y - Z

Books have a substantial influence on the destruction of the forests of the Earth. For example, it takes 17 trees to produce one ton of paper. A first printing of 30,000 copies of a typical 480-page book consumes 108,000 pounds of paper, which will require 918 trees!

Waite Group Press™ is against the clear-cutting of forests and supports refor-estation of the Pacific Northwest of the United States and Canada, where most of this paper comes from. As a publisher with several hundred thousand books sold each year, we feel an obligation to give back to the planet. We will therefore support organi-zations that seek to preserve the forests of planet Earth.

Message from the
Publisher

WELCOME TO OUR NERVOUS SYSTEM

Some people say that the World Wide Web is a graphical extension of the information superhighway, just a network of humans and machines sending each other long lists of the equivalent of digital junk mail.

I think it is much more than that. To me, the Web is nothing less than the nervous system of the entire planet—not just a collection of computer brains connected together, but more like a billion silicon neurons entangled and recirculating electro-chemical signals of information and data, each contributing to the birth of another CPU and another Web site.

Think of each person's hard disk connected at once to every other hard disk on earth, driven by human navigators searching like Columbus for the New World. Seen this way the Web is more of a super entity, a growing, living thing, controlled by the universal human will to expand, to be more. Yet, unlike a purposeful business plan with rigid rules, the Web expands in a nonlinear, unpredictable, creative way that echoes natural evolution.

We created our Web site not just to extend the reach of our computer book products but to be part of this synaptic neural network, to experience, like a nerve in the body, the flow of ideas and then to pass those ideas up the food chain of the mind. Your mind. Even more, we wanted to pump some of our own creative juices into this rich wine of technology.

TASTE OUR DIGITAL WINE

And so we ask you to taste our wine by visiting the body of our business. Begin by understanding the metaphor we have created for our Web site—a universal learning center, situated in outer space in the form of a space station. A place where you can journey to study any topic from the convenience of your own screen. Right now we are focusing on computer topics, but the stars are the limit on the Web.

If you are interested in discussing this Web site or finding out more about the Waite Group, please send me e-mail with your comments, and I will be happy to respond. Being a programmer myself, I love to talk about technology and find out what our readers are looking for.

Sincerely,

Mitchell Waite

Mitchell Waite, C.E.O. and Publisher

200 Tamal Plaza
Corte Madera, CA 94925
415-924-2575
415-924-2576 fax

Website:
http://www.waite.com/waite

CREATING THE HIGHEST QUALITY COMPUTER BOOKS IN THE INDUSTRY

Waite Group Press

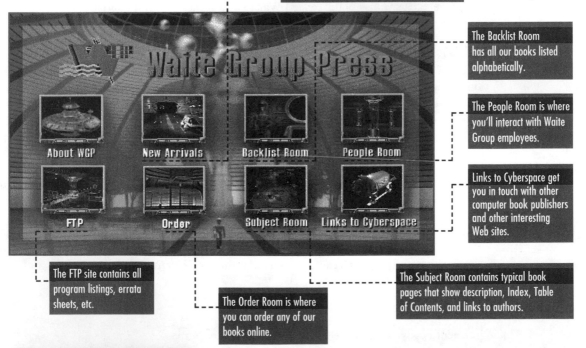

This is a legal agreement between you, the end user and purchaser, and The Waite Group®, Inc., and the authors of the programs contained in the disk. By opening the sealed disk package, you are agreeing to be bound by the terms of this Agreement. If you do not agree with the terms of this Agreement, promptly return the unopened disk package and the accompanying items (including the related book and other written material) to the place you obtained them for a refund.

SOFTWARE LICENSE

1. The Waite Group, Inc. grants you the right to use one copy of the enclosed software programs (the programs) on a single computer system (whether a single CPU, part of a licensed network, or a terminal connected to a single CPU). Each concurrent user of the program must have exclusive use of the related Waite Group, Inc. written materials.

2. The program, including the copyrights in each program, is owned by the respective author and the copyright in the entire work is owned by The Waite Group, Inc. and they are therefore protected under the copyright laws of the United States and other nations, under international treaties. You may make only one copy of the disk containing the programs exclusively for backup or archival purposes, or you may transfer the programs to one hard disk drive, using the original for backup or archival purposes. You may make no other copies of the programs, and you may make no copies of all or any part of the related Waite Group, Inc. written materials.

3. You may not rent or lease the programs, but you may transfer ownership of the programs and related written materials (including any and all updates and earlier versions) if you keep no copies of either, and if you make sure the transferee agrees to the terms of this license.

4. You may not decompile, reverse engineer, disassemble, copy, create a derivative work, or otherwise use the programs except as stated in this Agreement.

GOVERNING LAW

This Agreement is governed by the laws of the State of California.

LIMITED WARRANTY

The following warranties shall be effective for 90 days from the date of purchase: (i) The Waite Group, Inc. warrants the enclosed disk to be free of defects in materials and workmanship under normal use; and (ii) The Waite Group, Inc. warrants that the programs, unless modified by the purchaser, will substantially perform the functions described in the documentation provided by The Waite Group, Inc. when operated on the designated hardware and operating system. The Waite Group, Inc. does not warrant that the programs will meet purchaser's requirements or that operation of a program will be uninterrupted or error-free. The program warranty does not cover any program that has been altered or changed in any way by anyone other than The Waite Group, Inc. The Waite Group, Inc. is not responsible for problems caused by changes in the operating characteristics of computer hardware or computer operating systems that are made after the release of the programs, nor for problems in the interaction of the programs with each other or other software.

THESE WARRANTIES ARE EXCLUSIVE AND IN LIEU OF ALL OTHER WARRANTIES OF MERCHANTABILITY OR FITNESS FOR A PARTICULAR PURPOSE OR OF ANY OTHER WARRANTY, WHETHER EXPRESS OR IMPLIED.

EXCLUSIVE REMEDY

The Waite Group, Inc. will replace any defective disk without charge if the defective disk is returned to The Waite Group, Inc. within 90 days from date of purchase.

This is Purchaser's sole and exclusive remedy for any breach of warranty or claim for contract, tort, or damages.

LIMITATION OF LIABILITY

THE WAITE GROUP, INC. AND THE AUTHORS OF THE PROGRAMS SHALL NOT IN ANY CASE BE LIABLE FOR SPECIAL, INCIDENTAL, CONSEQUENTIAL, INDIRECT, OR OTHER SIMILAR DAMAGES ARISING FROM ANY BREACH OF THESE WARRANTIES EVEN IF THE WAITE GROUP, INC. OR ITS AGENT HAS BEEN ADVISED OF THE POSSIBILITY OF SUCH DAMAGES.

THE LIABILITY FOR DAMAGES OF THE WAITE GROUP, INC. AND THE AUTHORS OF THE PROGRAMS UNDER THIS AGREEMENT SHALL IN NO EVENT EXCEED THE PURCHASE PRICE PAID.

COMPLETE AGREEMENT

This Agreement constitutes the complete agreement between The Waite Group, Inc. and the authors of the programs, and you, the purchaser.

Some states do not allow the exclusion or limitation of implied warranties or liability for incidental or consequential damages, so the above exclusions or limitations may not apply to you. This limited warranty gives you specific legal rights; you may have others, which vary from state to state.